CATASTROPHE

CATASTROPHE

RISK AND RESPONSE

RICHARD A. POSNER

UNIVERSITY PRESS

2004

UNIVERSITY PRESS

Oxford   New York
Auckland   Bangkok   Buenos Aires   Cape Town   Chennai
Dar es Salaam   Delhi   Hong Kong   Istanbul   Karachi   Kolkata
Kuala Lumpur   Madrid   Melbourne   Mexico City   Mumbai   Nairobi
São Paulo   Shanghai   Taipei   Tokyo   Toronto

Copyright © 2004 by Oxford University Press, Inc.

Published by Oxford University Press, Inc.
198 Madison Avenue, New York, New York 10016

www.oup.com

Library of Congress Cataloging-in-Publication Data
Posner, Richard A.
Catastrophe : risk and response / by Richard A. Posner.
p.   cm.
Includes index.
ISBN 0-19-530647-3
1.   Emergency management.   2. Disasters.   3. Risk assessment.   4. Technological
innovations—Moral and ethical aspects.   I. Title.
HV551.2.P675   2004
363.34—dc22   2004009728

3   5   7   9   8   6   4

Printed in the United States of America
on acid-free paper

Preface

Certain events quite within the realm of possibility, such as a major asteroid collision, global bioterrorism, abrupt global warming—even certain lab accidents—could have unimaginably terrible consequences up to and including the extinction of the human race, possibly within the near future. The scientific and popular literature dealing with possible megacatastrophes is vast. But law and the social sciences, with the partial exception of economics—there is an extensive economic literature on global warming—have paid little attention to such possibilities. This seems to me regrettable. I am not a Green, an alarmist, an apocalyptic visionary, a catastrophist, a Chicken Little, a Luddite, an anticapitalist, or even a pessimist. But for reasons explained in chapter 1, I have come to believe that what I shall be calling the "catastrophic risks" are real and growing and that the social sciences, in particular economics, statistics, cognitive psychology, and law, have an essential role to play in the design of policies and institutions for combating them.

As may the mathematical methods sometimes used in the analysis of extreme events, such as the promisingly named "catastrophe theory," which has some economic applications[1] and is used in some of the studies I cite; or chaos theory,[2] or the branch of statistics known as reliability theory, which is used "where a single copy of a system is designed: space ships, huge dams, nuclear research equipment, etc. All these objects must be extremely reliable. At the same time we very often have no prototype or any previous experience. How to evaluate their reliability? In what terms? What is the 'confidence' of such evaluation?"[3] Lack of relevant previous experience is one of the frequent characteristics of the catastrophic risks discussed in this book.[4] But apart from a brief discussion of chaos theory in chapter 1, I do not employ these methods. They are highly technical, and I have wanted to make the book intelligible to the general reader, including the mathless lawyer, so no math beyond the junior high school level is employed. Nor for that matter is any knowledge of economics, statistics, or the other fields on which I draw presupposed—not even law.

Granted, there are dangers in an age of specialization in attempting to bring different disciplinary perspectives to bear on the analysis of catastrophic risks—or indeed in attempting to analyze the different risks in a lump. No one individual can be a master of all these perspectives or an expert in the full range of risks. But specialization has its drawbacks and the occasional generalist study its advantages; and it is difficult to see how the catastrophic risks can be understood and dealt with sensibly unless they are occasionally viewed together and from all relevant points of view.

The germ of the book is a review I did of Margaret Atwood's 2003 novel *Oryx and Crake*.[5] Set in the near future, her novel depicts the virtual extinction of the human race by a bioterrorist against a background of global ruination caused by uncontrolled technological advance. I was curious whether there was any scientific basis for her dark vision—and discovered that there was and that the social sciences were not taking it as seriously as it deserved. The law was paying no attention at all, because law is court-centric and there have been no cases involving catastrophic risks in the sense in which I am using the term, and because a cultural gulf separates lawyers from scientists.

I had agreed to review Atwood's novel because of my growing interest not in catastrophe as such but in technology, an interest awakened by a trial that I had recently conducted involving the validity and infringement of the patent on the antidepressant drug Paxil.[6] At the trial, distinguished scientists testified about fascinating but abstruse issues of biochemistry and I was led to wonder whether the law's conventional methods for resolving science-laden legal disputes were adequate in an era of increasing scientific complexity. The research that I have done for this book has convinced me that law is indeed lagging dangerously behind an accelerating scientific revolution.

So rapid is the advance of science that some of the scientific findings reported in this book will undoubtedly have changed by the time the book is published. Nevertheless I hope that my discussion of the analytical techniques and institutional reforms necessary to meet the social challenges of modern science is sufficiently general to retain, for a time anyway, its relevance in the face of continuing scientific advances.

I have received a great deal of help with this book. Amanda Butler, Nicole Eitmann, Roger Ford, Adele Grignon, Phil Kenny, Carl LeSueur, Grace Liu, Paul Ma, Gavin Martinson, and especially Paul Clark and Liss Palamkunnel, provided exemplary assistance with the research required for the book. I had fruitful discussions concerning the subject matter with Gary Becker, Shana Dale, Daniel Dennett, Timothy Ferris, Michael Fisher, Christine Jolls, Barry Kellman, Lawrence Lessig, Daniel Levine, John Mearsheimer, Eric Posner, Stanley Sokul, Stephen Stigler, Larry Summers, Cass Sunstein, and John Yoo, as well as with distinguished scientists who gave generously of their time to this scientific innocent with his dumb questions: Stephen Berry, John Deutch, Henry Frisch, Robert Haselkorn, Richard Kron, Raymond Pierrehumbert, and Chung-I Wu. I also wish to acknowledge the helpful suggestions and leads of Michael Aronson, Edward Castronova, Kenneth Dam, Eric Drexler, Dedi Felman, Andrew Franknoi, Howard Kunreuther, Herbert Lin, Richard Lindzen, William Nordhaus, Mark Siegler, Jonathan Wiener, and an anonymous reader for the Oxford University Press. Andrew Baak, Gary Becker, Eric Drexler, Jonathan Masur, John Mearsheimer, Shelley Murphey, Todd Murphey, Martha Nussbaum, Ian Parry, Charlene Posner, Eric Posner, Martin Rees, Jay Richardson, Cass Sunstein, Victoria Sutton, and John Yoo gave me valuable comments on portions of the manuscript itself; David Friedman's and Scott Hemphill's detailed comments on the entire manuscript deserve a special acknowledgment. An early version of the book formed the basis of a talk that I gave at the University of Chicago's Workshop on Rational Choice in the Social Sciences. I thank the participants in the workshop for their comments.

Contents

Contents

CATASTROPHE

Introduction

You wouldn't see the asteroid, even though it was several miles in diameter, because it would be hurtling toward you at 15 to 25 miles a second. At that speed, the column of air between the asteroid and the earth's surface would be compressed with such force that the column's temperature would soar to several times that of the sun, incinerating everything in its path. When the asteroid struck, it would penetrate deep into the ground and explode, creating an enormous crater and ejecting burning rocks and dense clouds of soot into the atmosphere, wrapping the globe in a mantle of fiery debris that would raise surface temperatures by as much as 100 degrees Fahrenheit and shut down photosynthesis for years. The shock waves from the collision would have precipitated earthquakes and volcanic eruptions, gargantuan tidal waves, and huge forest fires. A quarter of the earth's human population might be dead within 24 hours of the strike, and the rest soon after.

But there might no longer *be* an earth for an asteroid to strike. In a high-energy particle accelerator, physicists bent on re-creating conditions at the birth of the universe collide the nuclei of heavy atoms, containing large numbers of protons and neutrons, at speeds near that of light, shattering these particles into their constituent quarks. Because some of these quarks, called strange quarks, are hyperdense, here is what might happen: A shower of strange quarks clumps, forming a tiny bit of strange matter that has a negative electric charge. Because of its charge, the strange matter attracts the nuclei in the vicinity (nuclei have a positive charge), fusing with them to form a larger mass of strange matter that expands exponentially. Within a fraction of a second the earth is compressed to a hyperdense sphere 100 meters in diameter, explodes in the manner of a supernova, and vanishes.

By then, however, the earth might have been made uninhabitable for human beings and most other creatures by abrupt climate changes. Here is a possible scenario: A sudden steep increase in global temperatures is produced by the continued burning of gasoline and other fossil fuels (fossilized remains of ancient organisms—hence carbon compounds, which when burned give off carbon-based gases) and the deforestation of the Amazon rain forest. The burning and deforestation inject into the atmosphere carbon dioxide and other gases that retain the heat reflected from the earth's surface. The higher temperatures resulting from the increased atmospheric concentration of these "greenhouse" gases cause the Greenland and Antarctic ice caps to melt, raising ocean levels to a point at which the world's coastal areas are inundated and melting the permafrost in Alaska and Siberia. The melting releases immense quantities of methane, the most heat-retentive of the greenhouse gases, which causes more melting of the permafrost, a further release of methane, and a further warming effect, resulting in a runaway greenhouse spiral that destroys agriculture in the tropics because the warming is too sudden to enable the crops to be adapted to the new conditions. European agriculture is destroyed as well because the melting of the north polar ice cap dilutes the salty water of the North Atlantic, causing the Gulf Stream to straighten out and flow due north, so that it no longer heats Europe. Europe lies at a high latitude, and without the warming effect of the Gulf Stream quickly becomes as frigid as Siberia.

Worse threatens. Higher temperatures increase the amount of water vapor in the atmosphere. So there are more clouds, and they may be opaque to the sun but not to the heat radiated back from the earth. If so, surface temperatures will begin to fall, causing precipitation increasingly to take the form of snow rather than rain, forcing a further drop in surface temperatures. The upward spiral of the earth's temperature has been reversed but only to usher in an equally disastrous downward spiral ending in "snowball earth"—the entire planet encased in thick ice pierced only by the tips of a few volcanoes.

Yet before any of these dramatic climatic changes occurred, the human race might have exterminated itself through engineered plagues devised and disseminated by lunatics inspired with apocalyptic visions: With the aid of gene-splicing kits stolen from high school classrooms, religious terrorists and rogue scientists create a strain of the smallpox vaccine that is incurable, is immune to vaccine, and kills all its victims, rather than just 30 percent as in the case of natural smallpox. In a single round-the-world flight, a biological Unabomber, dropping off inconspicuous aerosol dispensers in major airports, infects several thousand people with the juiced-up smallpox. In the 12 to 14 days before symptoms appear, each of the initially infected victims infects five or six others, who in turn infect five or six others, and so on. Within a month more than 100 million people are infected, including almost all health workers and other "first responders," making it impossible to establish and enforce a quarantine. Before a vaccine or cure can be found, all but a few human beings, living in remote places, have died. Lacking the requisite research skills and production facilities, the remnant cannot control the disease and soon succumb as well.

What is catastrophe?

None of these disasters (which along with a number of others form the subject matter of chapter 1) is certain to occur. But any of them might, with more than trivial probability. The catastrophic asteroid strike and the abrupt climate spirals are part of the earth's prehistory. They have happened before; they could happen again. Should either of the other two megacatastrophes sketched above occur—the world-ending lab accident or the devastating bioterrorist attack—it would be an example of modern technology run amok. So might be abrupt global warming, and not just because internal combustion engines and electrical generation are products of technology; technology affects the climate indirectly as well as directly by its positive effects on the growth of the economy and of world population. Both are factors in global warming and in another of the catastrophe scenarios as well—a precipitous and irreversible loss of biodiversity.

All these disasters and more would be catastrophes in the sense the word bears when used to designate an event that is believed to have a very low probability of materializing but that if it does materialize will produce a harm so great and sudden as to seem discontinuous with the flow of events that preceded it. The low probability of such disasters—frequently the *unknown* probability, as in the case of bioterrorism and abrupt global warming—is among the things that baffle efforts at responding rationally to them. But respond we must; at least we must consider seriously whether to respond; for these events can happen, and any of them would be catastrophic in the sense of cataclysmic rather than the milder sense in which a hurricane or earthquake might be termed "catastrophic"[1] because its unexpected severity caused large losses to property owners and insurance companies.[2] One definition of "catastrophe" given by *Webster's Third New International Dictionary* is "a momentous tragic usually sudden event marked by effects ranging from extreme misfortune to utter overthrow or ruin." Concentrate on the top of the range ("utter overthrow or ruin") and you will have a good grasp of how I use the word in this book.

The catastrophes that particularly interest me are those that threaten the survival of the human race. Even so lethal an event as the great flu pandemic ("Spanish influenza") of 1918–1919, which is estimated to have killed between 20 and 40 million people worldwide,[3] or the AIDS pandemic, which may well exceed that toll—already more than 20 million have died in sub-Saharan Africa alone,[4] though over a much longer period of time and out of a much larger world population—is only marginal to my concerns. Pandemics are an old story, and can kill substantial fractions of local or regional populations. But they have never jeopardized the survival of the human race as a whole, as bioterrorism may do.

I forgo consideration of the moral disasters to which continued technological advances may conceivably give rise. The prominent bioethicist Leon Kass contends that "technology is not problem but tragedy." By this he doesn't mean that technology may destroy us physically, which is my primary concern, although enslavement of the human race or its subjection to totalitarian tyranny would be genuine catastrophes even in my austere sense of the word. He means that "homogenization, mediocrity, pacification, drug-induced contentment, debasement of taste, souls without loves and longings—these are the inevitable results of making the essence of human nature the last project for technical mastery."[5] Kass is the chairman of President Bush's Council on Bioethics, which recently issued a report that warns

> of a sex-unbalanced society, the result of unrestrained free choice in selecting the sex of children; or of a change-resisting gerontocracy, with the "elders" still young in body but old and tired in outlook. And there are still uglier possibilities: an increasingly stratified and inegalitarian society, now with purchased biological enhancements, with enlarged gaps between the over-privileged few and the under-privileged many; a society of narcissists focused on personal satisfaction and self-regard, with little concern for the next generation or the common good; a society of social conformists but with shallow attachments, given over to cosmetic fashions and trivial pursuits; or a society of fiercely competitive individuals, caught up in an ever-spiraling struggle to get ahead, using the latest biotechnical assistance both to perform better and to deal with the added psychic stress.[6]

Kass is right that technology can have social consequences. Think of how the Internet has given rise to an enormously increased volume of pornography and how the abortifacient ("morning after") pill may soon write finis to the right-to-life movement.[7] The transformation in the social role of women in the last half century, with resulting effects on marriage and divorce rates, extramarital sex, and the status of homosexuals, is the result to a significant degree of technological progress. Technological progress has produced labor-saving household devices, safe and effective contraception that interferes minimally or not at all with sexual pleasure, an abundance of jobs that do not require masculine physical strength, and a drastic decline in infant mortality, which has reduced the amount of time that women need to be pregnant in order to be confident of producing a target number of children who will survive to adulthood. The combined effect of these developments has been to reduce the demand for marriage and increase the demand for extramarital sex, the public role of women, the age of marriage and of giving birth, the incidence of births out of wedlock, and tolerance for sexual deviance (a word rapidly going out of fashion), while reducing the overall birth rate and the amount of time that mothers spend with their children. Developments in communications technology may have had equally profound and, to the conventional-minded, disturbing effects.

Do the social and moral consequences of modern technology (many of them presciently depicted in Aldous Huxley's satiric novel *Brave New World*)—consequences fostered by an outlook that regards our biological nature as merely a set of "unsolved technical problems"[8]— portend moral decay? Radical change, probably;[9] moral decay, perhaps, but I do not attempt to deal with the question in this book.

What if anything should society be doing to try to prevent the catastrophes with which I shall be dealing? "If anything" is an important qualification. Not all problems are soluble, and we mustn't merely assume that we can do something about the catastrophic risks that cloud the future. We must first of all try to get a handle on their true gravity, which is a function both of the probability that one or another of them will materialize if we do nothing and of the awfulness of the consequences if that happens. Then we must weigh the costs that would have to be borne, and the psychological and political obstacles that would have to be overcome, in order to implement effective methods of reducing the risks.

The analytical and institutional challenges are formidable. In part this is because of the centrality of science and science policy[10] to the catastrophic risks and their prevention. A number of the risks are actually the product of scientific research or its technological applications.[11] Some are preventable by modern technology—and often by modern technology alone. Of still others technology is both cause and potential cure. The intertwining of catastrophe and technology is thus a major concern of the book. The challenge of managing science and technology in relation to the catastrophic risks is an enormous one, and if it can be met it will be by a mosaic of institutional arrangements, analytical procedures, regulatory measures, and professional skills. I am particularly interested in determining the positions that law, policy analysis, and the social sciences should occupy in that mosaic. At present, none of these fields, with the principal exception of economic analysis of global warming, is taking the catastrophic risks seriously and addressing them constructively. This has partly to do with features of the risks that make them intractable to conventional analytical methods, although I shall argue that cost-benefit analysis of possible responses has unexplored potential.

In the case of law, neglect of the catastrophic risks is part of a larger problem, that of the law's faltering struggle to cope with the onrush of science.[12] It is an old story,[13] but a true one, and becoming more worrisome by the day. Think for example of how law has been challenged by scientific progress that has enlarged our knowledge of causal relations. In the old days, the only ascertainable cause-and-effect relations tended to be of the "*A* hit *B*" or "*A* ran down *B*" variety: one cause that was of interest to the law and one readily identifiable effect, following closely upon the cause. Modern science enables remote causes to be identified and diffuse effects traced to them. A radiation leak in year *y* might create 10 excess cancers in a population of 100,000 people in year *y* + 20, giving rise to baffling questions of who should be permitted to sue for damages and in what amount.[14] The Delaney Amendment to the Food, Drug, and Cosmetic Act, forbidding sale of any food additive containing carcinogens in however small a quantity,[15] became obsolete and had to be partially repealed[16] when the advance of science enabled such minute quantities of carcinogens to be detected that plainly harmless substances were being outlawed. Falling detection limits are also generating patent-infringement litigation over accidental "appropriations" of minute amounts of patented compounds.[17] Such problems are real and from the standpoint of the legal profession and the legal system serious.[18] But they are not catastrophic in the sense in which I am using the term, and so they do not belong to my subject.

The sheer difficulty of modern science is one obstacle to coping with catastrophic risks. Another is the bafflement that most people feel when they try to think about events that have an extremely low probability of occurring even if they will inflict enormous harm if they do occur. The human mind does not handle even simple statistical propositions well, and has particular difficulty grasping things with which human beings have no firsthand experience.[19] By definition, we have little experience with low-probability events and often none at all, so that such events can be apprehended only in statistical terms. The two difficulties, that of grasping the significance of low-probability events and that of thinking in statistical terms, thus are closely related. Both appear to be evolutionarily adaptive, moreover—"hard-wired" in our brains—and therefore tenacious. Because mental capacity and therefore attention are limited, human beings would not have survived in the dangerous circumstances of the ancestral environment had they been prone to let their attention wander from situations fraught with a high probability of immediate death, as when being attacked by a predator, requiring maximum alertness, to low-probability menaces—which anyway they couldn't have done much about. It is only when the overall probability of death declines, which happened after our biological evolution was essentially complete, that it becomes rational to focus on eliminating small risks. So it is not surprising that evolution did not produce an ability to think clearly about such risks as a standard part of our mental skill set.

The mental exertion required to think about things that one has not experienced is a form of imagination cost and a clue to why people do better in dealing with probabilities when they are restated as frequencies (such as "once in a thousand years" rather than "a one-in-a-thousand chance").[20] The frequency format implies that one is being asked about things that have happened—which may justify an inference that they will happen about as often in the future—rather than about things that haven't happened yet though they may in the future.

Probabilities are related to frequencies through the law of large numbers.[21] The probability that a balanced coin fairly tossed will come up heads on the first toss is 50 percent, but if the coin is tossed only once or twice heads are quite likely not to be observed. In 100 tosses, however, there will be about 50 heads, and in 1 million tosses the number of heads will be very close to 500,000 and the probability will have been transformed into a frequency. But suppose there's a one in a thousand chance that the coin when tossed will land on its edge rather than on either of its sides. Suppose further that the coin is tossed only once a year. Then in a thousand years the coin can be expected to be observed on its edge only once. So if we decide at the outset that we don't want the coin to land on its edge, we will be deciding on the basis of probabilities, not frequencies, as it is unlikely that tossing the coin once or a few times will enable us to observe an actual edge-landing. But it requires more mental effort to act on the basis of probabilities than on the basis of frequencies. Anyone who doubts this will be disabused by reflection on the inability even of experts and responsible officials to take the risk of a 9/11-type terrorist attack seriously until it actually happened, though the risk was well known.

Not that frequencies—experience rather than prediction—are an infallible guide. Obviously one can go wrong in assuming that the future will repeat the past. That is the pitfall that philosophers discuss under the rubric of the fallacy of induction. But it is the kind of assumption that comes naturally to people, whereas thinking in terms of numerical probabilities is learned behavior—and not learned well, because it is not taught well and often is not taught at all. Systematic biases that cause erroneous judgments are less likely to afflict people who are experienced in the relevant activity,[22] however, and so experts may be able to help the general public respond intelligently to risk.

A related distinction to bear in mind is between notional and motivational belief. It is possible to affirm a proposition on which one would never act, simply because the proposition was not felt deeply enough to impel action. Everyone knows that he or she will die someday, and maybe sooner rather than later, but a great many people do not act as if they knew it. They take foolish risks, avoid doctors, don't make a will, and let the premiums on their life insurance lapse, because they *feel* invulnerable though they *know* they aren't.

There is tension between the psychological and economic accounts of behavior, both of which I employ in this book; the former emphasizes irrationality and the latter rationality. But it may be possible to dissolve much of the tension by redescribing the kinds of irrational behavior emphasized in recent cognitive psychology, such as the difficulty with the handling of probabilities that I have just been discussing, as behavior in response to costs of processing information. This is in contrast to the costs of *acquiring* information, which have been a staple topic in economics for almost half a century. (The union of rational-choice economics with cognitive psychology, the latter emphasizing the discrepancies between rational and actual human behavior, is thus sometimes termed "behavioral economics.") But whether or not fully compatible with rational-choice economics, the findings of cognitive psychology are indispensable to understanding the human response to phenomena that lie as far outside the ordinary experience of people as the catastrophic risks do.

The interdisciplinary perspective employed in this book yields some fresh, and to a degree paradoxical, insights. For example, when probabilities of death are very low, estimates of the value of life may be depressed to the point at which the cost in human lives of a maximum disaster—right up to and including the extinction of the human race—would be lower than that of a disaster that killed many fewer people. What is more, an uncritical belief that saving lives is always a good thing may impede effective responses to some catastrophic risks.

Another paradox is that the existence of reputable scientific dissent from a consensus (for example, on the likely consequences of global warming) may justify *greater* expenditures on averting a catastrophe than if the consensus were unchallenged, even though the dissenters will be arguing for lower expenditures. And, speaking of global warming, we shall see that a tax on emissions of greenhouse gases might arrest global warming even if the demand for fossil fuels were completely unresponsive to higher prices in the short run. We'll also see that the propriety of curtailing civil liberties in response to the threat of catastrophic risks created by terrorist groups or deranged scientists ought to depend on whether such a curtailment would *itself* create a catastrophic risk. Furthermore, when conditions are changing rapidly, predictions based on simple extrapolation from past experience are likely to be completely unreliable. This last point is not very fresh, but it deserves emphasis because of the frequency with which connoisseurs of catastrophe tell us that bioterrorism, for example, is a minor threat because few people have been killed by it in the entire course of human history.

The organization of this book

The principal catastrophic risks, as they now appear, can be divided into four more or less homogeneous classes, all discussed in chapter 1. The first consists of natural catastrophes, such as pandemics (widespread, often global, epidemics) and asteroid collisions. Technology did not create or augment the risks in this class (with a partial exception regarding pandemics), but is critical to the response.

The second class consists of laboratory or other scientific accidents, for example accidents involving particle accelerators, nanotechnology (the manipulation of atoms and molecules to create new molecules and other structures—a nanometer is a billionth of a meter), and artificial intelligence. Technology is the cause of these risks, and slowing down technology may therefore be the right response.

The third class consists of other unintentional albeit man-made catastrophes, such as exhaustion of natural resources (the traditional, yet least likely, disaster scenario), global warming, and loss of biodiversity. Both global warming and biodiversity depletion are consequences of energy generation, land clearing, gene splicing, and other human activities that affect climate and genetic variety. The fourth and final class of catastrophic risks consists of deliberately perpetrated catastrophes, comprising "nuclear winter," bioweaponry, cyberterrorism, and digital means of surveillance and encryption. Because the employment of these tactics by nations, at least on a global scale, is unlikely at present (except in the case of surveillance and encryption), this category largely equates to technological terrorism.

One catastrophic risk within each of the four classes receives particular emphasis not only in chapter 1 but throughout the book: asteroid collisions in the first class, particle-accelerator disasters in the second, global warming in the third, and bioterrorism in the fourth—the four that I sketched at the outset of this introduction. Chapter 1 describes them at length and with many references to the scientific literature in order that the reader will understand the scientific reasoning and evidence that have persuaded me that these are risks worth worrying about.

Chapter 2 explores why such risks are analytically, psychologically, politically, economically, and practically so difficult to cope with or even to perceive. The obstacles include science fiction, doomsayers (and the occasional Pollyanna), politics as seen through the lens of public-choice theory, scientific illiteracy and science worship, externalities and the lack of a good theory of technological change, and the cognitive limitations mentioned already that people brush up against in dealing with very small probabilities. The chapter introduces the term "economy of attention"[23] to name the deficiencies in mental capacity and institutional resources that make it difficult to think constructively about all the low-probability disasters at once, and identifies fallacies in previous considerations of the catastrophic risks. One of these is an interesting selection fallacy: *by definition*, all but the last doomsday prediction is false.[24] Yet it does not follow, as many seem to think, that *all* doomsday predictions must be false; what follows is only that all such predictions but one are false.

What can be done to improve the assessment of the catastrophic risks and of the possible responses to them is the subject of chapter 3. My focus there is on analytical techniques, centrally cost-benefit analysis, the use of which by U.S. government agencies to evaluate proposed regulations of health and safety is now standard.[25] Two points need to be emphasized when a proposed regulation is aimed at preventing a harm that has only a probability, and not a certainty, of occurring unless the regulation is adopted. The first is that the probability of an event is a function of the interval under consideration. The probability of an asteroid collision is much greater in the next thousand years than in the next six months. (Most of the probability figures in this book are annual probabilities.)

Second, the simplest way to capture in quantitative terms the probabilistic character of a harm is to multiply the cost that the harm will impose should it occur by the probability that it will occur. The product is the "expected cost" of the harm; equally it is the expected benefit of a measure that would prevent the harm from ever occurring. The expected cost (benefit) of a 1 percent chance of $1,000 is $10.

Cost-benefit analysis is not yet being used to evaluate the possible responses to the catastrophic risks. That is a shame. Such analysis is invaluable in revealing both anomalies in public policy and opportunities for improving policy. Granted, it is also exceptionally difficult to apply to these risks. One reason is uncertainty about their gravity, an issue entangled with doubts about the feasibility of monetizing death. There is also uncertainty concerning the benefits of risk-creating scientific and technological endeavors and the proper discounting (weighting) of risks likely to materialize only in the distant future.[26]

The limitations of cost-benefit analysis that will be flagged in chapter 3 raise challenging issues of rationality. We usually think of rationality as a means of fitting means to ends and sometimes also of weighing ends in light of ultimate goals such as welfare or happiness (the same analytic procedure but with immediate ends being redefined as means to ultimate ends). But how are rational decisions to be made if means cannot be weighed and compared because essential information is unobtainable?

Admitting the difficulties, I am nevertheless optimistic about the potential of cost-benefit analysis to shape sound responses to the catastrophic risks. I shall suggest ways of eliding the conceptual and measurement problems—such ways as inverse cost-benefit analysis and the tolerable-windows approach. I shall show how one might be able to skirt many of the difficulties and some of the expense of curbing global warming by reconceiving proposals for taxation of greenhouse-gas emissions so that emission taxes are seen as a means of inducing technological breakthroughs (without which global warming is very unlikely to be checked) rather than of bringing about immediate substitution away from activities, such as the burning of fossil fuels, that produce such emissions.

Chapter 4 examines a number of possible institutional reforms at the law-science interface that may aid in coping with the catastrophic risks. They have mainly to do with the role of lawyers, courts, regulation, and international organizations in the control of the risks. I also discuss specific policies (other than the fiscal policies discussed in chapter 3) for controlling them. The policies include various police measures, some already adopted, to deal with deliberate catastrophic risks, primarily that of bioterrorism. Both the actual and the proposed policies have received little disinterested analysis, having become caught up in partisan bickering and treated as a provocation by civil libertarians. Civil-liberties concerns are unlikely to be a persuasive counterweight to concerns with public safety until civil libertarians begin to identify and if possible quantify the concrete benefits that they envisage from adhering to principles that may be making the world vulnerable to a catastrophic terrorist attack. On the other side of the political divide, the knee-jerk conservative reflex against surrendering any U.S. sovereignty to international organizations is as blind to the need for difficult trade-offs as the civil libertarian's refusal to take threats to life and limb seriously.

Some useful distinctions

Several distinctions, some already hinted at, cut across the organization of the book and should be borne in mind throughout. One is the distinction between the promotion of technology and its control. Another is the distinction between, on the one hand, natural and man-made catastrophes that technology might prevent, and, on the other hand, catastrophic risks brought about or made more dangerous by technology. These distinctions are needed in order to avoid giving the analysis too negative a cast. Modern science and technology have enormous potential for harm. But they are also bounteous sources of social benefits. The one most pertinent to this book is the contribution technology can make to averting both natural and man-made catastrophes, including the man-made catastrophes that technology itself enables or exacerbates. For example, breakthroughs in the technology of utilizing sunlight and wind as sources of energy could alleviate the problem of global warming—itself a product in large measure of technological progress (as manifested mainly in the internal combustion engine and the generation of electricity from coal, oil, and natural gas)—by enabling the substitution at reasonable cost of these clean forms of energy for fossil fuels.

Other benefits of modern science must be kept in mind as well. As much as 30 percent of the growth in total output of goods and services in the twentieth century may have come from scientific and technological innovation rather than from increases in the amount of labor or capital inputs into production.[27] And *measured* progress, such as growth in GDP,[28] understates the actual increase in social welfare that innovation has brought about. Think not only of the improvements in the quality of products and services (ranging from automobiles to dentistry) and the flood of entirely new products and services, but also of the increase in longevity, which is estimated to have added as much to personal welfare as the increase over the same period in personal income.[29]

Another important distinction is between catastrophes that portend the extinction of the human race in the long run and catastrophes that may bring about its extinction in the foreseeable future—before the end of the current century, say. This distinction will enable me to make analysis less intractable by downplaying catastrophes that are likely to occur only in the *exceedingly* remote future. Some people think it important that the human race survive for millions, even billions or trillions, of years. Worried therefore about the expansion of the sun into the earth's orbit, which is expected to occur in a few billion years,[30] they want us to begin thinking seriously about colonizing other planets. Dinosaurs had a "run" of more than 100 million years but then became extinct, and it might seem tragic that such a fate awaits us unless we do something.

Most people who think along these lines do so not because they have too much imagination but because they have too little. They have great difficulty understanding what an incredibly long time even 1 million years is from a human standpoint—that it has room for 200 civilizations as long-lived as ours has been (dating human civilization from the earliest, the Sumerian, to leave a written record). A span of a million years, let alone of a billion or a trillion, belongs to a timescale that cannot have real meaning for human beings living today. The human mind does not readily grasp the human significance of very large (also very small) numbers—as in Stalin's sinister quip that one death is a tragedy, a million deaths a statistic.

I suspect that for most people who worry about whether the human race will be around in a million years the *psychological* difference between a hundred and a million years is slight. That doesn't mean that people are dummies. It means rather that the human brain reached its present capacity in prehistoric times, when people lived in small groups, used simple tools, and had to devote their entire mental capacity to coping with their visible, audible, and tangible environment. An ability to grasp the significance of the immensely large and immensely small magnitudes that preoccupy scientists and characterize the kind of risks with which I'm concerned in this book, like the closely related ability to deal with probability and statistics, would have had no survival value. Consider such magnitudes as the following, all of great interest to scientists but incomprehensible to the laity: If an apple were as large as the earth, and its constituents similarly magnified, one of its atoms would be as large as a normal apple. An atom, moreover, is mostly empty space, with the nucleus, in which the mass of the atom is concentrated, occupying less than a trillionth of that space. The nucleus itself is a composite of smaller particles—protons and neutrons— themselves composed of still smaller particles—quarks. All matter and energy may be composed ultimately of still smaller entities called "strings"; if an atom were the size of the universe, a string would be the size of the average tree.[31] That's toward the lower end of the (known) size scale; toward the upper end is the universe itself, composed of billions of galaxies, each consisting of billions of stars. And there may be even smaller particles than strings and there may be a multitude of universes, perhaps superimposed but invisible to each other because occupying different spatial dimensions.

A compelling reason for not giving a great deal of thought to the remote future is the difficulty, often the impossibility, of making accurate predictions beyond a few years. People in the year 1000 could have had only the vaguest conception of what the world would be like in the year 2004, and we can have only the vaguest conception of what it will be like in the year 3000, let alone the year 1,000,000. We have better predictive methods than people in 1000 did, but on the other hand the rate of technological change is higher now than it was then. Lacking the requisite foreknowledge we can't know what we should be doing now to forestall the disasters that are possible, maybe even likely, on that timescale.

So I'm not going to worry very much about the prospects for perpetuating the human species indefinitely, although I shall have to touch on the issue in chapter 3 in discussing the use of cost-benefit analysis as a tool of catastrophic-risk assessment. But catastrophes that might cause the extinction of the human race, or inflict some lesser but still cataclysmic harm, by the beginning of the next century are certainly worth thinking about. Many of the children and most of the grand-children of the people living today can be expected, barring such a catastrophe, to survive into the twenty-second century.

There's a lot of room, though, between a hundred years in the future and a million years, and I am not sure that we should be cavalier about what may happen in a thousand years. Suppose that in 4 A.D. the Romans had started up a particle accelerator that created a risk, albeit very small, of destroying the earth. (Such an accelerator *was* started up, at Brookhaven National Laboratory, in 2000, as we shall see in chapter

1.) Suppose the annual risk of such a disaster was one in a million and that each year's risk of disaster was independent of every other year's risk in a statistical sense. Then the risk of a disaster occurring sometime within the next 2,000 years that would end human history before or during our lifetime would have been an uncomfortably large 1 in 500.[32] (The formula—which recurs throughout this book—for the probability of surviving n periods when there is a probability p of death in each period and the n probabilities are independent of each other is $(1 - p)^n$. For $p = .000001$ and $n = 2,000$, the probability of survival is .998, so the probability of death is .002.) Do we think it would have been responsible for the Romans to have taken such a risk, merely because it would be slight if it were truncated at a hundred years?

This example suggests that the reason human survival beyond, say, the twenty-second century has little resonance with most of us is merely that the future is hazy; the haziness illustrates the operation of imagination cost. The future that is now the present was as hazy to the Romans as our future is to us. But that would not have been a good reason for their risking the destruction of the human race in what to them was the remote and therefore weightless future. Where the example is misleading, however, is in failing to extrapolate from the Romans' assumed ability (assumed in my example, that is—obviously the assumption is contrary to fact) to build a particle accelerator 2,000 years ago. If they had had *that* much knowledge in 4 A.D., then probably within a few hundred more years they would have learned how to avoid an accelerator disaster, and so the risk of extinction by 2004 would have been smaller than 1 in 500. Nevertheless the example is relevant to whether we should be utterly insouciant about the fate of our remote descendants ("remote" on the scale of thousands, not millions or billions, of years). It does not answer the question how much we "owe" the remote future, but the answer may not be important. The threat that the catastrophic risks pose in the *near* future, the current century, may be a sufficient basis for taking effective action now to prevent the risks from *ever* materializing.

A complication in my decision largely to ignore the remote future is that low-probability events can happen at any time. Suppose the kind of asteroid collision that is believed to have done in the dinosaurs 65 million years ago occurs on average only once in 65 million years. (We'll see that astronomers actually reckon the probability as between 1 in 50 million years and 1 in 100 million years.) This implies that such a strike is *un*likely to occur in this century, not that we are "due" for it. Asteroid strikes are independent events in the statistical sense, the sense in which the fact that a tossed fair coin comes up heads does not affect the probability that the next toss will also come up heads. An event that occurs every 65 million years is as likely (unlikely) to occur this year or this decade or this century as it is to occur in any other year, decade, or century. It's not like the sun's expanding into the earth's orbit, which we have reason to think has essentially a zero probability today and will continue to do so for eons but will then begin to rise, eventually to one.

The reason for the hedge in "essentially" is that I want to avoid making claims of metaphysical certainty. From a scientific standpoint, anything is possible. But some possibilities really are too remote to be worth worrying about, such as the possibility that my next breath will create a black hole or that the entire human population will be persuaded to commit suicide. To put this differently, we have to be selective in responding to the catastrophic risks because if we allow our imaginations to multiply their number indefinitely we'll end up doing nothing about any of them.

And that would be tragic. For while it would be reassuring to think that only a lunatic fringe of Greens and Chicken Littles is worried that nature or technology may destroy or immiserate the human race, this just is not so. From the other end of the political spectrum from the Greens, I quote David Friedman, a libertarian economist fiercely hostile to government regulation but who has a Ph.D. in physics and a keen interest in science and technology:

> The next century [meaning the next 100 years, not the twenty-second century] or so is radically uncertain, with plausible outcomes ranging from the extermination of our species to the conversion of humans to more or less immortal near-gods. But it isn't clear that increasing "regulation" makes the adverse outcomes less likely or the good outcomes more. We don't have a decent mechanism for centralized control on anything like the necessary scale. What is true is that our decentralized mechanisms, which work well on a large scale, depend on a world where there is some workable definition of property rights in which the actions that a person takes with his property have only slight external effects, beyond those that can be handled by contract. Technolog-

ical progress might mean that no such definition exists—in which case we are left with zero workable solutions to the coordination problem.[32]

The danger is real; it is also underappreciated. The cure is elusive.

It is sobering to reflect on some implications of the fact that our universe contains many billions of galaxies, each composed of billions of stars, most older than our sun.[33] Given those numbers, there probably are billions, maybe trillions, of planets, on some of which intelligent life almost certainly evolved long before it evolved on earth. So it is surprising that no intelligent beings have developed a technology that would enable them to explore the universe and discover, and make some kind of contact with, us. Of course the only planets inhabited by intelligent life may be so far away that they would have had to reach scientific maturity many millions of years ago to have been able to communicate with us, given that no signal can (scientists firmly believe) travel faster than light. Another possibility, however, is that whenever a race (and it could be a race of robots that had taken over from the "natural" race that had created them—one of the doomsday scenarios that I examine in chapter 1) reaches the level of technological sophistication, which we are rapidly approaching, at which it would be possible to make contact with intelligent life elsewhere in the universe, it destroys itself. It has unleashed forces that it cannot control. It has been the victim of the tendency of technological advance to outpace the social control of technology.[34]

1

What are the catastrophic risks, and how catastrophic are they?

The number of extreme catastrophes that have a more than negligible probability of occurring in this century is alarmingly great, and their variety startling. I want to describe them and in doing so make clear the importance of understanding what science is doing and can do and where it is leading us. I begin with the natural catastrophes and move from there to the man-made ones, which I divide into three groups: scientific accidents, other unintended man-made catastrophes, and intentional catastrophes.

Natural catastrophes

Pandemics

The 1918–1919 flu pandemic is a reminder that nature may yet do us in. The disease agent was an unexpectedly lethal variant of the commonplace flu virus. Despite its lethality, it spread far and wide because most of its victims did not immediately fall seriously ill and die, so they were not isolated from the healthy population but instead circulated among the healthy, spreading the disease.[1] No one knows why the 1918–1919 pandemic was so lethal, although it may have been due to a combination of certain features of the virus's structure with the crowding of troops in the trenches and hospitals on the Western Front (where the pandemic appears to have originated near the end of World War I), facilitating the spread of the disease.[2] The possibility cannot be excluded that an even more lethal flu virus than that of the 1918–1919 pandemic will appear someday and kill many more people. There is still no cure for flu, and vaccines may be ineffective against a new mutant strain—and the flu virus is notable for its high rate of mutations.[3]

Another great twentieth-century pandemic, AIDS, which has already killed more than 20 million people,[4] illustrates the importance to the spread of a disease of the length of the infectious incubation period. The longer a person is infected and infectious yet either asymptomatic or insufficiently ill to be isolated from the healthy population, the farther the disease will spread before effective measures, such as quarantining, are taken. What has proved to be especially pernicious about AIDS is that its existence was not discovered until millions of people had been infected by and were transmitting the AIDS virus (HIV), which has an average infectious incubation period of 10 years. Given the length of that period, the only thing that may have prevented AIDS from wiping out the human race is that it is not highly infectious, as it would be if HIV were airborne rather than being transmissible only by being introduced into a victim's bloodstream. Even by unsafe sex it is "generally poorly transmitted. For example, the probability of transmission from a single anal receptive sexual contact with an infected partner is estimated at 1 in 100 to 1 in 500."[5] However, the length of HIV's infectious incubation period and the difficulty of transmission may be related; for, given that difficulty, were the virus unable to "hide" from its host's immune system for a considerable time, it would be detected and destroyed before it had a chance to replicate itself in another host.[6]

AIDS illustrates the further point that despite the progress made by modern medicine in the diagnosis and treatment of diseases, developing a vaccine or cure for a new (or newly recognized or newly virulent) disease may be difficult, protracted, even impossible. Progress has been made in treating AIDS, but neither a cure nor a vaccine has yet been developed. And because the virus's mutation rate is high, the treatments may not work in the long run.[7] Rapidly mutating viruses are difficult to vaccinate against, which is why there is no vaccine for the common cold and why flu vaccines provide only limited protection.[8] Paradoxically, a treatment that is neither cure nor vaccine, but merely reduces the severity of a disease, may accelerate its spread by reducing the benefit from avoiding becoming infected. This is an important consideration with respect to AIDS, which is spread mainly by voluntary intimate contact with infected people.

It might seem that the role of technology in relation to naturally occurring diseases would be wholly positive. Not so. Modern transportation, especially by air, facilitates the rapid spread of new diseases, as does crowding in huge cities, especially in poor countries.[9] These may be factors in the increased number of emerging (new) and "re-emerging" diseases, such as tuberculosis, in recent decades.[10] And the promiscuous use of antibiotics has spurred the evolution of antibiotic-resistant, potentially lethal bacteria.[11] (The effect is similar to that of pesticides in promoting the evolution of pesticide-resistant pests.)[12] I call it "promiscuous" because neither the patient nor his doctor is likely to consider the effect of prescribing the antibiotic on the evolution of resistant disease strains. But it may be offset by the benefit to the patient, and may even be neutralized by the fact that curing an infected person shortens the time during which he or she can infect other people.

Crowding in huge cities may not seem related to technology, but it is, albeit indirectly. For it is largely a consequence of population growth and economic development,[13] both of which are strongly influenced by technological progress, particularly in public health and agriculture.[14]

Yet the fact that *Homo sapiens* has managed to survive every disease to assail it in the 200,000 years or so of its existence is a source of genuine comfort, at least if the focus is on extinction events. There have been enormously destructive plagues, such as the Black Death, smallpox, and now AIDS, but none has come close to destroying the entire human race. There is a biological reason. Natural selection favors germs of limited lethality; they are fitter in an evolutionary sense because their genes are more likely to be spread if the germs do not kill their hosts too quickly. The AIDS virus is an example of a lethal virus, wholly natural, that by lying dormant yet infectious in its host for years maximizes its spread. Yet there is no danger that AIDS will destroy the entire human race, that is, its host population.

The likelihood of a natural pandemic that would cause the extinction of the human race is probably even less today than in the past (except in prehistoric times, when people lived in small, scattered bands, which would have limited the spread of disease), despite wider human

What are the catastrophic risks, and how catastrophic are they?

23

contacts that make it more difficult to localize an infectious disease. The reason is improvements in medical science. But the comfort is a small one. Pandemics can still impose enormous losses and resist prevention and cure: the lesson of the AIDS pandemic. And there is always a first time.

That the human race has not yet been destroyed by germs created or made more lethal by modern science, as distinct from completely natural disease agents such as the flu and AIDS viruses, is even less reassuring. We haven't had these products long enough to be able to infer survivability from our experience with them. A recent study suggests that as immunity to smallpox declines because people are no longer being vaccinated against it, monkeypox may evolve into "a successful human pathogen,"[15] yet one that vaccination against smallpox would provide at least some protection against; and even before the discovery of the smallpox vaccine, smallpox did not wipe out the human race. What is new is the possibility that science, bypassing evolution, will enable monkeypox to be "juiced up" through gene splicing into a far more lethal pathogen than smallpox ever was.

Asteroids

A risk of natural catastrophe that cannot be blamed on technology to even the slightest degree is that of a collision between an asteroid or comet and the earth.[16] I'll ignore comets—only about 1 percent as many comets as asteroids approach close enough to the earth to pose a danger of collision[17] and in addition their cores are made of ice, which makes them less dangerous than asteroids (most of which are rocks, but some of which may be ice too),[18] though some scientists believe that the danger of comets is being seriously underestimated.[19] I'll also ignore "meteorites" in the sense of either really tiny asteroids or mere shards of an asteroid or a comet that happen to break off and fall to earth; they are too small to have catastrophic effects.

A billion asteroids orbit the sun in a belt between Mars and Jupiter. If they all stayed in the belt, they would pose no danger of colliding with the earth. But because of changes over time in their orbits, some of them have strayed and now occupy orbits close enough to the earth's to create a risk of collision. It is estimated that 1,148 asteroids with a diameter of 1 kilometer or more should be considered potentially hazardous near-earth objects because their orbits bring them at times within 7.5 million kilometers of the earth and they are big enough to do tremendous damage. A collision between one of these PHOs and the earth is expected to occur every 500 to 1,000 years.[20] These estimates are based on the frequency of past collisions of asteroids with earth and other planets and with our moon, as well as on calculations of the orbits of those asteroids that have been identified as near-earth objects.

An asteroid that struck what is now Mexico 65 million years ago, though estimated to have been only 10 kilometers (slightly more than 6 miles) in diameter when it entered the earth's atmosphere, is believed to have caused the extinction of the dinosaurs, along with many other forms of life.[21] A similar collision is believed to have occurred 250 million years ago, wiping out 90 percent of the species living then.[22]

Not all geologists and paleontologists agree that the asteroid strike was the sole or major cause of the extinction of the dinosaurs.[23] And among those (the majority) who think it was, there is disagreement over the form of the destruction caused by the strike. The dominant view is that dust from the shattered asteroid blocked sunlight, shutting down photosynthesis, which caused the dinosaurs to starve to death. An alternative view that is gaining ground is that dust alone couldn't have caused the extinction of the dinosaurs; rather, the impact of the asteroid ignited forest fires all across the earth, engendering vast clouds of smoke and soot augmented by clouds of sulfuric acid resulting from the asteroid's having vaporized sulfate rock in the earth when it hit.[24] If the second theory is correct, collisions with asteroids having a diameter of between 0.6 and 1.5 kilometers would be less destructive than adherents of the dust theory would predict, because such collisions would not produce huge clouds of soot and sulfates.[25] But there is little doubt that a collision with an asteroid having a diameter of 10 kilometers might cause the near or even total extinction of the human race by a combination of fire, concussion, enormous tidal waves, and the blocking for several years of the sunlight required for crops and other plant life. "By this size [10 kilometers], most of the world's [human] population would almost certainly perish."[26]

Even a collision with a much smaller asteroid—1.5 to 2 kilometers— might kill a billion or more people.[27] Collisions with asteroids of that size are believed to occur on average only once in 500,000 to 1 million years.[28] But the literature also contains an estimate of a 1/360,000 annual probability that an asteroid with a diameter of at least 1.7 kilometers will collide with the earth, with horrendous effects,[29] including a death toll that might reach 1.5 billion.[30] In contrast, a collision with an asteroid 10 kilometers or larger is expected to occur only once in

What are the catastrophic risks, and how catastrophic are they?

25

50 million to 100 million years,[31] and only one of the current near-earth objects identified so far is this large. But as of April 2003, only 645 of the estimated 1,148 near-earth objects had been identified, and 22 of the 645 (including the one giant) have a diameter of at least 3.5 kilometers and another 96 have a diameter of at least 1.8 kilometers.[32] There may be as many as 300,000 near-earth objects with a diameter of at least 100 meters, although 100,000 is considered the best estimate.[33]

Nor should the destructive effects of the innumerable smaller asteroids be ignored. An asteroid that may have been no more than 50 meters in diameter exploded five miles above the Tunguska River region of Siberia in 1908, generating a quantity of energy equivalent to that of 10 to 15 megatons of TNT, the equivalent of an early hydrogen bomb.[34]

Table 1.1 summarizes the types of asteroid collision, with associated probabilities and consequences. Note however that in most cases these are *maximum* consequences: a Tunguska-sized asteroid, for example, will have the consequences listed in the second row of the table only if it explodes above or near a large city, which is extremely unlikely because large cities occupy only a minute fraction of the earth's surface. The damage done by a colliding or exploding asteroid will vary with its closing speed and density, as well as with its size and where it hits. Thus, if an asteroid explodes far enough away from the earth, as most incoming asteroids do, there is no harm, and likewise if it shrinks to a harmless size as a result of the heat of the atmosphere or melts in that heat because it is made of ice. Not much comfort can be taken from shrinkage of a large asteroid during its descent through the earth's atmosphere, however. That shrinkage is the by-product of the release of destructive energy that heats the column of air in the path of the plunging asteroid. That is why estimates of the effects of asteroid strikes are based on the size of the asteroid when it begins its descent through the atmosphere.

Because of the small size even of asteroids large enough to cause colossal destruction, and the high speed (it might easily be as high as 25 miles per second)[35] at which an asteroid would hit the earth unless it had disintegrated in the atmosphere, an impending collision would not be discovered more than a second or two before impact unless a telescope happened to be pointed in the right direction. And if the asteroid's presence were discovered, there would be no way to prevent the collision. However, a network of earth- or space-based telescopes, deployed to maintain continuous surveillance of the entire sky so that asteroids approaching the earth from any direction would be

Table 1.1. Impact Effects of Near-Earth Objects

NEO diameter	Yield (megatons)	Crater diameter (km)	Average interval between impact (years)	Consequences
	<10			Upper atmosphere detonation of "stones" (stony asteroids) and comets; only "irons" (iron asteroids <3%), penetrate to surface
75m	10 to 100	1.5	1,000	Irons make craters (Barringer Crater); stones produce air-bursts (Tunguska). Land impacts could destroy area the size of a city (Washington, London, Moscow).
160m	100 to 1,000	3	4,000	Irons and stones produce ground-bursts; comets produce air-bursts. Ocean impacts produce significant tsunamis. Land impacts destroy area the size of a large urban area (New York, Tokyo).
350m	1,000 to 10,000	6	16,000	Impacts on land produce craters; ocean-wide tsunamis are produced by ocean impacts. Land impacts destroy area the size of a small state (Delaware, Estonia).
700m	10,000 to 100,000	12	63,000	Tsunamis reach hemispheric scales, exceed damage from land impacts. Land impacts destroy area the size of a moderate state (Virginia, Taiwan).
1.7km	100,000 to 1 million	30	250,000	Both land and ocean impacts raise enough dust to affect climate, freeze crops. Ocean impacts generate global scale tsunamis. Global destruction of ozone. Land impacts destroy area the size of a large state (California, France, Japan). A 30-km crater penetrates through all but the deepest ocean depths.
3km	1 million to 100 million	60	1 million	Both land and ocean impacts raise dust, change climate. Impact ejecta are global, triggering widespread fires. Land impacts destroy area the size of a large nation (Mexico, India).
7km	10 million to 100 million	125	10 million	Prolonged climate effects, global conflagration, probable mass extinction. Direct destruction approaches continental scale (Australia, Europe, USA).
16km	100 million to 1 billion	250	100 million	Large mass extinction (for example K/T or Cretaceous-Tertiary geological boundary).
	>1 billion			Threatens survival of all advanced life forms.

Source: Report of the [U.K.] Task Force on Potentially Hazardous Near Earth Objects 16 (Sept. 2000).

spotted, could be built that would give warning months, years, or even centuries in advance that a dangerously large asteroid was likely to hit the earth.

It takes many observations of an astronomical body to be able to determine its precise orbit, a complication being that an asteroid's orbit is subject to slight perturbations, mainly from Jupiter's gravitational field, that have a cumulatively significant effect on its orbit. These perturbations and therefore the asteroid's exact orbit can be determined with enough observations, but the precision required would be very great. A 1-centimeter change in orbit when an asteroid was still some distance from the earth could cause the asteroid, though it seemed to be heading straight for the earth, to miss it by a safe margin—or an asteroid that seemed certain to miss the earth by a safe margin instead to hit it.[36]

Once an asteroid was determined to be on a collision course with the earth, it might be possible, depending on the size and distance of the asteroid, to use missiles tipped with nuclear or other explosives to change its orbit, or perhaps spacecraft carrying rockets that would be fastened to the asteroid to change its orbit by a steady pushing, which would actually exert greater force than an explosion—yet might take years to accomplish.[37] Successful deflection would depend on the missile's (or spacecraft's) being able to intercept the asteroid while it was still far from earth. For once it was near, its path could no longer be altered enough to avoid the collision. And merely blowing it up might not reduce its lethality. The rain of fragments could be as destructive as a single impact,[38] or even more so, though mainly because there would be a greater likelihood that one of many fragments would hit a populated area than that a single intact asteroid would.[39] Successful deflection of incoming asteroids, whether by pushing or blasting, would also require knowledge that we do not yet have concerning the structure and composition of the asteroids.

Because of such uncertainties, an asteroid defense probably would not be airtight. The farther in the future the estimated date of impact was, the more time there would be to deflect the asteroid but also the greater the likelihood of an error, including an error that resulted in nudging the asteroid *into* a collision course with the earth. But unless the risk of such an error were significant, even an imperfect defense would be beneficial. If the point of impact could be determined only a few weeks in advance, evacuation of the population in its vicinity might save millions of lives even if the impact itself could not be prevented.

As this example shows, prevention is not the only possible response to a risk. This is true even when the risk is of extinction. Were it known that the human race would become extinct in 10 years, people would respond by reducing their savings rate, since savings are a method of shifting consumption to the future. The response would reduce, however slightly, the cost of the impending extinction.

The risk of extinction is only one of the risks created by the asteroid menace, and it is the aggregation of risks that should be the focus of concern. Clark Chapman and David Morrison estimate that the chance of being killed by an asteroid of any size is approximately the same as that of being killed in an airplane crash or a flood.[40] John Lewis estimated that there is a 1 percent chance of an asteroid one or more kilometers in diameter hitting the earth in a millennium, and that such a hit would kill an average of one billion people.[41] This figure equates to an expected annual death rate from such strikes of 10,000. Elsewhere in his book, it is true, Lewis estimated an annual death rate of only 1,479 even when the 1-kilometer threshold was dropped and all possible asteroid (and comet and meteorite) collisions were considered.[42] But that figure was based on a Monte Carlo simulation (Monte Carlo simulations map probabilities onto timescales, showing when a probabilistic event might occur on the timescale covered by the simulations) that was truncated at 10,000 years; thus a very rare, very destructive asteroid collision might not show up in the truncated simulation but would if the simulation covered a longer interval.

Other natural catastrophes

Other natural catastrophes besides pandemics and asteroid collisions are of course possible, including a volcanic eruption in Yellowstone National Park that might be a thousand times more powerful than that of of Mount St. Helens—an eruption that had the explosive energy of 24 megatons of TNT, about twice that of the Tunguska asteroid explosion.[43] Volcanic eruptions have, however, less cataclysmic potential than pandemics or asteroid strikes. There is usually some warning, and the upper bound of destruction is lower, in part because few volcanoes are located in heavily populated areas. (Vesuvius, near Naples, is an exception.) But major volcanic eruptions are far more frequent than serious asteroid collisions, and so the expected cost of the former may be equal to or, in all likelihood, greater than that of the latter, though this may depend on whether the harm of extinction deserves a special weight, an issue I take up in chapter 3.

What are the catastrophic risks, and how catastrophic are they?

29

There have been horrendous earthquakes, of which the great Lisbon earthquake of 1755, which is estimated to have killed 60,000 people, is very far from having been the largest; an earthquake in Shensi, China, in 1556 is estimated to have killed more than 800,000 people.[44] But earthquakes, like volcanoes, do local rather than global damage. I shall skip over these and other natural catastrophes and move to the man-made ones.

Scientific accidents

The strangelet scenario

Several types of catastrophe that might result from scientific accidents (the sort of thing most famously dramatized by Mary Shelley's novel *Frankenstein*) deserve consideration. Another, the accidental production of lethal new germs, I defer to the discussion of bioweaponry later in the chapter.

As explained by Sir Martin Rees, professor of physics at the University of Cambridge and the United Kingdom's Astronomer Royal, the physics of subatomic particles is not so well understood that the following end-of-the-world scenario can be dismissed as total fantasy. Collisions of atomic particles in very powerful particle accelerators, though perhaps no more powerful than an existing accelerator, the Relativistic Heavy Ion Collider at the Brookhaven National Laboratory in Long Island (RHIC), might conceivably produce a shower of quarks that would

> reassemble themselves into a very compressed object called a strangelet. . . . A strangelet could, by contagion, convert anything else it encountered into a strange new form of matter. . . . A hypothetical strangelet disaster could transform the entire planet Earth into an inert hyperdense sphere about one hundred meters across.[45]

Rees considers this "hypothetical scenario" exceedingly unlikely, yet points out that even a probability of 1 in a billion is not wholly negligible when the result, should the improbable materialize, would be so total a disaster.

Concern with possible catastrophic consequences of particle-accelerator experiments led the director of the Brookhaven National Laboratory to commission a risk assessment, by a committee of physicists chaired by Robert Jaffe, before authorizing RHIC to begin operating in June 2000.[46] In a synopsis of the assessment, the director, John Marburger, offered this lucid summary of the strangelet doomsday scenario:

> All particles ever observed to contain "strange" quarks have been found to be unstable, but it is conceivable that under some conditions stable strangelets could exist. If such a particle were also negatively charged, it would be captured by an ordinary nucleus as if it were a heavy electron. Being heavier, it would move closer to the nucleus than an electron and eventually fuse with the nucleus, converting some of the "up" and "down" quarks in its protons and neutrons, releasing energy, and ending up as a larger strangelet. If the new strangelet were negatively charged, the process could go on forever.[47]

That is, the strangelet would keep growing until all matter was converted to strange matter.

The possible catastrophes examined by the assessors were not limited to a strangelet disaster. They included creating a black hole that would swallow the earth and maybe the rest of our solar system as well, and destroying the entire universe by causing a phase transition. What we call "space" may conceivably "exist in different 'phases,' rather as water can exist in three forms: ice, liquid, and steam. . . . Some [physicists] have speculated that the concentrated energy created when [subatomic] particles crash together could trigger a 'phase transition' that would rip the fabric of space itself," destroying all the atoms in the entire universe.[48] However, these consequences seem much less likely even than a strangelet disaster. One minor though intriguing reason for thinking this is that if there is intelligent life elsewhere in the universe, as seems highly likely from the sheer number of planets (see the introduction), some civilization more advanced than our own would already have built a particle accelerator as powerful as RHIC, precipitating a phase transition that would have destroyed the universe.

RHIC (pronounced "Rick" by insiders) is not actually the world's most powerful accelerator. Collisions at Fermilab's Tevatron accelerator (in Batavia, Illinois) between individual protons and antiprotons generate energies greater than those at RHIC. The difference is that by colliding and shattering gold nuclei, which are far more massive than a single proton or antiproton—each gold nucleus contains 197 protons and neutrons—experiments at RHIC produce an unprecedented volume of quarks (the constituents of protons and neutrons), which might

What are the catastrophic risks, and how catastrophic are they?

31

include a large number of strange quarks, though none has been detected. It is the possibility of producing a shower of strange quarks that gives rise to anxiety about their clumping to form a strangelet that might have a negative charge and set off the chain reaction described by Rees and Marburger.[49]

To add to one's worries, the Center for European Nuclear Research (CERN), in Geneva, is planning to begin operating an accelerator—the Large Hadron Collider—in 2007 that will outdo RHIC in luminosity. "Luminosity" is the scientific terms for how likely it is for collisions to occur in an accelerator. The more that occur, the more quarks, including strange quarks, are likely to be produced. It is the enhanced luminosity of RHIC, compared to existing accelerators, that creates concern that particle collisions in RHIC might cause a strangelet disaster. In addition, Brookhaven is seeking funding for a $150 million upgrade of RHIC ("RHIC–II"), to begin operating in 2010, that will enable particle collisions with up to 40 times the luminosity of RHIC.[50]

It is tempting to dismiss the risk of a strangelet disaster on the ground that the mere fact that a risk cannot be shown to be precluded by a law of nature is not a sound reason to worry about it. Should I be afraid to swim in Loch Ness lest I be devoured by Nessie? This question was put to me by a physicist who is deeply skeptical about the strangelet scenario. The question is not well formed. The interesting question is whether a sea "monster" of some sort, perhaps a dinosaur that managed to avoid extinction, or, more probably, some large sea mammal, may be lurking somewhere in the lake. No law of nature forbids that there shall be such a creature in a deep Scottish lake, and although none has been found despite extensive searches, and many fraudulent sightings have been unmasked,[51] it is unclear whether the entire lake has been searched.[52] It seems extraordinarily unlikely that there is anything that would qualify as a "Loch Ness Monster"—but would one want to bet the planet that there is not?

Or consider the proposition that no human being has ever eaten an entire adult elephant at one sitting. Philosophers use such propositions to argue that one can have empirical certainty without a confirming observation. Yet although there is no known instance of such a meal, it is conceivable that modern technology could so compact an elephant as to make it digestible in one sitting, and it is also conceivable, though only barely, that someone, somewhere, has successfully employed that technology. It is *exceedingly* unlikely (even if one throws in the possibility that someone has succeeded in breeding a miniature elephant), but, again, one wouldn't want to bet the planet on its not having occurred.

Experiments conducted in RHIC are expected to produce 200 billion collisions of gold nuclei;[53] one would like to be more confident that none of them will cause a strangelet disaster than one is confident that there is no large sea animal in Loch Ness or that no human being has ever devoured an adult elephant at one sitting. The RHIC assessors concluded, however, that the risk of a strangelet disaster was too slight to worry about (the accuracy of their assessment has been questioned, as we shall see in chapter 3),[54] and the accelerator went into operation with no untoward consequences.

"With no untoward consequences"—and so, one may be inclined to remark, the assessors were vindicated and another Chicken Little scenario laughed away. But were they vindicated, really? And should the fact that the world has survived four years of experiments at RHIC make us smile at those who thought permitting such experimentation might result in the destruction of the earth? The answer to both questions is no. It's not as if any responsible person had thought the probability that the first experiment conducted at RHIC would have catastrophic consequences was 100 percent, or anywhere close to that figure. The fact that the accelerator has operated without incident for four years tells us nothing about the probability of catastrophe except that it is indeed less than 100 percent in four years. Suppose the assessors had thought the probability zero, and the critics of RHIC had thought it was .0000001 (one in 10 million) per year. Uneventful operation for four years would not enable a choice to be made between these two estimates. Yet as we shall see in chapter 3, the choice might be crucial to whether the project could have passed a cost-benefit test had it been subjected to one (it was not).

Now it is true that the best reason for not betting the world on there not being a Loch Ness Monster or that no human being has ever eaten an entire adult elephant at one sitting is that winning the bet wouldn't yield a significant benefit to offset the risk, tiny as it is. So if experiments in RHIC are likely to yield a significant benefit, we might be quite rational to accept the remote possibility of even complete disaster. As we shall see in chapter 3, however, it is uncertain whether such experiments are likely to yield a significant benefit.

An exceedingly modest variant of the strangelet doomsday scenario, yet still a frightening portent, occurred a few years ago and merits no-

What are the catastrophic risks, and how catastrophic are they?

33

tice. It involved the AIDS drug ritonavir (trade name Norvir). Two years after Abbott Laboratories began commercial production of the drug, a previously unknown polymorph (that is, a different crystalline form of the drug's active ingredient) appeared in Abbott's Illinois plant. Immediately the old form began converting to the new, because the new form was more stable. (Later-appearing polymorphs tend to be more stable than earlier-appearing ones. The less stable a crystal is, the more likely it is to convert to a more stable crystalline form, and once it has converted it is unlikely to convert back.)[55] The conversion precipitated a market crisis because the new form did not have the therapeutic properties of the old. Fortunately (or so it seemed), the new form had not yet been observed in the plant in Italy where the bulk ritonavir was manufactured for shipment to the Illinois plant to be made into pills. But shortly after a visit to that plant by Abbott scientists from Illinois, the new form showed up there too, probably as a result of "seeding" of the plant by minute crystals—perhaps no more than a few tens of molecules in size[56]—that had adhered to the scientists' clothing. As a result, the plant could no longer produce the old form.[57]

Crystal conversion by seeding is becoming more common, apparently because conversion from one crystalline form to another is impeded by impurities; they interfere with the formation of new crystalline forms. Impurities in the manufacture of chemicals are becoming less common, because of improvements in the technology of manufacturing. It is another example of how technological progress can cause trouble.

The relevance of crystal conversion by seeding to the strangelet scenario lies in the fact that the mechanism of that conversion is not yet well understood,[58] just as the behavior of the most fundamental constituents of the universe is not yet well understood—which is why physicists want ever more powerful particle accelerators. High-energy physicists know a great deal more about those constituents than they did 100 years ago or even 20 years ago, but they will acknowledge that they probably know very little relative to what there is to know about such things.

The analogy of strangelets to crystals must not be pressed too hard. The bonds that hold atoms together in a crystal are weaker by several orders of magnitude than those binding the particles in an atom's nucleus.[59] They can usually be severed by the application to the crystal of moderate amounts of heat or pressure or by placing the crystal in a solvent, such as water. The energies required to decompose a subatomic particle into its component quarks (including the strange quark—the bad guy in the strangelet doomsday scenario) are greater still by several orders of magnitude.[60] Probably the energies deployed in particle accelerators are too weak to set off the kind of chain reaction envisaged in the strangelet scenario, or to create black holes, a new big bang, or a catastrophic phase transition, as distinct from the kind of chain reaction sparked off by the seeding of Abbott's Italian plant by tiny crystals, especially since strange quarks are expected to decay very rapidly. But we cannot take too much comfort from the difference between the two phenomena. Size is not important to setting off a chain reaction. A minimum crystal, consisting of just a few atoms, may be large enough to convert an adjacent, less stable crystal, which in turn becomes a converter of its neighbors; by this means, conversion proceeds exponentially.[61] It is conceivable that the same type of chain reaction could be started by a tiny strangelet.

Omnivorous nanomachines

Martin Rees, a highly distinguished physicist whose calm but frightening book has been respectfully reviewed in reputable scientific journals,[62] worries also about the potential effects of laboratory accidents involving nanomachines. He has in mind machines, not yet designed or built but on the horizon, that would be measured in nanometers, which are billionths of a meter.[63] (A nanometer is roughly four times the diameter of an atom.) Nanotechnology has many other uses besides the as yet hypothetical one of creating nanomachines. For example, by rearranging the atoms in carbon molecules, nanotechnologists can create superstrong carbon filaments.[64] And in combination with bioengineering, nanotechnology may soon enable the economical manufacture of computer chips the size of molecules.[65] But Rees's concern lies elsewhere.

Living cells contain machines, such as the ribosome, that manufacture protein molecules out of simpler molecules that enter the cell from the bloodstream. Cells thus engage in "self-assembly," the process by which "components, either separate or linked, spontaneously form ordered aggregates,"[66] but the ribosome within a cell performs its manufacturing operations under dictation by a genetic program. Chemical or physical means (the latter including microscopes equipped with tips that can move and position individual atoms and molecules)[67] may someday be used to create similar machines ("assemblers") at the nanometric level. Self-assembly is important because nanosized ma-

What are the catastrophic risks, and how catastrophic are they?

35

chines are too small to be economically created by building them one by one; they have to be able to build themselves. "Systematic organization of matter on the nanometer length scale is a key feature of biological systems. Nanotechnology will allow us to place components and assemblies inside cells and to make new materials using the self-assembly methods of nature."[68]

Nanotech self-assembly is illustrated by a process by which germanium atoms, when deposited in the correct number on a properly prepared silicon surface, form themselves into a pyramid by the interactions of the atoms with each other.[69] In other words, the germanium atoms build their own pyramid. Already self-assembly is being used to create nanowire elements and molecular computer chips.[70]

And still this is not what Rees is worried about. He is worried about a possible further step—nanomachines that would be general-purpose assemblers, just like living cells, which manufacture proteins *and themselves*.[71] The distinction is between self-assembly, in which small, relatively simple parts combine to form somewhat more complex structures, as in the example of the germanium atoms, and self-replication, in which a complex system reproduces itself, thus creating additional self-reproducers, on the model of cell division. In short, Rees is worried about artificial life. Conceivably nanomachines could be "designed to be more omnivorous than any bacterium, perhaps even able to consume all organic materials. Metabolising efficiently, and utilising solar energy, they could then proliferate uncontrollably, and not reach the Malthusian limit until they had consumed all life."[72] Self-replication implies exponential growth, sorcerer's apprentice–fashion: 2 becomes 4, 4 becomes 8, and so on. With an unlimited power source enabling rapid replication and hence multiplication, the creatures might smother the earth.

The word "designed" in the passage I just quoted from Rees suggests deliberate rather than accidental creation of an extinction technology. But the monster—"gray goo" engulfing the world—might be created accidentally if nanomachines with the basic abilities required for self-replication were built. The danger is taken seriously enough by leading nanotechnologists to have impelled them to issue guidelines limiting the power supply for nanomachines to power sources that, unlike sunlight, are not found in the natural environment.[73] The contention by the distinguished chemist Richard Smalley that self-replicating nanomachines will never be created is hardly reassuring, given the record of scientists' "never" predictions.[74]

Nanotechnology has many beneficial applications and is being subsidized by the U.S. government to the tune of almost $750 million a year.[75] As far as I know, none of this money is being allocated to research into the dangers that the technology poses, or into guiding research away from self-replication and into safer methods of producing nanomachines, such as autoproduction, in which nanosized assemblers would create nanomachines in the desired quantity but would not replicate themselves. (The sense, doubtless, is that since the danger of omnivorous nanomachines lies in the future, though probably only by a decade or two, we can postpone consideration of it.) The exquisite difficulties in dealing with a dangerous technology that might also be the solution to problems created by other dangerous technologies are illustrated by the possibility that slightly less voracious nanomachines than those feared by Rees might alleviate the problem of global warming by devouring carbon dioxide molecules in the air.[76]

The dangers of nanotechnology are not limited to self-replicating nanomachines. As Eric Drexler explains in a private communication,

> Molecular manufacturing will be able to produce aerospace systems orders of magnitude cheaper than today's, with lighter structures and engines, superior sensors, and a billion times more onboard computer power. The enormous productive capacity of molecular manufacturing has an ominous weapons potential, and this has nothing to do with self-replication. Imagine cruise missiles that after traveling thousands of miles (as existing cruise missiles can do) release smaller missiles that travel tens of miles and release wasp-sized missiles that can fly for miles to specific targets. On arrival, these small machines could take action (lethal or nonlethal), or could land, watch, and communicate with one another and a command center. They could wait for hours or years, then take off again to reposition or strike. A million tons of such weapons, with imaginative use of payloads, sensing, and coordination, could be a potent means of global conquest and control.

Genetically modified crops

The strangelet doomsday scenario, polymorphic crystalline conversion, and nanometric omnivores, diverse as these phenomena (actual or envisaged) are, all exemplify uncontrolled replication. We can

What are the catastrophic risks, and how catastrophic are they?

37

think of Rees's hypothetical omnivores, for example, as cancer cells raised to new orders of reproductive frenzy. The structure of even the simplest form of life is immensely complex, but my earlier reference to crystals should remind us that the line between the living and the non-living is somewhat fuzzy. Crystals display several lifelike characteristics: a relatively high degree of complexity, a responsiveness to environmental stimuli (the conversion phenomenon) greater than one expects from inanimate matter (compare crystal conversion to a stone's splintering when struck by a hammer), and the ability to replicate themselves (the conversion phenomenon viewed from the standpoint of the seeds). We can think of Rees's omnivores as standing midway between crystalline and true life, much like viruses, which "belong in the twilight zone between the living and nonliving worlds."[77] A virus is a fragment of genetic material, either DNA or RNA, encapsulated in proteins. The fragment is not alive, but if it gets into a cell, the cell will replicate the viral material.[78] Laboratory accidents involving natural viruses and other natural disease agents could have catastrophic consequences as well.

Another well-known replicator is the plant we call the weed (actually a number of different plant species). Its capacity for replication and its robust health—properties that together make it destructive of other plant life—in moderation improve agricultural yields. And so we are beginning to see the hybridization of weeds with crops, a form of gene splicing (more precisely, recombinant DNA technology) that produces genetically modified crops (GMCs), also called transgenic crops. But "in moderation" is an important qualification. The danger once again is that the process might get out of hand—that juiced-up weed genes introduced into crops might escape, through sexual reproduction (transfer of pollen from stamen to pistil), into natural flora of the same species, causing the natural flora to become destructively aggressive and herbicide resistant—to become, in short, *much* weedier.[79] (So Rees's feared nanomachines could be thought of as inorganic superweeds.) Alternatively, a genetically modified plant or animal, such as a growth-enhanced salmon, might, if loose in the wild, outcompete and destroy native species, contributing to the loss of biodiversity discussed in a later section of this chapter. Bioconfinement, as by sterilizing genetically modified plants or animals in an effort to isolate them from natural populations, may be of only limited efficacy against these dangers.[80]

Indur Goklany believes that the benefits of genetically modified crops clearly exceed the costs,[81] and of course he is not alone in this belief.[82] But he does not consider the possibility of disastrous effects on native species. And the principal benefit of GMCs that he perceives— that without them it may be impossible to support a world population in 2050 that is 50 percent greater than today's population[83]—neglects the social costs of population growth, such as an increase in the production of greenhouse gases (more on this later). This neglect is surprising because Goklany recognizes global warming as a serious problem.[84]

Artificial intelligence

Speaking of borderlands between life and nonlife, there may some day, perhaps some day soon (decades, not centuries, hence), be robots with human and eventually (but decades, not centuries, later) more than human intelligence. It wasn't long ago that people thought a chess machine could never beat a grand master; we now know better. With improvements in voice- and face-recognition software, neuroscience, robotics, communications, digitization, and artificial intelligence, there are now robot soccer teams, albeit the players are only the size of coffee cans and move on wheels.[85] Of greater portent, electrodes planted in monkeys' brains enable the animals to control robotic arms, connected by wire to the electrodes, by sheer thought.[86] Similar electrodes in human brains, connected wirelessly to robots, would open up new vistas in warfare.

The next step would be to replace the human brain with an equally intelligent robot's brain. No law of science decrees that life shall always be constructed, and by "nature," not man, from certain compounds of carbon. Superintelligent robots with a silicon or other inorganic base (or an organic one, for that matter) may be the next stage in evolution. Human beings may turn out to be the twenty-first century's chimpanzees, and if so the robots may have as little use and regard for us as we do for our fellow, but nonhuman, primates. The robots may kill us, put us in zoos, or enslave us, using mind-control technologies to extinguish any possibility of revolt, as in the movie *The Matrix*, which I discuss in the next chapter.

This prospect has become obscured by a debate over whether robots can ever develop consciousness, by a related debate over the possibility that artificial intelligence can ever transcend merely algorithmic computation (the sort of thing computers do so well),[87] and by the fallacy of believing that robots will never develop emotions and therefore will forever be harmless. The first debate, and the fallacy, owe much

What are the catastrophic risks, and how catastrophic are they?

39

to Ray Kurzweil's book *The Age of Spiritual Machines.* The word "spiritual" says it all. Kurzweil envisages a merger between robotic and human beings by the end of this century.[88] He believes that no human capacity is beyond the foreseeably enlarged mental capacity of machines, which is sensible, but he looks forward to the development of such machines without misgivings, which is more dubious. He reminds one of those astronomers who, with the support of NASA, are trying to advertise our existence to possible intelligent life in other solar systems. "Pioneer" spacecraft carried plaques depicting a male and female figure, the solar system's place in the galaxy and the earth's location within that system, and the hydrogen atom, while "Voyager" spacecraft, which at this writing are nearing the edge of the solar system, carry gold-plated copper records with pictures of life on earth, greetings in 80 languages, and a selection of music beginning with Bach.[89] Our eager searchers for extraterrestrial life are heedless of the danger that beings more intelligent than we—and many planets, perhaps a million in our galaxy alone, may be inhabited by beings as intelligent as we[90]— might, if they discovered our existence, want to destroy us or put us in zoos, and be capable of doing so. Like Kurzweil, the searchers subscribe to the unwarranted belief that intelligence and goodness (*our* conception of goodness, moreover) are positively correlated, or that progress is always—progressive, which if true would mean that the twentieth century had been less violent than the nineteenth; in fact, it was more violent.

There is more reason to worry about robots than about extraterrestrials. Extraterrestrial beings who have the requisite technology may already have discovered us, by means of ultrapowerful telescopes or other detection devices. (The devices would have to be ultrapowerful because the intensity of electromagnetic radiation decreases with distance. Radio waves emanating from human activities on earth are therefore exceedingly weak at interstellar distances—indeed, most of those waves are bounced back by the atmosphere, though this would not be true of waves emanating from spacecraft.) If so, there is no need to try to make ourselves known to them and anyway nothing we can do to protect ourselves. Fortunately, the danger is pretty slight because of the distances involved. Radiation traveling at the speed of light takes four years to reach Alpha Centauri, the star nearest our sun, and 30,000 years to reach the center of our galaxy (the Milky Way). So unless the aliens are perched on a neighboring planet, we are safe from them.

And if they are perched on a nearby planet, they know all about us and can pounce at any time and as there is nothing we can do about it we might as well not worry. Another possibility is that any intelligent life in other solar systems that might have done us harm destroyed itself by attaining a level of scientific sophistication at which the destructive potential of science got out of hand and destroyed the civilization that created it[91]—the level we may be approaching.

To return to the danger posed by advances in artificial intelligence, robots may not need to achieve consciousness—which is to say self-consciousness, as distinct from merely being awake, that is, switched on—in order to surpass us. Nor is it reassuring that current robots, including the limbless robots we call computers, are not programmed with emotions. A robot's potential destructiveness does not depend on its being conscious or able to engage in nonalgorithmic calculation of the sort involved in many human and animal intellectual processes. The game of chess is modeled on war, though it is immensely simpler, if only because the possible moves are more limited and there is no resource constraint. Still, it may be a portent of things to come that computers, playing chess algorithmically rather than, as human players do, intuitively, can now beat the best human players—something unforeseen until quite recently. Robots several generations from now may be able to beat any nation in a war. It might seem that, lacking emotions, a creature, however intelligent, would not actually *do* anything, that it would have no motivations. But single-cell organisms act as if purposefully, without having a suite of emotions. A nation or terrorist group that wanted to use robots to wage war could easily program them to be destructive. Unless carefully programmed, the robots might prove indiscriminately destructive and turn on their creators.

Moreover, although the human brain, with its 100 billion neurons and 100 trillion connections among them, is enormously more complex than any current computer—maybe a million times more complex[92]—no known principle of nature decrees that neuroscientists shall never, ever, reverse-engineer the brain and use the information gleaned to duplicate the brain by means of nanotechnology. A nanotube, which is a strand of molecular carbon only one atom in thickness, can conduct electricity and is therefore a candidate to succeed the much larger silicon chip and become the basis of a computer comparable in power and compactness to the human brain. We may even be within reach of creating minute quantum computers of immense power. "It has been claimed

What are the catastrophic risks, and how catastrophic are they?

41

that a classical computer could take as long as the age of the universe to factor a 200-digit number into its prime cofactors. . . . It is possible that a quantum computer could factor that number in minutes."[93]

Anyway compactness is not critical. In "grid" computing, advanced software is used to organize a large number of small computers into a single system. The Internet connects tens of millions of computers; the aggregate computer power is comparable to that of a human brain. The problem of creating a computer with the capability of the human brain is not hardware but software—designing programs that would create out of the multitude of computer circuits the immensely complex processing networks found in brains. But the problem may not be insoluble, and Kurzweil probably is correct that "once a computer achieves a human level of intelligence, it will necessarily roar past it"[94] because it calculates much faster than the human brain; signals move through neurons in chemical waves, which are much slower than electrons moving in electric circuits.

With superhuman intelligence may come self-consciousness, which we human beings, after all, have managed to attain with merely human-level intelligence—and chimpanzees with less. And then the situation could get completely out of hand. Once robots have not only superhuman intelligence but also emotions and self-consciousness, they may begin to reflect on whether it makes sense to allow themselves to be bossed around by a dumber species, and they may decide to act on their reflections.

It might seem that to "decide" implies the possession of free will, and how could a machine be endowed with *that* faculty? But to "decide" need imply nothing more mysterious than to act in conformity with the result of a cost-benefit analysis or some other decision procedure. A chess-playing computer "decides" to make the move that gives it the best chance of winning. Its decision is as if purposive, though presumably there is no self-awareness of decision making. A robot equipped with a cost-benefit algorithm that specified safety or survival as the transcendent benefit might "decide" that its best course was to enslave or destroy the human race.

Even if robots never develop the ability or inclination to take over the world, in the hands of human beings they could still constitute weapons of mass destruction comparable to the most destructive forms of nuclear and biological warfare. For this purpose, all that would be necessary would be for the robots to be able to identify and destroy human targets—a capability close to being achieved by the Unmanned

Aerial Vehicles that the United States used in the Afghan war in 2001,[95] and later in Yemen — and to reproduce. The latter possibility is foreshadowed by experiments with robots that "hunt" their own sources of energy (catching 100 slugs an hour and using the slugs' rotting bodies to generate electricity),[96] that repair and maintain themselves,[97] and that assemble themselves.[98] Imagine these capabilities married to the latest triumph of robotics—the creation of a

> physically implemented robotic system that applies techniques from artificial intelligence to carry out cycles of scientific experimentation. The system automatically originates hypotheses to explain observations, devises experiments to test these hypotheses, physically runs the experiments using a laboratory robot, interprets the results to falsify hypotheses inconsistent with the data, and then repeats the cycle.[99]

Other unintended man-made catastrophes

Global warming

To return to ritonavir for a moment, Abbott managed without too much difficulty to create a new crystalline polymorph that had the therapeutic properties of the one that had disappeared through conversion. But the costs of eliminating the hazards thrown up by technology can be staggering. This is strikingly the case with regard to global warming and makes assessment of the magnitude of the global-warming problem a matter of high urgency. According to the statistician Bjørn Lomborg, the costs of arresting global warming could be many trillions of dollars greater than the costs of global warming itself.[100] This is in contrast to the modest costs of substitution for the chlorofluorocarbons that were destroying the ozone layer in the stratosphere. That substitution is the success story of international efforts to control environmental hazards,[101] though Rees claims that "it was a technological accident and quirk of chemistry that the commercial coolant adopted in the 1930s was based on chlorine. Had bromine been used instead, the atmospheric effects would have been more drastic and longer-lasting."[102]

Lomborg is Greenpeace's bête noire, an "anti-gloom environmental propagandist," according to Rees.[103] His analysis of global warming is indeed deficient.[104] Yet even he accepts an estimate of $5 trillion for the social costs (discounted to present value) of global warming,[105]

What are the catastrophic risks, and how catastrophic are they?

43

while William Nordhaus, the leading economic expert on global warming, estimates its social costs at only $4 trillion.[106] What Lomborg is really pointing to is not an exaggerated concern with the dangers of global warming but an absence of institutional controls that has let it get out of hand.

The $4 trillion and $5 trillion estimates of the social costs of global warming are, however, misleading in two respects. First, because they are present-value estimates, the proper comparison is not with the world's annual output of goods and services but rather with the stock of physical and human capital that generates that output. For the United States alone, with its $10 trillion annual GDP, the value of that stock is probably at least $100 trillion, compared to which $5 trillion is merely large. Also, $5 trillion is a much smaller percentage of Gross World Product, estimated by the World Bank at $31.4 trillion in 2001, than of the U.S. GDP. GWP is much the better benchmark because the costs of global warming will be widely diffused; indeed, probably few of those costs will be borne by the United States.

But in another respect the $4 trillion and $5 trillion estimates understate the potential menace of global warming. They are based primarily on the destructive effect of higher temperatures on agriculture in developing countries[107] and on increased flooding because of partial melting of the Greenland and Antarctic ice caps and other temperature-related factors.[108] The consequences of global warming may be much worse, especially if the warming is abrupt—as it may be.

To understand the danger, one must understand how human activities can affect the earth's climate.[109]

Although carbon dioxide and other "greenhouse gases," such as methane, are only a small component of the atmosphere, they make the earth habitable because they don't block any sunlight from reaching the earth but do reflect heat radiated skyward from the earth's surface. Without them, the earth's climate would be frigid.[110] A secondary effect arises from the fact that water vapor has a very substantial greenhouse effect if it remains dissolved in the atmosphere rather than returning to earth as rain or snow. The warmer the atmosphere, the greater its water-retention capacity and so the more water vapor remains in the atmosphere, amplifying the warming effect of the other greenhouse gases.

The percentage of greenhouse gases in the atmosphere has been rising steadily since the Industrial Revolution, with much of the increase occurring in the last thirty years. The main causes of the increase appear to be twofold. First is the burning of ever-greater amounts of fossil fuels—principally oil, natural gas, and coal—to produce energy. (Another possible cause, just beginning to receive attention, is also a product of burning: soot.)[111] The fossil fuels are carbon based, and burning them produces carbon dioxide as a by-product.

Second is deforestation. Trees absorb carbon dioxide; and burning down a forest, which is the usual method of deforestation, like other forms of oxidization of carbon-based matter releases carbon dioxide, both from the trees themselves and from the soil beneath them.[112] Deforestation must be distinguished from a forest's steady state, in which the absorption of carbon dioxide by photosynthesis is offset by the trees' emission of carbon dioxide when they respire at night (although their net intake of carbon dioxide greatly exceeds the amount they emit)[113], by the eating of leaves and other forest debris by animals, and by decay, which returns carbon to the soil, where some of it is converted to carbon dioxide and methane that eventually return to the atmosphere. (If trees are cut down to produce wood for construction, the effect of decay in eventually liberating carbon dioxide is attenuated.) But there is a lag in the process by which forests generate carbon dioxide to offset their absorption of it by photosynthesis. The result of the lag is that the destruction of a forest has an immediate effect in reducing the absorption of atmospheric carbon dioxide that is in addition to the release of carbon dioxide into the atmosphere when trees are destroyed by being burned.[114]

Increased burning of fossil fuels is a result of economic growth, and deforestation is a result primarily of growth in population. So with both the world economy and world population growing, it is no surprise that emissions of greenhouse gases are growing too.

The higher the percentage of greenhouse gases in the atmosphere, the warmer the climate is likely to be, and beyond some point there could be catastrophic effects on human welfare that are reflected imperfectly in the dollar estimates of the harms from global warming.[115] These effects are powerfully evoked in Margaret Atwood's novel *Oryx and Crake*, which describes the destruction of the nation's coastal regions (Harvard gone the way of Atlantis) and horrific daily thunderstorms, "the coastal aquifers turned salty and the northern permafrost melted and the vast tundra bubbled with methane, and the drought in the midcontinental plains regions went on and on, and the Asian

What are the catastrophic risks, and how catastrophic are they?

45

steppes turned to sand dunes."[116] That is no fantasy. The sober economist William Nordhaus offers the following list of possible "catastrophic consequences" of global warming:

> major surges of the West Antarctic ice sheets, leading to a sea-level rise of 20 feet or more; unexpected shifts in ocean currents, such as displacement of the warm current [the Gulf Stream] that warms the North Atlantic coastal communities; a runaway greenhouse effect in which warming melts tundras and releases large amounts of additional GHGs [greenhouse gases] like methane; large-scale desertification of the current grain belts of the world; very rapid shifts in temperature and sea levels; or the evolution and migration of lethal pests in new climatic conditions.[117]

Neglect of such possibilities undermines the optimistic assessment of the effects of global warming by another economist, Thomas Gale Moore.[118] He presents a "best-case" analysis. He also neglects transition costs. If agriculture in India is destroyed by global warming, it won't be child's play to relocate it to Greenland, even if Greenland has warmed to the point where it can grow tropical crops.

The key question is how *rapidly* catastrophic climate changes might occur. If they occur gradually, there will be time either to adapt, as suggested by Moore, or to apply a technological fix. Stated differently, if they occur gradually, they won't really be catastrophic. But "in a chaotic system, such as the earth's climate, an abrupt climate change always could occur" as a result of an external shock—a "forcing," and "the more rapid the forcing the more likely it is that the resulting [climate] change will be abrupt on the timescale of human economies or global ecosystems."[119] (An analogy is "leaning slightly over the side of a canoe will cause only a small tilt, but leaning slightly more may roll you and the craft into the lake.")[120] The increase in the percentage of greenhouse gases in the atmosphere is a "forcing," and "abrupt" could be as short as a decade.[121] So not only can the possibility of catastrophic climatic change not be relegated to the remote future, but it may be impossible to mitigate the catastrophe by adaptive changes in human activity, as by relocating agriculture from southern to northern climes and moving coastal cities inland.

The idea that what is bad for the tropics is good for the polar regions is questionable on another ground besides the staggering transition costs that would be incurred if global warming were sudden. Both are regions in which the seasonal temperature range is slight compared to that of the temperate zones. Fauna and flora adapted to living in such a region are more vulnerable to temperature change than those native to areas of greater seasonal variation in temperature. If the polar regions become warm enough for agriculture to flourish, they will be too warm for polar bears, penguins, seals, and other cold-weather animals to survive in. The implications for human welfare, setting aside (though there is no reason to set aside) any distress people may feel at the destruction of such lovely fauna (apart from zoo specimens), are unclear. They belong to the general issue of biodiversity loss, which I take up later in this chapter.

The human implications of global warming would be unmistakable if the ice sheets that cover Greenland and Antarctica melted,[122] raising ocean levels to the point at which most coastal regions, including many of the world's largest cities, would be inundated. Or if the dilution of salt in the North Atlantic as a result of the melting of the north polar ice cap, the ice of which is largely salt free, diverted the Gulf Stream away from the continent of Europe.[123] The dense salty water of the North Atlantic blocks the Atlantic currents from carrying warm water from the South Atlantic due north to the Arctic, instead deflecting the warm water east to Europe. That warm-water current is the Gulf Stream.[124] If reduced salinity in the North Atlantic allowed the Gulf Stream to return to its natural northward path, the climate of the entire European continent would become like that of Siberia, and Europe's agriculture would be destroyed.

Worse is possible, such as the runaway greenhouse effect that Nordhaus mentions.[125] Suppose rising temperatures released methane, which is 20 times more efficient than carbon dioxide at trapping heat, from the soil and from the bottom of the oceans, resulting in further warming and so in further releases of methane. Methane is found in great quantity not only in soil and ocean bottoms but also in permafrost, which is already beginning to melt. The melting of glaciers, a parallel phenomenon to the melting of permafrost, can also result in large releases of methane into the atmosphere.[126] A runaway methane greenhouse effect might be augmented by the effect of higher air temperatures in increasing the amount of water vapor in the atmosphere.

It is even conceivable that because increased rainstorms mean more clouds, and some clouds prevent sunlight from reaching the earth without blocking the heat reflected from the earth's surface, global

What are the catastrophic risks, and how catastrophic are they?

47

warming could precipitate a new ice age—or worse. Falling temperatures might cause more precipitation to take the form of snow rather than rain, leading to a further drop in surface temperatures and creating more ice, which reflects sunlight better than seawater and earth (both of which are darker than ice) do, further reducing surface temperatures to the point of producing a return to "snowball earth."[127] The snowball-earth hypothesis is that 600 million years ago, and maybe at earlier times as well, the earth, including the equatorial regions, was for a time entirely covered by a layer of ice several kilometers thick except where the tips of volcanoes peeped through. The downward temperature spiral may have been precipitated by a decline in the amount of greenhouse gases in the atmosphere as a result of a change in the location and configuration of the continents that brought them closer to sources of moisture, causing increased rainfall that scrubbed carbon dioxide out of the atmosphere.[128]

The hypothesis is controversial. It is unclear whether the conditions required for the initiation of snowball earth were ever present,[129] and whether current or foreseeable conditions could cause such initiation. What is most suggestive about the example is the ominous tipping or feedback effect that it illustrates (the canoe analogy). A relatively small change, such as an increase in rainfall caused by global warming, or an increase in the fraction of precipitation that is in the form of snow rather than rain, could trigger a drastic temperature spiral. The runaway greenhouse effect involving methane illustrates the same process in reverse, and, as in the rainfall example in the preceding sentence, one spiral can trigger the opposite spiral.

It is because of such dizzying possibilities that the climate system is "chaotic" in a sense that can be made more precise with the aid of Figure 1.1 and the distinction that it illustrates between linear and nonlinear functions. An example of a linear function would be a demand function in which the price of some good declines by 2 percent for every 1 percent increase in the quantity sold, a relation that can be graphed as a straight line. One could imagine a similar function relating global temperature to the atmospheric concentration of greenhouse gases, and that concentration in turn to the annual amount of greenhouse gases emitted into the atmosphere, such that if emissions were known to be growing at a rate of 1 percent a year we might know that temperature would rise by 0.1 percent a year.

A nonlinear function, however, might produce the sawtooth pattern of Figure 1.1.

Figure 1.1. A Chaotic Function

The equation $x_{t+1} = 1.9 - x_t^2$ is plotted against time (the horizontal axis), with x being given an initial value of 1 and the solution to the equation in period one becoming the value of x in period two, the solution in period two the value of x in period three, and so on.[130] So in period one $x_{t+1} = .9$, which becomes x in period two, generating $x_{t+1} = 1.09$ in period two, which becomes x in period 3, and so on. The result is a chaotic system in the strict mathematical sense. The example shows how a deterministic system (there is no randomness in the graph—every point on it is determined by the equation) can yield abrupt, irregular swings. The earth's climate appears to be chaotic in this sense, and unfortunately the equation that would enable its chaotic pattern to be predicted has not been discovered.

Nordhaus has tried to factor catastrophic global warming into his cost-benefit analysis of measures for limiting emissions of carbon dioxide and other greenhouse gases.[131] His latest study estimates losses from abrupt catastrophic warming that range from 22.1 percent of GDP for the United States and a number of other countries and regions to 44.2 percent for Europe and India.[132] Large as they are, these figures, even though they weight loss of output by a risk-aversion factor, may be too low. The weighted average loss, 30 percent,[133] is similar to that experienced in the worldwide economic depression of the 1930s.[134] That is a subcatastrophic event in my austere sense of "catastrophic," especially since the loss was not permanent. If it had been, this would imply that, had the depression never occurred, the GWP would be 43 percent greater today than it is, for that is the percentage increase necessary to bring 70 percent back up to 100 percent.

A more fundamental point is that no probabilities can be attached to the catastrophic global-warming scenarios, and without an estimate of

What are the catastrophic risks, and how catastrophic are they?

49

probability an expected cost cannot be calculated. This raises a question about Nordhaus's $4 trillion estimate of the present value of the social costs of global warming. Although between one-half and two-thirds of the $4 trillion is an estimate of expected loss from abrupt, catastrophic global warming,[135] that is the roughest of his estimates, and he acknowledges elsewhere that despite his own efforts "there is virtually no linked [economic] research on abrupt climate change."[136] The scientific study of climate has not reached the point of being able to offer precise, accurate predictions because it has not mastered the enormous complexity of the forces that affect climate, such as solar fluctuations, air pollution (which has a cooling effect and thus reduces global warming[137]—Greens, take note), and clouds, which can either warm or cool the earth's surface depending on their height, thickness, and other characteristics.[138] There are, as we have already glimpsed, a number of ominous feedback possibilities.[139] And here is a benign example: deforestation increases the amount of carbon dioxide in the atmosphere, but the increased atmospheric carbon dioxide stimulates the growth of the remaining forests. Global warming may have caused an overall increase in vegetation.[140]

Yet with all the complexities and uncertainties of climate science acknowledged, it remains reasonably certain that the earth has been growing warmer for the last century and a half and at a rate much higher than in most earlier periods in the earth's history,[141] that the increase in the percentage of greenhouse gases during this period is the major cause of this growth and is due largely to increased burning of fossil fuels and other human activities, and that if emissions continue to grow at the rate at which they've been growing in recent decades the percentage of greenhouse gases in the atmosphere will double within 50 to 100 years.[142] Total annual emissions of carbon dioxide from fossil-fuel burning, cement manufacture, and gas flaring alone (that is, disregarding deforestation) rose from 1.6 billion tons in 1950 to 5.3 billion tons in 1980, 6.1 billion in 1990, and 6.6 billion in 2000,[143] and undoubtedly are still rising, though probably at a slower rate.

The rise in global temperatures has already caused a noticeable melting not only of the Alaskan and Siberian permafrost, but also of the polar ice caps.[144] That melting, together with the warming of the oceans (water expands when heated) has caused sea levels to rise,[145] though it should be noted that the melting of the north polar ice cap, as distinct from the melting of the ice sheets that cover Greenland and Antarctica, does not directly contribute to higher sea levels. The north polar ice cap floats on water, and so, as it melts, it displaces less water. The main significance of its melting is the possible effect on the Gulf Stream.

It is not certain that the warming trend will continue even if no efforts are made to limit emissions, for there are other influences on global climate besides the percentage of heat-retaining gases in the air. Between 1900 and 1910 the earth's average temperature declined, and it didn't change between 1940 and 1980, even though emissions of greenhouse gases were growing in both periods.[146] Cutting the other way, however, is the fact that even drastic limits on greenhouse-gas emissions will not actually arrest the warming trend; it will just slow it down,[147] because carbon dioxide is only gradually removed from the atmosphere by being absorbed by the oceans.

Most climate scientists believe that the warming trend will continue but is unlikely to reach a catastrophic level in the near future. The maximum rise in sea levels predicted to occur in this century, according to the scientific consensus, is 0.88 meter, which is less than three feet.[148] The average temperature at the earth's surface is expected to increase by between 1.4 and 5.8 degrees Centigrade (2.5 and 10.4 degrees Fahrenheit).[149] The upper end of that range estimate is alarming but may be an exaggeration.[150] It ignores the possible substitution of new, "clean" energy sources (that is, sources that do not generate energy by burning fossil fuels) as the relative price of the new sources, such as solar batteries,[151] falls because of growing scarcity of fossil fuels and continued advances in the technologies of clean substitutes.

But will fossil fuels become scarce, and will those advances continue, and at what rate? No one can be sure of the answers. And "clean" must be qualified: a determination of how clean a fuel is must consider the conditions of its manufacture. Although hydrogen is a clean fuel in the sense that burning it for energy does not give off carbon dioxide, the current methods of manufacturing hydrogen require large quantities of fossil fuels, so that on balance the substitution of hydrogen for gasoline to power automobiles, for example, would not reduce overall emissions of greenhouse gases.[152]

Nuclear energy, which currently supplies less than 20 percent of worldwide electricity demand, is fully clean. But it is no panacea, because it is much costlier than power generation by plants that burn coal or natural gas, because of the difficulty of disposing of radioactive wastes, because of the danger of a catastrophic meltdown of a nuclear plant — either accidental (as at Chernobyl) or caused by terrorists —

What are the catastrophic risks, and how catastrophic are they?

51

because of the risk of terrorists' obtaining fissionable materials from such plants, and because of public fears of nuclear power that even if they are excessive are stubborn and constitute an inescapable political reality. An authoritative recent study, while favoring nuclear energy, acknowledges all of these as unresolved problems and with respect to proliferation risks alone concludes that "if the nonproliferation regime is not strengthened, the option of significant global expansion of nuclear power may be impossible."[153]

The adoption of clean energy sources as a result simply of a fall in their relative price must be distinguished from their adoption as a deliberate method of forestalling global warming. Like switching to agricultural methods less sensitive to the effects of extreme heat than the methods currently employed, a substitution of clean fuels that was dictated by fears of global warming would be a form of remediation and thus would belong on the cost side of the analysis. That is even more clearly the case with regard to carbon sequestration (that is, preventing carbon dioxide from entering the atmosphere or removing it from the atmosphere), for which there is no market in the absence of regulatory limits on carbon dioxide emissions.

If global warming is gradual, the costs of adjustment or adaptation or melioration, though stiff, will be bearable and there is no immediate need to impose draconian limits on greenhouse-gas emissions. It is the risk of abrupt global warming that brings the global-warming issue squarely within the compass of this book. Optimists will point out that the earth's climate has been relatively stable for the last 10,000 years or so, suggesting robustness in the face of forcing events. The optimism is unfounded. The era of stability (the "Holocene," as it is called) is atypical of the earth's geological history. The period that preceded it, known as the "Younger Dryas," was a scene of abrupt climate changes[154] of the sort that if they happened today could have catastrophic consequences for human welfare. The period started with a plunge to ice-age temperatures and ended with a rise in temperature of 8 degrees Centigrade (14.4 degrees Fahrenheit) within about a decade.[155] Because there are no written records for the period and only limited archaeological evidence, we can have no clear idea of the effects of that sudden warming on human welfare. But given the frosty climate when it began, they were almost certainly beneficial.[156] The effects of global warming are relative not only to the amount of warming but also to global temperatures when it starts. Today a temperature increase similar to the one that closed the Younger Dryas would be starting from a much higher level, and modern people face few difficulties in keeping warm in cold climates. Today a 14-degree increase in average global temperatures within the space of a decade would be a global catastrophe.

Greater temperature swings in even shorter periods only slightly earlier than the Younger Dryas have also been recorded.[157] Climatologists cannot specify the conditions that cause such changes and so cannot assess the probability that the stress that greenhouse-gas emissions are placing on the environment will trigger them. Changes in the atmospheric concentration of carbon dioxide may have caused the temperature oscillations in the Younger Dryas,[158] and though those changes were not due to human activities, they are a portent of what may happen as a consequence of those activities. No species has so stressed the environment as modern human beings are doing, and at an accelerating pace as China, India, Brazil, and other large, poor countries modernize rapidly. The human impact on the climatic equilibrium is inherently unpredictable.

Some global-warming skeptics, less moderate than Lomborg, deny that there is a global-warming problem, or at least a problem related to human activities, at all. These radical skeptics, such as Patrick Michaels, point out that climatologists have a vested interest in whipping up fears of global warming because the greater the fears, the more research grants climatologists can obtain.[159] (Their incentives are the opposite of those of particle physicists, who, desiring ever more powerful particle accelerators, are inclined to minimize the dangers that such accelerators may create.) Fair enough; it would be a mistake to suppose scientists to be completely disinterested, and when the science is inexact or unsettled the normal self-interested motivations that scientists share with the rest of us have elbow room for influencing scientific opinion. To this it can be added that the climatic and other environmental effects of burning fossil fuels are red flags to the Greens, and so in a basically serious book about global warming we find such absurdities as the claim that communism collapsed "in no small part because the nineteenth-century ideology of Karl Marx paid little attention to the effects of environmental degradation."[160] There is suspicion that climate scientists are influenced by Green thought.

The other side of this coin, however, is that Michaels's own research, along with that of other global-warming skeptics, is financed by the energy industries.[161] And it may not be very good research. Richard Lindzen, a professor of meteorology at M.I.T. who is one of the scientifically most distinguished global-warming skeptics, has been quoted

What are the catastrophic risks, and how catastrophic are they?

53

as saying that Michaels comes to the climate debate from the "scientific backwater of climatology. He doesn't really know physics and he should."[162] And Ross Gelbspan has pointed out that

> the most outspoken scientific critiques of global warming predictions rarely appeared in the standard scientific publications, the "peer-reviewed" journals where every statement was reviewed by other scientists before publication. With a few exceptions, the critiques tended to appear in venues funded by industrial groups and conservative foundations, or in business-oriented media like the *Wall Street Journal*.[163]

The insurance industry, which is not a hotbed of leftist thought and has a significant financial stake in evaluating catastrophic risks correctly, is taking global warming seriously.[164]

There are more reputable global-warming skeptics than Michaels, although their ranks appear to be diminishing.[165] I mentioned Richard Lindzen.[166] The best known, however, is S. Fred Singer, author of *Hot Talk Cold Science*.[167] Singer denies that there is any credible evidence of global warming. He relies heavily on temperature measurements by satellites, as distinct from earth stations, many of which are near cities, which are hotter than rural areas; but recent, more sensitive satellite sensors *have* detected warming.[168] Singer also denies that if there is global warming it is due to human activities and argues that in any event global warming will be very gradual and will confer net benefits on the world. The reasons he offers for these conclusions are difficult to evaluate. His book was published by a conservative think tank rather than by an academic press; he does not cite any work by himself that was published in a journal that specializes in climate science or related fields; the tone throughout the book (and in his other writings on global warming as well)[169] is highly polemical; and he rarely cites or engages with scientists who believe that global warming is occurring, is caused by human activities, and is likely to have adverse effects. He contends that potential "climate 'disasters'" (by which he seems to mean any harmful global warming) "exist only on computer printouts and in the feverish imagination of professional environmental zealots."[170] By "computer printouts" he means the findings generated by "general circulation models" used by climate scientists to explain and predict climate change. The models are admittedly imperfect, but their imperfections do not warrant dismissing fears of global warming as fanciful. And not all climate scientists who are concerned about global warming are "professional environmental zealots."

He claims that because "nearly all research is funded by government," which he thinks does "not look kindly on research proposals that could demonstrate environmental 'hazards' to be not serious or even nonexistent," "essentially no research funds are provided to document and quantify some of the undeniable benefits from man's impact on the environment."[171] Government is not the only source of research funds; industry has an incentive to fund studies skeptical of global warming, and, as we know, it does fund them.

Singer kisses off fears of "a runaway climate warming, or other catastrophe" on the sole ground that carbon dioxide levels "have been many times higher in the past than today's value without causing irreversible climate catastrophes. . . . Major and rapid temperature changes have occurred not only during glacial periods of the last 2 million years, but even during the Holocene of the past 11,000 years."[172] Much turns on what one means by "irreversible" (Singer doesn't say). There is a sense in which no climate catastrophes are irreversible; even snowball earth was a temporary phase in the earth's climate history, and likewise the sudden warming at the end of the Younger Dryas—which Singer doesn't mention. Nor does he mention the possibility of a runaway methane warming effect or a flipping of the Gulf Stream.

All this said, Singer and the other skeptics may be correct. I am not a scientist and have no authority to make judgments on disputed scientific questions. And yet, paradoxical as this may seem, estimates of the harm from global warming are not highly sensitive to the views even of highly reputable skeptics. Suppose the relevant scientific community agreed that there was a 95 percent probability that between now and 2100 the average global temperature would rise by between 2.5 and 10.4 degrees Fahrenheit (call this range the "confidence interval"), with a mean of 6.45 degrees. Given risk aversion, an increase in the confidence interval, with the mean unchanged, would increase the expected benefits of controlling greenhouse gas emissions. For present purposes, risk aversion (discussed at greater length in chapter 3) just means that people weight heavily the worst possible outcomes in a distribution of possible outcomes. To widen the confidence interval is to make the worst outcomes worse, which spells added disutility to the risk averse. It's the difference between having, on the one hand, a 50 percent chance of winning $1,000 in a lottery and a 50 percent

What are the catastrophic risks, and how catastrophic are they?

55

chance of losing $1,000, and, on the other hand, a 50 percent chance of winning $100,000 and a 50 percent chance of losing $100,000. A risk-averse person would prefer the former gamble to the latter.

So suppose 5 percent of climatologists don't think the temperature increase by 2100 is likely to fall in the 2.5 to 10.4 degree range; they think a likelier range is 0 to 1 degree, with a mean of 0.5. These are the skeptics. If they are balanced by another group of climatologists who challenge the consensus from the other side, as it were—call them the alarmists—the only effect will be to widen the confidence interval (the mean estimate will be unchanged) and thus increase the perceived disutility of global warming. If there are no alarmists, the mean estimate of the temperature increase will fall when the skeptics' estimate is factored in, but the fall will be only from 6.45 to 6.02 degrees.

It would thus be a mistake to say that because some climatologists doubt there is a global-warming problem, we can ignore the problem until climatologists get their act together and forge a unanimous agreement on the problem and its solution. The maximum effect of such doubt should be to reduce the optimal expenditure on dealing with the problem. And this is provided that the doubting Thomases are not balanced by alarmed Thomases. If they are, then (to repeat) the optimal expenditure on combating global warming would, given risk aversion, rise, not fall.

If we inquire into the *source* of the skeptics' doubts, moreover, we may conclude that their doubts actually increase the confidence interval rather than just reduce the mean estimate and that the first effect may dominate. The skeptics point to the inability of climate models to explain the historic pattern of climate change. It is that very inability, for example to explain the temperature spike at the end of the Younger Dryas, that engenders fear that human beings may be courting disaster by emitting carbon dioxide in such quantities as we are doing into the atmosphere, because we do not have a complete understanding of the effect of environmental change on climate. Consider the argument that because the climate in the Middle Ages was warmer than it is today, even though the level of carbon dioxide emissions was much lower, emissions may not be causing the current warming.[173] Put aside the question whether the premise is accurate[174] and the non sequitur of arguing that because other conditions may cause global warming besides carbon dioxide emissions, carbon dioxide emissions do not. The interesting point is that if the causes of global warming are multiple and, as the skeptics emphasize, uncertain, the risk of abrupt climate change is enhanced. The conditions that warmed the earth in the Middle Ages (if they did) may recur, amplifying the effect of carbon dioxide emissions on global temperatures. A contemporary example is Alaska, which in the last 30 years has been warming at a faster rate than anywhere else in the world ("winters have warmed by a startling 2–3 ˚C, compared with a global average of 1 ˚C"), as a result of a combination of the increased concentration of greenhouse gases in the atmosphere with other climate factors.[175]

Although derisory about the general circulation models on which predictions of global warming are based, Singer does not claim to have a better model and does not deny that "some global warming may occur in the future" as a result of rising atmospheric concentrations of greenhouse gases (he does not doubt that they *are* rising), caused in turn, as he also does not deny, by the burning of fossil fuels and by other human activities. He is sufficiently concerned about global warming to advocate speeding up the absorption of atmospheric carbon dioxide by the oceans by adding nutrients designed to increase the number of phytoplankton, which devour carbon dioxide.[176] He acknowledges that "there are still unanswered questions that need to be settled by additional research."[177]

Conservatives seize on the existence of doubt about the magnitude or causality of global warming to oppose emission controls,[178] while liberals seize on doubt concerning the likelihood of bioterrorism to oppose limitations on granting visas to foreigners to do research on lethal pathogens. In neither case is the existence of doubt a valid ground for rejecting expert opinion. Doubt properly is an input into analysis rather than a substitute for analysis.[179] Singer's basic error is to suppose that the *only* rational response to the existence of doubt is to conduct research aimed at dispelling it.

The approach of merging probabilities that I have suggested for accommodating doubters will not work when probabilities cannot be assigned to particular outcomes[180] (which unfortunately is the case with respect to abrupt global warming), nor when scientific opinion is polarized and the feasible responses to the risk are discontinuous. Suppose 90 percent of climatologists believe that measures to prevent abrupt global warming will be ineffective unless $100 billion is spent on them, but they have no confidence that spending more will yield any further benefit, while 10 percent of climatologists believe that mea-

What are the catastrophic risks, and how catastrophic are they?

57

sures to combat global warming have zero value. If $100 billion is spent, the skeptics' position has been given zero weight, while spending anything less than $100 billion is tantamount to giving zero weight to the majority view. The only choice is between the extreme positions,[181] and it would have to be made on the basis of risk aversion and confidence or skepticism concerning the epistemic significance of a scientific consensus as distinct from scientific unanimity. It would be like having to decide whether to have surgery that one of ten equally reputable physicians thinks necessary but the other nine do not. The patient cannot split the difference by opting for one-tenth of the operation.

It remains to consider who should count as a "reputable" member of the relevant scientific community for purposes of summing scientific opinions and, within that community, who has relevant expertise with regard to the specific issue under consideration. Scientists who publish on global warming or closely related topics in refereed journals can be assumed to have relevant expertise, and those are the scientists whose views, adjusted for the doubts and other qualifications that they express, should be included in the canvass of scientific opinion. From an electronically searchable database of 46 journals of "meteorology and atmospheric sciences," I picked the top 20 journals as measured by "impact factors" designed to identify the most influential journals in a field and identified 330 articles published in these journals in 2002 and 2003 that mentioned global warming. I examined every fifth article, a total of 67, with randomized replacement for articles in the initial sample that mentioned global warming only in passing. In 53 of the 67 articles it was apparent that the author or, more commonly, authors believed both that human activities were causing global warming and that there would be adverse consequences, although some of the articles emphasize other contributory factors. Two of the 67 articles are somewhat skeptical (though neither is as skeptical as Singer's work is), five mentioned global warming only in passing, and the remaining seven were noncommittal.[182] The ratio of "believers" to skeptics is thus an impressive 53:2.

Exhaustion of natural resources

The least likely man-made disaster is the one that, over the years, has received the most attention,[183] though this is changing. I refer to the exhaustion of natural resources—including the very fossil fuels that so distress the Greens because of the effect on global warming. It is true that, at least as long as the extraction of natural resources is confined to our planet, those resources are finite in a literal sense. But it is unlikely that they are finite in relation to a realistic estimate of human demands. The reason is the price system. When a good becomes scarcer, its price rises, producing two effects. People buy less of it because substitutes are now more attractive, and additional money is invested in increasing its production. The earth is estimated to contain between 4 and 6 trillion tons of fossil fuels economically recoverable at 2002 market prices. But should they all be used up, as much as three times the quantity could be obtained at higher cost from the methane on the ocean floors.[184] Natural gas consists mainly of methane, which therefore amounts to a huge untapped source of natural gas. The Greens, were it not for their uncritical hostility to capitalism, should find the operation of the price system reassuring. For it implies that the consumption of fossil fuels and the resulting emissions of carbon dioxide will decline as higher prices caused by growing scarcity induce the substitution of clean fuels.

The analysis is equally applicable to water, a focus of current concern by environmentalists. Although 72 percent of the earth's surface is ocean, fresh water is in short supply in many inhabited parts of the world, and some environmentalists are predicting disaster.[185] One might expect them to welcome global warming, which is expected to increase the amount of precipitation. But it may do so mainly in areas that do not face a water shortage;[186] moreover, the demand for water will be greater the warmer the climate becomes. In any event, a catastrophic global water shortage is almost inconceivable. The scarcer fresh water becomes, the more economical will desalination become, and also the greater will be the incentive for water-saving measures ranging from subsurface irrigation to chemical toilets (conventional toilets use an immense amount of water).

There is no *fundamental* economic difference between water viewed as a natural resource and oil, gas, or coal. If anything, the comparison favors water, because it is not depletable, though that difference is not fundamental if I am right that the price system will prevent oil, gas, or coal from running out before there are feasible substitutes. What is worrisome, however, is that shortages of water, though only short term, might have severe political consequences in tense, dry regions, such as the Middle East. But the risk of a global catastrophe seems negligible.

What are the catastrophic risks, and how catastrophic are they?

59

Loss of biodiversity

The process just described by which markets adjust smoothly to scarcities in natural resources will not work when the resources in question are animal or plant species that have no commercial value. Even species that do have commercial value can be endangered, most obviously but not only if absence of property rights or of rights-mimicking regulation results in too-rapid exploitation with little or no concern for conservation and renewal. This problem has been studied extensively with regard to fishing, and let me begin there.

If the spawning grounds for some species of edible fish are neither owned by anyone nor subject to regulation that mimics ownership by limiting access, fishermen may overfish until the species is extinct. Whether they will or not depends on the costs of fishing, the rate of reproduction of the fish, and market prices. But the important point is that a fisherman who limits his catch will not be benefiting himself in the least. He will just be leaving more fish for his competitors to take unless he is able to make a legally enforceable agreement with them to limit the amount of fishing that all do. As there will usually be too many fishermen for such an agreement to be feasible,[187] there is no self-regulating economic process to assure the survival of edible fish species.

This problem of collective action can be, and to a degree has been, solved by a combination of nations' extending their claims to exclusive control of fishing from 12 to 200 miles from their coasts, so as to enable them to regulate all fishing within that zone,[188] and international treaties regulating fishing.[189] It is in the collective economic interests of the fishing nations to preserve most commercially valuable species, though not all, as we shall see. Because there are fewer fishing nations than there are individual fishermen, forging an agreement among nations is more feasible than leaving the control of overfishing to the market.

Many of the methods used to prevent overfishing are, it is true, inefficient compared to either user fees or "cap and trade" regulations modeled on the successful system of tradable permits to emit sulfur dioxide (the cause of acid rain). In cap and trade an overall emissions ceiling is fixed, permits are issued allowing members of the industry to emit up to a fixed level lower than before the cap was imposed, but the permits are tradable, which creates a market in which the firms that can reduce their emissions at lowest cost sell their permits to the those whose costs are higher; the result is that overall emissions are brought down to the ceiling at the lowest possible cost. An example of an inefficient method of trying to prevent overfishing is truncating the fishing season. This may have little effect beyond motivating fishermen to buy larger boats in order to increase their catch during the shortened season.[190]

Even with proper regulations, a commercially valuable species may become extinct, at least if narrowly economic criteria are applied and catastrophic risk ignored. The reason this can happen ("efficient extinction") is that the rate at which a species reproduces may be lower than the market discount rate.[191] Suppose the discount rate is 10 percent but the reproduction rate is only 2 percent. To hold off harvesting the species in order to have 2 percent more to harvest in a year would not make commercial sense unless rising scarcity was expected to raise the future price of the species by (almost) 10 percent. Deferring harvesting would be like buying a bond that paid 2 percent interest when the interest rate on bonds of comparable quality was 10 percent.

The concern about extinction of plant species is based in part on the potential medicinal value of plants[192] and can be alleviated by an improved system of property rights[193] because medicinal applications have commercial value. Like their animal counterparts, plant species that have no perceived commercial value are less likely to survive and may in fact be disappearing rapidly because of human activities.

We must not take for granted that the extinction of species that have no commercial value, or less value than the cost of averting their extinction, is a social problem, let alone one that poses a catastrophic risk to human welfare. (We'll see later that it's not even clear that number of species is the relevant variable for assessing the ecological impact of human activity.) After all, extinction is at the heart of the gale of creative destruction (as Joseph Schumpeter characterized innovation) that we call evolution. Evolution is species competition. The losers in that competition dwindle, and if because of the toll taken by predators or disease or diminished food supply their rate of reproduction falls below the replacement level, eventually they disappear completely.

Extinction is not *always* a consequence of inferior adaptability, at least in the normal sense of the word "adaptability." The dinosaurs were better adapted to the global environment than the mammals that were contemporary with them; the mammals were merely niche animals in the age of the dinosaurs.[194] But maybe the dinosaurs just *seemed* better adapted; maybe it was the mammals who were better adapted,

What are the catastrophic risks, and how catastrophic are they?

61

because asteroids are part of the environment and the mammals, unlike the dinosaurs, survived the impact of the asteroid that exterminated the dinosaurs. More precisely, *some* species of mammals survived; many others became extinct along with the dinosaurs.[195] One theory of why some survived is that while the interruption of photosynthesis destroyed the living plants on which the dinosaurs depended for food, some mammals were able to live off leaf litter and other dead plant matter, and also off the corpses of the many animals killed in the disaster, until the sky cleared and photosynthesis resumed.[196] This theory offers a basis for hoping that at least some human beings would survive an equivalent asteroid collision, since we are omnivores.

The dinosaurs' fate has a further implication for the concerns of this book. The dinosaurs had a run of more than 100 million years before becoming extinct. They must therefore have been a robust form of life, able to adapt to a variety of environmental changes. Human beings, in contrast, have been around for only about 200,000 years. The comparison is a little misleading because dinosaurs are a collection of species rather than a single species, and individual dinosaur species may not have survived as long as the collectivity did, just as, while mammals have survived to the present, a number of mammalian species, such as the woolly mammoth and the saber-toothed tiger, have not. My point is only that we cannot have as much confidence in our survival prospects as dinosaurs, had they been thinking beings, would have believed in their heyday that *they* had; we have not been subjected to as rigorous a "test of time." The fact that we are more intelligent than dinosaurs enables us to cope better with certain environmental changes, but it also exposes us to risks that dinosaurs did not face. They didn't have to worry about disastrous lab accidents or bioterrorists.

It is believed that as many as 99.9 percent of all the species that have emerged on earth may have become extinct,[197] whether through competition or catastrophe. Yet the remaining variety of species is formidable; indeed, for all we know there may be more species on earth today than at any previous time.[198] No one knows either how many species there are—estimates range from fewer than 4 million to 100 million,[199] though most of the estimates are clustered between 10 million and 14 million[200]—or how many there were a year ago or 10 years ago or 1,000 years ago. As a result, no one knows how many species have become extinct because of human activities.

The oft-repeated estimate that 40,000 species are becoming extinct every year has been derided as groundless[201] but is more accurately described as exceedingly speculative. The fossil record suggests that the average number of extinctions before human beings were around to cause more of them did not exceed 10 a year,[202] and it seems unlikely that we would be causing 4,000 times that number. But who knows? The distinguished evolutionary biologist Edward O. Wilson has predicted that by the year 2030 a fifth of all species will be either extinct or on the verge of extinction unless dramatic measures are taken to save them.[203] In making that prediction he didn't indicate how many species he thinks there are today. But elsewhere he says that the median estimate is 10 million,[204] and if that is the number he is using, then he is predicting that in roughly a quarter of a century two million species will become extinct or will be verging on extinction—which is 80,000 a year.

This figure, even when halved, must be taken with more than a grain of salt—the data concerning extinctions are awful, as all reputable ecologists admit.[205] But it cannot be considered wholly irresponsible.[206] The rapid increase in the human population, shown in Figure 1.2, is causing the widespread destruction of habitats. That destruction endangers the species whose habitats they are, as does the human propensity to introduce new predators into the habitats of animals and plants that are defenseless against them.[207] Human hunting, logging, herbicides, and pollution play a role in extinctions too. As does global warming,[208] and only in part because polar and tropical species tend to be adapted to only a narrow range of temperatures.[209] Even in the temperate zones, fauna may be threatened, notably fish, which have limited tolerance for changes in the temperature of the streams, ponds, and other bodies of water in which they live.[210]

Summarizing a variety of approaches to the vexing task of estimating the rate at which species are becoming extinct, Robert May and his associates conclude that if current trends continue, we face impending extinction rates "at least four orders-of-magnitude faster than the background rates seen in the fossil record."[211] Four orders of magnitude is 10,000, so if the background rate is 10 extinctions per year a rate of extinction four orders of magnitude greater would be 100,000 extinctions per year. May and his associates, however, estimate the background rate at only at one per year,[212] so they are expecting "only" 10,000 annual extinctions. But this is still a number sufficiently greater than the background rate, whatever exactly it is, to arouse concern that human activities are reducing biodiversity substantially,[213] with unknowable but probably adverse consequences.

What are the catastrophic risks, and how catastrophic are they?

63

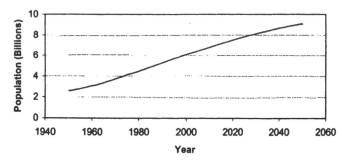

Figure 1.2. World Population. *Source:* U.S. Census Bureau.

There are reputable scientists (Lomborg is not a scientist) who believe that ecologists have seriously underestimated the background rate of extinctions and seriously overestimated the current rate; re-estimates have produced dramatically reduced figures for the increase in the extinction rate caused by human activity.[214] Still, "there is little doubt that species are going extinct extremely rapidly and that we are in the midst of a major extinction interval."[215] Even Lomborg thinks that the current extinction rate is 1,500 times the natural background rate.[216]

The catastrophe that ended the reign of the dinosaurs was serendipitous from the standpoint of our own species. Had the dinosaurs survived, large mammals, such as primates, would probably not have evolved—there wouldn't have been room for them in ecological space—and so there would be no human beings.[217] This illustrates the point that without periodic extinctions "biodiversity would increase exponentially. . . . Rather soon, the system would saturate: speciation would have to stop because there would be no room for new species." Extinction "creates space for evolutionary innovations."[218] A really new life form is likely to be vulnerable when it first appears, requiring a shakedown period to get the design flaws out. It is more likely to survive that initial period of vulnerability the less competition it has from other species.

But to commend the beneficent effects of extinction is to take a very long view indeed. Those who operate on a human timescale will find it difficult to work up enthusiasm about the benefits of mass extinctions in producing new life forms millions of years hence, when in the nearer term reducing genetic diversity by man-made extinctions may deprive humanity of potentially valuable resources—perhaps even indispensable ones, though that seems unlikely. Anyway it is doubtful that extinctions are really creating more space for new species to occupy eventually; the ecological space that the extinction of existing species creates is filled primarily by human beings rather than by new forms of life.

One may be tempted to discount the gravity of the problem of diminishing biodiversity by noting the existence of organizations that collect and conserve specimens of endangered plant and animal species both in their original habitats and in special facilities elsewhere ("ex situ," as it is said), such as San Diego Zoo's "Frozen Zoo," which preserves cells from hundreds of animal species by freezing them; the cells can be cloned to produce new members of the species.[219] But these conservation efforts have only a limited significance. Not only is there no census of species, but it is infeasible to conduct one, because many species, especially those in danger of extinction, have minute populations and restricted habitats, often in hard-to-reach places. As a result, we do not know how many of the species that are not being conserved will become extinct unless heroic measures are taken to preserve their habitats.

If we take a strictly anthropocentric view of catastrophic risks, eschewing philosophical questions,[220] we must ask what exactly humankind loses by extinctions. Maybe nothing beyond the charm of unusual life forms if extinctions are considered one by one; what is worrisome from the point of view of this book is the unknown consequences of mass extinctions. If millions of species will become extinct within the foreseeable future, there is a risk, though probably a very slight one, of true ecological catastrophe because of the interdependence of species. If a species that is the main food source of another species disappears, the other species may become extinct too, while at the same time still another species, which may have been the main food source of the first, may explode, wreaking havoc. The organic world is a network, and severing a network at one point can have disastrous effects at others. An example is the fate of Steller's sea cow (a relative of the manatee), which became extinct in the eighteenth century. A major factor in its extinction, it appears, is that fur hunters depleted the local otter population. The otters fed on sea urchins, and with the otters gone the sea urchin population exploded. The sea urchins' diet was kelp, as was the sea cows', and the depletion of kelp by the increased population of sea urchins reduced the sea cows' food supply and hence

What are the catastrophic risks, and how catastrophic are they?

65

their population, increasing their vulnerability to hunters, who finished them off.[221]

Thus far I have been assuming, consistent with most discussions of biodiversity loss, that "species" is the correct unit of analysis. It may not be. First, "species" is not a well-defined concept. The usual understanding of a species is of a set of organisms that interbreed. This doesn't work for organisms that reproduce asexually. One reason that estimates of the number of species differ is that the estimators don't agree on what should count as a species.

Second, and more important, the number of species is only a very crude index of genetic diversity,[222] which is the real value at stake. There may be greater genetic diversity among several species each of which belongs to a different genus (the next higher grouping of organisms) than among a larger number of species all belonging to the same genus. And there is considerable genetic diversity within as well as across species.[223] Think of the different breeds of dogs and cats or the differently colored birds of the same species. For that matter, think of the genetic differences between two members of the same family unless they are identical twins. The larger the population of a species, the more genetically diverse it is likely to be. This effect may be offset by the squeezing, perhaps to extinction, of the population of another species. But by the same token the extinction of one species may allow the population of a genetically more diverse one, or the populations of many more species, to expand. Were the human race to become extinct, the amount of genetic diversity in the global ecosystem would increase. And though there is much concern about "exotics"—species newly introduced to an area that ravage local organisms that haven't evolved defenses effective against the newcomers—the introduction of a new species may at least improve the prospects for its survival by diversifying its habitat.

All this said, it seems a fair guess that if (a big if, however) 20 percent of existing species are doomed to extinction within the next quarter century, there will be a significant reduction in overall genetic diversity, especially since the environmental conditions that would bring about such a decline in the number of species would probably also diminish the populations of the surviving ones and therefore reduce within-species genetic diversity as well. Indeed, selective breeding for the "best" livestock and crop plants has already caused a marked diminution in livestock breeds and plant varieties, with resulting loss of genetic diversity.[224]

As suggested by my reference to diversification, the anthropocentric significance of genetic diversity from the standpoint of this book is that it is a kind of insurance policy. The less genetic diversity there is, the greater the potential impact on human welfare of plant disease, climate change, and other environmental stressors;[225] imagine if the only surviving variety of tree when Dutch elm disease struck had been Dutch elm. There doesn't seem to be any danger that mass extinctions will lead to the extinction of the human race. But there may be a slight risk of destroying most human agriculture through the kind of domino effect that I mentioned earlier, where the disappearance of a species or other group reverberates up and down the food chain, with potentially catastrophic effects if a very large number of species go extinct in a short period of time. I do not know how to measure these risks, which depend on the fragility of the ecological equilibrium. But we may be playing with fire in permitting species to disappear at as fast a rate as many ecologists believe we are doing.

The best-known public effort to retard the rate of extinctions is the Endangered Species Act.[226] The act is designed to save species that are in danger of extinction by forbidding their destruction and by requiring the formulation and implementation of "recovery plans" designed to increase the populations of the endangered species. Some 1,100 species have been listed as "endangered" or, if they are slightly less imperiled, "threatened." This is probably only a small fraction of the species in the United States that are threatened with extinction. Moreover, there are recovery plans for only 40 percent of the listed species, and in the 30 years that the statute has been in effect only 11 listed species have recovered sufficiently to be removed from the list,[227] although many listed species may have been saved from extinction. Because having a listed species on one's property can prevent development of the property, and the costs are not reimbursed by the government, "landowners have strong incentives"—to which they are known sometimes (no one knows how often) to yield—"to minimize the risk of economic loss to a taking under the Act by hindering the gathering of information about species on their land, or at the extreme, by destroying potential habitat overtly before the species are listed and covertly afterwards."[228] In any event, if the median estimate of the number of species in the world—10 million—is accepted and the rate of extinctions is anywhere near what ecologists like Edward Wilson and Robert May believe, it is apparent that the act is making only a trivial contribution to reducing the rate.

What are the catastrophic risks, and how catastrophic are they?

67

A note on population

Biodiversity reduction and global warming are linked not only in being environmental problems, but also causally; I mentioned that a significant increase in global temperatures will place a heavy stress on animals and plants that are adapted to only a narrow temperature range. The two risks are also linked in their relation to population growth and economic development. The more human beings there are, and the more prosperous they are, the more land will be cleared and the more fossil fuels will be burned in internal combustion engines and electrical generating plants. The clearing of land is likely to reduce the number of species, and both it and the burning of fossil fuels cause emission of greenhouse gases.

Conceivably, regulatory measures, including land-use controls and emission taxes, or market-driven substitution of cleaner fuels, will bail us out, although that may require revolutionary advances in technology.[229] Alternatively, world population growth may level off and even begin to decline—eventually. But when will that be, and at what level will the population top out? No one knows, because the determinants of population change are numerous and difficult to predict.[230] Moreover, population is likely to keep growing even after the birthrate falls below the replacement level if earlier population cohorts, which are larger because their members were born when the birthrate was higher, have not reached the age at which they will be having their own children.

A glance back at Figure 1.2 will reveal a predicted rise in the world population from its current level of about 6 billion to 9 billion by 2050. Wolfgang Lutz has distilled from a variety of projections a range of world population estimates for that year of 6.5 billion to almost 14 billion people, with the likeliest estimate 10 billion.[231] Meanwhile, per capita production is expected to grow by more than 2 percent a year during this century.[232] If world population increases at an annual rate of 1 percent and per capita production at an annual rate of 2 percent, for a total annual growth in production of 3 percent, then GWP will increase almost fourfold by 2050 ($1.03^{46} = 3.895$). This implies greatly increased stress on the environment, suggesting that biodiversity loss and global warming will become increasingly serious problems in the coming decades unless measures are taken now to begin to ameliorate them. Like global warming, biodiversity depletion is irreversible in the short run.

Granted, if all population growth occurs in the poorest countries, the rate of per capita growth in production is likely to decline. But that may not benefit either the climate or biodiversity. Population growth rather than economic growth drives deforestation, and deforestation both increases atmospheric carbon dioxide and promotes extinctions.[233]

The effect of a growing world population on the catastrophic risks casts doubt on a common criticism of stringent environmental controls: that they increase mortality.[234] Banning DDT, the critics point out, has increased the incidence of malaria. More generally, because income and longevity are positively correlated, costly environmental regulations reduce longevity by reducing incomes. Such regulations are not the best, and may not even be a rational—they are certainly not an intended—method of population control; compared to birth control, they are cruel. But in a complete analysis their effect in limiting population and thus reducing catastrophic risks would count as an offset to their cost.

For the analysis to be *really* complete, however, any positive externalities of population growth would have to be considered along with the negative ones. These would include enabling increased specialization of labor, an important source of efficiencies, and accelerating the expansion of the stock of useful knowledge. The second effect comes about not only because there are more potential producers but also because there may be increasing returns to the production of knowledge, especially scientific knowledge.[235] On the one hand, it is true, increasing the number of innovators increases the probability of simultaneous invention, which reduces the returns to innovation. But this effect may be outweighed by that of increased innovation in expanding the knowledge base on which future innovators build.

In addition, the expansion of the market for new products and services that is brought about by an increase in the population may increase the rate of technological advance by offering the prospect of larger profits from successful innovation.[236] Most costs of creating intellectual property, of which scientific and other technical knowledge is an important type, are fixed rather than variable. This means that an expansion in output will yield revenues that are only slightly offset by the costs of the expansion, and the difference is available to cover the fixed costs of research and development. To illustrate, if fixed costs are $10, variable cost is $1 per unit of output, and price is $2, then at an output of 10 units total revenue will be $20 and will just equal total

What are the catastrophic risks, and how catastrophic are they?

69

costs of $20 ($10 + [10 × $1]). But at an output of 20 units, total revenue will be $40 and will exceed total costs [$10 + [20 × $1]) by $10.

A further effect of increased population—the increase in total human welfare if additional people derive greater utility from living than the disutility they impose on the existing population—has dubious normative significance for reasons that will be explored in chapter 3. But if additional people derive positive utility from living without causing existing people to lose any of *their* utility, then there is a net gain in global utility. It doesn't matter whether the additional people derive less utility from life than the existing population. If in a two-person society A has utility from living of 100 and B of 90, killing B does not increase welfare even though it raises average utility from 95 to 100.[237]

But we must consider two negative externalities of population growth that are highlighted by consideration of the catastrophic risks. The first is the danger of catastrophe that is created by headlong technological advance, more precisely by the fact that technological progress is much more rapid than progress in developing and implementing methods of controlling the dangers that technology creates. Just compare scientific progress since 1800 with the progress in politics, law, and morals over the same period. Not that there hasn't been progress in those spheres; the domain over which human activity is governed by rational processes has expanded greatly.[238] It's just been slower. The difference is due partly to the fact that science has better methods of testing its hypotheses, partly to its dealing (by choice!) with more manageable subject matter, and partly (a related point) to its being less buffeted by politics. The faster the rate of scientific progress, the greater and more dangerous is likely to be the relative lag in progress in social control. The chapters that follow will reveal how daunting the challenge of effective social control of scientific and technological risk is already.

Second, given a fixed though tiny percentage of individuals assumed to have the skills and motivation to devise and carry out a scheme of catastrophic destruction, any increase in world population increases the absolute number of those dangerous individuals, just as the more planets there are, the likelier it is that at least one of them contains intelligent life. It might require only a handful of deranged or fanatical individuals with the relevant technological skills to cause a global catastrophe.

To sound a frequent note in this book, not enough is known for the positive and negative externalities of continued population growth to be quantified. Risk-averse people may therefore favor policies that limit that growth, such as subsidizing contraception and abortion, fostering urbanization (but remember that this could increase the risk of natural pandemics), restricting family welfare payments, substituting social security for dependence on one's adult children for support in one's old age, and, what is probably most efficacious, subsidizing women's education and job opportunities in order to increase the opportunity costs of bearing and raising children.

Notice, finally, that the greater the dangers posed by continued population growth, the less catastrophic certain catastrophic events might turn out to be, such as a pandemic that, in Malthusian fashion, thinned out the world's population.

Intentional catastrophes

"Nuclear winter"

During the half century of the cold war (1947–1989), the catastrophic risk that attracted the most attention was that of a nuclear and, beginning in the 1950s, a thermonuclear war[239] (that is, a war with hydrogen bombs rather than just atomic bombs). Before the first test explosion of an atomic bomb in 1945, there was some concern in scientific circles that a nuclear explosion could ignite the entire atmosphere.[240] But the risk was considered very small, and anyway risk taking is the order of the day in wartime; and of course the risk did not materialize. Although there has long been loose talk about how a nuclear war might cause the extinction of the human race, this was never a danger if attention is confined to atomic bombs. A Hiroshima-sized bomb can cause a great loss of life, and a thousand of them much more. There were almost 150,000 deaths in Hiroshima; multiply that number by a thousand and the total number of deaths rises to 150 million. But this is only 2.5 percent of the world's population today, a percentage not much greater than the percentage of the world's population killed in World War II (some 40 to 50 million, out of a world population of 2.3 billion—so about 2 percent), though the loss was spread over six years. Still, 150 million is an appalling number of human deaths—and it is an underestimate, because there would also be radioactive contamination of human and other habitats, resulting in many illnesses

What are the catastrophic risks, and how catastrophic are they?

71

and some deaths. But the human race would survive. This is less certain if we imagine an all-out war with hydrogen bombs, which could produce consequences similar to that of a major asteroid collision, in particular the destruction of most agriculture by the creation of dense clouds of debris that would shut down photosynthesis, maybe for years.[241] Martin Rees, however, says that the "best guess" is that even a full-scale hydrogen-bomb war would not cause "a prolonged worldwide blackout."[242]

To wage thermonuclear war was never an option seriously considered by the United States or the Soviet Union, but the danger of an accidental all-out thermonuclear war was not trivial. There were a number of false alarms during the cold war—occasions on which one side thought the other had launched a first strike against it.[243] That was why both sides developed a second-strike capability, that is, a capability of inflicting a devastating retaliation after a surprise attack. Nevertheless, had either nation been convinced that the other had launched a first strike, it would have been strongly tempted to respond in kind immediately rather than wait to see how much of its second-strike capability survived the strike against it. At the same time, the nuclear "balance of terror" may have averted a nonnuclear World War III, which could have been immensely destructive. This is a genuine though paradoxical example of the occasional beneficent effects of technology in reducing catastrophic risks created by technology.

The problem of false alarms that might touch off a thermonuclear war has become less serious. The United States and Russia (the only nation formerly part of the Soviet Union to retain nuclear weapons) are no longer enemies. It is inconceivable that either nation would launch a first strike against the other, and so a false alarm would instantly be recognized as being just that. An accidental launch remains a possibility, however, though presumably a remote one; and even though it would be unlikely to provoke a war, a single hit with a hydrogen bomb could kill millions of people. China, moreover, has thermonuclear weapons and an increasing capability of delivering them over long distances, and somewhat tense relations with the United States, particularly over Taiwan; we may someday find ourselves confronting China in much the same way that we confronted the Soviet Union during the cold war. Other, weaker nations have or are on the verge of acquiring nuclear arms, but the only ones that are hostile to the United States— namely North Korea and Iran—are unlikely to be permitted to acquire thermonuclear weapons, and without them they are too overmatched by the United States to pose a serious threat. Unless completely irrational, their leaders are deterred from using nuclear weapons against us.

But this is cold comfort, and not only because irrational behavior is not unknown among dictators; ruling by intimidation has a tendency to produce paranoia and intellectual isolation. Nations have other enemies besides the United States. A nuclear war between India and Pakistan loomed as a possibility in 2002 because of the asymmetry in conventional military strength between the two nations; and had Saddam Hussein obtained nuclear weapons, as we know at one time he wanted to do, a nuclear war in the Middle East would have become a possibility. Apart from the great destruction that even a war waged with a small number of atomic bombs would create, there is the danger that such a war would escalate, bringing in additional nuclear powers. For example, should a terrorist group based in Pakistan succeed in detonating a nuclear bomb in Israel, Israel might well launch a retaliatory nuclear strike against Pakistan, itself a nuclear power. India might take the opportunity to finish with Pakistan, provoking nuclear retaliation by a desperate Pakistan. All three of these nations, moreover, are at least potential thermonuclear powers. And conceivably, though improbably, China could be sucked into a nuclear war between India, which is a rival of China, and Pakistan.

Is the danger of a missile attack with nuclear or thermonuclear weapons against the United States sufficiently great to justify the creation of a defense against ballistic missiles? There are complex issues of cost and efficacy that I will not attempt to address, except to note that antiballistic missile (ABM) research and development probably would not, as one might think it might, contribute significantly to an effective defense against asteroid strikes. An asteroid defense is a much easier project because asteroids come one at a time and cannot use decoys to attempt to overwhelm the defense.

The main objective of an ABM defense, moreover, is not so much to prevent an attack from succeeding as to deprive potential enemies of a bargaining chip. If in 2003 Saddam Hussein's Iraq had had the capability of A-bombing the United States or even Israel, we might have hesitated to invade Iraq because of the risk that, faced with defeat and overthrow, he would decide on national suicide and induce the Iraqi military to implement his decision. North Korea may be playing this game with us.

The gravest nuclear threat today comes not from rogue states but from terrorists (or from a combination: North Korea, perhaps, selling

What are the catastrophic risks, and how catastrophic are they?

73

fissile material to terrorists). One danger is that a terrorist group will actually build an atomic bomb. The design of these weapons is well known, and although their construction is costly and requires considerable engineering sophistication, it may not be beyond the ability of a well-financed group if it can get its hands on plutonium or highly enriched uranium—and that is not out of the question either.[244] I mentioned the possibility that North Korea would sell fissile material to terrorists. More ominous (because fear of retaliation may deter North Korea from knowingly selling fissile material to a group that might use it against a nuclear power, such as the United States) is the possession by a number of the former communist nations of nuclear reactors that burn weapons-grade nuclear fuel; the precautions against theft from these facilities are often weak.[245] The security of Pakistan's nuclear arsenal is also in doubt. Pakistan is an unstable, ill-governed nation that may one day come under the control of Islamic extremists and that has an acknowledged history of contributing to nuclear proliferation.[246] But probably the greatest danger resides in Russia's huge stocks of weapons-grade nuclear materials; "much of this material is not adequately protected against theft or diversion," and there have been in fact a number of thefts.[247] All in all, there may be enough plutonium outside secure military installations to furnish the raw material for 20,000 atomic bombs.[248]

A group as small as "two or three people with appropriate skills could design and fabricate a crude nuclear explosive" that would explode with an energy equivalent to 100 tons of TNT—50 times the energy of the nonnuclear explosion that destroyed a federal building in Oklahoma City in 1995, killing more than a hundred people.[249] Greater dangers include the dangers of terrorists' stealing a nuclear bomb (if manufactured from plutonium, a nuclear bomb having an energy equivalent of 20,000 tons of TNT—the energy of the bomb dropped on Nagasaki—need be no larger than an orange),[250] crashing an airplane into a nuclear reactor (the United States has more than 100 nuclear power plants),[251] or stealing radioactive materials that if used to coat a conventional bomb would produce a weapon that could cause extensive radioactive contamination.[252] As is generally true of novel man-made threats, the risk of a nuclear terrorist attack cannot be quantified. But it does not seem insignificant.

The expected costs of an atomic attack by terrorists may well be greater than those of "nuclear winter," if the probability of the former is as much greater as that of the latter as seems to be the case, even though the risks of nuclear terrorism that I have sketched, unlike the risk of nuclear winter, are subcatastrophic from the standpoint of this book. But that is small comfort. The expected costs of a subcatastrophic disaster may exceed those of a catastrophic one, since the probability of the lesser disaster may be higher and expected cost is the product of probability and consequence (subject to a possible adjustment for risk aversion). Anyway it is unclear what additional measures should be taken to prevent an accidental war involving thermonuclear weapons beyond those already being taken by the existing thermonuclear powers (the United States, Russia, the United Kingdom, France, and China) to ward off what is after all a danger that has been recognized for half a century; and so the prospect of nuclear winter does not figure largely in this book. A source of considerable worry, however, is that while only the five nations just mentioned are known to have hydrogen bombs, three other nations—Israel, India, and Pakistan—are believed either to have them or to have the capability of producing them. If they do not have them already, they probably will have them soon.

Bioterrorism

As we know from the earlier discussion of AIDS, a bacterium or virus that was new and fatal and easily spread (probably by being airborne), for which there was no vaccine or cure, and that had a long infectious incubation period during which it was difficult to detect, could trigger a pandemic that would kill all or most human beings. If instead it killed all plants,[253] the destructive effect on human beings would be almost as great.[254]

No existing germ has all the desired properties, as far as anyone knows. Anthrax, for example, though highly lethal, is not contagious, and so is more like a chemical weapon than a biological one (as are toxins, such as ricin, which are not germs at all). A natural pathogen that kills its entire host population, and therefore itself, is, as I noted at the beginning of this chapter, not fit in an evolutionary sense. That is why we are unlikely to be wiped out by a natural pandemic, though it could happen as the result of a mutation that produced a "suicidal" pathogen. But an existing pathogen might be enabled by gene splicing or other biological or chemical manipulation to cause the extinction of the human race. Smallpox virus is the prime candidate to be such a pathogen, as we'll see, but it is not the only one.

I have captioned this section of the chapter "bioterrorism" because the threat of biological attack is primarily a terrorist threat rather than

What are the catastrophic risks, and how catastrophic are they?

75

a state threat, and this for two reasons: the difficulty of preventing the spread of disease to one's own people and that states can be deterred from using biological weaponry against powerful nations like the United States, though they might use it against weaker nations, and there is always a risk that such use would cause a pandemic. Bioterrorism[255] is a growing threat for several reasons: advances in biotechnology; the fact that effective measures against one type of terrorist threat, such as airplane hijacking, cause terrorists, who in this and other respects are quite rational,[256] to substitute other methods of attack;[257] and the shift in the character of terrorist groups in recent years from ones with limited political agendas, such as the Irish Republican Army and the Palestine Liberation Organization, to ones, most notoriously but not only Al Qaeda, that "are potentially more dangerous because they have fluid objectives, perceive fewer political or ethical constraints on the scope of their actions, are often interested in violence for its own sake, and are less easily deterred by threats of punishment."[258] It is true that no terrorist group that has aims short of destroying the human race would knowingly launch a biological attack that had a substantial probability of causing that destruction, and true too that suicide terrorism is more likely to be effective the more limited its aims,[259] as there is no negotiating with, no yielding to the demands of, a terrorist bent on destroying the world. Yet terrorist groups may have apocalyptic aims and make world suicide their goal. And terrorist groups having more limited aims may miscalculate the lethality of the means they employ to achieve them.

Conceivably a single deranged individual could produce and disseminate a lethal pathogen. The creation of biological weapons through gene splicing[260] and their dissemination does not require elaborate facilities, sophisticated materials and equipment, a large number of workers, or an extensive or complicated delivery system.[261] High school students do gene splicing, and the requisite knowledge is available on the Web.[262] Granted, the preparation and dissemination of a lethal pathogen are far more difficult than the creation and dissemination of a computer virus by a lone hacker operating a laptop with a link to the Internet. Laboratory facilities and experience in biotechnological research, rather than just abstract knowledge of methods and materials, would be necessary to fabricate a juiced-up pathogen and aerosolize it for maximally effective dissemination. But the requisite facilities and technical personnel are found in many countries, not all of which have or enforce tight legal controls on bioengineering.

One of these countries is the United States. Many of our college laboratories contain poorly guarded lethal pathogens for use in agricultural research financed by the Department of Agriculture.[263] The Soviet Union had a huge bioweaponry program,[264] and some of the scientists who worked in it emigrated after the Soviet Union's collapse—most to developed countries but some perhaps to nations that harbor or are friendly to terrorists or incapable of eliminating them, and they may have taken samples with them to their new employers. There are still closed laboratories in Russia in which experiments with lethal pathogens are believed to be taking place. North Korea has a biological warfare program[265] and might in its economic desperation sell information about it to nations that allowed the information to come into the hands of terrorist groups or could not prevent such seepage. Iraq certainly *had* a biowarfare program; do we know where all the Iraqi scientists who worked in it are today? Other nations thought to have biological weapons or bioweapon programs are China, Egypt, India, Iran, Israel, Libya, Pakistan, Sudan, and Syria,[266] though Libya's is being dismantled.

Terrorist groups have a proven interest in bioweaponry.[267] Of the 36 known foreign terrorist organizations listed by the State Department in its 2002 report on global terrorism, nine either have links to Al Qaeda or Osama bin Laden or are believed to have biological or chemical weapons or (as in the case of Al Qaeda) an interest in acquiring them.[268] (The United Nations lists 199 organizations affiliated with Al Qaeda alone.)[269] Aum Shinrikyo, the Japanese group that released sarin in a Tokyo subway in 1995, killing a dozen people, had earlier made repeated though unsuccessful efforts to develop a biowarfare capability.[270] Some terrorist groups almost certainly have enough money to be able to hire scientists and technicians and buy the necessary materials and equipment for them—Aum Shinrikyo even succeeded in recruiting scientists as members.[271] And while it is doubtful that a single individual (a biological Unabomber) would have the full range of skills necessary to design and fabricate bioweapons all by himself, he might be able to enlist the necessary technical assistance without revealing his sinister purpose, perhaps by pretending to be developing a vaccine. And we know from the long search for the Unabomber that an "amateur terrorist"[272] is especially difficult to catch because he leaves a smaller footprint than a group.

Several years ago a team of Australian biologists developed a lethal virus by accident while trying to invent a contraceptive vaccine for

What are the catastrophic risks, and how catastrophic are they?

77

mice as a means of pest control.[273] They injected mouse DNA containing the gene IL-4, which produces a compound called interleukin–4, into mousepox virus in a successful effort to enhance the virus. They then infected mice with the enhanced virus, which they hoped would stimulate an immune response that would make the mice infertile. Mousepox is closely related to smallpox but is far less lethal, and indeed it is virtually harmless to the strain of mice involved in the experiment. The spliced mousepox virus, however, was not only more potent than the natural virus but so lethal that it killed even mice that had been vaccinated against mousepox.[274]

This example shows how a laboratory accident may produce an unusually dangerous strain of a natural disease agent that, should it escape from the lab, could start an uncontrollable pandemic.[275] But it is the implications of such accidents for bioweaponry that I want to explore. The Australian scientists published an article describing the enhanced mousepox virus[276] and in a part of the article captioned "materials and methods" provided in effect a blueprint for any bioterrorist able to obtain a virus that causes disease in human beings and might be enhanced by the method employed by those scientists.[277]

The smallpox virus is stable in aerosol form and has an infectious incubation period of seven to seventeen days.[278] Even when symptoms do appear, at the end of that period, they frequently are mistaken for those of other diseases, such as flu or even chickenpox.[279] The aerosols of smallpox virus in the exhalations of an infected person carry for several meters,[280] so that, without an effective vaccine, hospital workers and family members would be quickly infected by the first wave of infected persons, especially if the disease hadn't been identified.

The average reproduction rate of smallpox—that is, the number of persons likely to be infected by contagion from one infected person, a number that varies not only with the contagiousness of the disease and the length of time before the infected person dies and so ceases to be contagious but also with the density of population and frequency of interactions among people and of course the extent and efficacy of vaccination—is 5.5.[281] Suppose a terrorist infected 1,000 people at widely separated locations, each of the victims infected on average 5.5 others within three days, who in turn infected on average 5.5 others in the same period, and this continued for three weeks, that is, for seven rounds. By then more than 150 million people would have become infected ($1,000 \times 5.5^7$). Border controls and other methods of preventing terrorists from achieving physical proximity to their victims, which are the methods recommended for preventing suicide terrorism,[282] would not work against this type of attack. An innocent person flying from Athens airport to the United States who had been infected with smallpox at that airport could become the port of entry for smallpox in the United States.

With smallpox spreading as the result of an attack such as I have described and the vaccine ineffective—for I am assuming a "juiced-up" smallpox virus similar to the juiced-up mousepox virus created by the Australian plant scientists—and no cure, only isolation (of everyone known to be infected or to have been exposed to the disease in question) or quarantining (isolating everyone who *might* have been exposed to it) could limit the further spread of the disease. Quarantining is the more costly measure, both to those administering it and to the population at large, because more people are subject to it,[283] but it is hard to see how it could be avoided in the case of a large-scale outbreak of smallpox. Yet it might well be ineffectual. The relatively long infectious incubation period of smallpox would allow the disease to spread to a great distance before a quarantine could be imposed.[284] Many health workers would be infected, and those who were not, lacking vaccine protection, would be reluctant to approach infected persons, and if they did their ranks would be rapidly thinned as they caught the disease. If the terrorist avoided detection, he could continue spreading the disease even after known victims had been quarantined, until he himself became disabled by it. Isolated human populations might escape infection but might not be viable in a world from which most of the human race, perhaps including all the urban populations and all health workers, had vanished.

The occasional outbreaks of smallpox in modern times before its eradication were quickly contained.[285] But these were isolated outbreaks rather than implementations of a plan of widespread destruction. And many potential victims, plus hospital and other public health workers, had been vaccinated. A terrorist who got hold of smallpox virus, gene spliced it as was done with the mousepox virus, grew the virus in living cells, and extracted modest quantities of the virus in fluid form could place the fluid in aerosolizers that he would unobtrusively deposit in airport departure lounges, shopping malls, movie theaters, indoor stadiums, and other enclosed spaces in which people congregate. The aerosolizers would spray an invisible mist that could infect hundreds or even thousands of people within a few minutes at each location, all of whom would then be carriers.[286] Within weeks, hun-

What are the catastrophic risks, and how catastrophic are they?

79

dreds of millions of people around the world would be infected, and the disease would be unstoppable. A bizarre wrinkle is that airports are beginning to install air fresheners, which a terrorist could switch with dispensers of aerosolized bioweapons without anyone noticing.

Smallpox virus may be difficult for terrorists to get hold of. The disease was declared eradicated in 1980 (the last known outbreak was in 1977), and the only known specimens are under lock and key in two laboratories, one in the United States and the other in Russia. But there is suspicion, though no hard evidence, that stocks of smallpox virus exist elsewhere.[287] And it is possible that vaccinia virus, which is used to vaccinate human beings against smallpox and is much more widely available than the smallpox virus itself, might be reengineered to be as lethal as the smallpox virus.[288] Flu virus, gene spliced to be more lethal than the natural virus and to be vaccine resistant, is another candidate for a devastating bioweapon. It is more difficult to work with than smallpox because of its high rate of mutation, but this difficulty could be overcome by continued rapid progress in biotechnology.

The mousepox experiment has been replicated by microbiologists at St. Louis University—with the difference that they inserted the IL-4 gene into a different part of the virus, the effect being to make it even more lethal than the Australian plant scientists had made it. The St. Louis researchers announced the result of their experiment publicly even before submitting it for publication in a scientific journal.[289] The leader of the research team "emphasized repeatedly" that the juiced-up mousepox "'can't affect humans.'"[290] He was being disingenuous. People aren't susceptible to mousepox; that is true. But the significance of the gene-spliced mousepox virus is that inserting the IL-4 gene into the *smallpox* virus might produce a strain of smallpox against which the existing vaccine would be ineffective. The St. Louis team said that their "research could help deter terrorism by demonstrating the emergence of more potent medical defenses." They added that a combination of an antiviral drug (cidofovir) with human smallpox vaccine "saved some mice" and that combining cidofovir with "a monoclonal antibody drug that fought the effect of interleukin−4" did even better.[291] A bioterrorist reading the article would realize that he should be looking for something to add to smallpox virus to counter the effect of cidofovir and monoclonal antibody drugs. The sort of research done by the St. Louis scientists may be essential in combating bioterrorism, but publicizing the research could destroy its value in that regard. And the drugs that they think would be effective against a juiced-up smallpox are not stocked in sufficient volume to stop a pandemic.

A molecular virologist has developed "a genetically engineered Ebola that will enable researchers to mutate the virus at will to see which of its genes and proteins are most responsible for its deadly effects."[292] Apart from the value of such an invention in developing a cure, a mutant virus might be the basis for a vaccine; the most common type of vaccine is simply a weakened disease agent. Moreover, a broad-spectrum vaccine is more valuable than one that is effective against only one strain of a virus, and to develop such a vaccine requires knowledge that may be obtainable only by mutating the virus into more lethal forms. In addition, genetic engineering can be used to create more effective vaccines and ones that cause fewer allergic reactions.[293]

So far, so good; but in the wrong hands Ebola might be mutated (for example by injecting a toxin into the virus) into a form that would increase its infectiousness and defeat any vaccine or cure that had been developed for the natural form of the virus. Indeed, according to Kanatjan Alibekov (now Ken Alibek), the former chief scientist of the Soviet Union's biowarfare program, the Soviets succeeded in weaponizing Marburg Variant U, a cousin of Ebola. They processed Variant U into an inhalable dust so potent that just a few microscopic particles of the dust would kill.[294]

The case of the genetically reengineered Ebola vaccine underscores the dilemma of "dual use" technology, that is, a technology, such as gene splicing, that has beneficent as well as destructive applications. As Ebola illustrates, the beneficent uses are not limited to combating bioterrorism; natural germs remain, as we saw at the beginning of this chapter, a deadly threat. The lethal pathogens that bioterrorists might try to juice up might spread naturally. An attempt to ban gene splicing would thus impose large social costs to the extent that the ban was effective. But the point is academic, because the attempt would be futile. The potential benefits of the technology would create irresistible pressure for continued development. If the United States banned it, development would simply gravitate to another country.

Combating bioterrorism is complicated by an ominous feedback effect. To deal with the threat of bioterrorism we need to train more biochemists in virology and related disciplines in order to staff the laboratories working on vaccines, cures, and methods of detection. But the more biochemists there are who have such training, the greater the

What are the catastrophic risks, and how catastrophic are they?

81

number of people who know how to alter, create, and distribute such agents. However minute the percentage of them likely to be enlisted in a campaign of terrorism (provided the percentage exceeds zero), the more biochemists there are, the more potential bioterrorists there are. The danger is particularly acute with regard to biochemists who come to the United States from unfriendly nations, or nations in which a substantial slice of the population is fiercely hostile to the United States although the government is friendly to us, for advanced training and then return to their home countries.

In part because scientists' salaries are low relative to those of highly educated Americans in medicine, law, and business—for example, in 1999 the median salary of physical scientists who had received their doctorate within the preceding three years was only $52,000[295]—a great many of the scientists and technicians currently working in the United States are foreigners who may return home some day. Only half the technical employees of the National Institutes of Health are U.S. citizens.[296] And in the last thirty years the number of American graduate students in physics has fallen by almost half, while the number of foreign students has almost doubled and now exceeds the number of American students.[297]

Foreign students from terrorist-friendly nations who remain in the United States are less likely to do us harm than those who return to their nations. And if all did remain, then welcoming such students might be a means of depriving terrorists of their ablest potential recruits. But as we'll see in chapter 4, not all remain. Indeed, persons who enter the United States on a student visa are normally required to return to their native country for a period of time before settling in the United States permanently.

The danger of a cataclysmic bioterrorist attack seems so great that one may wonder why we are still here. Maybe my analysis underestimates the obstacles to such an attack. Academic-style analysis has a tendency to overlook practical difficulties and in particular to underestimate the time and the practical know-how that it takes to cross the bridge from an idea to its implementation. (The other side of "imagination cost" is that we can think quicker than we can do.) Maybe spiking smallpox virus is harder than it looks—those Australian plant scientists were using cutting-edge methods and equipment. To launch a devastating biological attack, a terrorist group or deranged scientist would have to obtain a suitable pathogen, engineer it to maximize its lethality and defeat any existing vaccine, handle it without infecting themselves before they could complete their work (since they would have no vaccine protection), aerosolize it—the most difficult stage[298]—and disseminate it. Failure or discovery at any stage would spell ruin and is likelier the more stages there are—though the terrorist attacks of September 11, 2001, had been years in preparation and involved a significant number of people, probably at least 100, yet were not foiled.

Difficulties are made to be overcome. We may have been spared a devastating bioterrorist attack thus far only because terrorists have yet to grasp the full implications of the biotech revolution and equip themselves to take advantage of it. A more reassuring possibility is that even terrorists don't want to kill everybody, especially the members of their own families, and they may realize that the scope of a bioterrorist attack may be impossible to limit. They may also, reflecting on the extraordinary disruption caused by the small-scale anthrax attack in the eastern United States in the fall 2001 that killed only five people, decide that a bioterror attack that killed thousands, or millions, but not billions of people would nevertheless cause an entirely satisfactory degree of chaos. But there may be terrorists who do not blanch at risks to their families and who welcome Armageddon. And there is also the "mad scientist" risk. Although scientists have a lower incidence of mental illness than other professional and creative people,[299] a number of scientific and technical workers are mentally ill[300] and people can be profoundly deranged (by our lights, at least) without having a diagnosable mental illness: Hitler, for example, and probably Osama bin Laden and Saddam Hussein.

Because the biotech industry is expanding rapidly and the costs and skills required for gene splicing are falling, the danger of bioterrorism is rising. We may be safe today, but not tomorrow. We may have gained some time as a result of the disorganization of Al Qaeda, brought about by the vigorous response of the United States and other nations to the 9/11 attacks. And we are more alert to the risk of terrorist attacks, including attacks utilizing weapons of mass destruction, than we were before that watershed event. But in time Al Qaeda may regroup or successor organizations achieve a high level of coherence and effectiveness, including effectiveness in neutralizing our intelligence operations. What is certain is that the technology usable for bioterrorism will improve, perhaps through a merger with nanotechnology. Such a merger might enable the smallpox virus to be synthesized, so that bioterrorists would no longer have to buy or steal it. The polio virus has already been synthesized. "Binary" methods of pro-

What are the catastrophic risks, and how catastrophic are they?

83

duction, in which the DNA of a virus is divided during the "spiking" stage to reduce risk to the handler and the separated pieces are "stitched" back together after the processing is complete, are on the way too. So are "stealth" viruses that, like the AIDS virus, have a very long infectious incubation period.[301]

Bioweaponry is often bracketed with chemical as well as nuclear weapons as weapons of mass destruction. Chemical weapons have been used by terrorists and under optimal conditions could inflict heavy casualties.[302] But they are highly unlikely to inflict casualties on the potential scale of nuclear and biological weaponry. They do not have the destructive force of nuclear weapons; they are not contagious, like many biological agents; and they can be neutralized by special clothing and other gear.

Cyberterrorism

It is natural to move from biochemical viruses to computer viruses; indeed the proliferation of the latter may be a portent of proliferation of the former. Viruses are only one form of cyberterrorism,[303] but I will begin with them.

Computer viruses are usually created by lone individuals who are skilled in computer technology and do not need expensive equipment. These viruses can spread very rapidly. The Internet is to the computer virus as the atmosphere is to an airborne biological virus, although the broader problem is computer interconnectivity—the Internet is only one, though the largest, computer network.

The potential danger is illustrated by the Melissa virus of 1999, a bit of software uploaded into the Internet in the form of an innocuously labeled document that when downloaded burrowed into the recipient's email address book and sent itself to the first 50 names in the book the next time the computer was online. Each of the recipients thus became the "carrier" of the virus to those addressees. Millions of computers were infected within a short time.

The annual cost of computer viruses to society has not been estimated with any precision. But it may amount to billions of dollars in interruption of service and in countermeasures by software companies, Internet service providers, the information-technology staffs of Internet users, and law enforcement personnel, not to mention the diversion of a valuable resource, namely the time of the hackers, to a socially unproductive activity. Computer viruses are not an extinction event; indeed at present they are more a nuisance than a serious problem. Their chief significance for the type of risk on which I focus in this book may be as evidence that there are indeed a great number of antisocial geeks, such as "computer skilled, but anti-social individuals who deliberately disrupt computer systems merely for the joy and personal satisfaction which comes from such achievement."[304] The most dangerous geeks, however, are those whose expertise is in biochemistry rather than computer programming.

If it is true that computer viruses are costing the U.S. economy $13 billion a year, as one estimate has it,[305] still that is only slightly more than one-tenth of 1 percent of GDP. But that is now, and the costs may rise rapidly. The number of viral infections of computers is increasing— from 6 in 1988 to 82,084 in 2002 and 76,404 in just the first half of 2003, almost doubling in the third quarter to 114,855[306]—and the total social costs are likely to rise more rapidly than the number and lethality of the computer viruses because we are in an arms-race situation, with hackers' efforts to devise ever more damaging computer viruses being matched by ever more sophisticated defenses. So far the defense is ahead. Most of the damage from computer viruses is sustained by unsophisticated Internet users who fail to take elementary precautions, such as deleting suspicious messages (especially email attachments) without downloading them and updating their antivirus software conscientiously. Computer viruses are usually detected quickly and slain by software patches distributed over the Internet within hours or even minutes of the launch of the virus. But the balance may shift in favor of the offense in the future, as technology evolves.[307] There are signs of this in a recent flurry of computer viruses skillfully disguised as security patches distributed by Microsoft!

"More than 800,000 hazmat [hazardous materials] shipments occur daily in the United States. . . . Terrorists could hack into and misuse information systems to identify and track such shipments in order to attack them at high-consequence locations," or even to "cause an accident resulting in the release of hazardous materials . . . by seizing control of railroad switches or signals." They might also "exploit vulnerabilities in transportation information systems to mask" shipments of weapons of mass destruction into the United States.[308] Conceivably a computer virus that evaded countermeasures that now seem adequate could disable all the military's computers during a war or, as in the science fiction movie *Terminator 3: The Rise of the Machines*, gen-

What are the catastrophic risks, and how catastrophic are they?

85

erate a credible report of an imminent nuclear strike by a hostile nation or a terrorist group. Even a virus that "merely" destroyed the World Wide Web or disrupted Internet communications for a period of weeks could trigger a major economic depression.[309] Optimists will point out, however, that most existing operating-system software predates computer viruses—indeed, predates the Internet—and future operating-system software will be less vulnerable.

A distinct form of cyberterrorism is the "insider attack."[310] Someone who has or gains physical access to a computer network inside the government or an industry may be able to obtain highly sensitive information or engage in acts of sabotage, destroying valuable data or perhaps even reprogramming computers to direct destructive acts.[311]

Digitization: surveillance and concealment

A different type of computer-related threat to social welfare arises from the effect of digitization of data on surveillance on the one hand and on concealment on the other. Surveillance involves both spying and analysis. Our police and intelligence agencies may soon be able to monitor all electromagnetic transmissions occurring anywhere on earth (phone calls, email, etc.), to eavesdrop on most face-to-face conversations as well, for example by deciphering the window vibrations caused by the human voice, and to maintain continuous video surveillance of all public spaces.[312] Digitization and computerized data processing will enable the stupendous mass of data obtained by such methods to be stored, sorted, pooled, interpreted, and identified with specific individuals, as well as enabling the collection, exchange, storage, and retrieval of all personal records (medical, financial, etc.) that are in electronic form, as all soon will be. In the wake of the 9/11 attacks, law enforcement authorities have, for example in the MATRIX project (see the next chapter), pooled more and more of the information about individuals that is contained in different databases. In the not very distant future, advances in digitization may enable the inexpensive creation of a comprehensive, continuously updated, readily accessible dossier on every human being on earth, containing a complete record of his or her conversations, purchases, computer files, health, travels, and other circumstances and activities both personal and professional. Even so innocuous-seeming an innovation as electronic toll collection, such as the popular E-Z Pass system, produces records that if retained and sorted would provide a comprehensive picture of an individual's daily travels.[313]

Comprehensive surveillance capability will not be a public monopoly. The European Union recognizes this; its privacy directive is applicable mainly to private rather than governmental databases.[314]

The psychological damage from impairing personal privacy to the degree that technological progress portends could be considerable, though there is a tendency to exaggerate it. The inhabitants of primitive societies have little privacy, because of the physical circumstances of their lives and because secrecy is more dangerous to social order when effective institutions of law enforcement have not emerged.[315] Yet these peoples do not appear to suffer from more hang-ups than we moderns do. Celebrities and politicians seem able to adjust to loss of privacy—and not all of them are exhibitionists. Maybe the rest of us will adjust as well.

Privacy is, moreover, an ethically and economically equivocal good, and not merely in an age of terrorism. Its operative meaning is concealment. The loss of utility from not being able to conceal discreditable facts about oneself might be balanced by the gain in transparency of transactions, both personal and commercial. It would be psychologically painful to lose one's own privacy, but reassuring to be able to place more trust in other people because they had lost their privacy.

Loss of privacy would, however, tend to make people more conformist, more guarded and circumspect, less communicative; and the result would be a reduction in creativity and innovation. Blackmail, identity theft, and other crimes based on the possession of private information would flourish, moreover, and huge "defense" costs would be incurred to preserve a remnant of privacy in the face of highly effective methods of surveillance both private (including criminal) and public. Defense costs would be incurred even if all phone conversations, letters, and email were monitored by means impossible to thwart. People would substitute methods of communication that while less efficient would be less easily monitored. Or they would simply not divulge discrediting information though it might be of great social value, such as that they were infected by a communicable disease.[316] And the demand for methods of encryption would soar, touching off an arms race between surveillance and encryption; the costs of the arms race would be socially wasted, or largely so.

Most of the costs that I have emphasized so far could arise as just the unintended by-products of innocent information-gathering activities. But a particular danger is the power that advanced techniques of digital surveillance would deliver into the hands of government to

What are the catastrophic risks, and how catastrophic are they?

87

snoop into every nook and cranny of people's private lives. The loss of all political liberty as a result of pervasive governmental surveillance, as in the society depicted in George Orwell's *Nineteen Eighty-Four*, would bear an uncomfortable resemblance to our becoming slaves of superintelligent robots.

We can push the analysis a bit further by distinguishing *solitude* from *secrecy* as forms of privacy. Solitude fosters individualistic attitudes, while conversely the constant presence of other people or sense of being under constant surveillance enforces conformity. Secrecy, in the sense of concealing from the world not only what one is thinking but also what one is communicating to friends or other intimates "in private," enables subversive thinking and planning to be hidden from the authorities. Thus secrecy, unlike solitude, has a social as well as a private dimension. Being able to hide one's thoughts is important, but so is privacy of communication. "Secret conversation" is not an oxymoron. The planning of organized activity is impossible without communication; less obviously, productive *independent* as well as collective thinking requires having someone to bounce ideas off. And few people are sufficiently independent minded to cling to an unorthodox idea if they don't know that others share it. We want to be part of a herd even if it is a very small one.

So privacy is a political good.[317] But it is not an unalloyed one. Charismatic political leadership—the most dangerous kind—depends on the leader's ability to control public information about himself. The same technological advances that have made it costly for private persons to protect their privacy have, by making government more transparent, made it harder for public officials to conceal bad acts—including snooping into the private affairs of the citizenry. And against the feared loss of personal privacy it can be argued that digitization and computer technologies actually enable more effective concealment of electronic communications than used to be possible. Double-key encryption systems enable individuals to encrypt email and other electronic communications (such as Internet telephony) more effectively than the encoding devices traditionally used to conceal telegraphic and telephonic communications. But because unbreakable encryption facilitates terrorist and other criminal activities,[318] we can expect governments to seek to limit it, for example by forbidding it to be used against surveillance by the government itself. This movement is well under way but may have started too late—software for effective encryption is already widely available, and there are thousands of competent programmers in foreign countries who are beyond the reach of U.S. law. Yet one can imagine surveillance being able to defeat even the strongest encryption: if I am being watched while typing on my computer, it doesn't matter that I may be able to encrypt unbreakably the message that I am typing.

The main point, however, is simply that encryption is part of the problem that gives rise to privacy-eroding surveillance rather than being the solution. It is not a good solution, because it is too dangerous; it would tilt the balance too far back in favor of privacy. Comprehensive surveillance may not be a good solution either, but David Brin may be correct that it is inevitable and that we must, and will, learn to live with it.[319]

David Friedman argues that we can have our cake and eat it—allow encryption and leave it to the market to de-encrypt, by the same mechanism that causes students to waive their federally conferred right to privacy in their college transcripts.[320] No one is forced to do business with someone who refuses to turn over relevant financial, health, and other information, and refusal is a signal that you have something to hide from your would-be transaction partner. All this is true, but it is not an answer to the use of encryption by criminals or, more to the point of this book, terrorists. Yet if encryption is prevented, government is strengthened, with the potentially disastrous political consequences that I have mentioned.

Catastrophic synergies and lesser-included catastrophes

The dangers posed by the catastrophic risks are magnified by the fact that some of the risks are positively correlated. Not all, of course; an asteroid collision wouldn't increase the likelihood of a strangelet disaster, and if a world-ending strangelet disaster occurred, all the other catastrophic risks would be moot. However, an asteroid collision of less than catastrophic proportions could interact with global warming to precipitate catastrophe; and we have seen that global warming and loss of biodiversity are likely to go hand in hand because global warming is one of the risk factors for loss of biodiversity and because population growth, which we can assume will continue for some time, increases both catastrophic risks. We also saw how cyberterrorism would

What are the catastrophic risks, and how catastrophic are they?

89

increase the risk of terrorist attacks with weapons of mass destruction, as could encryption if it makes terrorist communications secure—as could, for that matter, the social and economic disorganization that would be bound to follow a major asteroid collision or a lethal pandemic. In addition, any major attack by terrorists with such weapons would create fertile conditions for the imposition of public-safety measures that would jeopardize privacy and liberty. Critics of the Bush administration believe that the administration used the 9/11 attacks as a pretext for adopting measures that threaten to destroy civil liberties. However that may be, imagine an attack that was 10 or 100 or 1,000 times more destructive than the 9/11 attacks, and then imagine the likely response of any president.

In a full analysis of catastrophe, the expected cost of the extreme events that are the focus of this book would have to be enlarged to take account not only of the interactions just discussed but also of the multitude of lesser-included catastrophes that are possible—the small but destructive asteroid collision, the pandemic that kills "only" a few million people in a short span of time, the strangelet scenario in which only a nuclear explosion results,[321] and so on. Think of the economic, political, and social dislocations caused by the 9/11 attacks[322] and now think of the dislocations that would follow a bioterrorist attack that killed not 3,000 but 30,000 people.

Some types of risk, it is true, have what is called a "catastrophic distribution," which means that almost all the harms to which the risk gives rise will be inflicted by one or a small number of the possible incidents. For example, it has been estimated that three-fourths of the fatalities caused by all asteroid collisions that occurred in a period of 10,000 years would result from the single largest hit.[323] This may be one reason so little thought is being given to the risk of asteroid collisions. "The overwhelmingly most likely number of people to die by a globally catastrophic [asteroid] impact in the foreseeable future is zero. The juxtaposition of the small probability of occurrence balanced against the enormous consequences if it does happen makes the hazard of 'impact winter' very difficult to think about."[324] (A related phenomenon is the tendency to overinsure against high-probability losses and underinsure against low-probability ones.)[325]

The bioterrorism risk distribution is different and makes the threat more palpable and therefore easier to take seriously. Because of variations in the lethality, incubation period, and infectiousness of different germs, not to mention wide variations in the aims and capabilities of different terrorist groups, there is an enormous range of potential casualties from bioterrorist attacks. To focus on the worst case is to underestimate the aggregate threat posed by bioterrorism greatly, whereas to focus on the worst asteroid strike is to underestimate the danger to human life by only 25 percent.

What are the catastrophic risks, and how catastrophic are they?

91

2

Why so little is being done about
the catastrophic risks

I have said that the dangers of catastrophe are growing. One reason is the rise of apocalyptic terrorism. Another, however—because many of the catastrophic risks are either created or amplified by science and technology—is the breakneck pace of scientific and technological advance. A clue to that pace is that between 1980 and 2000 the average annual growth rate of scientific and engineering employment in the United States was 4.9 percent, more than four times the overall employment growth rate.[1] Growth in the number of scientific personnel of the other countries appears to have been slower, but still significant, though statistics are incomplete.[2] Of particular significance is the fact that the cost of dangerous technologies, such as those of nuclear and biological warfare, and the level of skill required to employ them are falling, which is placing more of the technologies within reach of small nations, terrorist gangs, and even individual psychopaths. Yet, great as it is, the challenge of managing the catastrophic risks is receiving less attention than is lavished on social issues of far less intrinsic significance, such as race relations, whether homosexual marriage should be permitted, the size of the federal deficit, drug addiction, and child pornography. Not that these are trivial issues. But they do not involve potential extinction events or the modestly less cataclysmic variants of those events.

So limited is systematic analysis of the catastrophic risks that there are no estimates of what percentage either of the federal government's total annual research and development (R & D) expenditures (currently running at about $120 billion), or of its science and technology expenditures (that is, R & D minus the D), which are about half the total R & D budget, are devoted to protection against them.[3] Not that R & D is the only expenditure category relevant to the catastrophic risks. But it is a very important one. We do know that federal spending on defense against the danger of terrorism involving chemical, biological, radiological, or nuclear weapons rose from $368 million in 2002 (plus $203 million in a supplemental appropriation) to more than $2 billion in 2003.[4] That is a step in the right direction. But most of these expenditures are for medical defenses against biological agents (see chapter 3); I argue in chapter 4 that police measures are not receiving as much attention as they should.

Cultural factors

Scientific illiteracy

One reason for widespread indifference to the catastrophic risks is the abysmal state of scientific knowledge[5] among nonscientists. Scientific ignorance is a well-known factor in the public's systematic misperceptions of the risks of different hazards,[6] and while such ignorance could exacerbate fears of what science might do to us, it seems, rather, to allay them.

Although American elementary and junior high school students do better on tests of scientific knowledge than their counterparts in most other countries,[7] by the last year of high school they are performing below the level of their foreign counterparts.[8] Despite this, the overall scientific literacy of the U.S. population is greater than that of the populations of the European Union, Japan, and Canada.[9] And Americans are more attentive to science than these other populations.[10] But this isn't saying much. Only a third of American adults know what a molecule is, 39 percent believe that astrology is scientific, and 46 percent deny that human beings evolved from earlier animal species.[11] Only 52 percent do *not* believe in astrology, 50 to 60 percent believe in ESP, only a little more than half know that it takes the earth a year to revolve around the sun (some don't know it takes a year; some don't know the earth revolves around the sun), about a third believe in UFOs, and similar percentages believe in ghosts and in communication with the dead.[12] It is possible that science is valued by most Americans merely as another form of magic.

The findings recited above, which are based on surveys, should be taken with a grain of salt (a point I make in a related context, that of "contingent valuation" surveys, in the next chapter). People lose facility with taking tests after they leave school and are surprised, freeze, and forget what they know when a question of fact (rather than of opinion) is sprung on them by a pollster. But the sheer amount of evidence of scientific ignorance is impressive. One study found that fewer than 20 percent of Americans can understand the *New York Times*'s Tuesday science section.[13] Morris Shamos estimates that "the fraction of Americans who might qualify as true scientific literates in this sense is 4 to 5 percent of the adult population, nearly all being professional scientists or engineers."[14] By "this sense" he means that

> the individual ... is aware of some of the major conceptual schemes (the theories) that form the foundations of science, how they were arrived at, and why they are widely accepted, how science achieves order out of a random universe, and the role of experiment in science. This individual also appreciates the elements of scientific investigation, the importance of proper questioning, of analytical and deductive reasoning, of logical thought processes, and of reliance upon objective evidence.[15]

Shamos's criteria can be criticized as too demanding; yet Jon Miller's less demanding criteria for what he calls "civic scientific literacy" yield an estimate that only 17 percent of the adult U.S. population was scientifically literate in 1999,[16] though this was a significant increase over his estimate of 12 percent for 1995. Imagine a population that had a *verbal* literacy rate of only 17 percent. And by his measure only 5 percent of the population of the European Union is scientifically literate.[17]

I must be careful in using such loaded terms as "abysmal" and "illiteracy." No one thinks our educational system abysmal because it produces few students who are literate in Hittite, Tamil, or Esperanto. The benefits of scientific education have to be compared with the costs, which include not only the educational programs that would have to be abandoned or curtailed to make way for more science teaching but also and more pertinently the scientific and technical manpower that would be diverted from research to teaching.[18] That is a particular concern with respect to high school science education, where the problem is not that students aren't required to study math and science but that the quality of instruction in these subjects is often low.[19] To improve that quality substantially would require teacher salary increases[20] that the taxpayer is unwilling to fund.

Colleges, however, might reorient their curricula toward math and science without increasing the overall expense of college education substantially, especially if, as I believe, the emphasis ought to fall on increasing the scientific literacy not of the population as a whole but of an elite consisting of the very bright students who go on to become officials and other policy makers and opinion leaders. Bright students have little to lose by substituting math and science for courses in postmodern literary criticism and cultural studies, sociology, women's studies, black studies, journalism, the Holocaust, film—and, in law school, constitutional law and other highly politicized legal subjects. (Little chance, though, of substitution against so popular a field as film!) Society would not be worse off even if by concentrating on technical fields the bright students failed to become cultured persons in the sense in which "culture" denotes familiarity with the classics of the Western philosophical, literary, and artistic traditions. It is a myth that culture is civilizing in the sense of making people less likely to engage in genocide and other atrocities[21] or that it has other social benefits. What would be unfortunate, however, would be the substitution of science courses for foreign language study, given the global aspect of the catastrophic risks and the resulting need for international cooperation in dealing with them.

In the United States—one of the world's most religious non-Islamic nations and seemingly becoming more so by the day—widespread scientific illiteracy has a connection with religiosity. For there is tension (chronicled in the magazine *Skeptical Inquirer*) between the scientific and the religious worldviews, however much mainstream religious and scientific leaders deny it. Resistance to the teaching of evolution in high school, a resistance widespread particularly in the South, is only the best-known manifestation of this tension.

More important than religiosity, however, is the sheer difficulty of modern science, a difficulty symbolized by the profoundly counter-intuitive (as well as formidably mathematized) principles of modern quantum theory, such as:

- Electrons are only probabilities until they are observed.[22]
- Atomic particles cannot be motionless even at a temperature of absolute zero because then their motion—zero—and their location would be simultaneously determined, violating the uncertainty principle.[23]
- Whereas "for waves on the ocean, it is the water that 'waves,'" and "for sound waves in the air, it is the molecules that comprise the air" that wave, "for matter it is *the probability of finding the particle* that waves."[21]
- The motion of an atomic particle can be influenced by the simultaneous motion of another atomic particle located so far away from it that any force or signal emanating from the second particle would have to travel faster than the speed of light (an impossibility, according to the special theory of relativity) in order to affect the first particle.[25]

Not all science is as difficult as quantum theory, but most of it is difficult enough to baffle the lay mind. Even when not highly mathematized it uses mathematical and statistical procedures that lay people don't understand, is extremely complicated, employs a strange and intimidating vocabulary, and deals with unimaginably long spans of time (in such fields as cosmology, geology, and evolutionary biology) and unimaginably small objects and processes (such as cell replication), or with unimaginably short spans of time (in the field of high-energy physics) and unimaginably large objects (in the field of astronomy). "Laypeople possess scarcely any understanding, and much misunderstanding, of what science is doing and can do. . . . That the masses remain unenlightened . . . is not attributable to lack of missionary efforts, but to the recondite nature of modern science."[26]

If political leaders, lawyers, judges, journalists, and other members of the governing class have no interest in and feel for science, they are unlikely to attend closely to either the dangers or the opportunities that modern science creates. The problem is particularly acute for members of the legal profession because so many of them deliberately turned their back on science when they decided to go into law. Whereas modern science is heavily dependent on mathematics, the law's methods place overwhelming emphasis on verbal skills. Law thus provides a refuge for bright youngsters who have "math block," though this usually means only that they shied away from math and science courses in college because they could get higher grades with less work in verbal fields and as a result never became comfortable with mathematical concepts or operations.[27] Few people have "math block" in the sense of a psychological impediment to learning math at a level consistent with their general intellectual abilities; indeed only about 6 percent of the school-age population has a math learning disability. "A neurological deficit that results in persistent difficulty in processing numbers" must not be confused with "mathematics phobia" resulting from "negative experiences in [students'] past or a simple lack of self-confidence with numbers."[28]

Anyone admitted to an elite law school can learn enough math to be able to understand fundamental scientific principles, the character of scientific research, and the mentality of scientists and engineers, though he or she would in most cases be unable to understand the mathematics employed by advanced practitioners in particle physics and other scientific disciplines, use scientific terminology correctly, or avoid making mistakes. By way of comparison, economists are now using esoteric mathematical and statistical methods and a good deal of jargon, yet lawyers who practice in fields in which economics is important do not consider themselves incapable of learning enough economics to be able to understand the relevant economic principles and communicate effectively with economic expert witnesses.

A factor in the scientific illiteracy of the elite is advanced college placement. It often means that high school students can take undemanding math and science courses that enable them to satisfy college requirements in these subjects and thus be excused from taking the demanding college counterparts of those courses. As a result, they may take no math or science at all in college and by the time they graduate will have forgotten the science and math they learned in high school.

Science worship

Ignorance of science coexists dangerously with an uncritical veneration of science and scientists. The enormous success of science in enlarging human knowledge and devising new and improving old products and services has not only engendered a highly positive view of science on the part of Americans;[29] it has also tended to occlude the dangers that continued scientific progress poses and to create an attitude of "leave science policy to scientists." Scientists are viewed as magicians whose magic we are happy to consume without seeking to understand the tricks that produce it. That is why scientific ignorance tends to allay rather than to exacerbate fear of science. We think of science as the key to our comfort, prosperity, longevity, and geopolitical power, and we resist thinking that our dependence on it may prove to be a Faustian pact.[30] Even the practical benefits of science are exaggerated, because people forget that technological progress, which is what mainly contributes to human well-being, is not always a matter of applying scientific principles. Often it is inductive and atheoretical.[31] The wheel preceded physics, spectacles preceded optics, surgery preceded physiology, and even many modern inventions, including Band-Aids and lawn mowers, are based on practical know-how rather than on scientific theory.[32]

Still, science has contributed so greatly to human welfare and possesses so much unrealized potential to continue doing so that to think of it as a source of equally great dangers has a killjoy air and is likely to be dismissed as Luddite. To emphasize those dangers is to invite the riposte that the only way to combat dangers created or exacerbated by technology is with more technology—and to a great extent this is true. This may explain the surprising finding that three-quarters of the U.S. population believe that the emission of carbon dioxide and other gases is raising global temperatures and approve international efforts to control these emissions.[33] The emissions are due largely to technology, but to the "old" technology of the internal combustion engine and electrical generation, not to modern science. You can be for science and against global warming, just as you can be for recombinant DNA but against bioterrorism, the bioterrorists being bad people who might get hold of and pervert the fruits of modern science.

A common mistake is to suppose that scientists are such admirable people that they can be safely entrusted with the ultimate responsibility for guiding scientific research. In fact they are no more admirable than any other type of worker. Neither selection nor self-selection for a scientific career is based on admirableness. Though the conventions and protocols of science enforce on scientists, in comparison to astrologers and English professors—and lawyers—a high degree of objectivity *when they are doing science*, it does not follow that such individuals can be depended on to be objective policy analysts. That is a role for which they are not trained (but is anyone?) and that does not impose the constraints that science imposes. Scientists' policy analyses are as likely to be deformed by career, financial, and ideological considerations as those of nonscientists. This might not matter if the aims of science and public policy were the same, but they are not. Scientists want to advance scientific knowledge rather than to protect society from science; the policy maker's ordering of values is the reverse. Not that scientists are indifferent to public safety; but it is not their business and sometimes it is in competition with their business.

Scientists resent the imposition of legal controls on scientific research and are insensitive to the degree to which that resentment rests on self-interest. Barry Bloom, dean of the Harvard School of Public Health, criticizes the editors of leading scientific journals for having taken the position that "an editor may conclude that the potential harm of publication outweighs the potential societal benefits." Bloom calls this "a chilling example of the impact of terrorism on the freedom of inquiry and dissemination of knowledge that today challenges every research university."[34] He seems to think that freedom of scientific research should enjoy absolute priority over every other social value. Such a belief comes naturally to people who derive career advantages from being able to engage in a particular activity without hindrance.

Bloom is incensed at limitations on allowing foreigners to study science in American universities. Under the rubric of "Advancing Openness," he advocates changes in existing regulations (see chapter 4) to enable any foreigner who obtains a visa for studying science in the United States to pursue any area of scientific research, however sensitive and whatever the student's likely motive.[35] Bloom's concern is understandable in terms of professional self-interest. As I noted in chapter 1, our universities are heavily dependent for graduate students on foreigners. According to Bloom, 24 percent of the graduate students at Harvard are foreign.[36]

Nuclear scientists and scientists employed in weapons laboratories have long accepted the necessity of tight controls on their research. But until recently biology was unregulated, and biologists are finding it difficult to adjust to a regulatory regime. I remind the reader of the mousepox experiments and the dangers of open publication of research that, even if innocent in design—even if designed to protect against bioterrorism—furnishes potential terrorists with a recipe for making devastating biological weapons. There is also a psychological factor at work. Scientists are reluctant to acknowledge even to themselves that their research may in the long run do more harm than good. That is one reason science policy cannot be entrusted solely to scientists.

I have been emphasizing character and perspective, but it is not even clear that scientists are smarter in the relevant sense (an essential qualification) than people of comparable standing in other professional fields. They are smarter *at science*, and many of them, especially mathematicians and physicists, have higher IQs than nonscientists of comparable professional achievement.[37] It doesn't follow that they can do better than the math and science dummies at social policy, with respect to which verbal and social skills, common sense, worldly experience, and ability to evaluate character and to divine motivation may be more important than mathematical or other abstract analytical skills, or intuitions about the laws of physics or the behavior of nonhuman life forms. People who spend their professional lives studying atoms or amoebas are not necessarily well equipped to deal effectively with human social problems, including the regulation of science and technology. (Primatologists, on the other hand. . . .)

Because scientists are usually quicker witted than their peers in "mushy" fields, they sometimes think they can deal more intelligently with nonscientific questions than nonscientists can. They fancy that they can opine broadly yet authoritatively on issues of science policy that are not actually scientific in character. (I give some examples later.) In short, they exaggerate the degree to which IQ can substitute for knowledge and experience. A number of brilliant scientists did turn out to be distinguished administrators and savants, such as James Conant and J. Robert Oppenheimer, and, among the living, James Watson and David Baltimore. Nevertheless, "training in physics hardly qualifies a man to dictate public policy."[38]

Science fiction

Another reason for the widespread neglect of catastrophic risks, whether they are natural and hence perhaps amenable to technological reduction or man-made and therefore probably created or at least exacerbated by technology, is a "boy who cried wolf" phenomenon, examined in this and the next section.

Catastrophe in general has always held a strong attraction for readers and writers of fiction, and the relationship between technology and catastrophe has made it natural for science-fiction writers to make technologically induced catastrophes a major theme along with such natural catastrophes as asteroid collisions. Fiction writers are privileged to exaggerate. Also, there is selection bias when one is talking about doomsday: no prediction of doomsday can be accurate except the last one, since after doomsday there are no more readers or writers. (But this is true only of *literal* doomsday, not of the lesser catastrophes predicted by Paul Ehrlich and other Greens, which I discuss later.)

Because of these things, catastrophe-oriented science fiction, as distinct from comedic and utopian science fiction, is dominated by depictions of catastrophe that turn out to be false even when they are seriously intended rather than mere literary devices. I'll begin with some examples drawn from the upper tail of the quality distribution of futurist literature (a better term than "science fiction," a category dominated by works of only modest literary merit) and end with a quartet of catastrophe movies. The literary examples are H. G. Wells's *Time Machine*, Aldous Huxley's *Brave New World*, George Orwell's *Nineteen Eighty-Four*, and Margaret Atwood's *Oryx and Crake*.

These novels and others that could be picked instead[39] use the method of prediction known as naive extrapolation. That is, they identify a dominant contemporary trend and explore the ominous consequences if it continues indefinitely. For Wells, writing in 1895 and mesmerized by Darwinism, the trend was, he thought (mistakenly, as it turned out), the polarization of England's classes. The time traveler travels 800,000 years into the future and discovers an England occupied by two human species, the Eloi and the Morlocks. The former are the childish, physically and mentally degenerate descendants of the nineteenth-century English upper class. The latter are the equally degenerate descendants of the lower class. The Morlocks live underground (Wells was struck by the tendency of manual labor, not limited to mining, to move underground) and produce the goods that the Eloi, who have no skills and do no work, need for survival. In exchange, as it were, the Morlocks prey on the Eloi, eating them when they can find them outdoors at night. It is a neat example of symbiosis.

For Huxley, writing during the worldwide depression of the 1930s, the great social problem was that, as he and others believed (again incorrectly), technological progress was creating chronic widespread unemployment by enabling more output to be produced by fewer workers. The solution, he thought, would require central planning to bring production and consumption into phase. Borrowing ideas from an insightful work of futurism by the English scientist J. B. S. Haldane,[40] Huxley sketched a future in which technology—helping to solve the problem it had created—would enable the creation of genetically distinct classes, ranging from high-IQ Alphas to near-moronic Epsilons, each perfectly adapted to performing a particular task. Technology would thus enable the central planners to avoid overproduction while providing employment for everyone.

In the 1940s the focus of concern shifted to another type of centralization: the extinction of liberty by totalitarian governments. And so we have Orwell's vision of a near future in which Soviet techniques of social control would be perfected and universalized. He was wrong too—which is not to deny the pertinence of *Nineteen Eighty-Four* to the analysis of the possible political consequences of pervasive government surveillance of private conduct, which I sketched in chapter 1.

The predictions of these distinguished writers went awry because the writers were insufficiently attentive to forces in society that would tend to retard and eventually reverse contemporary trends. (An underlying reason, of which more later, is the psychological tendency to see a pattern where there isn't one.) Some trends are self-correcting; as I noted in chapter 1, if petroleum is becoming scarce, its price will rise, inducing substitution and also a wider search for reserves. Other trends, provided they are not irreversible, as global warming may be, will be stopped by collective action when their costs rise to a level high enough to activate the political process. Others, however, such as the risk of a disastrous asteroid collision, fit neither category. The risk of such a collision is not, so far as anyone knows, growing, and obviously there is no tendency for the risk to correct itself. But the *perception* of the risk may grow, perhaps to the point at which collective action is triggered.

Futuristic novels are better regarded as conditional predictions, that is, warnings, rather than as unconditional predictions—that "this is what the future holds." In some of these novels the future is allegorical. H. G. Wells's *War of the Worlds* is about the horrors of war and (again reflecting his Darwinian preoccupations) adaptive fitness (the Martian invaders die because they have no natural immunity against bacteria); he didn't really expect Martians to invade the earth. But the only point relevant to my concerns is that the body of futurist writing taken as a whole describes catastrophic risks that have failed to materialize, and this tends to make people blasé about catastrophe. You watch a movie in which an asteroid collides with the earth and causes cataclysmic damage but write it off as science fiction rather than recognizing it as a more or less realistic depiction of a possible though unlikely real-life event.

Margaret Atwood's 2003 novel *Oryx and Crake*, which I mentioned in the preface and from which I quoted briefly in chapter 1, is a distinguished addition to doomsday fiction. Set in the near future, it depicts a world that is a recognizable version of our own but ravaged by severe global warming, biodiversity depletion, the final destruction of privacy by the electronic media (as in such Web sites as "nitee-nite .com," where one can watch people committing suicide), and the permeation of the atmosphere not only by pollutants but also by new germs. The world is dominated by a technocratic elite that inhabits sealed-off "Compounds." A member of the elite—a brilliant, geeky, faintly autistic scientist-executive named Crake, employed by a company engaged in advanced bioengineering—grows dissatisfied with the human race and decides to destroy it and replace it with one of his own design. The mode of destruction that he successfully employs with the aid of only one (unknowing) accomplice is a biological attack similar to the hypothetical enhanced-smallpox attack that I discussed in chapter 1, though as in most science fiction of biological disaster the pathogen resembles Ebola because, being hemorrhagic, it causes a more gruesome death.

Atwood's novel differs from the others I've discussed not only in being too recent to have been overtaken by events, but also in emphasizing catastrophic risks, notably global warming and bioterrorism, that are not self-correcting. True, like any other risk, the bigger these risks grow the greater will be the pressure to do something. But in the case of global warming, as we shall see, the political and economic obstacles to doing anything are formidable and in the short run probably insuperable, while delay in responding is allowing the atmospheric concentration of greenhouse gases to rise inexorably and perhaps irreversibly. The risk of bioterrorism is growing too, and the obstacles to controlling it are, as we shall see, especially daunting.

A question raised by Atwood's novel and other works of science fiction that deal with contemporary hazards is whether they might not operate to alarm—which would be all to the good—rather than, as I am suggesting, to lull. On the one hand there is the prevalent view that anything that is science fiction is, as it were by definition, harmless make-believe. On the other hand there is the power of art, both high and popular, to stir emotion and even incite political action. Some people think that *Uncle Tom's Cabin*, published in 1852, although not a work of literary distinction, was one of the catalysts of the Civil War. And Orwell's great satires *Animal Farm* and *Nineteen Eighty-Four* may have helped to turn people against Stalinism. My guess is that *Oryx and Crake* is pretty much preaching to the converted—although my own interest in catastrophic risks was stimulated by her novel and I do not share her leftish political views. President Bill Clinton was so alarmed by Richard Preston's bioterrorism novel *The Cobra Event* (1997) that he advocated, well before the 9/11 attacks, a major effort to prevent bioterrorism.[41] But as far as awakening people's concern about such risks is concerned, one would expect disaster movies, with their powerful visual impact in this era of highly realistic cinematic special effects, to be the Paul Reveres of catastrophe.

A prime prospect might seem to be *Armageddon*, a 1998 Hollywood movie about a narrowly averted collision between a huge asteroid and the earth. Unlike so many science-fiction movies, *Armageddon* doesn't involve any extraterrestrial beings; it's squarely about one of the catastrophic risks discussed in this book. There are other movies about the danger of asteroids colliding with the earth as well, such as *Deep Impact*, *Meteor*, and *Asteroid*, plus a notable novel, *Lucifer's Hammer*, by Larry Niven and Jerry Pournelle (1977), but *Armageddon*'s remarkable special effects set it apart.

The movie starts promisingly with a reminder that an asteroid only about six miles in diameter wiped out the dinosaurs, and is punctuated with frightening scenes, some quite realistic, of meteorites (shards of the asteroid that seems about to collide with the earth) striking the earth; especially powerful is the scene of a meteorite destroying Paris, though the implication that meteorites have an affinity for the best-known cities is absurd. There is even a mordant reference to the fact (and it is a fact, as we'll see in the next chapter) that NASA isn't spending enough on detection of near-earth objects to be confident of spotting even large ones in time to do anything to deflect them.

But as a wake-up call to a genuine menace the movie is spoiled by three things. The first is its message, which is that Americans (and specifically an ethnically diverse group of middle- and lower-class Americans) can do anything, no matter how impossible it looks—the asteroid is the size of Texas, and it will hit the earth in 18 days and kill all life on it, even the bacteria—and also that it is America's destiny to save the world. I like the message, but it is not calculated to incite calls for a reallocation of NASA's budget. Second, the asteroid is too large. Not only are we not in danger of being struck by an asteroid that large, but its size is gratuitous, since an asteroid many times smaller would have the same terminating effect on the human race. Apart from the fleeting reference to the dinosaur buster, there is no suggestion in the movie that smaller near-earth objects are worth worrying about. One reason the asteroid in the movie is outsize is that for dramatic reasons it has to shed large meteorites that shower down on the earth, two spacecraft have to land on it and the crew of one undertake a hair-raising journey to reach the other, and a hole 800 feet deep has to be dug so that an A-bomb can be dropped down and blow the asteroid into two pieces that will pass on either side of the earth. If an asteroid the size of Texas (800 miles across) were somehow not noticed until it was within 18 days of hitting the earth (very unlikely), there would be no way to deflect it; and it certainly could not be blown up with a single atomic bomb, or, for that matter, with millions of hydrogen bombs.

Another asteroid-collision movie, *Deep Impact*, is more realistic but less entertaining and popular—partly because it *is* more realistic and therefore more ominous. The asteroid (actually a fragment of a comet) that strikes the earth in *Deep Impact* is only two miles across. Interestingly, one reason the asteroid in *Armageddon* is so huge is that the director "didn't think the audience would believe something 5 or 6 miles long could kill the Earth."[42] By thus pandering to the audience's scientific ignorance, the movie occludes the existence of any real danger of a catastrophic asteroid collision.

Another notable catastrophe film is *Outbreak* (1995), a fast-paced and skillfully acted movie about the threat of a biological holocaust. In the movie the U.S. Army in the 1960s—when we had in fact a biological-warfare program—has developed a lethal, Ebola-like virus and tested it in an African civil war. Having satisfied itself that the virus is lethally effective, the army bombs the test site to destroy all traces of the experiment. But the virus has spread to the area's monkeys, and a descendant of them, a carrier of the disease though not itself infected, is unwittingly brought to the United States 30 years later, and soon the disease breaks out in a town in California. An evil army general (Donald Sutherland) wants to bomb the town in order to preserve the secret of the virus for weapon purposes, even though a heroic army doctor (Dustin Hoffman) has found the simian Typhoid Mary and by extracting antibodies from it (for remember that the monkey itself, though a carrier, is immune) has developed a vaccine. The evil general is thwarted and the town saved.

The scenes of sick and dying people, of panic induced by the rapid spread of an unknown fatal disease, of the overwhelming of local health facilities, and of the ugliness of a quarantine are brilliant and terrifying. And the possibility that a biological-weapon project could accidentally loose a lethal pathogen on the world is real. There is also a history of our military authorities' concealing the results of experiments with novel weaponry. But the movie's emphasis on the struggle between the evil general and the heroic doctor (and there is also of course a romantic subplot, as in *Armageddon*) situates the movie in the world of make-believe and by doing so allays the anxieties that the biowarfare setting might otherwise have engendered in viewers.

The most recent of the science-fiction disaster movies, *The Day after Tomorrow* (2004), is the first to deal with global warming. It is too recent for one to know what effect if any it will have on the public's perceptions. Environmentalists have hailed it as a timely and terrifying warning; spokesmen for the energy industries have derided it as scientifically preposterous. There is a sense in which it is both. The movie depicts the form of abrupt global warming in which a warming spiral precipitates a freezing spiral. We know from chapter 1 that such a sequence—though one hopes it is extremely unlikely—is not impossible, even in the near term. But in the movie, the transition from global warming to a new ice age far more severe than the last ice age (though not as bad as "snowball earth") takes place in just a few days, which is impossible; it would take years. And the movie has the standard Americans-can-do-anything, happy-endings-are-always-possible theme that alleviates fears created by the disaster special effects, arresting as they are. There was a missed opportunity, because abrupt global warming is more easily visualized than most catastrophes, given the frequency of extreme weather conditions.

The finest of the recent catastrophe films is *The Matrix* (1999), set almost two centuries hence and distinguished not only by astonishing special effects (since transcended, however, owing to the rapid progress of digitization, including by *The Matrix*'s otherwise disappointing sequels) but also by very fine acting, editing, pace, and the timely and ingenious twist that it gives to the old theme of mind control; think of such classics as *The Manchurian Candidate* and *The Invasion of the Body Snatchers*, or for that matter *Nineteen Eighty-Four* or even the Grand Inquisitor parable in *The Brothers Karamazov*. The other movies I've discussed are entertainment, instantly recognized as such and dismissed as serious warnings, even when rather grim, as is true of *Deep Impact*. *The Matrix* is something more.

Superintelligent robots ("sentient [computer] programs") have conquered the world and enslaved mankind—one of the catastrophe scenarios that I described in the first chapter. Human beings are programmed to believe that they are living normal lives in 1999, but actually they are inhabiting a virtual reality in which they are fed flawless impressions of an external world. They are like "brains in a vat," a subject of philosophical speculation from Descartes to Robert Nozick, except that they are entire bodies in a vat because the robots need human bodies as a power source. So instead of the monkey moving the robot by means of brain waves—see chapter 1—the robot is moving the monkey by means of brain waves. (By a bizarre coincidence, "MATRIX"—short for "Multistate Anti-Terrorism Information Exchange"—is the name the U.S. Department of Justice has chosen for an ambitious program of linking federal, state, and commercial databases in order to enable a vast range of information to be assembled concerning any individual in whom law enforcement authorities have an interest.)[43]

So realistic is the world created by the "matrix"—this video-game world, though because the games are played in the head rather than at a console none of the players except the handful of rebels know they're playing—that the death of a person's "avatar" (one's virtual self, the self that plays the game) causes the physical body to die unless one is exceptionally strong-minded. The only human being strong-minded enough to survive a virtual death is Neo, the movie's hero, who returns to life after having been killed in virtual reality while killing not only the programmed human beings whom he encounters there as police or other pliant tools of the robots but also, unprecedentedly, some of the robots themselves.

The movie's merger of physical space with cyberspace is a clue to how the evolution of robots and, what is closely related, continued advances in digitization may one day create a world much like that depicted in *The Matrix*. Such "online digital worlds" as The Sims, EverQuest, Lineage, There, and Second Life are portents. Second Life, for example, allows one to "create beautiful scripted 3D objects in a totally live online environment — from weapons to clothing lines to motorcycles. Explore a rapidly changing and expanding world simulated on over 100 servers (with new land added almost daily), containing hundreds of thousands of user-created objects, daily and nightly hosted events, games to play, and people to meet. Buy and sell land, create a business, or exchange virtual for real currency. It's up to you." According to Second Life's home page (from which the above description is quoted), *Time* magazine has described Second Life as "the Matrix minus the evil machines."

Apart from the idea of the human body as an energy source ("milking" the inert human body for electricity would consume more energy, to keep the body alive, than it would produce), the scientific premises of *The Matrix* appear to be reasonable extrapolations from known scientific principles and existing technology.[44] I mentioned the monkey that moves the robot with brain waves. Paralyzed people who in a forthcoming experiment will have chips implanted in their brains "to enable them to operate a computer by thought alone . . . will have a cable sticking out of their heads to connect them to computers, making them look something like characters in 'The Matrix.'"[45] And just months ago the MIT Media Lab Europe created Mind Balance, a video game in which the player wears a headset that picks up his brain waves noninvasively (the monkey had electrodes planted in his brain) and uses them to make the moves in the game.[46] The next step will be for the headset to "broadcast" the moves of the other players directly to the player's brain. And here is the economist Edward Castronova on the feel of existing, not imagined, online digital worlds:

> VWs [virtual worlds] offer something that is perhaps a bit more than a mere entertainment to which the players have become addicted. Rather, they offer an alternative reality, a different country in which one can live most of one's life if one so chooses. And it so happens that life in a VW is extremely attractive to many people. A competition has arisen between Earth and the virtual worlds, and for many, Earth is the lesser option.[47]

As it was for Cypher, the traitor in *The Matrix*.

Yet the fairy-tale elements of *The Matrix* (for example, strong-minded as Neo is, he would have died had it not been for a kiss by the heroine, in a gender reversal of *Sleeping Beauty*), the uplifting intimation that in the end humanity (led, as in *Armageddon*, by a racially and gender diverse group of ordinary Americans—a group that by definition can accomplish anything) will prevail because robots live by rules and human beings are free, and the insistent parallels to the Christ story and Jewish messianism,[48] along with the fact that the movie is set safely, as it were, in the future, prevent it from being terrifying. Few viewers come away from the movie thinking that digitization, artificial intelligence, and robotics endanger the future of humankind—though, *pace* Ray Kurzweil, who doesn't buy "the Matrix scenario of malevolent artificial intelligences in mortal conflict with humans,"[49] they do. Paul Fontana may well be right that "the instant cult status of *The Matrix*" is "due to the subtext of exile, restoration, and the fulfillment of eschatological hope."[50]

The Matrix claims that mind will in the end conquer matter but simply assumes that the mind will be human and the matter inorganic. This is an echo of the fallacious optimistic view, which I discussed in chapter 1, that robotic intelligence can never surpass that of the human race. A further problem with *The Matrix* as warning—it is the endemic problem with prophecies of doom—is that it is the latest in a *very* long series of science-fiction novels and movies about robots rebelling against their human masters.[51] (A notable precursor, with some thematic similarities, is the *Terminator* series.) The impression created is that such rebellion, and the ensuing enslavement or extermination of humans by the robots, is *only* a science-fiction theme. And speaking of *Terminator*, notice how in *Terminator 2: Judgment Day* the terrifying theme of robots' achieving consciousness and precipitating a nuclear holocaust is undercut by the appearance of a robotic savior from the future, who like the Tin Man in *The Wizard of Oz* acquires (figuratively speaking) a heart.

Earlier I suggested a tension between the religious and the scientific worldview. Reflection on the movies that I have been discussing suggests a more direct tension between religiosity on the one hand and the recognition of the gravity of the catastrophic risks on the other. The most influential religions in the United States are Christianity and Judaism, and they are both messianic: everything is to come right in the end. The messianic theme is prominent in science fiction—indeed in all the science-fiction movies that I have discussed—and blunts an awareness of looming disasters. A benign providence would not permit the human race to become extinct—unless it was arranging a better life for us in the hereafter. Science fiction casts a salvific aura over science and the future.

I am not trying to put down science fiction. I admire the works that I have been discussing, especially the novels and *The Matrix*. Much of science fiction (especially what insiders call "hard" science fiction) is solidly grounded in science. Science fiction most famously but not only by Jules Verne predicted scientific discoveries and technological applications long before they came to pass.[52] *Oryx and Crake* and *The Matrix* may be genuinely prophetic, in accordance with Stephen Hawking's dictum that "today's science fiction is often tomorrow's scientific fact."[53] The vivid depiction of a squalid human future in such works should give us pause. But the psychological impact is weakened by the connotation that "science fiction" bears as the antithesis of science, as when a scientific claim is dismissed as "the stuff of science fiction."[54] It is not that "fiction" is really the antithesis of "fact," but that to gain and grip an audience a work of the imagination, be it a novel or a movie, has to season fact with fantasy, and by doing so it relinquishes scientific authority. On balance, science fiction probably impedes rather than advances the recognition of the catastrophic risks that endanger us. Consistent with this suggestion, there is evidence that the reading or viewing of science fiction encourages an optimistic view of science.[55]

Scientific doomsters

The second component of the "boy who cried wolf" phenomenon is the frequency with which credentialed scientists make irresponsible doomsday predictions. In 1970 Paul Ehrlich, then as now a biology professor at Stanford, offered the following rash predictions, all quickly falsified:

- Americans will probably be subjected to water rationing by 1974 and food rationing by the end of the decade, [and] . . . hepatitis and epidemic dysentery rates could easily climb by 500 percent in this country between 1970 and 1974 on account of crowding and increasingly polluted water.[56]
- Most American women do not realize that by having more than two children, they are unknowingly contributing to the early death of those children.[57]
- [DDT and other pesticides] may have already shortened by as much as a decade the life expectancy of every American born since 1946.[58]
- The [global] death rate will increase until at least 100–200 million people per year will be starving to death during the next 10 years.[59]
- It is conceivable that in a decade or two all marine fishing, both commercial and sport, will have ceased because of irreversible changes in the oceans.[60]

Other extreme statements made by Ehrlich in 1970, the year of the first Earth Day, include that 65 million Americans might starve to death in the 1980s, that hundreds of thousands of Americans might die in "smog disasters" in the 1970s, and that DDT and other pesticides might well reduce Americans' life expectancy to 42 by 1980.[61] Ehrlich and the economist Julian Simon made a bet in 1980 that the composite price of a menu of commercially valuable metals picked by Ehrlich would rise over the next decade because of a growing scarcity of raw materials. The price fell, so he lost the bet.[62] It did not occur to Ehrlich that a rise in the price of raw materials would be a good thing from his standpoint, as it would reduce output and with it such undesirable byproducts as carbon dioxide emissions.

Carl Sagan, another well-known scientist, predicted at the outset of the 1991 Gulf War that if Saddam Hussein set fire to the Kuwaiti oil fields (as he did),

> the net effects will be very similar to the explosion of the Indonesian volcano Tambora in 1815, which resulted in the year 1816 being known as the year without a summer. There were massive agricultural failures in North America and in western Europe, and very serious human suffering and, in some cases, starvation. Especially for south Asia that seems to be in the cards, and perhaps for a significant fraction of the northern hemisphere as well.[63]

No such disaster ensued from the fires.

Scientists overestimated the radiation hazards from atomic warfare[64] and may well be exaggerating the current rate of biodiversity loss. And remember the Y2K scare?[65] And fears that an atomic explosion would ignite the atmosphere? After enough false prophecies of doom, people stop paying attention.

Worse, the pratfalls of doomsters such as Ehrlich arm those who have an ideological or economic motive for minimizing estimates of catastrophic risk. They can plausibly depict the doomsters as intellectually reckless and ideologically motivated, because the doomsters attribute catastrophic dangers to capitalist excess, such as the high level of consumption in the United States and the emission of carbon dioxide by the country's immense volume of vehicular traffic. Concern with catastrophic risks becomes associated in the public mind with left-wing anarchists, radical Greens, and other cranks, producing the backlash discussed in the next section of this chapter.

Satirizing the cranks, Margaret Atwood in *Oryx and Crake* invents a futile protest against a new genetically modified coffee ("Happicuppa") that is putting small coffee growers out of business,

> a Boston Coffee Party sprang up. There was a staged media event, boring because there was no violence—only balding guys with retro tattoos or white patches where they'd been taken off,

and severe-looking baggy-boobed women, and quite a few over-weight or spindly members of marginal, earnest religious groups, in T-shirts with smiley-faced angels flying with birds or Jesus holding hands with a peasant or God Is Green on the front. They were filmed dumping Happicuppa products into the harbour, but none of the boxes sank. So there was the Happicuppa logo, lots of copies of it, bobbing around on the screen. It could have been a commercial.[66]

The optimistic backlash

Polarization of views is a marked tendency of public-intellectual discourse.[67] Intellectuals appeal to a popular audience by taking extreme positions that arrest attention and differentiate the speaker or writer from his competitors in the public-intellectual market. Environmental extremists, such as Paul Ehrlich, have learned this lesson well. At the same time, their extremism makes them broad targets—but the tendency of public-intellectual discourse toward extreme positions leads the attackers to overshoot the mark. An early example is a book by John Maddox called *The Doomsday Syndrome* (1972), which uses the excesses of Ehrlich, Barry Commoner, Rachel Carson, and other well-known environmentalists to disparage doomsday scenarios. The book is well written and well informed, but the author's impercipience regarding advances in bioengineering and computerization is striking. Not that he could be expected to have predicted them; but he shouldn't have thought he could see the future clearly enough to dismiss the risks that continued advances in these fields might create.

A more recent example is an article by the well-known science journalist Gregg Easterbrook.[68] A full-bore attack on those, including highly reputable scientists such as Martin Rees, who have expressed concern about catastrophic risks, the article opens in the jocular tone signaled by the title ("We're All Gonna Die! But It Won't Be from Germ Warfare, Runaway Nanobots, or Shifting Magnetic Poles: A Skeptical Guide to Doomsday"):

Omigod, Earth's core is about to explode, destroying the planet and everything on it! That is, unless a gigantic asteroid strikes first. Or an advanced physics experiment goes haywire, negating space-time in a runaway chain reaction. Or the sun's distant companion star, Nemesis, sends an untimely barrage of comets our way. Or . . . [69]

After more in this vein, Easterbrook gets down to cases. He makes some good points, such as that chemical warfare is unlikely to cause catastrophic casualties, because of rapid dispersal of poison-gas clouds. But when he turns to the kind of disaster risks discussed in chapter 1 of this book, he commits a series of logical and factual errors.

He states that "biological weapons have never lived up to their billing in popular culture," that "evolution has spent millions of years conditioning mammals to resist germs," and that "no superplague has ever come close to wiping out humanity before, and it seems unlikely to happen in the future." All true, but misleading (obviously mammals have not been conditioned to resist *all* germs) or irrelevant, including "have never lived up to their billing in popular culture" or "it seems unlikely to happen in the future."[70] The fact that something is unlikely to happen is no reason to ignore the risk of its happening, especially when the "it" may be the extinction of the human race. A sensible person is concerned with probabilistic as well as certain death and so doesn't play even one round of Russian roulette (even—I argue in the next chapter—if offered a huge sum of money to play), though he will probably survive it. Nor does a sensible person give controlling weight to the fact that a risk has not yet materialized. You would be dumb to cross a street against the light on the ground that no one had ever been run down at that particular intersection. You would be especially dumb to do so if until today the street had been used only by rickshaws. Until gene splicing, which is recent, and the emergence, also recent, of apocalyptic terrorism, the danger of bioterrorism may have been slight, although Japan killed thousands, perhaps hundreds of thousands, of Chinese with biological weapons during World War II;[71] but it is slight no more.

Evolutionary pressures, as we know, tend to limit the lethality of natural pathogens. That is why the earliest forms of a new pathogen tend to be the most virulent: the most virulent die out and are succeeded by less virulent forms that spread farther because their hosts live longer and so infect more other creatures with the disease. But we know that a pathogen like the smallpox virus could be juiced up in the laboratory to a level of lethality that might bring about the extinction of the human race, even though this would be a maladaptive consequence from the standpoint of the virus, which would become extinct along with the host population.

Easterbrook acknowledges that bioweapons "may turn increasingly troublesome as time passes and knowledge of biotechnology becomes harder to control."[72] But he overlooks the corollary that we should begin worrying now, especially since the danger of bioterrorism, unlike that of nanotechnology or artificial intelligence, exists now, rather than just lying in the future; knowledge of dangerous biotechnology is already uncontrolled. He concedes that "perhaps one day some aspiring Dr. Evil will invent a bug that bypasses the immune system." But these bugs exist already; otherwise we wouldn't need vaccines and antibiotics. And AIDS, for example, destroys the immune system. Easterbrook acknowledges the possibility "that existing pathogens like smallpox could be genetically altered to make them more virulent (two-thirds of those who contract natural smallpox survive)."[73] But he does not mention the greater danger that the smallpox virus can, like the mousepox virus, be genetically altered to make vaccination ineffective.

Easterbrook misdescribes the strangelet scenario as one in which the entire universe is destroyed. So he is reassured by the fact that the universe has survived for 15 billion years. In fact, as we know, the strangelet scenario is about the destruction of the earth, not the universe.

Though prominent nanotechnologists take the concerns about runaway nanomachines seriously enough to have agreed to limit the power supply for such machines, Easterbrook derides the "gray goo" scenario on a ground earlier proposed by the physicist Freeman Dyson that since the top speed of a swimmer or flyer moving under its own power (stored internal energy) is proportional to its length, a nanorobot could not move faster than a tenth of an inch per second.[74] But Dyson had arbitrarily assumed constant internal power per unit of volume. Many short birds can fly faster than long ones because they have greater internal power. Moreover, the speed of nanomachines need not be limited by their internal power, because they could be carried by winds at high speeds. And the size of a robot constructed on the basis of nanotechnology is unrelated to the size of the nanoparticles of which it is composed. A human being is composed of molecules, but it is not constrained to move as slowly as molecules. In fact, a human being is constructed on the principles of nanotechnology.

Easterbrook has written seriously in the past about environmental problems, and the article that I am criticizing has a sober discussion of global warming.[75] But the discussion ends on a note of ridicule and belittlement: "So be prepared: Stock lots of sweaters and a few Hawaiian shirts. The weather can be tricky this time of year."[76]

He actually exaggerates the danger of asteroid collisions by saying that there are at least 1,100 near-earth objects "big enough to cause a

Chicxulub strike,"[77] a reference to the asteroid collision that is believed to have wiped out the dinosaurs. The figure (actually 1,148, and merely an estimate) refers to the number of near-earth objects with a diameter of 1 kilometer or more.[78] As noted in chapter 1, very few of these have a diameter as great as 10 kilometers, the estimated size of the dinosaur buster; only one that large has been detected thus far in the search for near-earth objects. Easterbrook concludes sensibly that our lack of a plan to develop a technology that could prevent such collisions "may be unwise" and that "perhaps NASA ought to take more seriously research into how to block a killer rock."[79] (The hesitation in "may" and "perhaps" makes no sense given Easterbrook's belief that there are 1,100 near-earth objects as dangerous as the dinosaur slayer.) But that conclusion, which may be influenced by his exaggeration of the danger, is inconsistent with the title and tone of the article and with his overall conclusion that

> we fret about proliferating nanobots or instant cosmic doom when we ought to be devoting our time and energy to confirmed worries like 41 million Americans without health insurance. A high-calorie, low-exertion lifestyle is far more likely to harm you than a vagrant black hole. . . . It makes far more sense to focus on mundane troubles that are all too real.[80]

The fallacy, a recurrent one in debates over public policy,[81] is to think that we have a choice between only two policies: we can either expand health insurance or take measures against catastrophic risks. We can do both. We would just have to give up something else. If the something else, for example subsidizing U.S. farmers or textile manufacturers, is a less valuable use of our resources, then giving it up in order to provide both more health insurance and more safety would be a good trade.

Another of Easterbrook's articles commits the closely related "one risk at a time" fallacy. He thinks that maybe society "can only conquer one risk at a time," and if so we should disregard the risk of biological weapons because there is "a weapon that we know can kill in vast numbers, because it already has: the [atomic] bomb."[82] It's not true that society can conquer only one risk at a time, nor that a hypothetical risk cannot be compared with one that has actually materialized in the past, as if only frequencies and never probabilities could furnish rational motives for action. We don't have to await a massive bioterrorist attack in order to have sufficient confidence in the danger to take preventive measures. That would be like saying that the United and the Soviet Union should not have taken measures to prevent an accidental thermonuclear war until millions of people were killed by a hydrogen bomb.

What I have called the optimistic backlash against the doomsters actually is not merely reactive; it has roots in a long history of technological optimism in American culture.[83] People have difficulty holding in their head at one and the same time that modern technology is creating both enormous benefits *and* enormous risks, and that both the benefits and the risks are growing—the latter quite possibly more rapidly—with continued technological progress. This difficulty, which is rooted in the mental quirk that psychologists call "cognitive dissonance," is of a piece with the tendency of people to write down risks to safety when they perceive benefits to an unsafe activity and write them up when they perceive no benefits.[84]

Optimism about science is a natural reflex of scientists, for career and psychological reasons, and is reinforced by a concern that fear of catastrophic risks provides support for curtailing civil liberties. So M. F. Perutz writes that international criminal law could be an effective weapon against individuals who develop or use biological or chemical weapons— a counsel of futility, at least if the concern is with suicidal terrorists or other undeterrables. He also quotes with approval, as a warning against "preemptively undermining U.S. civil liberties in the name of enhancing homeland defense," the inconsequent observation that "seventy [biological attacks] have occurred in the last century causing nine deaths, but only eighteen of these seventy attacks were made by terrorists."[85] In like vein, Stephen Moore and Julian Simon state that "the risk of dying from a terrorist incident is miniscule [*sic*]. Less than 1,000 Americans die from terrorist attacks every year, which accounts for far fewer deaths than from falling off a ladder at home or from riding a bicycle."[86]

Perutz ends his article with the reckless claim that "the still-prospering tobacco industry poses a proven threat to health and life that is many thousand times greater than the potential threat of bioterrorism."[87] The *potential* threat of bioterrorism, being unlimited, is vastly greater than the danger from smoking cigarettes. Perutz also ignores the fact that smokers *voluntarily* assume the risk of disease and death; no one voluntarily assumes the risk of being sickened or killed by bioterrorists, unless it is the bioterrorists themselves. And notice his commission of the "dominant risk" fallacy. To reason that if risk *A* is greater than risk

B one should pay no attention to *B*, whatever its absolute size, is like telling a person who has cancer not to seek treatment for a broken arm.

In a similar article, Freeman Dyson dismisses the dangers posed by nanotechnology on the additional ground (besides speed) that nanotechnologists have not yet succeeded in constructing an assembler, let alone a self-replicating one that would be the equivalent of a cell.[88] (Since his article was published two years ago, primitive nanotech assemblers have been built, as we saw in chapter 1.) This is like pointing to twentieth-century experience with biological warfare and saying there is nothing to worry about. We have to deal with twenty-first-century hazards.

Dyson goes on to note that the international community of biologists agreed at the Asilomar Conference in 1975 on guidelines designed to minimize dangers from gene-splicing experiments, and that the guidelines, though soon relaxed,[89] continue to be observed. He calls the experience "a shining example of responsible citizenship, showing that it is possible for scientists to protect the public from injury while preserving the freedom of science."[90] All it shows is that scientists may *sometimes* be able to protect the public from *some* of the adverse consequences of scientific progress without compromising freedom of scientific inquiry. Scientists were unable to protect the public from nuclear-weapons proliferation or chemical and biological warfare, though some of them tried. Others were busy developing the weaponry. There are millions of scientific workers in the world.[91] They cannot be cajoled into forming a united community of conscience.

Dyson believes that we are significantly better off as a result of the Biological Weapons Convention,[92] signed by major nations including the United States and the Soviet Union in 1972, even though the Soviet Union flouted it from the start (which was easy to do because the convention made no provision for monitoring or enforcing compliance), with consequences that may yet be felt. Compliance with the convention is, Dyson acknowledges, unverifiable, which means that any nation that wants to develop bioweaponry can do so with impunity. Many nations have not signed the convention, and we know from chapter 1 that a number of nations have bioweapons programs. We also know that the danger of biological attacks comes mainly from terrorists and psychopaths. To that danger the convention is virtually irrelevant.

Dyson concludes by citing John Milton's assertion that "books should not be convicted and imprisoned until they have done some damage."[93]

If only "some damage" were the worst danger humanity faced from the continuing advance of science! After someone learns from a book how to destroy a goodly part of the world's population, it will be too late to "convict and imprison" the book.

Limited horizons

Still another cause of society's failure to take catastrophic risks seriously is the difficulty, which is at once philosophical and political, of knowing how seriously to take small probabilities of immense harm, even if those probabilities are known. If the annual probability of a catastrophic collision with an asteroid is 1 in 65 million, it is exceedingly unlikely that such a collision will occur within current politicians' terms of office, or lifetimes, or their children's or grandchildren's or even great-grandchildren's lifetimes; and after that who cares? In fact the annual probability of a catastrophic asteroid collision, albeit not one so catastrophic as to endanger the survival of the human race, is much greater than 1 in 65 million, as we know from chapter 1. But it is still very small. Politicians are unlikely to win points for preventing something that is highly unlikely to happen in the foreseeable future. And so sufficient unto the day is the evil thereof.

This type of thinking is not irrational, or even demonstrably wrong. It is unclear what regard we should have for our remote descendants, and whether the lack of regard for them that we seem to manifest in our behavior reflects limited altruism or limited foresight or a rational hunch that technology will bail us out the way it has done ever since we came down from the trees. Whatever the cause of our insouciance about catastrophic risks, a politician who wants to raise taxes today to minimize the risk of catastrophes a thousand years hence will be cutting his throat. And in an age of rapid technological advance there may be good reasons for doing nothing today and waiting for the progress of science and technology to provide cheap solutions for problems more likely to materialize in the remote than in the near future. A related argument, however—that it is foolish to transfer wealth from the present to future generations because the secular trend in income suggests that future generations will be wealthier than ours—doesn't work with regard to catastrophic risks because a catastrophe in the sense in which I am using the word would dramatically reduce the wealth of future generations, possibly to zero.

Bjørn Lomborg makes a technology-will-save-us argument for going slow in trying to curtail carbon dioxide emissions in order to reduce the rate of global warming.[94] He points out that the cost of solar energy has been falling, and, if it continues to do so, then—since the cost of fossil fuels is not falling—solar energy will become increasingly competitive with those fuels, their consumption will fall, and emissions of carbon dioxide will decline. Similarly, if no technology is available today to avert collisions with asteroids but is quite likely to be developed, without any force feeding, in the not-too-remote future, we might as well wait, because the probability of a disastrous asteroid collision is substantial only when the period over which the probability is calculated is very long. Recall from the introduction that the probability of surviving n periods in each of which there is an (independent) probability of disaster of p is $(1 - p)^n$. If the annual probability of disaster is .0001, the probability of surviving for 1 year is 99.99 percent, but the probability of surviving for 100 years is only 99 percent and for 1,000 years only 90 percent. (Recall also the Monte Carlo simulations of asteroid impacts, in chapter 1.) The possibility of an asteroid collision illustrates this point better than global warming does because increases in the atmospheric concentration of greenhouse gases may as a practical matter be irreversible.[95]

Doubt concerning what if anything we owe our remote descendants, and the desirability, if the costs of responding to catastrophic risks are falling over time, of delaying our response to them, are things to take into account when considering how best to respond. They do not justify dismissing the risks out of hand, but they may constitute a politically compelling excuse for doing so, as we'll see with respect to the ill-fated Kyoto Protocol on global warming.

Psychological factors

False positives

If people living near high-voltage electrical transmission lines notice an unusual number of cancers in the neighborhood, they are likely to attribute it to the lines. When it is pointed out to them that a random series will often contain a run (as in the series 1 1 1 1 0 0 1 0 1 1 0 0 0 0 0 0 0 0 1 1 1 0 1 1 1 0 1 1 1 1 0 0 0 0 1 1 1 1 0 1 0 1 0 0 1 1 1 0 1 0 0 0 0 1 1 0 1 0 1 0 1 0 1 0 0 1 1 0 0 0 0),[96] they are nonplussed because to the statistically unsophisticated a run is a pattern and a pattern holds meaning. Once again we are in the presence of an evolutionarily adaptive limitation of human cognitive ability. Pattern recognition is key to an animal's survival; and we are animals. It has greater survival value than computational power does, and it is the thing that we still do better than computers do. False positives in pattern recognition—seeing as patterns what are really just coincidences—are less dangerous for a creature than false negatives—failing to recognize the patterned behavior in the lion's striding toward you. And so our minds are biased in favor of committing the former error.[97] The upshot has been a drumbeat of false alarms (included those sounded by writers of futurist fiction) about technological hazards: Love Canal, brain cancer from using cellphones, serious illnesses and deformities from silicone breast implants, and so forth—with the result both that fear of technological hazards has become associated in the sophisticated public's mind with ignoramuses and trial lawyers and that technology managers devote a disproportionate amount of their safety-related activities to reassuring panicky neighbors.[98] A modest goal of educational reform would be to require all college students to take a statistics course.

The economy of attention

For people accustomed to dealing just with everyday dangers and ignorant of science, the catastrophes that modern technology, or nature at its most ferocious (such as when it did the dinosaurs in), could unleash are incomprehensible. People can understand something as limited in scope and incremental in consequence as the atomic explosions that devastated Hiroshima and Nagasaki. Conventional bombing had already done comparable damage to German cities and to other Japanese cities. And thermonuclear as well as nuclear explosions have been photographed and the photographs widely disseminated. But people have difficulty understanding the energies in the universe that might be released by scientific accident or deliberate manipulation.

This is not to say that people are stupid. It is to say that because the human mind is limited, people can't think about every danger that may beset them. Just as in the ancestral environment it wouldn't have made sense to neglect a 1 in 10 chance of being eaten by a predator in order to focus on a 1 in 1,000 chance of being struck by lightning—especially since early man lacked the scientific tools for estimating slight probabilities and devising effective measures for eliminating or reducing them—so modern man as well, his brain no larger than that of his ancestors, must make choices about which risks to worry about. There are many things worth thinking about, and thought devoted to one of them is unavailable for any of the others. (So there is a kernel of truth in Gregg Easterbrook's argument that if we start worrying about low-probability risks we may be led to neglect more serious problems.)

Nor can the amount of thought be nicely proportioned to the importance or unimportance of the subject. Below some threshold the thought devoted to a question will bring the inquirer no closer to an answer. We would have to devote a *lot* of thought to asteroid collisions and how to prevent them in order to devise a sensible response. And it would be demanding and therefore difficult thought because of the difficulty people have in comprehending small probabilities. It is not a serious problem for experts, but they would have to expend effort to persuade the public to support so weird-sounding a project as an asteroid defense.

There is thus an argument for ranking risks by their expected costs and deliberately disregarding the lowest-ranked ones. There is even an argument for giving attention that is disproportionate from a strict expected-costs standpoint to those risks that are easier to think about because the probability of their materializing is greater, or (a related point) because they have materialized in the past and so we have actual experience with them—we don't have to imagine them. No asteroid collision with the earth has ever been observed by a human being who left a record of the sighting, and so it requires a much greater effort of imagination to think seriously about the danger of an asteroid collision than it is to think seriously about the possibility of nuclear war.[99]

Recall from chapter 1 one of John Lewis's estimates of the expected annual number of deaths from asteroid collisions: 1,479. This exceeds the average annual number of deaths from airline crashes. One thing that makes the public worry less about the risk of asteroid collisions than about airline crashes is that airline crashes occur every few years, whereas apparently there hasn't been a major asteroid strike since 1908 and it occurred in an uninhabited area. No human beings are known to have been killed by the Tunguska asteroid—the principal victims probably were reindeer. Airline crashes thus are "available" to the mind in a way that asteroid collisions are not. Yet because expected cost is the product of probability and magnitude, risks having very different probabilities and therefore availabilities can have the same expected cost. The expected cost of a 1 in 1 billion chance of a $1 billion loss is the same as that of a 10 percent chance of a $10 loss—$1—but there is a psychological asymmetry in the response to expected costs that are based on such divergent probabilities. That asymmetry would undoubtedly dominate even if the 1 in 1 billion chance were 2, or 3, or 10 in 1 billion, though the expected cost of the lower-probability event would then be a multiple of the expected cost of the higher-probability event.

Another difference between airline crashes and asteroid collisions, which may not seem related to probabilities but is, is that one can *do* something about the risk of being killed in an airline crash—not fly, or fly less frequently, or fly only on major airlines—and one cannot do anything about asteroid collisions except write one's Congressman. Yet most people who are afraid to fly substitute another method of transportation, namely driving, that is more dangerous than flying. Either they misunderstand the probabilities (perhaps because they overestimate their driving skills) or the thought of death in an airplane crash arouses a sense of dread that dominates a comparison of probabilities.

What I am calling the "economy of attention" is related to the psychologists' concept of the availability heuristic—the tendency of people to attach disproportionate weight to salient, arresting events.[100] In the conditions of the ancestral environment, it made sense for human beings to be hyperalert to clear and present dangers, because those were the only ones they could do anything about. Being an evolved mental trait, this disposition has persisted into modernity, further undermining our ability to understand more than notionally, and respond intelligently to, slight risks of immense losses.

Temperament

I mentioned earlier the optimistic backlash against the doomsters. I was commenting on content rather than on temperament, but temperament is part of the reason for the difficulty of getting people to focus constructively on the catastrophic risks. Some people have a natural bent toward optimism; their outlook is sunny. Others are naturally pessimistic; they have a tendency toward depression. In still others neither characteristic is strongly marked, and it is among those people that support for constructive responses to the catastrophic risks must be sought. Optimists would tend to be hopeful that effective responses to these risks could be devised and implemented, but, being optimists, they would heavily discount the risks themselves. They are not fearful of low-probability events, however dreadful. Pessimists would tend to worry about the risks—even to exaggerate them—but would despair of being able to do anything about them. Optimists are hopeful but fearless; pessimists are fearful but hopeless. (So pessimists are more imaginative than optimists.) Though for opposite reasons, neither group is strongly motivated to think seriously about devising effective responses to catastrophic risks. The two groups together are not the entire population, but they are a large part of it and this operates as a drag on the prospects for adoption of proposals for dealing with the risks.

Economic factors

The economics of innovation

A further difficulty in coming to grips with technology-related risk is that of fitting technology, as distinct from investment, consumption, family, law, politics, and other major human activities well studied by the social sciences, into an analytical framework. The natural candidate to be the framework for analyzing technology is economics. Technological progress is costly and so must be financed, whether by public or private subsidies or by the creation of property rights in commercially valuable products of technology in order to provide incentives for market participants to finance the necessary technology themselves. Technology has not only costs but also, obviously, benefits; as I noted in the introduction, it is a principal engine of economic growth.

But it turns out to be an unruly subject for economic analysis. To begin with, uncertainty seems to be at its core. A new technology is something that is invented, and invention means discovering something that no one knew. There is no algorithm for discovering nature's secrets and putting them to work in the service of human desires. The most promising economic theory of invention sees it as a semi-blind process analogous to natural selection. Competing inventors take different paths none of which can be confidently expected to be successful, and the one that turns out to be best survives and the others fall by the wayside.[101] It might turn out to be best for reasons that had not been in the minds of the inventors, because inventors cannot know for sure where their work will lead. Scientific progress is unpredictable because it is a byproduct of exploring the unknown parts of the universe.

Because the path of science is unpredictable, so are its consequences, and all the more so because they tend not to be concentrated on the individuals or other entities that develop or apply the science. The benefits and costs of ordinary physical products accrue primarily to seller and buyer. But science, including the useful science that we call technology, is basically information, and information is difficult to sequester (you can't put it in your pocket or build a fence around it) and as a result tends to be appropriable by third parties without their having to compensate the creator, the "owner," of the information. Because information is in effect self-replicating, both the benefits and costs of technology tend to be external to the inventor and his immediate customers. The externalization of benefits makes it difficult for the inventor to recover his investment in developing the technology (many or even all the beneficiaries will be able to appropriate the technology without paying him anything for it) and so has given rise to the elaborate system of intellectual property rights that courts enforce, such as patent rights, designed to internalize those benefits.

The externalization of the costs of invention, which is unaffected by intellectual property law, makes the inventor irresponsible. The major costs that the invention creates may fall largely on others, as in the case of inventions that have destructive applications, such as encryption and recombinant DNA.

With the benefits and costs of technological progress falling to such a large extent on third parties rather than on the inventor and his customers alone, the market cannot be relied upon to generate the optimal rate and direction of inventive activity. But because those benefits and costs are also very difficult to predict, government cannot do a good job of guiding and controlling inventive activity either. That is why technology seems to drive society rather than vice versa and to be a source of both great hope and great danger.

The problem of technological uncertainty is compounded by secrecy. While information has a natural tendency to spread, there are incentives for concealing it and often effective means of doing so. Large industrial and military installations are not readily concealable, but much basic research and laboratory-scale production are. And so are the plans of small terrorist groups and, a fortiori, of individual "mad scientists" fantasizing about destroying the world. Hence the ambivalence with which we regard encryption.

Global decentralization

Still another economic obstacle to dealing effectively with the catastrophic risks is the difficulty of solving problems when the solutions require international cooperation. That is the case with respect to most catastrophic risks almost by definition; the harmful consequences of a true catastrophe are unlikely to be limited to a single nation. It is one thing for the United States to decide to curb its emissions of carbon dioxide; there are political obstacles, but they can be overcome if the benefits are palpable and clearly in excess of the costs. It is quite another for the United States to negotiate with the other nations of the world a solution to the global-warming problem that does not burden us unduly. The transaction costs are immense, which is one reason for the failure of the Kyoto Protocol of 1997, and are growing. There are 193 nations; in 1950 there were only 87.[102]

A further complication is that the wealthy countries of the northern hemisphere are the principal emitters of greenhouse gases but the poor countries of the equatorial belt are the principal prospective victims of global warming, and they cannot afford to compensate the wealthy countries for incurring the costs involved in substantially curtailing those countries' emissions. That is one reason the United States has refused to ratify the Kyoto Protocol, which requires developed nations to reduce their greenhouse-gas emissions to 7–10 percent below the 1990 level (7 percent for the United States). The United States would have borne almost two-thirds of the estimated $800 billion cost of compliance with the protocol[103] yet because of our temperate climate would have derived little benefit from it, unless of course compliance would stave off global catastrophe. Actually, the cost may be exaggerated. Reduced consumption of fossil fuels by net importers of such fuels, including the United States, would reduce the price of those fuels by reducing world demand,[104] and this effect would partly offset the costs to the wealthy nations of capping their emissions. But only partly. In contrast, the nations that signed the Montreal Protocol, which limits the emission of chlorofluorocarbons in order to preserve the stratospheric ozone shield against ultraviolet radiation, and thus has a parallel structure to the Kyoto Protocol, obtained sufficient benefits from *unilaterally* curtailing their emissions that the protocol itself may merely have codified the voluntary cutbacks by individual nations that preceded it.[105]

The problem with the Kyoto Protocol is not only that the United States would have borne a disproportionate share of the costs of compliance. It is also that incurring those costs would have represented a poor investment for the United States from a conventional economic standpoint even if we were more vulnerable than we think we are to the potential harms from global warming unless it is abrupt. (We have some vulnerability to being harmed even by gradual global warming, primarily though not only in our extensive coastal areas.)[106] Partly because of the slow rate of oceanic absorption of atmospheric carbon dioxide, as a result of which emissions of carbon dioxide have a cumulative effect on the atmospheric concentration of the gas, and partly because the Kyoto Protocol does not limit the emissions of developing countries at all, even full compliance with the protocol would be unlikely to have much effect on global temperatures, flooding, and so on until the twenty-second century (at least if a distinct benefit of emissions controls—technology forcing, which I discuss in the next chapter—is ignored). According to Nordhaus and Boyer, the protocol's discounted present benefits would be only about $120 billion for the entire world, compared to discounted present costs that might well exceed $800 billion,[107] even assuming compliance in an efficient manner.[108]

Nordhaus and Boyer used discount rates for high-income countries that did not exceed 3 percent.[109] Even 3 percent may seem awfully low. But they were trying to measure the pure rate of time preference (that is, of preference for present over future consumption) without add-ons for expected inflation or for the risk of nonpayment, which are components of interest rates on loans. There is no reason to include an inflation estimate in a discount rate unless the future costs or benefits being discounted include such an estimate, and it makes sense to ignore inflation at both ends.[110] But these are side issues; at *any* nonnegligible discount rate, the present value of remote future benefits will be computed as slight. The same, of course, is true of remote future costs. But the costs of compliance with the Kyoto Protocol would be steep from the outset, while significant benefits would probably not begin to accrue for another century. It is in a case of such marked asymmetry in the time profiles of benefits and costs that discounting to present value can make a huge difference.

The disappointing cost-benefit ratio need not be decisive. We may have a strong desire to prevent global warming in future centuries, not just our own century; maybe we don't want to discount the future costs of global warming at all. But just who is this "we"? The democratic majority in the United States is insufficiently altruistic to be willing to incur heavy costs for the benefit of foreigners, let alone their remote descendants. Think of how few resources we are willing to commit to foreign aid except when there are urgent political or geopolitical reasons (Iraq, Israel, Egypt, Pakistan, etc.). From the standpoint of the American public, the Kyoto Protocol would be a foreign-aid program to dwarf our formal foreign-aid programs, and the beneficiaries, not even having been born yet, would be completely invisible.[111]

Overlooked by the drafters of the protocol was the possibility of reducing emissions at less cost to the United States by creating a system of tradable emissions permits (a cap-and-trade system), as in the successful emissions-trading system for sulfur dioxide, the cause of acid rain. Then a developing country that could abate its emissions at lower cost than the United States could sell emission permits to U.S. emitters. That would reduce the cost of our "foreign aid" because the same reduction in emissions would be obtained at a lower cost than if the U.S. emitters could comply with their limits only by reducing their own emissions all the way down to those limits.

I shall come back to the costs and benefits of the Kyoto Protocol and its alternatives in the next chapter. For now the point to emphasize is that the decentralization of the international community is an obstacle to dealing with catastrophic risks. And not just global warming. It would make it impossible to discourage free riding on investments in an asteroid defense. The United States would have to take the lead in creating such a defense because of its wealth and because it is the only nation that has the technological sophistication to design and construct the surveillance and interception technology that such a defense, to be maximally effective, would require. Granted, the United States has no monopoly of space science; and here I note the interest shown by the United Kingdom in creating an asteroid defense in conjunction with other European nations as well as with the United States.[112] But the United States would have to take the laboring oar. Its scientific and technological preponderance remains awesome. Total U.S. R & D expenditures are approximately equal to the combined R & D expenditures of Japan, Germany, France, the United Kingdom, Italy, Canada, and Russia.[113] A third of all scientific and technical articles in leading international journals are authored by Americans.[114] It comes as no surprise that a report commissioned by the United Kingdom's Minister for Science states that "the United States is doing far more about Near Earth Objects than the rest of the world put together,"[115] though it is actually doing little.

The United States would have no means of compelling the rest of the world to contribute to the cost of a defense against asteroids, even though the rest of the world would benefit. Were there enough free riding, the United States might lose interest in asteroid defense, even if it had any to begin with. But the expense of an asteroid defense would probably be so small relative to the U.S. economy—a few billion dollars spread over a number of years—that the effect even of widespread free riding on our willingness to invest in such a defense would be slight. It might seem that free riding would never discourage such investments; that the only question would be the net benefit of the investment to the United States. But nations worry about relative as well as absolute power (and therefore wealth) because they are in potential military competition with other nations.[116] The United States would be reluctant to adopt a policy that increased its wealth by 10 percent but doubled China's. Furthermore, no nation wants to get a reputation for being good for a free ride. These considerations might induce the United States to take a strong stand in negotiations for a global response to the asteroid threat, and when bargainers take strong stands they may fail to reach agreement. Each may be unwilling to be the first to flinch, lest it develop a reputation as an easy mark—the very thing it sought to avert by taking a strong stand in the first place.

Speaking of military competition, however, there is nothing like a common enemy to induce nations to cooperate with one another, and near-earth asteroids are enemies of all nations. In fact, the risk of a catastrophic asteroid strike is pretty much uniform across countries, except those that have long coastlines relative to their size, since a large asteroid striking an ocean would create enormous tidal waves. Although the larger the country the more likely it is to be struck by an asteroid, the smaller the country the more devastating the strike is likely to be. If the asteroid that exploded above Siberia in 1908 had exploded above Belgium instead, Belgium might have been devastated.[117] Even so, small countries, such as Iceland, Denmark, and probably Belgium, would be tempted to free ride on a project led by the United States to create a global defense against asteroid collisions, just as small NATO countries free ride on the defense expenditures of the large ones. The small countries would hope that the asteroid defense would be built even if they contributed nothing to the cost. For in that event they would benefit along with the United States and any other contributors to the project, yet at zero cost.

U.S. strategy would be to try to convince other countries that unless they anted up their fair share of the project, the United States wouldn't go ahead with it, so their ride wouldn't be free—or rather, wouldn't be a ride. But the wealth and power of the United States would tend to deprive the threat of credibility. The free riders would know that if the United States thought the risk of a devastating asteroid collision worth attending to, it *would* attend to it, even without the cooperation of other countries. It would thus be a help if a blocking minority in the U.S. Congress had such a passionate commitment to fairness that other countries would know that unless they contributed significantly to global projects, Congress would not appropriate money for them. That would make a tough negotiating posture credible. But, as I said, the total cost of an asteroid defense seems too slight for free riding to be a serious deterrent to the United States. (Free-riding hasn't destroyed NATO.) The problem is not free riding; it is that asteroids are not yet perceived to be a significant enemy.

The primacy of national self-interest, and the consequent difficulty of organizing collective action to respond to a global problem, also complicate efforts to meet the threat of bioterrorism, because of the dual-use character of biotechnology. As the likeliest target of such terrorism, the United States might be thought willing to go it alone. But if we impose security-motivated controls on our biotech research, the research will be shifted to countries that won't impose such controls. They won't impose them because they want the fruits of such research, not to create bioweapons but to produce pharmaceuticals (including vaccines against lethal pathogens) and increase crop yields.

In the wake of the Australian mousepox experiment discussed in chapter 1, a committee of the National Research Council of the National Academies of Science and Engineering recommended requiring that proposals of biological experiments that could help terrorists or hostile nations be reviewed in advance by biosafety committees at research facilities and by an advisory committee in the Department of Health and Human Services.[118] Yet the dangerous research that stimulated this recommendation was of course conducted in a foreign country, over which the proposed committees would have no jurisdiction. Well aware of the international dimension, the National Research Council committee pointed out that bioengineering research has become global.[119] Dangerous pathogens can be found in the laboratories of developing nations, such as Brazil, which has a significant biotech industry, heavily promoted by the Brazilian government.[120] And in Gabon, Belarus, Kazakhstan,[121] maybe Iran, and doubtless North Korea, as well. Australia is a well-governed modern nation; but these others? As Jonathan Tucker points out, "No comparable [to U.S.] security measures currently exist at thousands of research centers, clinical laboratories, and culture collections overseas that possess or work with dangerous pathogens and toxins."[122] Our own security measures aren't that great either, as I noted in chapter 1.

Another product of the biotech revolution—genetically modified crops—could also threaten human welfare. Yet the importance of agriculture to developing nations, coupled with the relative cheapness of biotechnological research and development, has produced an explosion of such R & D in Latin America, where "this new technique [gene splicing] is being developed in a superheated atmosphere of state promotion and corporate competition, in which bioscientists have a heavy financial and personal stake in the commercialization of techniques and products."[123] The problem of controlling biotechnical research is not a free-rider problem. The motive for refusing to follow the lead of the United States in imposing controls on such research would not be to obtain the benefits of the U.S. regulatory program without paying any of the costs. It would be to exploit the competitive opportunities that the program would open up for these nations by restricting U.S. research. But it is no less serious a problem for having a different character.

A similar but less serious problem would afflict unilateral U.S. efforts to slow down the development of ever more powerful (and possibly more dangerous) particle accelerators; they would be built abroad. Remember that the next RHIC-type accelerator scheduled to come on line is the Large Hadron Collider (LHC) of the European Center for Nuclear Research (CERN). The reason the problem is less acute than in the case of attempting unilateral control of biotechnology is that the economic benefits of high-energy physics research are much smaller—indeed, the net benefits may, as we'll see in the next chapter, be negative. (And there appear to be no military benefits.) We wouldn't lose much, besides some scientific prestige, if the center of such research moved elsewhere. Were the danger of the new accelerators perceived to be serious, there probably would be no great difficulty in negotiating an international agreement to rescind or delay projects such as the LHC or RHIC–II.

The problem of international anarchy is obscured by the fact that between the rise of the fascist dictatorships after World War I and the end of the Cold War in 1989, the principal man-made threats to human health and safety emanated from the handful of nations that qualified as "great powers." Other nations were either negligible because of poverty or dependent on one or more of the great powers because of weakness, colonial status, or economic domination. Our thinking has yet to adjust fully to the difference between the world before and the world after the cold war ended. The Soviet Union's collapse is merely the most dramatic of the changes that have led to our current highly decentralized international system, with its proliferation of small, autonomous nations (autonomous because they no longer fear invasion or subversion by great powers, though a few still do), its weakened governments and alliances, a consequent reduction in effective government regulation (consequent also on the sheer number of nations, which makes international coordination more costly to achieve), and a concomitant increase in the autonomy of markets, many global in scope or effects.

The combination of international capitalist competition unshackled by government with rapid technological progress is a libertarian's dream. But there is a downside that the economic concept of externalities illuminates. Individuals, corporations, and nations tend out of a natural selfishness not to take account in their decisions of the full costs that their activities impose on people with whom they have no actual or potential contractual relations. A polluting factory, even if untrammeled by law or regulation, will consider the effects of the pollution on its workers; it may have to compensate them in the form of a higher wage. It will not consider the effects on society as a whole, let alone on the inhabitants of foreign nations or the members of remote future generations. That is the economic rationale for placing regulatory limits, international as well as national, on pollution and other negative externalities. Free markets have many good effects, and most of the attacks against them—against "capitalism"—are wide of the mark. But the absence of an international environmental protection agency and other global regulatory mechanisms leaves the problem of negative externalities that spill over national borders unsolved.

The problem is especially acute with respect to those risks, such as bioterrorism, that do not depend on sponsorship by a powerful, or indeed by any, nation. Even if 191 of the 192 other nations of the world agreed with the United States to take steps to prevent bioterrorism, the holdout could acquire bioweapons that might wipe out a large portion of the human race. (In this regard, I note that only 148 nations have ratified the Biological Weapons Convention of 1972.)[124] Even if all 193 nations agreed to forswear bioweaponry, a small group of terrorists or even a single unbalanced scientist might be able to develop such weaponry because in many nations government is too weak to prevent terrorist cells and individual scientists from engaging in laboratory activities that could result in the development of lethal disease agents.

All this said, it would be a mistake to be entirely pessimistic about the prospects for effective international cooperation with respect to at least some of the catastrophic risks.[125] Free-riding and other collective-action problems often can be overcome, if the benefits of a solution exceed the heavy transaction costs. I instanced NATO, and there are many other examples. The problems cannot always be overcome; global warming poses a uniquely difficult collective-action problem because of an unusual alignment of risks and wealth. The fact that the severity of a risk differs across countries—even that the countries that create the risk are different from those at risk—is not an insuperable obstacle to effective international cooperation, provided the countries at risk can compensate the countries that create the risk for reducing it. Side payments are one method of inducing asymmetric risk reductions; pursuant to the Nunn-Lugar Act, Congress has appropriated some $4 billion in the last decade to help Russia dismantle its nuclear weapons and keep its fissionable materials secure.[126] There are limitations to this approach; as I noted earlier, nations are reluctant for reasons of security as well as (narrow) economic self-interest to transfer wealth to other countries. In the case of global warming, however, instead of poor countries placing rich countries at risk, it is rich countries that are placing poor countries at risk, and the latter cannot compensate the former. (I am exaggerating slightly. Poor countries emit carbon dioxide too, and their emissions are growing uncontrollably because such countries place development ahead of long-term harms.) But the perception of asymmetry can be reduced by emphasis on *catastrophic* risks, which as defined in this book are likely to have a global rather than merely regional impact. And note that wealthy Europe is one of the regions of the world most threatened by catastrophic global warming, since catastrophe might take the form of a "flipping" of the Gulf Stream.

The issue of a global defense against bioterrorism combines elements that we examined in connection with global defenses against asteroid collisions and global warming. On the one hand, the risk of a human-engineered pandemic is more or less evenly distributed across the world (like the asteroid risk), though it is somewhat greater in the poorer countries because of their inferior health services and in the United States as the prime target of the most sinister terrorists. On the other hand, it might be, or at least seem, prohibitively expensive for the wealthy countries to offer to pay the poor countries either to refrain from engaging in gene splicing or to create and administer effective controls, since one effect of such an offer would be to encourage poor countries to create research programs in order to be paid to shut them down or regulate them. Yet without the cooperation of the poor countries, the risk of bioterrorism cannot be controlled effectively.

Public choice

The term "public choice" refers to a body of scholarship in economics and political science that tries to explain public policy as the outcome of rationally self-interested behavior. The emphasis is on the role of interest groups. But that is inessential, and in my own recent work I have emphasized instead the role of the politician viewed as a "seller" of leadership and policies to a body of "consumers," the electorate, in a market in which the currency is votes rather than dollars.[127] The question I explore briefly here is whether the rational-choice model of political action can explain the pattern of response (more commonly lack of response) to the principal catastrophic risks.

We should consider whether any interest group that could overcome the free-rider obstacles to collective action would have an interest in supporting or opposing governmental efforts to reduce these risks, and whether an ambitious politician might rally the support of voters by making the prevention or reduction of such risks a priority. The answers vary across the spectrum of catastrophic risks. One method of slowing global warming would be to switch from electrical generating plants that burn coal, oil, or natural gas to nuclear power plants. But quite apart from the public's fear of nuclear power, environmental groups will not press for this solution because they contain "a large and dedicated antinuclear constituency," while the energy industry will not advocate nuclear power on the basis of its effect on global warming because the industry denies that global warming is a problem, or at least that it is a problem to which the industry contributes by burning fossil fuels.[128] And consumer groups may be concerned by the higher cost of nuclear power generation compared to power generation by plants that burn fossil fuels.

In the case of experiments in high-energy particle accelerators we know that particle physicists, along with the many technicians and other persons employed in the high-energy accelerator "industry," the suppliers of the expensive equipment used in these facilities, and the bureaucrats in the Department of Energy have professional or pecuniary stakes (or both) in such projects as RHIC, and hence an incentive to downplay risks. There are even emotional stakes. Particle physicists "are often depicted as involved in a 'religious quest,' handed them by Albert Einstein, or, as is commonly stated in the literature, the 'search for the Holy Grail'" of a unified theory of physical forces.[129] One doesn't allow low-probability risks to deflect one from such a search.

And because the risks involved in accelerator research are unlikely to materialize, and also esoteric, and doomsday scenarios are considered "science fiction" by most people, it would be difficult for a politician to make accelerator safety a selling point for himself to the electorate. He would look like a nut or a Chicken Little, especially since his opponents could tout the undoubted and very tangible benefits that past experiments in particle accelerators have generated in the form of medical treatments and computer technology. Nor is there a compact interest group, with stakes comparable to those of the people doing high-energy physics, that would benefit from the government's disinvesting in such research. It is true that solid-state physicists opposed the Superconducting Super Collider, which would have been a larger version of RHIC, costing billions of dollars; it was canceled by Congress in 1993 after construction had begun. I am informed (though have not been able to document) that the slaying of that project did not lead to increased federal spending on solid-state physics. Maybe it averted a cut in that spending, but I cannot verify that either. I do know that some of the ostensible savings from the cancellation went to finance RHIC.

Paradoxically, the difficulty of valuing basic research plays into the hands of the particle-accelerator community. It is curious to note that with the exception of a bulge for the Apollo space program, the share of the federal domestic discretionary budget devoted to nondefense R & D has remained constant at 10 percent for the last 40 years.[130] With the benefits of basic research impossible to quantify, zero-based budgeting is out of the question and inertia becomes a dominant factor in determining the size of the science budget. This may explain the fate of the Superconducting Super Collider. Because it was a proposed rather than an existing project, the inertia of politics worked against rather than for it. A further political vulnerability of the SSC was that it was located entirely in one state (Texas), a circumstance that narrowed its base of potential political support.

We'll see in the next chapter that there is some empirical support for the belief of economists that the social returns to scientific research exceed the private returns, and if this is true, then the political process is undervaluing such research. Public-choice theory suggests reasons: the costs are incurred in the present but the benefits are deferred and anyway uncertain; a major benefit of the most abstract research—quenching scientific controversy—accrues mainly to a tiny segment of the society, namely the scientific elite; the scientific community, because of the diversity of its research interests, cannot be welded into an effective interest group; nor does it have natural allies among the other interest groups. But this is in general, not in every case. Basic research that has foreseeable military or health applications has an advantage in the competition for public funds—and so does already-established "big science," such as space exploration or particle-accelerator research, where the inertial force of programs that defy cost-benefit analysis assures continued funding. This is another reason for uncertainty that the heavy public investment in particle accelerators is likely to generate continued net benefits. The size of the investment is not a responsible prediction of commensurate returns.

Federal financing of nanotechnology has reached the particle-accelerator level ($750 million a year), with nary a concern over safety. The reasons are easy to see. The commercial and scientific prospects for nanotechnology are immense, and the "gray goo" doomsday scenario not only unlikely but safely (or so at least it seems) in the future. And it is another subject about which the general public knows nothing and would be difficult to educate. So full speed ahead.

Public-choice analysis would predict the same for genetically modified crops—they promise immense benefits to world agriculture, and the dangers are esoteric and unlikely to materialize—were it not for the protectionist pressures of European farmers, to which the European Union has yielded to a significant extent,[131] as public-choice analysis would predict it would. Much European agriculture is high cost and therefore highly vulnerable to import competition. The higher agricultural prices that result from the protection of European agriculture against such competition provide large, concentrated benefits to farmers, while the cost is diffused over the entire European consuming public, which is too large and individually too little affected to be organized into an effective interest group. In addition, that public is easily frightened by Green warnings about the dangers of "tampering" with the food supply, especially in the wake of the mad-cow and foot-and-mouth epidemics, although such dangers as GMCs present have nothing to do with eating such crops. It is true that limits on GMCs hamper as well as help European agriculture, but the latter effect predominates.

The situation from a public-choice perspective is different again with respect to combating bioterrorism. Not because the probability of a devastating bioterrorist attack is completely unknown and thus cannot be reckoned slight. And not because the risk cannot be confidently supposed to lie in the future. For these things are true of most of the catastrophic risks. The difference is that the possible consequences of bioterrorism are very easy to imagine because they are similar to the consequences of natural disease epidemics, with which people have plenty of vicarious and even direct experience: we have all lived through a number of flu epidemics and are still living through the AIDS epidemic. And so far as interest-group pressures are concerned, while many biologists are worried that fear of bioterrorism will lead to intrusive regulation of biological research, others perceive professional opportunities in enlisting in the war against bioterrorism. U.S. demand for biologists is expanding, while competition from foreign biologists to meet that demand is shrinking because of the visa restrictions discussed in chapter 4. The war against bioterrorism may be a bonanza for biologists and others employed in biological research and production, while at the same time benefiting the public—a win-win scenario. Or maybe not, because those visa restrictions are reducing the number of foreign biotech students in the United States, which reduces the demand for American biology professors.

Analysis takes still another turn with respect to the issue of a defense against asteroid collisions. NASA is always in search of new projects, especially given the increasing controversy over the value and safety of manned space flight; and it has a $10 billion-plus annual budget, which it would very much like to retain in future years. One might suppose, therefore, that a multi-hundred-million-dollar project to defend against asteroid collisions would appeal to NASA, and maybe to the politically influential aerospace industry as well. Conceivably such a project would have been launched by now had it not been for the post–9/11 preoccupation with terrorism; an ambitious project for defending against asteroid collisions might seem a distraction from a more urgent defensive concern.

Furthermore, it is hard to convince the public that the threat of such collisions is anything more than science fiction, because we have no current or historical experience with such events.[132] And the probability of a devastating asteroid collision in the near future, while higher than the probability that RHIC will destroy the world, is small, and politicians have difficulty, as I have already suggested, appropriating the benefits of efforts to prevent disasters that are very unlikely to happen during their term of office. Suppose there is a 1 in 10,000 annual probability of a bioterrorist attack that will kill 1,000,000 people and a 1 in

100 annual probability of a bioterrorist attack that will kill 10 people. The expected cost in lives of the first attack is 100 and of the second only .1, yet the first is quite unlikely, and the second fairly likely, to occur within the career of the current office-holding politicians. (Indeed, an annual risk of 1 in 10,000 has only a 9.5 percent chance of materializing within 1,000 years.) The second risk is therefore likely to be weighted much more heavily than the ratio of the expected costs of the two attacks. Having a limited time horizon, politicians prefer policies that yield tangible benefits for constituents in the near term. Medicare pays a slice of every Medicare patient's medical bills, rather than just being major-medical insurance, so that the people covered by Medicare are constantly reminded that they are recipients of governmental largesse.

A further impediment to taking the asteroid threat seriously is that manned space travel appeals to the public despite its risks and expense. It lends a vivid human dimension to space exploration, which is immensely more appealing to the public and to astronomers and other scientists than cataloging and fending off orbiting rocks. The public likes to think of space as the new frontier, not as an attack path to the earth. NASA would therefore be swimming against the tide of public opinion if it pressed hard for an asteroid defense program. It isn't pressing at all, despite the recommendation of the task force it commissioned.[133] Nor would the Air Force like to be diverted from antiballistic-missile defense and other programs dear to it, especially those involving manned aircraft, to which the Air Force, still dominated by pilots, remains wedded.

The situation with respect to global warming rings another change on the public-choice theme. On the one hand, climatologists have a financial interest in stimulating public concern about global warming, are strongly backed by environmentalists and anticapitalists, and appeal to a public habituated to taking threats to the environment, including global warming, seriously. (An asteroid collision could do even more harm to the environment than global warming—actually, catastrophic global warming is one of the likely consequences of a cataclysmic asteroid collision—but, like an invasion by extraterrestrials, is rarely thought of as an *environmental* hazard.)[134] On the other hand, the costs of effective action against global warming appear to be very great and would be concentrated on particular industries and their customers—and the sparsely populated western states of the United States, with their immense driving distances, have disproportionate influence in the Senate because the Constitution entitles every state to the same number of senators as any other, regardless of population. Moreover, there is sufficient doubt about the magnitude of the global-warming threat, given the complexities and uncertainties of climate science, to enable those industries to advance plausible claims that the dangers of global warming are being exaggerated—and exaggerated by scruffy, rioting left-wingers to boot. Think of how, for many years, even slight scientific uncertainty enabled the tobacco industry to issue plausible denials that smoking was hazardous to health.

3

How to evaluate the catastrophic risks and the possible responses to them

To deal in a systematic way with the catastrophic risks identified in chapter 1 requires first assessing them and then devising and implementing sensible responses. Assessment involves first of all collecting the technical data necessary to gauge, so far as that may be possible, the probability of particular risks, the purely physical consequences if the risks materialize (questions of value are for later), and the feasibility of various measures for reducing either the risks or the magnitude of the consequences by various amounts. The next step in the assessment stage is to embed the data in a cost-benefit analysis of the alternative responses to the risk.

I am not proposing that cost-benefit analysis, at least as it is understood by economists, should be *the* decision procedure for responding to the catastrophic risks. But it is an indispensable step in rational decision making in this as in other areas of government regulation. Effective responses to most catastrophic risks are likely to be extremely costly, and it would be mad to adopt such responses without an effort to estimate the costs and benefits. No government is going to deploy a system of surveillance and attack for preventing asteroid collisions without a sense of what the system is likely to cost and what the expected benefits (roughly, the costs of asteroid collisions that the system would prevent multiplied by the probabilities of such collisions) are likely to be relative to the costs and benefits both of alternative systems and of doing nothing.[1] The "precautionary principle" ("better safe than sorry") popular in Europe and among Greens generally[2] is not a satisfactory alternative to cost-benefit analysis,[3] if only because of its sponginess—if it is an alternative at all. In its more tempered versions, the principle is indistinguishable from cost-benefit analysis with risk aversion assumed.[4] Risk aversion, as we know, entails that extra weight be given the downside of uncertain prospects. In effect it magnifies certain costs, but it does not thereby overthrow cost-benefit analysis, as some advocates of the precautionary principle may believe.

The difference cost-benefit analysis can make: the case of RHIC

Both the utility, and some of the problems, of applying cost-benefit analysis to the extreme events that are the subject of this book can be illustrated with reference to Brookhaven's Relativistic Heavy Ion Collider. RHIC cost $600 million to build and its annual operating costs were expected to be $130 million.[5] No attempt was made to monetize the benefits that the experiments conducted in it were expected to yield in each of the 10 years that the facility was planned to remain in operation, but to get the analysis going let me make a wild guess that the benefits can be valued at $250 million per year. In order to enable comparison with the up-front cost of the accelerator, the operating costs and anticipated benefits have to be discounted to present value. Discounting just means using an interest rate to make a future value equivalent to a present one. For example, at a 5 percent interest (discount) rate, receiving $100 a year for five years is the equivalent of receiving $432.95 now.

At a discount rate of 3 percent (the choice of discount rate is discussed in the next section of this chapter), RHIC's net present value would be $400 million. This figure is arrived at by subtracting from $2.1 billion—the present value of a stream of annual benefits of $250 million for 10 years discounted at 3 percent—$1.1 billion, the present value of the annual operating costs, similarly discounted, and $600 million, the accelerator's fixed costs.

But now suppose the cost of extinction of the human race, which as we'll see later in this chapter can be *very* conservatively estimated at $600 trillion (an estimate that therefore biases the analysis in favor of RHIC), is discounted by a .0000001 (1 in 10 million) probability. This is "discounting" in the sense not of reducing a future to a present cost but of determining the certain equivalent of an uncertain cost by multiplying the cost by the probability it will actually be incurred, the product of this multiplication being the expected cost of (in this case) extinction.

My choice of a 1 in 10 million annual probability of a strangelet disaster is arbitrary. For reasons that will become clearer in the last section of this chapter, no numerical probability can be responsibly assigned to such a disaster, though there have been efforts to do so. Arnon Dar and his colleagues estimated the probability of a strangelet disaster during RHIC's planned 10-year life as no more than 1 in 50 million,[6] which on an annual basis would be roughly 1 in 500 million. Robert Jaffe and his colleagues, the official risk-assessment team for RHIC, offered a series of upper-bound estimates, including a 1 in 500,000 probability of a strangelet disaster over the 10-year period, which translates into an annual probability of such a disaster of approximately 1 in 5 million.[7]

A 1 in 10 million estimate yields an annual expected extinction cost of $60 million for 10 years to add to the $130 million in annual operating costs. Discounting the total annualized costs of $190 million to present value at a discount rate of 3 percent yields a figure of $1.6 billion, which when added to the $600 million up-front cost exceeds the present value of the accelerator's benefits by $100 million ($2.2 billion minus $2.1 billion), as shown in Table 3.1.

So we see how doomsday risks, though involving very slight probabilities, could doom many projects—and not merely the marginal ones. But the opposite error must be avoided of supposing that "when the stakes are very high, no chance, however small, should be ignored."[8] Utterly trivial probabilities of even large harms must be ignored, or we shall be devoting all our resources to harm avoidance. But the probability of a disastrous accelerator accident may not be *so* small that it would be irrational to think we might want to take steps to reduce it still further, given the unspeakably horrible consequences should the probability become an actuality.

Table 3.1. Cost-Benefit Analysis of RHIC

Category	Costs (ex extinction risk)	Benefits
Total benefits		$250 mill. (???) × 10 (yrs.) = $2.5 bill.
Construction cost	$600 mill.	
Operating costs	$130 mill. × 10 (yrs.) = $1.3 bill.	
Operating costs discounted to present value at 3%	$1.1 bill.	
Benefits discounted to present value at 3%		$2.1
Total costs (construction plus discounted operating)	$1.7 bill.	
Net benefits		$400 mill.

	Costs (with extinction risk)	Benefits
Total (discounted; ex extinction)	$1.7 bill.	$2.1 bill.
Extinction	$60 mill. × 10 (yrs.) = $600 mill.	
Extinction (discounted)	$500 mill.	$2.5 bill.
Total (discounted)	$2.2 bill.	$2.1 bill.
Net benefits		– $100 mill.

But this analysis requires qualifications. If other nations were expected to build equally risky accelerators regardless of what the United States did, this would reduce the risk created by RHIC, just as taking measures to avoid dying from heart disease would have less effect on the risk of death if the risk of dying from cancer rose. (Or, if everyone died at 60, the risk of death from Alzheimer's would be trivial.) But because the risk of an accelerator catastrophe is very small, many risky accelerators would have to be built before the incremental risk of another accelerator fell so far that the outcome of the cost-benefit analysis would be altered significantly, just as, if the risk of dying from cancer rose by only one in a million, the effect of that increase on the benefits from avoiding death from heart disease would be trivial.

A more important qualification concerns the social benefits of increasingly powerful particle accelerators. Those benefits are difficult, maybe impossible, to determine; I plucked the figure of $250 million a year out of the air. Particle accelerators have played an important role in the growth of physical knowledge, knowledge that has in turn given rise to important products and services, including PET (positron emission tomography) scans, the ion-implementation method of manufacturing integrated circuits, and the development of superconductors.[9] But this history does not enable the benefits of an incremental increase in accelerator energies to be estimated. When the Superconducting Super Collider was under consideration (see chapter 2), the argument that particle physicists made for it was that it would enable them to get closer to discovering the fundamental laws of the universe,[10] not that it would yield improved products or services. The history of physics suggested that it would do that too—but which products or services, and of what value, and when, were impossible to predict.

About all that is clear is that the more basic the research conducted in a particle accelerator is, the more remote the practical applications of it are likely to be.[11] This suggests that my estimate of $250 million a year in benefits during the 10 years in which RHIC will be operating was a gross exaggeration. The experiments conducted at RHIC are unlikely to yield monetizable benefits in so short a time, and any benefits that accrue later may well be slight after being discounted to present value.

The futurity and uncertainty of basic research[12] that so exacerbate the difficulty of monetizing the benefits of RHIC underscore the larger problem of the lack of reliable methods of estimating the social value of R & D in general, government-supported R & D[13] in particular, basic research in general, and government-supported basic research in particular. The empirical literature on the social returns to R & D[14] does not focus on basic research because by definition such research lacks clearly foreseeable commercial applications. Looking back we can see that basic scientific research has contributed enormously to human welfare.[15] But there is a danger of exaggeration in measuring the value of basic research by its successes and ignoring the costly dry holes along the way. It is true that economists who specialize in the study of R & D believe that the private and social returns to basic research greatly exceed the returns to other activities.[16] Yet if this were really so, one would expect more and more private and public money to be invested in basic research until the point was reached at which the private returns, at least, to basic research would equal the returns to other productive activities, since until that point a reallocation of resources to basic research from other activities would increase overall output. (Suppose the rate of return to investing in R & D were 20 percent, but to investing in manufacturing only 3 percent; then clearly a reallocation of resources from manufacturing to R & D would increase overall returns.)

Private firms have only a limited incentive to conduct basic research[17] because they can't appropriate the remote commercial fruits. This is partly because basic research is not patentable (and anyway patent terms are relatively short); but it shouldn't be.[18] And partly because firms tend to have high discount rates (because they have profitable alternative investment opportunities), which shrink the value of distant commercial prospects. Firms have *some* incentive to conduct basic research, if only because it may give them a leg up in developing patentable applications—just not a very great incentive, and so the social returns to basic research may indeed exceed the private benefits. Therefore there is a case, though not a conclusive one given the incentives of universities and foundations to support basic research out of their own funds, for some public subsidization. And in fact in 1999 half of all basic research in the United States was funded by the federal government.[19] But there is no objective method of determining how much public money should be spent on basic research or how the money should be allocated among the different areas of science.

Within a narrowly defined area of science—once it is decided that the budget for high-energy physics shall be, say, $750 million in the next fiscal year—the money assigned to it can be allocated rationally among competing applicants on the basis of scientific merit as determined by committees of peers. There were good scientific arguments for allocating a big chunk of the high-energy physics budget to RHIC. But the question of what proportion of the overall federal budget to allocate to high-energy physics is unanswerable even in approximate terms. Cost-benefit analysis is not used to guide the award of federal research grants, and may not be usable for this purpose because of the impossibility of monetizing the benefits.[20]

Yet before throwing up our hands we should consider, with particular reference to RHIC, several possible methods for deciding how much public money should go to basic research. The first method is contingent valuation—asking a random sample of people (perhaps just taxpayers) how much each would be willing to pay to enable RHIC to be built and operate.[21] This is an unpromising approach, and not only because the respondents would not be asked to put their money where their mouth was. A more serious objection—more serious because no one supposes that surveys are worthless just because the respondents do not commit themselves to behaving consistently with their responses to the questions in the survey—is that people have trouble placing a money value on "products" remote from what they are accustomed to find offered for sale.[22] A related problem is that people may want to sound virtuous or informed in answering questions about public projects and so may exaggerate their actual willingness to pay for them.

An even greater problem with using contingent valuation to guide public investments is the absence of a budget constraint. Respondents in contingent-valuation surveys are not asked to allocate limited funds among an appropriately wide variety of alternative uses. It is one thing to ask people how much they would be willing to spend to enable further advances in fundamental physics; it is quite another to ask them how much they would be willing to spend to enable further advances in fundamental physics *and* to set aside a million acres in Colorado for wilderness *and* preserve historic buildings in Charleston *and* provide old-age homes for greyhounds. As the hypothetical choice set expanded, the respondents' willingness to spend on physics research would be bound to fall, perhaps to a trivial level.

But the decisive argument against using a contingent-valuation survey to evaluate RHIC is simply that very few people know enough about particle physics to have *any* opinion, let alone an informed one, on the desirability of RHIC relative to other projects, scientific and otherwise.

A more promising approach might be to try to measure the interest of the general public in the kind of discoveries that RHIC may enable physicists to make. Judging from the popularity of such books as Stephen Hawking's *Brief History of Time*, Steven Weinberg's *First Three Minutes*, and Brian Greene's *Elegant Universe*,[23] further discoveries concerning the physics of fundamental particles would confer utility on many people outside (as well as inside) the scientific community. And not only because of the light such discoveries would shed on cosmology, where physics joins astronomy, the enormous public interest in which cannot be doubted.[24] Popular interest in science is not limited to the visible universe. Brian Greene reports that "through public lectures on superstring theory I have given over the past few years, I have witnessed a widespread yearning to understand what current research says about the fundamental laws of the universe, how these laws require a monumental restructuring of our conception of the cosmos, and what challenges lie ahead in the ongoing quest for the ultimate theory."[25] High-energy physicists believe they're on the verge of dramatic breakthroughs in our physical knowledge, breakthroughs that will require ever more expensive high-energy particle accelerators to achieve.

But could the value to the general public of new discoveries in physics really be estimated from sales of books about physics oriented to a general audience? It would be impossible to infer from sales of existing books how the market would react to discoveries that might emanate directly or indirectly from experiments conducted in RHIC. And anyway the correct measure of the social value of books is not the revenues they generate, which are merely a wealth transfer from consumers to authors and publishers, but the difference between publishers' costs and the revenues publishers would obtain if they could engage in perfect price discrimination. In other words, the social value is the sum of the producer and consumer surplus created by sales of the book, and that is extremely difficult to estimate. But here, for what little they are worth, are some figures which suggest that the public's interest in science is rather limited. Of the 6,860 mass-market paperbacks published in the United States in 2001, only 86 were science books; and of the 380,012,000 copies of the 10,000 best-selling English-language books sold worldwide in 2003, only 959,000 were science books, which is only .2 percent of the total.[26]

The large space-exploration projects of the 1960s were sold to the American public in part as justified investments in ideological competition with the Soviet Union. That rationale is no longer available, though collaborative international scientific research—the hallmark of experimentation in the large research particle accelerators—may have some value in fostering good relations among nations' scientific elites.

It can be argued that even if public support for basic research in physics is unascertainable or hopelessly uninformed, government should promote the acquisition of scientific knowledge for its own sake rather than for its popularity or consumption value or any other instrumental consideration, just as the government promotes the arts, and culture generally, either for their own sake or, what is hardly more concrete, to enrich human life. The enrichment thesis descends from John Stuart Mill's distinction between the higher and the lower pleasures; the former are those of the mind and valuable even if not highly valued by *hoi polloi*. In testimony before Congress in 1969, the director of Fermilab, Robert Rathbun Wilson, when asked whether the Fermilab accelerator had any value for national security, replied that "it has nothing to do directly with defending our country except to make it worth defending."[27] Read literally, this is nonsense; but one sees what he was driving at and how it links up with Mill's distinction.

The problem with arguing that answers to scientific questions are valuable even if they don't satisfy any actual human curiosity is that the number of such questions is infinite. A rational decision about which to pursue could be based only on either the practical value of the answers or the curiosity of actual people, and not on some a priori prioritizing of scientific inquiries.[28] However, if the scientific elite can convince Congress to spend hundreds of millions of the taxpayers' money to learn more about the Big Bang, I would have to consider that an expression of democratic preference to which I should bow. I would still want to be sure that Congress understood the full costs of pursuing scientific knowledge *à outrance*, including the risk of catastrophic accidents.

A way of eliding the entire question of the optimal federal investment in high-energy particle accelerators would be to rescind federal funding of particle research and leave it to universities, foundations, research institutes, corporations, and wealthy individuals to fund research accelerators at whatever level seemed appropriate to these potential donors. That would provide a quasi-market test of the value of such research. It might seem that the costs of building and operating major research accelerators are too great to make private financing a realistic possibility. But Brookhaven and Fermilab, along with the Stanford Linear Accelerator Center (the three constituting the major research accelerators in the United States), though all are owned by the Department of Energy, are operated by university consortia or the equivalent; there is also some foreign-government funding. Most of the research conducted in the major accelerators, moreover, is joint among numerous scientists from all over the world; scientific articles reporting the results of experiments conducted in such accelerators typically list hundreds of authors. The aggregate resources of the universities and other institutions involved in such research, domestic and foreign, may well be great enough to fund it—without substantial or perhaps any federal assistance—at a level that accords due weight to safety. Indeed, the intellectual case for privatization of accelerator research seems compelling. But it would be politically unrealistic to imagine that the case will receive serious consideration. The fact that RHIC eludes measurement of the benefits side of cost-benefit analysis is a source of strength rather than weakness for the supporters of particle research because, as noted in chapter 2, it stumps people who want to argue that the costs exceed the benefits. It increases the inertia that tends to dominate governmental budgetary allocation decisions even when cost-benefit analysis is feasible.

A modest version of the precautionary principle

Although the benefits of RHIC cannot be quantified, any measure designed to reduce a catastrophic risk, such as the risk of a stranglelet disaster, that is created or exacerbated by scientific progress is likely to impede that progress. That would be obvious if the only measure that would prevent a strangelet disaster was shutting down RHIC; all the benefits of experiments in RHIC would be lost along with the costs. To help in striking the balance between progress and safety, let's consider whether the incremental benefits of scientific progress are likely to be smaller or greater than the incremental costs of the possible catastrophic byproducts of that progress. If smaller, this would argue for placing a thumb on the cost side of the cost-benefit analysis—a modest version of the precautionary principle.

I think that the downside of extinction probably does outweigh the upside of faster scientific progress:

1. Human happiness is easily impaired by an increase in the death rate due to war or disease, or by a decline in the standard of living, and a fortiori would be impaired by the sort of catastrophes with which this book is concerned. It is much more difficult to raise the happiness level. This is suggested by the fact that while wealthier people are usually happier (as measured, very imperfectly to be sure, by responses to survey questions) than poorer people in the same country, an increase in an individual's income tends not to produce a proportionate increase in his happiness, and average happiness is only slightly greater in wealthier than in poorer countries.[29] The fact that increases in a country's wealth, which are a function to a significant extent of technological progress, produce at most only slight increases in the average happiness of the population[30] implies that technological progress is, to a degree anyway, a running-in-place phenomenon so far as generating human happiness is concerned. Remember from the introduction "the conversion of humans to more or less immortal near-gods" that David Friedman described as the upside of galloping twenty-first-century scientific advance? It seems rather a dubious plus, and certainly less of

one than extinction would be a minus, especially since changing us into "near-gods" could be thought itself a form of extinction rather than a boon because of the discontinuity between a person and a near-god. We think of early hominids as having become extinct rather than as having become us.

Maybe, though, all Friedman means by a "near-god" is someone who lives far beyond the current human life expectancy; and we recall from the introduction that people derive great utility from extending their lives. But most people don't like to gamble on such extensions; they would rather have a reasonable assurance of living to 70 than a 50 percent probability of living to 50 and a 50 percent probability of living to 90.

And the more extravagant the conception of near-godhood, the less people will pay for it; the costs of imagining will go through the roof. It is one thing to lose what we have; we know what we have lost because we experienced it. It is another thing not to obtain something we might want, or think we might want. Since we do not have it, we may have difficulty imagining just what it would be like to have it. The costs of imagining are real costs and cannot be waved away as products of irrational thinking. Imagine trying to convince a poor person of what he is missing by not being able to afford caviar. Nor are there reputable experts to whom to delegate the task of imagining.

The cost of imagining is especially high when the object of the imagining is the afterlife, one version of near-godhood. That is a flaw in Pascal's famous wager. He argued that because the value of salvation to the individual was infinite, it would be rational to believe in God even if one thought the probability of his existence infinitesimal (because a minute percentage of infinity is still infinite), assuming that belief was a condition of salvation independent of the sect one chose to join (that is, assuming God is not "jealous" in the Old Testament sense). But if people cannot imagine infinite bliss, the value of salvation falls and the expected gain from believing in God can drop below the costs if the probability of his existing is reckoned to be slight. One observes that many rational people, even many people familiar with Pascal's wager, do not believe in God and that even among sincere believers few wish to trade years of life for years of afterlife by dying as soon as possible.

What Friedman really ought to be saying is that technology may eventually enable everyone on earth to live as well as Americans do.

That would be a fine thing, but most of the world's poor people would not gamble their existence on achieving that goal even if they had full information about how Americans live.

2. Risk aversion implies an asymmetrical attitude toward gains and losses. Because of diminishing marginal utility of income, most people would refuse to bet their entire wealth on a 50 percent chance of doubling it. Similarly, most people would not be willing to bet their lives on a 50 percent chance of obtaining twice or even 3 or 4 or 10 times their current felicity by becoming "an immortal near-god." To put it crudely, the decrease in utility from losing one arm would be greater than the increase in utility from acquiring a third arm. This is the core of an economically inflected precautionary principle.

3. Progress carries with it all sorts of unanticipated side effects, many negative. Technology has transformed the social role of women but as a byproduct has produced a high level of divorce and illegitimacy. Often, as Adam Smith and many others have remarked, people work hard for something only to find when they achieve it that they don't really want it. The only bright side of extinction of the human race would be to create space for new life forms to evolve, and even that would be missing from a strangelet disaster that reduced the earth's diameter to 100 meters.

For these reasons, it is not a compelling riposte to expressions of concern over low-probability disaster scenarios such as a strangelet disaster at RHIC that it is just as likely that RHIC will yield some enormous, at present wholly unforeseen and unimagined, human benefit. It is not as likely. The case for symmetry is more plausible when, as in the case of nanotechnology, technological breakthroughs, though perhaps pregnant with dangers, may offer the best prospect for reducing otherwise intractable risks of catastrophe. I have in mind the possibility that nanotechnology may eventually enable carbon sequestration to arrest global warming.

Discounting to present value

If a project will cost $4 today and produce a $5 value but not until 10 years from now, one cannot conclude that the net benefit of the project is $1, unless interest rates are zero. For if instead of spending $4 today one invested the money for 10 years, it would grow because of interest compounding, and if it grew to $6 this would mean that the $4 project had not been a good investment after all. This is the argument for using the rate of return on capital as the discount rate,[31] but there are alternative possibilities, as we shall see.

The effect of discounting on cost-benefit analyses of responses to catastrophic risks tends to be dramatic because the benefits of the responses are likely to be spread out over a very long time while many of the costs may have to be incurred in the present and near future. (RHIC is exceptional in that regard because it is intended to remain in operation for only a decade.) That is the situation whenever taking steps today will reduce the probability of very-low-probability events that loom as threatening only when summed over a considerable period of time. Though most of the costs of responding might have to be incurred up front, as in the case of an asteroid defense or ceilings on greenhouse-gas emissions, the benefits would include reducing the probability of disaster in the distant as well as in the near future and thus would be spread out over the future rather than concentrated in the present when most of the costs would be incurred.

The drama increases further when the annual expected costs, rather than being the same, are increasing. Global warming is illustrative.[32] The effect of greenhouse-gas emissions on the atmospheric concentration of those gases is as we know largely cumulative, so that even if the annual level of emissions does not increase but merely continues at its current level despite a growing population and increasing economic activity, the amount of atmospheric carbon dioxide will continue to rise. Yet the rise may not have serious consequences for human welfare until well into the future. Suppose that a $10 billion expenditure on capping emissions today would have no effect on human welfare during this century but, by slowing global warming, would produce a savings in social costs of $100 billion in 2100. At a discount rate of 3 percent, the present value of $100 billion a century from now is only $5 billion. That would make the expenditure of $10 billion today seem a very poor investment. (For the sake of simplicity I ignore benefits that are expected to accrue after 2100.) The same amount of money invested in financial instruments could be expected to grow to $192 billion by 2100, assuming a 3 percent real interest rate for the next 100 years (though in fact interest rates cannot be forecast over such a long period).[33] If the fund were then disbursed to the victims of global warming, they would be better off than if the $100 billion cost of global warming assumed to be incurred in that year had been averted. Less conservative investments, moreover, would yield larger expected returns—10 percent or more rather than 3 percent.[34]

But it is not a real alternative to spending $10 billion now to invest it in a fund for future victims of global warming. No such fund will be created, and so they will not be compensated. One reason it will not be created is the difficulty of committing governments to future action. If today Congress decided to establish a trust fund for the benefit of victims of global warming in the twenty-second century, there would be nothing to prevent a future Congress from diverting the fund to other purposes, unless the fund had actually been turned over to independent trustees, or to the United Nations or some other international organization, and that would be unlikely.

In circumstances such as these, discounting future to present values is not a method of helping people to decide how to manage their affairs in the way most conducive to maximizing their welfare. Rather it is a method of maximizing global wealth without regard to its distribution among persons. In the case of gradual global warming (the most likely type, though my particular interest is in the possibility of abrupt global warming), the victims are likely to be concentrated in poor countries, so that basing policy on the discounted costs of global warming would further immiserate the future inhabitants of those countries by increasing the authorized level of emissions harmful to them.

A discount rate based on market interest rates tends to obliterate the interests of remote future generations. The implications are drastic. "At a discount rate of five per cent, one death next year counts for more than a billion deaths in 500 years. On this view, catastrophes in the further future can now be regarded as morally trivial."[35] (To return to an example in the introduction, what right would the Romans have had to regard our lives as worthless in deciding whether to conduct dangerous experiments?) The trade-off is only slightly less extreme if one substitutes 100 years for 500. At a 5 percent discount rate, the present value of $1 to be received in 100 years is only three-quarters of a cent—and if for money we substitute lives, then to save one life this year we should be willing to sacrifice almost 150 lives a century hence.

And yet not to discount future costs at all[36] would be absurd, certainly as a practical political matter. For then the present value of benefits conferred on our remote descendants would approach infinity. Measures taken today to arrest global warming would confer benefits not only in 2100 but in every subsequent year, perhaps for millions of years. The present value of $100 billion received every year for a million years at a discount rate of 0 percent is $100 quadrillion, which is more than even Greenpeace wants spent on limiting emissions of greenhouse gases.

Because resources are limited, we couldn't make the expenditures called for by a cost-benefit analysis of catastrophic risks that eschewed discounting to present value even if we wanted to. What we could do would be to devote all our resources to catastrophe-averting projects above the modest expenditures necessary to maintain at a subsistence level the scientific and technical personnel employed on the projects. That is an absurd idea too. It is the absurdity of "total utility maximization," which might support such projects as reducing the human population to the level necessary to support as many sheep as possible, on the theory that the sum of the human and sheep utility under such a regime would exceed the present sum, given how many people but few sheep are miserable. To refuse to discount future costs is to say in effect that we should treat every potential human life, from now to when the sun expands into the earth's orbit (if the human population hasn't been relocated to another solar system by then), as having equal value, even though the effect would be to reduce the utility of the present generation and all foreseeable future generations as well to a minimal level.

The problem of how much weight to give to the welfare of remote future generations is the subject of an immense but inconclusive literature.[37] Perhaps, however, it can be finessed, at least to some extent. Here are some possibilities:

1. Richard Newell and William Pizer[38] argue that uncertainty concerning the future path of interest rates implies that the correct discount rate for very remote future harms is lower than the current rate. Suppose there's an equal chance that the applicable interest rate throughout this and future centuries will be either 1 percent or 5 percent. The present value of $1 in 100 years is 36.9 cents if the interest rate used to compute the present value is 1 percent but only .76 cents (a shade over three-quarters of a cent) if it is 5 percent. Now consider the 101st year and remember the assumption that the two alternative discount rates are equally probable. If the interest rate used to discount the future to the present value is 1 percent, then the present value of $1 at the end of that year will have shrunk from 36.9 cents to 36.6 cents. If instead the interest rate used is 5 percent, the present value of .76 cents will have shrunk to about .75 cents. This means that the *average* present value of $1 at the end of the 101st year will be 18.68 cents, implying

an average discount rate of less than 2 percent, rather than 3 percent. The reason is that the more rapid decline in value under the higher discount rate (5 percent) reduces its influence on present value. If, however, the discount rate oscillates between the two values rather than being either the one or the other throughout the entire period, the average rate will be close to 3 percent ($1.01^{50} \times 1.05^{50} = 1.0298^{100}$). But Newell and Pizer's assumption better reflects our profound uncertainty about the future. Martin Weitzman observes that "we tend not to attribute much weight to whether an event occurs three or four centuries from now,"[39] which implies a zero discount rate for costs incurred in that interval, or, more generally, as in Newell and Pizer's analysis, a flattening of discount rates over time.

2. A discounted present value can be equated to an undiscounted present value simply by shortening the time horizon for the consideration of costs and benefits.[40] For example, the present value of an infinite stream of costs discounted at 4 percent a year is equal to the undiscounted sum of those costs for 25 years, while the present value of an infinite stream of costs discounted at 1 percent a year is equal to the undiscounted sum of those costs for 100 years. The formula for the present value of $1 per year forever is $1/r$, where r is the discount rate. So if r is 4 percent, the present value is $25, and this is equal to an undiscounted stream of $1 per year for 25 years. If r is 1 percent, the undiscounted equivalent is 100 years.

One way to argue for the 4 percent rate (that is, for truncating our concern for future welfare at 25 years) is to say that we're willing to weight the welfare of the next generation as heavily as our own welfare but that's the extent of our regard for the future. One way to argue for the 1 percent rate is to say that we're willing to give equal weight to the welfare of everyone living in this century, which will include us, our children, and our grandchildren, but beyond that we don't care. Looking at future welfare in this way, we may be inclined toward the lower rate—which would have dramatic implications for willingness to invest today in limiting global warming. The lower rate could even be regarded as a ceiling. Most of us have some regard for human welfare, or at least the survival of some human civilization, in future centuries. We are grateful that the Romans didn't exterminate the human race in chagrin at the impending collapse of their empire.

3. Another way to bring future consequences into focus without conventional discounting is by aggregating risks over time rather than expressing them in annualized terms. If we are concerned about what

may happen over the next century, then instead of asking what the annual probability of a collision with a 10-kilometer-wide asteroid is, we might ask what the probability is that such a collision will occur within the next 100 years. An annual probability of 1 in 75 million translates into a century probability of roughly 1 in 750,000. That may be high enough—considering the consequences if the risk materializes—to justify spending several hundred million, perhaps even several billion, dollars to avert it.

4. Still another way to finesse the discount-rate issue is simply to ignore it on the ground that the discount rate is probably about the same as the rate of per capita economic growth. The approach might seem applicable only to economic losses, but that is not correct, because, as we'll see, value-of-life estimates are positively correlated with income. The drawback to this approach is that without discounting, the present cost of an infinite stream of future costs is infinite. That is not a compelling objection if we limit our consideration of the future to the next 50 years or so, but if we do that we'll be leaving the entire future beyond that point unaccounted for by our analysis.

Taxes, subsidies, and options: the case of global warming

At first glance, global warming seems like the poster child for the limitations of cost-benefit analysis. The fact that the benefits from controlling emissions of greenhouse gases probably lie in the distant future while many of the costs must be borne now if the situation is not to get out of hand not only presents an intractable problem of discounting to present value, as we have just seen; it also underscores the unreality of long-term predictions (despite which 100-year bonds at a fixed interest rate are issued occasionally)[41] concerning such imponderables as the rate and direction of technological change. And since the costs of remediation will be borne largely by the inhabitants of the wealthy countries, while the benefits will probably go largely to the descendants of the inhabitants of poor countries, the global-warming problem raises acutely the question what if any duties Americans should assume toward foreigners, more precisely the distant descendants of foreigners. The answer depends on ethical judgments.[42]

But we must not give up on cost-benefit analysis too soon. Let us to begin with not confuse costs that are merely difficult to measure with "costs" that cannot be measured even in principle. Such measures for preventing bioterrorism as placing biochemists under continuous surveillance, refusing to allow citizens of Muslim nations to study biochemistry at the graduate level in the United States, or invading hostile nations that are believed to possess weapons of mass destruction do not present the same kind of issue as deciding what we owe remote future generations and therefore what costs we should incur to help them. The latter issue, as my way of stating it ("what we owe") suggests, is ethical. The former, although often framed in ethical language ("civil liberties," "discrimination," and so forth), can be given an economic form. If we knew what the security measures that might be taken against the threat of bioterrorism would cost—with "cost" understood broadly to include the cost of inroads on privacy and liberty— we could use cost-benefit analysis to help us decide whether to take them. (I return to this question in the next chapter.)

Sometimes it is pretty clear that a nonmonetized cost merits a zero weight. It has been argued that a major cost of an asteroid defense is that it would militarize space. Missiles designed to deflect asteroids millions of miles from the earth might be effective for destroying spy satellites or knocking down incoming missiles. But this is extremely unlikely. A defense against ballistic missiles presents quite different technological challenges from a defense against asteroid collisions because there are countermeasures available to a missile offense, such as decoys, but not to dumb rocks, that must be neutralized for a missile defense to be effective. Space, moreover, is already militarized by ballistic missiles and spy satellites; an asteroid defense will not militarize it further. That may be why the Air Force is not interested in it.

In the case of global warming we may be able to elide the ethical problems that beset cost-benefit analysis by dropping the conventional assumption that the way taxes, tradable permits, or other methods of capping emissions of greenhouse gases (to simplify analysis, the only method of regulating emissions I'll discuss is taxing them)[43] work is by inducing substitution away from activities that burn fossil fuels and otherwise encouraging more economical use of such fuels. It is true that if taxes on gasoline rise, people will drive less and demand cars that are more fuel efficient, but to see what's wrong with assuming that the social benefits of emissions taxes lie in inducing such substitutions imagine (unrealistically) that the demand for fossil fuels is completely inelastic in the short run. Then even a very heavy tax on carbon dioxide emissions would have no short-run effect on the level of emissions, and one's first reaction is likely to be that, if so, the tax would be ineffectual. Actually it would be a highly efficient tax from the standpoint of generating government revenues (the basic function of taxation); it would not distort the allocation of resources, and therefore its imposition could be coupled with a reduction in less efficient taxes without reducing government revenues, although the substitution would be incomplete because, by reducing taxpayer resistance, more efficient taxes facilitate the expansion of government.[44]

More important from the standpoint of this book, such a tax might—paradoxically—have an even greater impact on emissions, precisely because of the inelasticity of short-run demand, than a tax that reduced that demand. With immediate substitution of alternative fuels impossible and the price of fossil fuels soaring because of the tax, there would be powerful market pressures to speed the development of economical alternatives to fossil fuels as energy sources. There would also be incentives to hasten the development of technologies for reducing atmospheric greenhouse gases directly, whether by removing carbon dioxide from the atmosphere through gene-spliced carbon-dioxide-devouring bacteria, piping carbon dioxide produced as an unwanted byproduct of electrical generation into porous underground rock formations or to the bottom of oceans, or reacting carbon dioxide with calcium or other minerals to form limestone or other carbonates.[45] None of these methods of carbon sequestration is economically feasible at present. But they may become so if heavy taxation of greenhouse-gas emissions stimulates greater R & D expenditures on the elimination of such gases. In both respects—hastening the development of economical clean fuels and of economical methods of carbon sequestration—an emissions tax would be technology forcing.

In the second respect, moreover, an emissions tax would be superior to a tax on the fossil fuels themselves (a gasoline tax, for example, or a tax on B.T.U. content). An energy tax is cheaper to enforce because there is no need to monitor emissions. But only an emissions tax would be effective in inducing carbon sequestration, because sequestration reduces the amount of atmospheric carbon dioxide without curtailing the demand for fossil fuels. A tax on gasoline will reduce the demand for gasoline but will not induce efforts to prevent the carbon dioxide emitted by the burning of the gasoline that continues to be produced from entering the atmosphere.

The analysis of technology-forcing emissions taxes is formalized in Figure 3.1. Two different demands for carbon dioxide are shown. D_1 is the less elastic demand, D_2 the more elastic. (The "demand" for emissions is derived from the demand for activities, such as power generation by coal-burning plants, that produce emissions as a byproduct.) The horizontal line P is the price (equals marginal cost) without an emissions tax, and $P + T$ is the price with a tax equal to T, which measures the social cost of emissions that is not reflected in the private cost. The tax reduces the output of emissions from $Q_{1,2}$ to Q_{1T} in the case of the less elastic demand and to Q_{2T} in the case of the more elastic demand. The reduction eliminates a deadweight social cost due to emissions that is equal to the triangle *bcd* in the case of the less elastic demand and *ace* in the case of the more elastic demand. Thus, the more elastic the demand, the greater the amount of social loss that is eliminated.

We can think of the two demand curves as short run (D_1) and long run (D_2). In the short run the demand for the activities that produce carbon dioxide emissions as a byproduct is inelastic[46] because it is difficult in the short run to substitute against those activities; the derived demand for the emissions is inelastic as well, given that carbon sequestration is at present uneconomical. In the long run the possibilities of substitution are much greater, so while in the short run the primary effect of an emissions tax is the price increase, in the long run the effect on emissions is substantial; in Figure 3.1, it is $Q_{1T} - Q_{2T}$.

Really dramatic long-run declines in emissions will require technological breakthroughs that steeply reduce the cost both of clean fuels and of carbon sequestration, rather than more insulation, less driving, lower thermostat settings, and other energy-economizing moves. And it is dramatic declines that we need. Even if the short-run elasticity of demand for activities that produce carbon dioxide emissions were -1 (that is, if a small increase in the price of the activity resulted in a proportionately equal reduction in the scale of the activity), a 20 percent tax on emissions would reduce the amount of emissions by only 20 percent (this is on the assumption that emissions are produced in fixed proportions to the activities producing them). Because of the cumulative effect of emissions on atmospheric concentrations of greenhouse gases, those concentrations would continue to grow, albeit at a 20 percent lower rate. Thus, although emissions might be elastic with respect to the tax, the actual atmospheric concentrations, which are the ultimate concern, would not be. In contrast, a stiff emissions tax might precipitate within a decade or two technological breakthroughs that would enable a drastic reduction of emissions, perhaps to zero. If so, the effect of the tax would be much greater than would be implied by

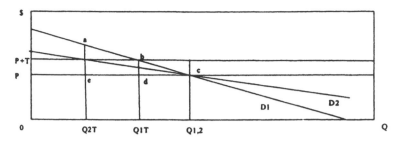

**Figure 3.1. Effect of Emission Taxes under Different Assumptions about the
Elasticity of Demand**

estimates of the elasticity of demand that ignored such possibilities.
The possibilities are masked by the fact that because greenhouse-gas
emissions are not taxed (or classified as pollutants), the private incentives to reduce them are meager.

Besides the effect on emissions, an emissions tax might as I suggested earlier improve the overall efficiency of the tax system if it were
substituted for particularly inefficient taxes, such as taxes on income
from capital.[47] The pairing of a stiff emissions tax with a reduction in
corporate income tax or personal income taxation of dividends may
seem politically bizarre. Actually it could be a stroke of political genius,
since liberals want emissions taxes and conservatives want lower taxes
on income from capital. Of course, the more effective an emissions tax
in reducing emissions, the less revenue it would generate.

Neglect of these possible effects of emissions taxes undermines
Bjørn Lomborg's claim (see chapter 1) that the costs of arresting global
warming will be greater—he thinks much greater—than the costs of
global warming itself. An emissions tax may be efficient to the extent
that the demand for fossil fuels both is inelastic in the short run (so that
the allocative effect of the taxes in inducing costly substitutions is minimized) *and* reduces the long-run costs of curbing greenhouse gases by
accelerating the development of clean fuels and efficient methods of
carbon sequestration.

Subsidizing research on measures to control global warming might
seem more efficient than a technology-forcing tax because it would
create a direct rather than merely an indirect incentive to develop new
technology. But the money to finance the subsidy would have to come
from tax revenues, and the tax (whether an explicit tax or inflation,
which is a tax on cash balances) that generated these revenues might

be less efficient than a tax on emissions if the latter taxed less elastic activities, as it might. A subsidy, moreover, might induce overinvestment. Even people ignorant of economics know that often it is futile to throw money at a problem. The problem may be serious and amenable to solution through an expenditure of resources, but above a certain level additional expenditures may contribute less to the solution than they cost. An emissions tax set equal to the social cost of emissions will not induce overinvestment, as industry will have no incentive to incur a greater cost to avoid the tax. If the social cost of emitting a specified quantity of carbon dioxide is $1 and the tax therefore is $1, industry will spend up to $1, but not more, to avoid the tax. If it can avoid the tax only by spending $1.01 on emission-reduction measures, it will forgo the expenditure and pay the tax.

A further advantage of a tax over a subsidy is that the government would not be involved in making the actual R & D decisions; the market would decide which technologies were the most promising. Government's inability to pick technological winners is well known. And third, despite my suggestion that new technology is likely to be the ultimate solution to the problem of global warming, methods for reducing carbon dioxide emissions that do not depend on new technology, such as switching to more fuel-efficient cars, may have a significant role to play, and the use of such methods would be encouraged by a tax on emissions but not by a subsidy for novel technologies, at least until those technologies yielded cheap, clean fuels.

The case for subsidy would be compelling only if inventors of new technologies for combating global emissions could not appropriate the benefits of the technologies and therefore lacked market incentives to develop them. But given patents, trade secrets, trademarks, the learning curve (which implies that the first firm in a new market will have lower production costs than latecomers), and other methods of internalizing the benefits of inventions, appropriability shouldn't be a serious problem. With two exceptions. The first is basic research (including research in climate science), which is not patentable and which as I said the commercial sector has limited incentives to conduct. The second is technologies for removing carbon dioxide from the atmosphere. Emitters would not pay for such a technology because it would not reduce their emissions and hence their taxes, in contrast to a technology for piping underground carbon dioxide produced in a coal-fired electric generating plant, which would have a ready market in electric companies faced with a heavy emissions tax. So there is a case for *some* public subsidy for R & D related to global warming, but a smaller one than would be optimal if an emissions tax didn't have a large technology-forcing effect, because, if it did, most of the work of inducing reductions in emissions would be done by the private sector under the pressure of the tax.[48] Even the residual subsidy could be largely avoided by giving emitters tax credits for reducing atmospheric carbon dioxide, such as by planting forests. The Kyoto Protocol actually contains a version of this suggestion.

Speaking of the Kyoto Protocol, the concept of an emissions tax as a technology forcer casts that ill-fated and much-derided measure in a more favorable light. On its face, the protocol is not only expensive[49] but ineffectual. It seems that all it would do, even if the United States ratified it, would be to roll back the annual level of greenhouse-gas emissions by the developed countries to their late-1980s levels—levels already so high that global warming would continue because of the cumulative effect of emissions on atmospheric greenhouse gases. And because developing nations have been exempted from the protocol's limits on emissions and some of those nations are industrializing (such as China) and deforesting (such as Brazil) so rapidly that within a few years developing nations will be producing more than half the world's greenhouse-gas emissions,[50] the overall annual level of emissions would continue to rise at only a slightly lower rate than contemplated by the protocol.

But this analysis ignores the effect of emissions in the nations subject to the protocol's ceilings in forcing greater R & D expenditures on clean fuels and carbon sequestration. If I am right that only a technological fix can halt global warming, then even if *only* the United States were required to limit its emissions (or did so voluntarily, for which there is some sentiment) the prospects for such a fix would be improved. An emissions tax geared to inducing a desired level of investment in those technologies needn't be as high as a tax designed to bring down emissions to the levels specified in the Kyoto Protocol immediately and needn't be imposed on developing nations.

A seductive alternative to the Kyoto Protocol is to do nothing at all about greenhouse-gas emissions in the hope that a few more years of normal (as distinct from tax-impelled) research in climatology will clarify the true nature and dimensions of the threat of global warming, and then we can decide what if any measures to take to reduce emissions. This might well be the right approach were it not for the practically irreversible effect of greenhouse-gas emissions on the atmospheric concentration of those gases. Because of that irreversibility, stabilizing the atmospheric concentration of greenhouse gases at some future date might require far deeper cuts in emissions than if the process of stabilization begins now. Making shallower cuts now can be thought of as purchasing an option to enable global warming to be stopped or slowed at some future time at a lower cost.[51] Should further research show that the problem of global warming is not a serious one, the option would not be exercised.

To illustrate, suppose there is a 70 percent probability that in 2024 global warming will cause a social loss of $1 trillion (present value) and a 30 percent probability that it will cause no loss, and that the possible loss can be averted by imposing emissions controls now that will cost the society $500 billion (for simplicity's sake, I'll assume the entire cost is borne this year). It might seem that since the discounted loss from global warming in 2024 is $700 billion, the imposition of emissions controls now would be cost justified. But suppose that in 2014 we shall learn for certain whether there is going to be the bad ($1 trillion) outcome in 2024. Suppose further that if we postpone imposing the emissions controls until 2014, we can still avert the $1 trillion loss. Then clearly we should wait, not only for the obvious reason that the present value of $500 billion to be spent in 10 years is less than $500 billion (at a discount rate of 3 percent it is approximately $425 billion), but also and more interestingly because there is a 30 percent chance that we won't have to incur *any* cost of emissions controls. As a result, the expected cost of the postponed controls is not $425 billion, but only 70 percent of that amount, or $297.5 billion, which is a lot less than $500 billion. The difference is the value of waiting.

But now suppose that if today we impose emissions controls that cost society $100 billion, this will, by forcing the pace of technological advance (I'll assume that this is their only effect—that there is no effect in reducing emissions), reduce the cost of averting in 2014 the $1 trillion loss brought about in 2024 by global warming from $500 billion to $250 billion. After discounting to present value at 3 percent and by 70 percent to reflect the 30 percent probability that we'll learn in 2014 that emissions controls are not needed, the $250 billion figure shrinks to $170 billion. This is $127.5 billion less than the superficially attractive wait-and-see approach ($297.5 billion minus $170 billion). Of course, there is a price to be paid for the modified approach—$100 billion. But the value is greater than the price.

This is an example of how imposing today emissions limits more modest than those of the Kyoto Protocol might be a cost-justified measure even if the limits had no direct effect on atmospheric concentrations of greenhouse gases. The option approach is applicable to other catastrophic risks as well, such as the risks associated with genetically modified crops.[52]

Global warming could be abrupt without being catastrophic, and catastrophic without being abrupt. But abrupt global warming is more likely to be catastrophic than gradual global warming because it would deny or curtail opportunities for adaptive responses, such as switching to heat-resistant agriculture or relocating population away from coastal regions. The example on the preceding page shows that the option approach is attractive even if the possibility of abrupt global warming is ignored; in the example, we know that we are safe until 2024. But the possibility of abrupt warming should not be ignored. Suppose there is some unknown but not wholly negligible probability that the $1 trillion loss from global warming will hit in 2014 and that it will be too late then to do anything to avert it. That would be a reason to impose stringent emissions controls earlier even though by doing so we would lose the opportunity to avoid their cost by waiting to see whether they would actually be needed. Since we don't know the point at which the atmospheric concentration of greenhouse gases would trigger abrupt global warming, the imposition of emissions limits now may, given risk aversion, be an attractive insurance policy.[53] An emissions tax that did not bring about an immediate reduction in the level of emissions might still be beneficial by accelerating technological breakthroughs that would result in zero emissions before the trigger point was reached.

The risk of abrupt global warming is not only an important consideration in deciding what to do about global warming; unless it is given significant weight, the political prospects for strong controls on greenhouse-gas emissions are poor. The reason can be seen in Figure 3.2, a graph that has been used without much success to galvanize public concern about global warming.

The shaded area is the distribution of predictions of global temperature changes over the course of the century and is at first glance alarming. But a closer look reveals that the highest curve, which is based on the assumption that nothing at all will be done to curb global warming, shows a temperature increase of only about 10 degrees Fahrenheit

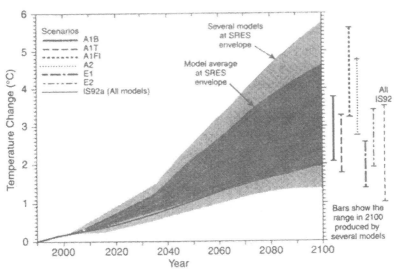

Figure 3.2. Global-Warming Predictions. *Source:* Union of Concerned Scientists, "Science of Global Warming: Future Projections of Climate Change," http://www.ucsusa.org/global_environment/global_warming/page .cfm?pageID=967 (visited Jan. 23, 2004).

over the course of the century. Such an increase would be catastrophic if it occurred in a decade, but it is much less alarming when spread out over a century, as that is plenty of time for a combination of clean fuels and cheap carbon-sequestration methods to reduce carbon dioxide emissions to zero or even (through carbon sequestration) below zero without prodding by governments. Given such an outlook, convincing governments to incur heavy costs now to reduce the 100-year increase from 10 to say 5 degrees is a distinctly uphill fight. There is also a natural skepticism about any attempt to predict what is going to happen 100 years in the future, and a belief that since future generations will be wealthier than our generation they will find it less burdensome to incur large costs to deal with serious environmental problems.

But once abrupt global warming is brought into the picture, any complacency induced by Figure 3.2 is quickly dispelled. For we then understand that the band of curves in the graph is arbitrarily truncated; that we could have a vertical takeoff, say in 2020, that within a decade would bring us to the highest point in the graph. And against *that* risk, a technology-forcing tax on emissions might well be effective even if only the major emitting countries imposed substantial emissions taxes. If manufacturers of automobiles sold in North America, the European Union, and Japan were hit with a heavy tax on carbon dioxide emissions from their automobiles, the fact that China was not taxing automobiles sold in its country would not substantially erode the incentive of the worldwide automobile industry to develop effective methods for reducing the carbon dioxide produced by their automobiles. Moreover, abrupt climate change might make future generations poorer than we are rather than richer—a possibility that might argue for using a negative rather than positive discount rate to determine the present-value cost of a future climate disaster.

Valuing human lives

Calculation of the benefits of catastrophic-risk reduction is complicated by the fact that most of those benefits are not economic in the narrow sense, though global warming is an exception. Most of its possible consequences, maybe even such catastrophic ones as the flipping of the Gulf Stream, are "economic" in the narrow sense of being readily monetizable. But not all. Increased deaths from floods and possibly from disease or starvation are among its consequences, and they are difficult to monetize. And a runaway greenhouse effect produced by a massive release of methane from soil and ocean bottoms could cause vast suffering, physical as well as financial, although I am assured by climate scientists that the earth does not contain enough methane to raise its temperature to that of Venus (> 800°F). Clearly the effect of an asteroid collision on the GDP is not what mainly worries us about such a prospect.

Valuing human lives is not, however, quite so arbitrary a procedure as it may seem. It sounds like an ethical or even a metaphysical undertaking, but what actually is involved is determining the value that people place on avoiding small risks of death. From data on wage premia in dangerous occupations, the response of housing prices to proximity to hazardous sites, seat-belt use, cigarette smoking, and other behavior toward risk, actual or perceived, of death, economists have calculated how much money the average person would demand to incur a given such risk.[54] Division of the "price" charged to bear a given risk by the risk yields the value-of-life estimate. Suppose the risk of death is .001 and the price demanded to bear the risk is $5,000; then the value of life would be $5 million ($5,000 ÷ .001). The range of estimates of the value of life so computed, based on U.S. data, is currently $4 million to $9 million, with a mean of $7 million.[55]

It might seem to follow that if the risk were not .001 but .000001, that is, 1 in a million rather than 1 in a thousand, the price for bearing the risk would be only one-thousandth as great ($5), yielding (by division of $5 by .000001) the same $5 million estimate of the value of life. But that is not necessarily correct. For there is no reason to think that the relation between the risk of death and the perceived cost of the risk is linear. Quite the contrary. Suppose the risk of death is not one in a thousand or one in a million, but one in two. Most people would demand an infinite amount of money to assume such a risk—which is to say, at that level of risk they would value their life at infinity. They would do so for the excellent reason that if they were dead they wouldn't get to enjoy the money they'd been given to assume the risk, and it is highly likely that they *would* be dead. But as is illustrated by the frequency with which people cross the street against the light or take unnecessary drives, most people are content to incur very small risks for negligible benefits because the likelihood that the risk will materialize and the benefit thus be snatched away is very slight.[56]

In other words, the function that relates risk to the cost that one is willing to pay to avoid it is probably asymptotic, as in $v = r/(1 - r)^{10}$, graphed in Figure 3.3, where v is the value to the average individual of avoiding risk r. The specific function is arbitrary, but it has value as an illustration. Notice that if the risk is zero, the cost that the individual is willing to pay to avoid it is also zero, while as the risk increases, v rises, eventually to infinity. In such a function, the compensation demanded for bearing risks that are just above zero (a risk of one in a billion, say, or even one in several million) is likely to be trivial, just as the compensation demanded for bearing risks at or above the Russian-roulette level is likely to be enormous. The risk may be so small that the difficulty, remarked several times in this book, that people have in grasping minuscule probabilities would cause them to ignore the risk completely and thus demand zero compensation for bearing it. In that event the curve depicted in Figure 3.3 would be kinked. It would intersect the horizontal axis slightly to the right of the origin and run along that axis from that point to the origin. The amount of compensation demanded to bear risks in this interval would be zero and therefore the value of life would also be zero, and so the social cost of the

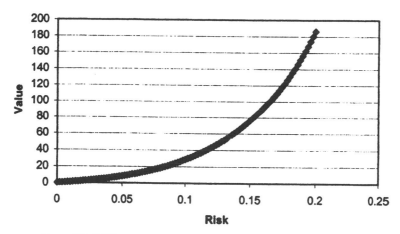

Figure 3.3. Willingness to Pay to Avoid Risk as a Function of the Risk

risk if it materialized, assuming its only effect was to kill people, would be zero too—no matter how many people were killed!

If Figure 3.3, despite its paradoxical character, captures at least some of the relevant reality, then because the value of life used in cost-benefit analysis of risky activities is just the cost divided by the risk, it is arbitrary to pick some consensus value based on small but not negligible risks, say $5 million, multiply it by the current world population of some 6 billion, and conclude that the benefit of averting an extinction event is $30 quadrillion. The $5 million estimate is unreliable, not only or even mainly because it is based on incomes in the wealthy countries— value-of-life estimates tend to be proportional to per capita income[57]— but because the risk of an extinction event is smaller than the smallest risks in the value-of-life studies from which the consensus value is derived. None of the studies involves a risk as small as one in a million.[58] The smallest risk is .000008, and almost all the studies involve risks that are between that figure and .00014, with the average being .0000915. Roughly, then, the range runs from 1 in 10,000 to 1 in 100,000.

Within that range the asymptotic relation in Figure 3.3 is not observed. That's not surprising, because the function has almost no curvature in this region. Which makes sense: if the asymptotic shape of the value of life function reflects the fact that it is difficult to compensate someone for bearing a risk that is quite likely to materialize and thus deprive him, in advance as it were, of the compensation for which he's negotiated, then when the risk is extremely small a further slight decline is unlikely to affect the value of life. And so as we continue to move down the function toward the zero origin, that value will not diminish significantly. But this neglects the possibility that as we get near the origin the function will become discontinuous because of people's innate tendency to disregard extremely low probabilities. Suppose, to return to the earlier example, that when the risk of death is only one in a million, the price for bearing the risk is not one-thousandth as great as when it is one in a thousand—that is, the price is not $5 rather than $5,000—but one hundred-thousandth as great, that is, 5 cents rather than $5; then (by division of 5 cents by .000001) the value of life would be not $5 million but only $50,000.

Studies of risk perception summarized by Chapman and Morrison find that on the one hand people tend to dismiss as beneath notice any risk of death lower than one in a million but that on the other hand they tend to weight heavily risks that are "dreadful" and "unknown," which might seem a good description of a catastrophic asteroid strike,[59] though people have a countervailing tendency to take natural catastrophes in stride.[60] We are in the presence of what Cass Sunstein calls "probability neglect," the inability of many, maybe most, people, much of the time, to respond rationally to very-low-probability risks.[61] This presents an analytical dilemma for the cost-benefit analyst. People may not demand any compensation at all for bearing risks that are only trivially greater than zero, in which event, as we know, the value of life implied by their behavior toward risk will be zero. But if the minute risk is of a "dreadful" catastrophe, they may demand a very high price to bear it, however slight it is, in which event the value of life implied by their behavior may be astronomical. Thus respondents in a post-9/11 survey expressed a willingness to pay higher airline ticket prices to reduce the risk of a terrorist attack to one in a million and slightly higher prices to reduce that risk to one in ten million.[62] The 9/11 aircraft hijackings and ensuing crashes were a prime example of a dreadful event. The article does not contain information from which the actual amount of money that the respondents would have been willing (more precisely, would have said they would have been willing) to pay for these risk reductions could be calculated. But suppose they would pay $25 per flight to eliminate the 9 in 1 million incremental risk; this would imply a value of life of $28 million.

The widespread indifference to those minute risks that are not "dreadful" may reflect not a clear-eyed, maybe macho preference for bearing a tiny risk rather than incurring even the slightest cost to avert it. It may instead reflect one or more of the following factors that should be familiar from earlier discussions: (1) a cognitive difficulty in thinking about rare occurrences in terms of probability rather than frequency;[63] (2) a related difficulty in thinking about things that lie outside one's experience ("imagination cost"); (3) what I am calling the economy of attention: people can't think about everything, and it may be efficient simply to dismiss very-low-probability events from their minds unless the expected costs of the events (not just the magnitude of the loss if the event occurs) are very great. If these factors explain the public's seeming indifference to most of the catastrophic risks—if the negligible value that people appear to attach to avoiding such risks is the result of a computational problem or an imagination cost or an attention cost, rather than a clue to actual preferences—the $50,000 estimate of the value of life that I suggested might be supported by the analysis underlying Figure 3.3 may be much too low.

Even a one in a million risk is not quite the long shot that it seems. For example, a one in a million risk of dying from arsenic in the water supply would translate into an average for the United States as a whole of almost 300 deaths a year. Even if individuals would write down such a risk to zero, to eliminate it at trivial cost might be a worthwhile social investment—something the public would be happy to pay for if it had all the facts.

The $50,000 value of life estimate may be too low for an additional reason: it ignores the fact that future generations can be expected (if doomsday is averted) to have higher incomes than the present one, and if so they will be willing to incur greater costs to avoid risks. The elasticity of the value of life with respect to income has been estimated to lie between .5 and .6,[64] implying that a 1 percent increase in income generates a .5 to .6 percent increase in the value of life—which is to say, in the demand for protection from lethal risks. Adjustment for this factor would tend to offset the effect of discounting to present value,[65] though in the present context not completely; for without discounting, the present value of the benefits of risk-avoidance measures would often approach infinity for the type of catastrophic risk with which this book is concerned.

The figure of 6 billion for the population at risk is undoubtedly too low. It ascribes no value to future humanity, which is as dubious a procedure as weighting the welfare of all future generations equally with that of the current one. Suppose as a crude adjustment we simply double the figure for the current population and, despite the reservations just expressed, multiply it by only $50,000. The resulting estimate of the benefits of averting an extinction event would be $600 trillion. This figure is surely a minimum estimate, and yet a surprisingly common reaction to the prospect of extinction is that if everyone dies at once and without any warning, there is *no* loss. What is true is that there is no *perceived* loss, no "conscious pain and suffering," as the tort lawyers say. And certain losses commonly occasioned by death, such as the grief and pecuniary losses of the decedent's survivors, are avoided. But few people are indifferent between living, on the one hand, and dying suddenly in their sleep, on the other, even if they have no dependents. They ascribe a positive value to continued life even though they know that if they died without warning they would not experience a sense of loss. And most people would be happier if they thought the human race, particularly including their own loved ones, would survive their own death, though some might feel a certain satisfaction in knowing they were the last generation on earth and so would not be missing out on experiences that other people would be having; they would not envy the living because there would be no living.

The greatest peculiarity of the approach that yields the $600 trillion figure by valuing an individual life at only $50,000 is that it implies paradoxical reversals. Suppose the risk of a hypothetical strangelet accident that would kill "only" 100 million people were 1 in 100,000. At such a probability, the implicit value of life derived in the studies noted earlier would be in the millions of dollars, and let us pick the current average figure for the United States of $7 million. Then the total loss from the "minor" strangelet accident would be $700 trillion—$100 trillion *more* than an accident that destroyed the entire human race. But if extinction of the human race as a result of a strangelet disaster were considered a "dreadful" risk and the value of life therefore written up to $28 million, as I suggested might accord with the terrorism survey, then the cost of such an event, even without regard to future generations, would be $336 quadrillion rather than $600 trillion. And at a risk of death greater than about .167 (the risk of death from playing one round of Russian roulette), the value of *one* life would be estimated as being at or near an infinite amount of money.

Given such paradoxes, it is tempting to accept that the value of life estimated at probabilities of death between 1 in 10,000 and 1 in 100,000 is a pretty good estimate for the value at probabilities of 1 in a million or 1 in 10 million (although not for probabilities of 1 in 2 or even 1 in

20). This would jack up the cost associated with catastrophes greatly and by doing so strengthen the argument that we ought to be doing more about them than we are doing. But for my purposes the approach that yields a precipitate drop in the value of life at extremely low probabilities of death has the virtue of being highly conservative, so that if we find (as I shall argue we should) that we are not spending enough on catastrophic-risk prevention even if the cost of the worst catastrophes is as modest as the approach implies, this should be a robust finding. Still, the breadth of the range of defensible estimates of the values of life at stake in catastrophic events is notable and disturbing and indicates an urgent need for further research.

Risk versus uncertainty

We know that people sometimes overreact, from a statistical standpoint, to a slight risk because it is associated with a particularly vivid, attention-seizing event. The 9/11 attacks have been offered as an illustration of this phenomenon.[66] But to describe a reaction to a risk as an overreaction is to assume that the risk is slighter than people thought, and this presupposes an ability to quantify the risk, however crudely. We do not have that ability with respect to terrorist attacks. About all that can be said with any confidence about 9/11 is that if the United States and other nations had done nothing in the wake of the attacks to reduce the probability of a recurrence, the risk of further attacks would probably have been great, although we do not know enough about terrorist plans and mentalities to be certain, let alone to know how great. After we took defensive measures, the risk of further large-scale attacks on the U.S. mainland fell. But no one knows by how much and anyway it would be a mistake to dismiss a risk merely because it cannot be quantified and therefore *may* be small—for it may be great instead. Unfortunately the ability to quantify a risk has no necessary connection to its magnitude. We now know that the risk of a successful terrorist attack on the United States in the summer of 2001 was great, yet the risk could not have been estimated without an amount and quality of data that probably could not have been assembled. To assume that risks can be ignored if they cannot be measured is a head-in-the-sand response.

This point is illuminated by the old distinction between "risk" and "uncertainty," where the former refers to a probability that can be estimated, whether on the basis of observed frequency or of theory, and the latter to a probability that cannot be estimated. Uncertainty in this sense does not, as one might expect, paralyze decision making. We could not function without making decisions in the face of uncertainty. We do that all the time by assigning, usually implicitly, an intuitive probability (what statisticians call a "subjective" probability) to the uncertain event. But it is one thing to act, and another to establish the need to act by conducting fruitful cost-benefit analyses, or using other rational decision-making methods, when the costs or benefits (or both) are uncertain because they are probabilistic and the probabilities are not quantifiable, even approximately. The difficulty is acute in some insurance markets. Insurers determine insurance premiums on the basis of either experience rating, which is to say an estimate of risk based on the frequency of previous losses by the insured or the class of insureds, or exposure risk, which involves estimating risk on the basis of theory or, more commonly, a combination of theory and limited experience (there may be some history of losses, but too thin a one to be statistically significant). If a risk cannot be determined by either method, there is uncertainty in the risk-versus-uncertainty sense; and only a gambler, treating uncertainty as a situation of extreme and unknowable variance in possible outcomes, will write insurance when a risk cannot be estimated. Or the government, as with the Terrorism Risk Insurance Act of 2002,[67] which requires insurance companies to offer coverage of business property and casualty losses due to terrorism but with the federal government picking up most of the tab.[68] The act excludes losses due to nuclear, chemical, or biological attacks, however, so it has limited relevance to the concerns of this book. Insurance companies are permitted to decline to cover such losses, and typically they do. As a result, estimates of the probability of such losses cannot be reliably estimated from insurance premium rates.

The role of uncertainty in cost-benefit analysis of the catastrophic risks is underscored by noting that a *complete* cost-benefit analysis of RHIC would involve (1) determining the cost of building the collider; (2) estimating its operating costs; (3) monetizing the scientific benefits of the experiments to be conducted in it; (4) estimating the cost to the United States and the world should there be a catastrophic accident, (5) estimating the probability of such an accident, (6) discounting the monetary amounts determined in steps (2), (3), and (4) to present value, (7) choosing the discount rate to use in step (6), and, finally, if the analysis yields a net benefit for the collider, (8) comparing that net benefit with the net benefits of alternative projects. Steps (1), (2), and, once the discount rate is selected, (6) are straightforward. But all the other steps in the analysis—monetizing the scientific benefits of the collider, estimating the social costs if a catastrophe occurs, estimating the probability of catastrophe, choosing the appropriate discount rate, and comparing the net benefits (if any) of the project with the net benefits of alternative projects—are profoundly uncertain, though not much turns on the choice of discount rate since the intended life of RHIC is only 10 years. I have mentioned the difficulties in estimating the social benefits of RHIC and the social costs of a strangelet disaster at RHIC. The difficulty of estimating the probability of such a disaster is as acute. There is no history from which to infer a frequency because RHIC is only four years old; there is no precedent for the heavy-ion collisions being performed in it; and scientific understanding of strange quarks has not progressed to the point at which a probability can be attached to a strangelet disaster as a matter of theory, though at least we know that it is not 100 percent over a four-year period and that the high-energy-physics community believes it to be extremely small.

It does not follow from such uncertainties, profound as they are, that cost-benefit analysis of measures for reducing catastrophic risks is hopelessly subjective. Even if point estimates of cost and benefit are infeasible, it may be possible, as we'll see in considering the tolerable-windows variant of conventional cost-benefit analysis, to estimate plausible ranges of costs and benefits, and the ranges may in turn, depending on the particular values picked to bound them, dictate a conclusion that the project is or is not cost justified. And I pointed out earlier that it may be possible to avoid having to monetize the cost of catastrophe (I give further examples in this chapter) and to surmount some of the difficulties involved in picking an appropriate discount rate by translating discount rates into time horizons.

The uncertainties involved in cost-benefit analysis should not be thought identical across all the catastrophic risks. A cost-benefit analysis of a system for detecting and deflecting incoming asteroids would not encounter the profound uncertainties regarding probabilities and benefits that afflict cost-benefit analysis of RHIC, while analysis of RHIC does not raise troublesome problems concerning discounting to present value, because of the project's short expected life. The major uncertainty attending cost-benefit analysis of asteroid collisions may be whether in calculating the social cost of such collisions extra weight should be given to an extinction event. Yet that issue could probably be elided. NASA could publish (1) the full menu of construction and operating costs for both the array of telescopes required for the reliable detection of potentially hazardous near-earth objects and the missiles or spacecraft and other apparatus required for deflection, and (2) the full range of possible collisions, with estimates of the deaths resulting from each and confidence intervals around each estimate. The government and the public would then have the information required for rationally deciding whether the nonmonetized benefits of the statistical lives saved by an asteroid defense were worth the costs of saving them.

The catastrophic risk that presents the most stubborn challenge to cost-benefit analysis is bioterrorism, because the probability of a bioterrorist attack, or rather the schedule of probabilities for the various forms that such an attack might take, cannot be estimated.[69] It is not only that terrorists are secretive as to plans and capabilities, but also that they—or at least the ones that have vague and encompassing aims—have such a wide range of potential means and targets to choose among and, if suicidal, cannot be deterred. Anyone who thinks terrorist attacks predictable should read what the director of the Defense Threat Reduction Agency of the Department of Defense wrote just months before September 2001: "We have, in fact, solved a terrorist problem in the last twenty-five years. We have solved it so successfully that we have forgotten about it; and that is a treat. The problem was aircraft hijacking and bombing. We solved the problem. . . . The system is not perfect, but it is good enough. . . . We have pretty much nailed this thing."[70]

Obviously *science* cannot predict where or when bioterrorists will strike, although it can say something about the likely means that they will employ, given feasibility and cost constraints, and much about the consequences of the various forms that a bioterrorist attack might take. But maybe the military and civilian intelligence services, the diplomatic service, and academic experts on terrorism can, by pooling their knowledge, produce reliable estimates of the probabilities of the various types of possible bioterrorist attack and the estimates can then be married to scientific expertise to produce a schedule of expected costs of bioterrorism and therefore a guide to responsive measures. As far as I am able to determine, however (which is not far, because I don't have any access to classified information), all that experts on terrorism are able to do, and even then only with a large error term, is to rank bioterrorist threats by *relative* likelihood—to say, for example, that a bioterrorist attack on Washington employing anthrax is more likely than an attack on London with smallpox. These rankings, while useful in establishing priorities within a fixed budget, do not enable expected costs to be calculated and thus a cost-benefit analysis to be performed.

Not that one can't find in the public record plenty of *discussions* of the probability of a devastating bioterrorist attack. But these discussions are speculative, polarized, and unquantified. Milton Leitenberg, who is to bioterrorism what S. Fred Singer is to global warming, thinks a bioterrorist attack unlikely unless continued harping on the danger gives terrorists ideas![71] (Which may mean that he is not *really* a skeptic.) Yet even before 9/11 revealed much about the aims and capabilities of international terrorist groups, there were warnings that advances in biotechnology (to which Leitenberg gives little attention) were creating a serious risk of a devastating bioterrorist attack.[72] Comparing Leitenberg's optimistic assessment with Laurie Garrett's earlier, pessimistic one, a defense official has remarked unhelpfully that "the likelihood is that reality lies somewhere in the middle."[73] He offers no evidence that the middle is a likelier place to find the truth than either extreme—or beyond.

There are, however, several possible methods of adjusting cost-benefit analysis to reflect the presence of radical, nonquantifiable uncertainty. They are discussed next.

Coping with uncertainty

Information markets

It's been suggested that "information markets" might be used to elicit information about the likely risks of particular bioterrorist attacks.[74] These are markets in which the "securities" traded are not stocks or other financial instruments, but predictions. The basic idea is a good one— that incentives matter, and therefore that predictions will be more accurate when there is a financial stake in accuracy, and the existence of a financial stake will elicit predictions from the most knowledgeable observers. The theory is fine but its applicability to terrorism is questionable. Terrorists could manipulate the market to generate inaccurate predictions or profit from their terrorism by making accurate ones. People who are not terrorists, moreover, or friends or family of, or sympathizers with, terrorists, are unlikely to have relevant information; and people hostile to terrorism have ample incentives to report any relevant information to the authorities. In addition, should bioterrorist attacks turn out to be infrequent (as we hope), it would be very difficult to verify the accuracy of the predictions; it would be like placing a bet on what the population of New York will be 100 years from now. But this is the least cogent objection to an information market in terrorism, because the pricing of the "securities" is based on probabilities rather than frequencies. Finally, as regards information markets for either natural catastrophes or accidental man-made ones, the man in the street has no useful information, and the information possessed by scientists and other experts gets elicited and shared without need to provide a direct monetary reward for being right.

A more promising approach, it might seem, would be to infer the risk of a bioterrorist attack from the premiums charged for insurance against such attacks. An insurance premium consists of (1) a loading charge to reflect the insurance company's administrative costs, plus (2) an estimate of the size of the loss insured against, should an event covered by the insurance occur, discounted by the probability that the event (in this case a bioterrorist attack) will occur. So the insurance industry's estimate of the probability of an (insured-against) catastrophe should be calculable from the terms of the insurance policy. Unfortunately, it seems that the insurance industry is no more able to estimate the probability of a terrorist attack than anyone else. In the wake of 9/11, insurance companies terminated coverage of losses due to terrorism (for which previously they had charged only nominal premiums), and though they were forced to restore coverage by the Terrorism Risk Insurance Act of 2002, the act, as I noted earlier, heavily subsidizes this insurance and makes it difficult to determine the industry's implicit estimate of the probability and magnitude of future terrorist attacks. Nor can insurance practices yield useful information about the likelihood of extinction events, since the end of the world or the human race is not an insurable loss. The act's exclusion of losses due to nuclear, chemical, or biological attacks suggests the marginality of insurance to the concerns of this book.

Inverse cost-benefit analysis

A helpful approach to cost-benefit analysis under conditions of extreme uncertainty is what I shall call "inverse cost-benefit analysis." Analogous to extracting probability estimates from insurance premiums, it involves dividing what the government is spending to prevent a particular catastrophic risk from materializing by what the social cost of the catastrophe would be if it did materialize. The result is an approximation to the implied probability of the catastrophe. Remember that expected cost is the product of probability and consequence (loss): $C = PL$. If P and L are known, C can be calculated. If instead C and L are known, P can be calculated: if $1 billion ($C$) is being spent to avert a disaster that if it occurs will impose a loss (L) of $100 billion, then $P = C/L = .01$.

If P so calculated diverges sharply from independent estimates of it, this is a clue that society may be spending too much or too little on avoiding L. It is just a clue, because of the distinction between marginal and total costs and benefits. The optimal expenditure on a measure is the expenditure that equates marginal cost to marginal benefit. Suppose we happen to know that P is not .01 but .1, so that the expected cost of the catastrophe is not $1 billion but $10 billion. It doesn't follow that we should be spending $10 billion, or indeed anything more than $1 billion, to avert the catastrophe. Maybe spending just $1 billion would reduce the expected cost of catastrophe from $10 billion all the way down to $500 million and no further expenditure would bring about a further reduction, or at least a cost-justified reduction. For example, if spending another $1 billion would reduce the expected cost from $500 million to zero, that would be a bad investment, at least if risk aversion is ignored. I discuss the implications of the total/marginal distinction below but ignore it for now.

The federal government is spending about $2 billion a year to prevent a bioterrorist attack (the president has requested another $2.5 billion for 2005, however, under the rubric of "Project BioShield"). I say "about $2 billion" because while the $2.6 billion that the president sought from Congress for 2004 for combating "catastrophic threats" covers chemical, nuclear, and radiological threats as well as bioterrorism, the emphasis is on the last.[75] The goal is to protect Americans, so in assessing the benefits of this expenditure I shall ignore casualties in other countries. Suppose the most destructive biological attack that seems reasonably possible on the basis of what little we now know about terrorist intentions and capabilities would kill 100 million Americans. We know that value-of-life estimates may have to be radically discounted when the probability of death is exceedingly slight. But there is no convincing reason for supposing the probability of such an attack less than, say, one in 100,000; and we know (well, think) that the value of life that is derived by dividing the cost that Americans will incur to avoid a risk of death of that magnitude by the risk is about $7 million. Then if the attack occurred, the total costs would be $700 trillion—and that is actually too low an estimate because the death of a third of the population would have all sorts of collateral consequences, mainly negative. Let us, still conservatively however, refigure the total costs as $1 quadrillion. The result of dividing the money being spent to prevent such an attack, $2 billion, by $1 quadrillion is 1/500,000. Is there only a 1 in 500,000 probability of a bioterrorist attack of that magnitude in the next year? One doesn't know, but the figure seems too low.

It doesn't follow that $2 billion a year is too little to be spending to prevent a bioterrorist attack; we mustn't forget the distinction between total and marginal costs. Suppose that the $2 billion expenditure reduces the probability of such an attack from .01 to .0001. The expected cost of the attack would still be very high—$1 quadrillion multiplied by .0001 is $100 billion—but spending more than $2 billion might not reduce the residual probability of .0001 at all. For there might be no feasible further measures to take to combat bioterrorism, especially when we remember that increasing the number of people involved in defending against bioterrorism, including not only scientific and technical personnel but also security guards in laboratories where lethal pathogens are stored, also increases the number of people capable, alone or in conjunction with others, of mounting biological attacks. But there *are* other response measures that should be considered seriously, as we'll see in the next chapter. And one must also bear in mind that expenditures on combating bioterrorism do more than prevent mega-attacks; the lesser attacks, which would still be very costly both singly and cumulatively, would also be prevented.

Costs, moreover, tend to be inverse to time. It would cost a great deal more to build an asteroid defense in one year than in 10 years because of the extra costs that would be required for a hasty reallocation of the required labor and capital from the current projects in which they are employed. And so would other crash efforts to prevent catastrophes. Placing a lid on current expenditures would have the incidental benefit of enabling additional expenditures to be deferred to a time when, because more will be known about both the catastrophic risks and the optimal responses to them, considerable cost savings may be possible. The case for such a ceiling derives from comparing marginal benefits to marginal costs; the latter may be sharply increasing in the short run.

Two further qualifications in evaluating the current response to the threat of bioterrorism require mention. The first concerns the way in which government expenditures are assigned to the different activities involved in combating terrorism. The expenditure category "catastrophic threats" in the federal budget is dominated by expenditures on identifying, detecting, and developing vaccines and cures for lethal pathogens. Expenditures classified elsewhere, however, such as expenditures on intelligence gathering, background checks, and border searches,[76] reduce the likelihood of bioterrorist attacks, though border searches very little because of the difficulty of detecting a lethal pathogen in a person's luggage. We should think of the catastrophic-threats category in the federal budget as addressed to the residual risk of a bioterrorism attack if the "forward" defenses fail (this is another marginal comparison); nevertheless, the estimate of that risk implied by the expenditures in that category still seems too low.

Second, expenditures on preventing bioterrorism are not limited to the federal government. States and cities, notably New York City, are also devoting resources to such prevention;[77] I imagine the aggregate amount is small, but I have not been able to obtain figures.

Current government expenditures on detecting and preventing asteroid collisions also seem too low. NASA spends about $3.9 million a year compiling its catalog of near-earth objects,[78] a preliminary defensive measure. But that is it, although the agency's program of research on "smaller Solar System objects," namely asteroids and comets, while not oriented toward defense against collisions, may yield knowledge that would be useful for such a defense,[79] for remember that knowledge of the composition, density, and other properties of a threatening asteroid are important to determining how best to alter its orbit. Other expenditures, actual and planned, and both private and public, relevant to an asteroid defense swell the total; I'll give examples. But the aggregate amount is small. Tellingly, NASA's annual reports do not contain a section on asteroid defense or near-earth objects. And the current expenditure level is so close to zero that the distinction between total and marginal benefits and costs has little significance.

We know that the expected costs of asteroid collisions are nontrivial though low and that methods of detection, mitigation, and (probably) deflection are feasible and are unlikely to break the bank. The report of the Near-Earth Object Science Definition Team, commissioned by NASA, which I cited in chapter 1, recommended a system of detection of all near-earth objects at least 140 meters in diameter that it estimated would cost $300 million to construct. Both the risks of asteroid collisions and the possible methods for detecting and intercepting asteroids that are on a collision course with the earth have been known for some time,[80] so the budget allocated to asteroid defense has had time to adjust, but hasn't done so. Granted, if the only asteroid collision we care about is one that would destroy the entire human race, $3.9 million a year may be enough, or even more than enough, to spend on defense against it, weird as this conclusion may seem. Dividing the cost of prevention by the cost of such a catastrophe to derive the implicit probability that the catastrophe will occur yields an estimated annual probability of 1.70 in 100 million ($10 million divided by $600 trillion is .0000000166), which is roughly equal to the mean estimate presented in chapter 1. That estimate was 1 in 75 million, which equates to 1.33 in 100 million.

But this calculation is based on a value of life of only $50,000 (the estimate that yields the $600-trillion loss figure). We recall that the UK task force estimated the annual probability of an asteroid collision that would kill 1.5 billion people as 1 in 250,000; and in that probability range the value of life is probably in the millions of dollars, although this has to be a guess, since the lowest probability in the value-of-life studies is a shade less than 1 in 100,000. Assume the value of life in the case of a 1 in 250,000 probability of death is $2 million. Then the expected annual cost of a collision that would kill 1.5 billion people would be $12 billion ($2 million × 1.5 billion [= $3 quadrillion] × .000004), which is many times greater than the U.S. government's annual spending on asteroid defense. More to the point, since most of the 1.5 billion victims would not be Americans, the *world's* annual spending on asteroid defense—which is probably only very slightly greatly than $3.9 million because no other country has gone beyond the talking stage so far as an asteroid defense is concerned—is too low. And this is ignoring the expected cost of a megacatastrophe that would be caused by a collision with an asteroid the size of the one that ended the reign of the dinosaurs.

Another approach to monetizing the asteroid threat builds on John Lewis's estimate (see chapter 1) that the expected annual number of deaths from asteroid collisions is 1,479. This we recall is a minimum estimate, which excludes the risk from the biggest asteroids. The probabilities that generate this modest estimate are higher than if deaths in the biggest possible asteroid collisions are included, but they are still low, and let me continue to use the ultraconservative estimate of $50,000 for the value of life in ultra-low-probability settings. This yields an annual expected cost of only $74 million, but this still is much more than NASA is spending. For a comparable annual expenditure, the system of detection proposed by the Near-Earth Object Science Definition Team could be built in a few years, followed by a system for intercepting asteroids found likely to collide with the earth.

I should mention here a proposal to build a Large-aperture Synoptic Survey Telescope (LSST). This $150 million instrument "could locate 90 percent of all near-earth objects down to 300 m in size, enable computation of their orbits, and permit assessment of their threat to Earth," while at the same time greatly increasing our knowledge of remote galaxies.[81] The telescope would not be a complete substitute for the telescopic array recommended by the NASA task force, even if the 10 percent of asteroids that would escape detection altogether are ignored. The LSST would spot an asteroid only when the asteroid crossed the section of sky swept by the telescope; the asteroid would not be monitored continuously even though its orbit might change after the initial observation. But the LSST would be a great start. Yet NASA refuses to fund it, so funding is being sought from the National Science Foundation and private sources. Lamentably, from the point of view of the concerns that animate this book, astronomers are much more interested in remote galaxies, study of which adds to knowledge of the origin, size, age, future, and composition of the universe than in local orbiting rocks. And so the extent to which the LSST, if it is built, will actually be used for the detection and evaluation of potentially dangerous asteroids is uncertain.

The federal government's science and technology budget allocates about $1.7 billion a year to climate-change research, including research on clean fuels and carbon sequestration as well as on improving predictions of global warming.[82] If the warming is moderate, the costs to the United States are likely to be modest, and $1.7 billion a year might actually be too much to spend on counteracting it. However, we know that abrupt, catastrophic global warming is a possibility and let me assume that if it occurred it would bring about a permanent reduction of one-fifth of GDP, which is currently $10 trillion. Because the $2 trillion a year loss is assumed to be permanent, the present value of the loss caused by such a disaster, at a 3 percent discount rate, is slightly more than $66.6 trillion. The annual probability of a global-warming disaster of the assumed magnitude (I ignore the complication introduced by the fact that it would probably take a decade for the disaster to unfold) cannot be estimated. Yet the probability cannot be assumed to be utterly trivial, so it is at least plausible that a level of carbon dioxide emissions taxes that induced a considerably although not astronomically

Table 3.2. Implied Annual Catastrophe Probabilities

Catastrophe	C	L	P (implied)
Bioterrorist attack (100 mill. deaths)	$2 billion	$1 quadrillion (U.S.)	.000002 (1 in 500,000)
Asteroid collision (1.5 bill. deaths)	$3.9 million	$3 quadrillion	.0000000013 (1 in 769 million)
Strangelet disaster	$0	$600 trillion	0
Catastrophic global warming	$1.7 billion	$66.6 trillion (U.S.)	.00000255 (1 in 388,000)

greater investment (largely private) than at present on averting such a disaster would be cost justified.

Table 3.2 summarizes the probabilities of catastrophe implied by current government expenditures to avert the four catastrophic risks that I have been discussing.

The distinction between total and marginal effects is only one qualification that must be borne in mind when reading this table. Notice that the table estimates the costs to the entire human race in the case of asteroid and strangelet disasters, but only the costs to the United States in the case of bioterrorism and catastrophic global warming. The reason is that no other nation is devoting significant resources to trying to prevent the first pair of disasters, while other nations are devoting significant resources to preventing the second pair; as I do not know the amount of those resources, I cannot assess the adequacy of the total expenditures worldwide. Moreover, even if the only costs of an asteroid or strangelet disaster that should be considered in determining how much the United States should spend to prevent such a disaster are costs to the United States, scaling down the cost figures in Table 3.2 accordingly would still indicate that we are spending too little. Dollar-weighted, the United States is about one-fourth of the world; remember that value-of-life estimates are increasing in per capita income, though the elasticity is less than one. And notice that $0 may overestimate the amount that we are spending to avoid a strangelet disaster, as it is uncertain whether the net social benefits of RHIC are positive even if safety considerations are ignored.

In fairness we should recognize that the concept of the economy of attention introduced in chapter 2 implies that it will sometimes be sensible to disregard low-priority projects entirely. This means that the function of threat assessment, in regard to catastrophic risks as well as to more familiar threats, is not only to rank threats by their expected cost but also to fix a cutoff point below which threats will be disregarded because they would require attention disproportionate to the social benefits that attention to them would confer. Time diverted to thinking about very-low-probability threats is unavailable for thinking about other threats unless the aggregate amount of attention to threats is increased, and that would require diverting intellectual effort from other activities. The Office of Science and Technology Policy in the executive office of the president has a staff of only 50, which for political, budgetary, and personnel reasons may be difficult to expand in the short run. If so, the office may be making a rational choice to devote no attention to the strangelet threat or the asteroid threat, on the ground either that threats of lesser catastrophes deserve more attention because their expected costs are greater or because they are more amenable to evaluation and response, or that other scientific projects altogether deserve more attention. The government cannot spend all its time conducting cost-benefit analyses of remote risks. Stated another way, the costs of responding to risks of disaster include the cost of assessing the risk and formulating the response—the cost, in short of conducting cost-benefit analyses—and may be considerable when opportunity cost (the forgone value of alternative uses of the time and other resources devoted to cost-benefit analysis) is included, as it should be, in the costs of such analysis.

But it is unlikely that ignoring the risk of a strangelet disaster or of an asteroid collision can be justified on this ground. Not only are these nonnegligible risks of huge catastrophes, but the costs of responding to them, even as expanded to take in the opportunity cost just mentioned, are moderate and, indeed, in the case of the strangelet risk, perhaps negative.

A final qualification is that the estimates of the expenditures required for an effective asteroid defense and for arresting global warming are too low. In the first case, they ignore other government programs, including other NASA programs for studying asteroids, that contribute at least indirectly to defense against the risk, and in both cases they ignore nongovernmental expenditures. The LSST, if it is built, will be financed in part by private universities; and many near-earth asteroids have been discovered by Lincoln Labs' LINEAR (Lincoln Near-Earth Asteroid Research) program, using two telescopes, although it does receive federal funding, some of it from NASA.[83] The federal government finances only about half the basic research conducted in this country, and some of the other half, which is financed by universities and private companies out of their own pockets, contributes to defending against catastrophes. In addition, some companies are voluntarily reducing their carbon dioxide emissions.[84] And investments in energy efficiency designed merely to reduce the cost of energy may reduce those emissions as a byproduct.

The tolerable-windows approach

Another way in which cost-benefit analysis can be used fruitfully even when there is great uncertainty about one or more of the components of the analysis is illustrated in Figure 3.4.

The marginal benefits and marginal costs of measures to reduce or eliminate a catastrophic risk are shown as functions of the quantity of precautions taken, with the optimal level of precautions (q^*) given by the intersection of the two functions. Suppose the optimum cannot be determined because of uncertainty about costs, benefits, the discount rate, or probabilities. We may nevertheless know enough about the benefits and costs to be able to create the "window" formed by the two vertical lines.[85] At the left side of the window frame the benefits of a further effort to eliminate or prevent the catastrophe in question comfortably exceed the costs, while at the right side the reverse is true. If we stay within the window, although we won't know whether our measures are optimal we'll at least have some basis for confidence that they are neither grossly inadequate nor grossly excessive. A particularly clear application is to the current funding of asteroid defense: it is likely that we are well to the left of the left side of the window.

Here is another example. The benefits of preserving the existing amount of genetic diversity cannot be quantified. But the cost of preserving samples of animals and plants, whether entire species or varieties within a species (such as different breeds of the same animal species), that are on the verge of extinction is probably small enough to put us to the left of the left side of the window. Indeed, since these samples can be preserved at low cost in the form of frozen seeds that can be resuscitated and made to germinate, large-scale efforts to preserve biodiversity by tightly limiting human land uses may not be cost justified. We cannot be sure because, as we know from chapter 1, there is no census of species and many of them have very small populations and those often in out-of-the-way places (such as ocean bottoms)— and these are the very species most at risk of extinction. It would be

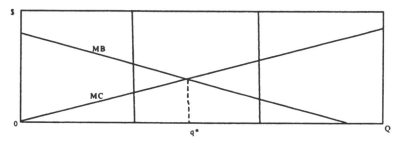

Figure 3.4. The "Tolerable Windows" Approach

infeasible to obtain and preserve specimens of all of them. Nevertheless, at least modest efforts to preserve specimens of species, or varieties, on the verge of extinction seem clearly worthwhile, and so that
is the place to start.

The place not to start in devising economically sensible solutions to
the problem of loss of biodiversity is illustrated by the Endangered
Species Act (see chapter 1) as it stood before being amended in 1978.
The original act did not permit the government to use cost-benefit
analysis to determine which species to list—any species known to be
endangered had to be listed—or how much to spend, or require private landowners to spend, to preserve the species. The 1978 amendment, passed in reaction to the notorious snail-darter case, required the
federal Fish and Wildlife Service, which administers the Endangered
Species Act, to consider the economic impact of a listing, and this
mandate has recently been interpreted to require cost-benefit analysis.[86] Because the annual costs of compliance with the act are probably in the hundreds of millions of dollars and it could cost billions to
save a fragile species picky about its habitat,[87] the trend toward subjecting proposed listings to cost-benefit analysis is probably a good
thing, though the estimation of benefits, which thus far has been based
largely on contingent-valuation surveys, has rightly been subjected to
sharp criticism.[88] Yet even if the benefits cannot be quantified, it is
surely valuable to policy makers and the public to know what the costs
are—they may be so great, in a particular case, as to compel an inference that we are to the right of the right side of the window.

A possible application of the tolerable-windows approach would be
a decision to postpone RHIC–II by five years. Since we don't know the
benefits and costs of such a project but do know that there is some,
though probably a very slight, risk of disaster that cannot be quanti-

How to evaluate the catastrophic risks and the possible responses to them

fied, there should be no felt urgency about starting the project "on time." If it is delayed, we shall gain an added margin of safety because additional years of fundamental physical research may improve the ability of physicists to estimate the risk of a strangelet disaster. Similarly, we might decide that nanotechnology, though an immensely promising technology and moreover one that may help us avert catastrophes such as abrupt global warming, should be subjected to some kind of safety regulation if this can be done without increasing its cost more than minimally. But of course such measures, if adopted by the United States unilaterally, will not succeed to the extent that they merely induce the dangerous research to gravitate to other countries.

Risk-risk assessment, and demonetizing death

A more familiar simplification of cost-benefit analysis than the tolerable-windows approach is risk-risk assessment, whereby the risks to life or health of alternative responses to some danger (including the alternative of doing nothing) are compared but no effort is made either to monetize them or to bring other costs and benefits into the analysis.[89] This approach can work well in simple cases—for example when a measure to prevent a 1 percent risk of death in an automobile accident would create a 2 percent risk of death in such an accident. It is also relevant to the dual-use dilemma that is created by efforts to prevent bioterrorism: measures that impede access to lethal pathogens may slow research into the development of effective medical responses to natural epidemics.[90]

But the utility of the method is greatly limited, because it leaves out considerations that may be critical to a responsible decision—namely other costs and benefits. For example, advances in medicine that reduce mortality may increase the rate of population growth, thereby contributing indirectly but not necessarily trivially to global warming, the costs of which cannot be reduced to lives lost, although abrupt global warming could cause a catastrophic loss of life. Population growth, as I pointed out in chapter 1, creates other negative externalities as well. They may or may not exceed the positive externalities; but the uncritical belief, which is standard in risk-risk assessment,[91] that "saving lives" is always on balance a good thing is an obstacle to responding intelligently to the catastrophic risks.

Despite the shortcomings of risk-risk assessment, it is a useful reminder that cost-benefit analysis can sometimes be simplified by leaving certain costs or benefits in nonmonetized form. A candidate for this approach is the benefits of avoiding minute risks of huge numbers of human deaths. Congress, or the public, could be told: there is one chance in 10 million of a world-destroying accelerator accident next year that could be avoided by closing down RHIC at a cost in benefits forgone estimated at $2.1 billion (the figure I used earlier in this chapter); decide whether you think the cost excessive. People can think about that trade-off as clearly as they could if the lifesaving benefits of closing down were monetized—maybe more clearly, since most of our decisions are based on trade-offs that are not completely monetized. For example, a person who is trying to decide whether to pay $100,000 for a new Mercedes-Benz is, if rational, making an implicit cost-benefit analysis. But he is not comparing two money prices. He is comparing the money price with the nonmonetized utility of owning the Mercedes. More precisely, he is comparing the nonmonetized utility of the various uses to which he could put the $100,000.

The point is that baffling questions can sometimes be made less baffling simply by being reframed.[92] But in this instance perhaps only slightly less baffling. One chance in 10 million is the kind of statistic that people have great difficulty ascribing real meaning to, though that doesn't prevent them from playing the lottery—or worrying about being killed in a plane crash, the odds of which happening, if it's a regularly scheduled U.S. airline, are not much shorter than 10 million to 1. (Admittedly that is a per-flight probability; the annual probability depends on how frequently one flies.) Further complicating my proposal regarding RHIC are the profound uncertainties associated with both the 1 in 10 million probability estimate and the $2.1 billion benefits estimate.

Politics, expertise, and neutrality: RHIC revisited

It may be objected that cost-benefit analysis is a waste of time because politicians are not welfare maximizers. They are not. But cost-benefit analyses can influence public policy even in a political system guided by self-interested politicians responsive to interest groups.[93] An interest group will not press for a project that does not confer net benefits on it. The greater the excess of benefits over costs, the likelier are the beneficiaries to be able to overcome the free-rider impediment to the formation of an effective interest group. The greater the excess of costs over benefits, the likelier are opponents to be able to organize effective resistance. So information about costs and benefits can influence political outcomes even if no political faction is committed to adopting only those policies that can pass a cost-benefit test.

National defense is a good example of a government program that exists because of a very great preponderance of benefits over costs, great as those costs, and uncertain as the benefits, are, rather than because national defense confers economic rents on some narrow interest group, though some people still believe that defense expenditures are the result of machinations by the "merchants of death." National defense is not only a good example, but a pertinent one. Measures for defending against catastrophic risks reflect concerns similar to those that motivate the nation's heavy military expenditures.

But we know from chapter 2 that there are all sorts of obstacles— political, psychological, economic, and cultural—to responding rationally to the catastrophic risks. And the problem seems general. Students of regulation have been sharply critical of the gross and seemingly irrational differences in the estimates of the value of life that are implicit in government regulation of different risks.[94] The range is from $100,000 for death in accidents involving unvented space heaters to $92 billion for death from the herbicides atrazine or alachlor in drinking water.[95] (These figures are derived as usual by dividing the cost of preventing the death by the probability that death would occur if the cost were not incurred.) Suppose NASA's asteroid-defense budget of $3.9 million a year is perfectly attuned to the public's valuation of lives lost in asteroid collisions and that John Lewis's estimate that the expected number of lives lost in such collisions is 1,479 deaths per year is correct. That is a global figure, and the U.S. population is only about 5 percent of the total world population, so let us reduce his number to 74. The implication is that NASA is valuing each of these lives at $52,700 ($3.9 million ÷ 74). This is not only considerably lower than the $7 million mean estimate in the scholarly literature, but little more than half the value of a life imperiled by an unvented space heater.

The differences among the value-of-life estimates probably can be explained by information costs; by psychological factors such as probability neglect, the availability heuristic, and the "dread" factor (notably absent in death by unvented space heater); by political factors; and by the asymptotic relation between risk and the value of life—notice that the $52,700 figure is close to what I earlier suggested might be defensible in the case of extremely improbable catastrophes that if they occurred might spell the end of the human race. The differences among the estimate may also be somewhat exaggerated by the critics.[96] Nevertheless, the criticism that government does not use consistent criteria to determine responses to risk has great force. And as Table 3.2 and the accompanying discussion suggested, the criticism applies as forcefully to the regulation of catastrophic risks as to the lesser risks on which the critics have focused. It underscores the importance of having cost-benefit analyses of responses to catastrophic risks conducted by neutrals, who do not have financial, political, or psychological stakes in how the analyses come out.

Consider the RHIC risk assessment that I first mentioned in chapter 1. The authors of the commissioned assessment[97] (not a cost-benefit or even risk-risk analysis, but merely an assessment of the risk of a planet- or universe-destroying accident) were selected by the director of the Brookhaven National Laboratory. Three of the four not only are experimental particle physicists who therefore have a career stake in increasing the power of particle accelerators; they were also planning to conduct experiments at RHIC—and are now doing so.[98] The fourth, the theoretician, was and is deeply interested in the results of the experiments.[99] Of course the risk assessment had to be carried out by physicists knowledgeable about particle accelerators, and of course no sane person would knowingly conceal the risk of destroying the world merely in order to indulge his scientific curiosity or enhance his career. What is more, Robert Jaffe, the leader of the assessment team, was one of the first scientists to draw attention to the potentially "apocalyptic" (his word) consequences of strangelets.[100] But career concerns can influence judgment in areas of scientific uncertainty, and scientists, like other people, can be overconfident. Should a strangelet disaster occur, moreover, only a minute fraction of the costs would be borne by the scientists who caused it. If it does not occur and RHIC proves to be a scientific success story, the physicists who conduct research at RHIC will appropriate the lion's share of the benefits (unless there are immediate commercial applications, which is not anticipated) in the form of prestige, career advancement, and personal satisfaction. Compare the reluctance of health-care workers to be vaccinated against smallpox because the vaccine sometimes produces serious side effects.[101] Should there be a smallpox pandemic, health-care workers would bear only a small fraction of the costs; it is that fraction, rather than the total, that motivates their decision on how much cost to bear to avert the pandemic.

The physicist Francesco Calogero has suggested that Brookhaven should have

> engage[d] two groups of competent experts, a "blue team" trying to make an "objective" assessment, and a "red team" (acting as devil's advocates) specifically charged with making a genuine effort at proving that the experiments are indeed dangerous—an effort that, if successful, might then be challenged by the blue team. . . . A debate might ensue, which, if conducted in a genuinely scientific spirit, would be quite enlightening for those who eventually had the responsibility of making a decision.[102]

Calogero was thus envisioning an adversary procedure similar to the clash of party-designated expert witnesses in a trial.

Confirming the possibly deforming effect of career concerns on objective evaluation, the physicist Adrian Kent points out a surprising blunder in one of the RHIC risk assessments (not the Jaffe team's): the statement that even under the most pessimistic assumption it would be safe to run experiments on RHIC for 5 million years.[103] What the authors meant was that the annual probability of disaster was only (at most) 1 in 5 million, not that if the probability materialized it would do so at the end of the period. In fact it would be far more likely to occur in year 1 than in year 5 million, because the probability that the earth would survive 5 million years in each of which there was a 1 in 5 million probability of its being destroyed is only 37 percent.[104]

The authors may have meant something different, though this is not clear. They may have meant that there is a .9999998 (that is, $1 - 1/5,000,000$) chance that the probability of a disaster in the first and every succeeding year of RHIC's operation (assumed to be planned for 5 million years rather than for the actual 10 years) is zero and a 1 in 5 million chance that it is one. This would equate to a 1 in 5 million probability of disaster next year (because $.9999998 \times 0 + .0000002 \times 1 = .0000002$), but also to a 1 in 5 million chance of the disaster's occurring at any time during the 5-million-year period, since the probability that there would be no disaster during the period would be .9999998.

Kent is also properly critical of the fact that having decided that the risk of disaster was negligible, the assessors did not bother to estimate its expected costs. He points out that even if the annual probability of a world-destroying catastrophe were only one in a billion, that would still imply an annual expected death toll (calculated by multiplying the number of persons who would be killed in such a catastrophe by the probability of the catastrophe's occurring) of six persons per year—and this is ignoring completely the effect of such a catastrophe in eliminating unborn future generations. An experiment expected to kill six persons a year would be unlikely to be undertaken unless the benefits were deemed substantial. But as we know, no effort to assess them was made, even though RHIC is a very costly undertaking quite apart from safety concerns.

Kent may have erred on the other side, however, by implicitly assuming that the proper value of life to use in a cost-benefit analysis of minute risks is great. I say "implicitly" because he used no dollar figures but assumed that if RHIC would cause 120 deaths in its planned life of 10 years it would be shut down.[105] Whether that is a large number or a small one in expected-value terms depends on the size of the population at risk. Twelve deaths a year in a world population of 6 billion translates into so slight an annual probability of death to any given person that, as we know from our earlier discussion, the dollar figure to use in valuing the risk may be very small. Were the $50,000 minimum estimate of the cost of a human death brought about by exceedingly unlikely catastrophes, such as an extinction-producing asteroid collision or lab accident, accepted and then multiplied by 120, the expected cost of the catastrophic risk created by RHIC over its entire 10-year planned life would be only $6 million. But we know that $50,000 may be way too low; multiply it by 10 or 100 and an expected death toll of 120 persons might become a decisive argument for shutting RHIC down.

Kent included in his risk assessment the threat to extremely remote future generations from an extinction event, without any discounting. He calculated that, barring disaster, the total number of human beings inhabiting the earth (not at one time, of course) between now and when the sun expands into the earth's orbit may reach 10^{17} (100 quadrillion).[106] But he cannot prove—no one can—that we should worry about the survival of the human race over such a long span of time. Notice that if we do worry about it, not only does the cost of a strangelet disaster if it occurs soar, but the probability of the disaster, assuming that equally dangerous accelerators succeed RHIC for the indefinite future, rises. Even if the annual risk of a strangelet disaster is only one in a billion, the probability that such a disaster will occur in the course of the next billion years is 63 percent—though long before that time is up science may have learned how to avert such a disaster, and so the probability estimate may be far too high.

Risk assessment is a seriously incomplete guide to decision making. Among the things it leaves out are the social benefits of dangerous technologies. Particle physics, continued progress in which depends heavily on experiments conducted in particle accelerators, has had a number of important practical applications, and by increasing our knowledge of fundamental physical forces it may enable us to head off the very laboratory accidents that could have catastrophic consequences. But by the same token the costs of particle accelerators that are unrelated to safety belong on the cost side of the cost-benefit analysis. The few particle accelerators used for fundamental research are expensive to build, maintain, and operate, relative to other scientific research facilities. The $750 million that the Department of Energy spends each year on the support of high-energy particle physics may be a legacy of the enormous prestige that accrued to nuclear physics from the success of the Manhattan Project. As we saw earlier in this chapter, it is uncertain not only whether RHIC would pass a cost-benefit test if all relevant costs and benefits were factored in, but also whether particle-accelerator research should be financed out of tax dollars at all. It seems anomalous that the government should spend virtually nothing to protect the nation from an asteroid collision while spending hundreds of millions of dollars every year to finance research that may be catastrophically risky yet seems to have no compelling claim to be financed by government rather than left to the private sector.

Even the technical analysis by the RHIC risk assessors may have been flawed. As a matter of theory, as the assessors pointed out,[107] strange quarks are expected to decay very rapidly and so would be unlikely to clump—though the creation of strangelets was one of the experimental results that it was hoped RHIC would yield.[108] Strange quarks are also expected to have a positive charge, in which event, even if they did clump, they would repel rather than attract any atomic nuclei in their vicinity, since nuclei have a positive charge.[109] If either expectation is correct, a contagion effect and resulting strangelet disaster would not occur. But not enough is known about strange quarks to exclude completely the possibility that some of them might have a negative charge and form a strangelet large enough (though it would still be smaller than an atom) and stable enough to convert atomic nuclei in its vicinity into a rapidly expanding and eventually all-devouring strangelet.[110]

Because of the theoretical uncertainties, the assessors added an empirical dimension to their analysis. They particularly emphasized the fact that the moon has existed for 4.5 billion years even though it has been continuously bombarded by cosmic rays that strike its surface, hitting heavy nuclei, such as iron nuclei, with much greater energy than the collisions in RHIC.[111] The magnets and other devices used to accelerate particles and ions in particle accelerators cannot achieve the force that propels cosmic rays despite the enormous mass of such rays at the speed they achieve. Yet the moon has not been converted to strange matter. (Because cosmic rays that hit the earth are slowed by the earth's atmosphere, the assessors thought the moon's survival for billions of years more significant than the earth's survival for an even longer period.)

The evidence is not conclusive. "A strangelet hypothetically produced in the collision would move with high speed relative to the lunar matter and would thus have a high chance of breaking up before coming to rest (to initiate the catastrophic scenario)," whereas a strangelet produced by a head-on collision in an accelerator would be almost at rest.[112] A crude analogy is to the difference between an accident in which one car hits another that is standing still and an accident in which two cars of the same weight traveling at the same speed collide head on. In the second accident both cars will stop when they collide, while the moving car in the first accident will shove the standing car forward; similarly, a cosmic ray hitting a fixed target such as the moon will tend to scatter the nuclei that it hits, making it less likely that they will clump than if the collision were head on.

The controversy over RHIC led the director-general of CERN (the European center for nuclear research, in Geneva) to commission a similar study by distinguished European physicists of the Large Hadron Collider that CERN plans to begin operating in 2007 and that will accelerate heavy ions at even greater energies than RHIC.[113] This brief, lucid study is reassuring, though not entirely so. The study acknowledges that "no estimates [presented in it] are absolutely assumption-free" and that "no first-principles theory of strange quark matter or strangelets exists at the moment."[114] But besides noting the unlikelihood as a matter of theory that strange quarks would clump or if they did that the clump would have a negative charge, the study makes the further theoretical point, based on a paper by one of the study's authors,[115] that a strangelet would not grow indefinitely because when it reached a size well short of disaster proportions its negative charge would turn neutral or positive.[116] For as the strangelet expanded, the strange quarks, because of their density, would sink beneath the surface, which would thus come to be dominated by the positively charged nuclei that the negatively charged strangelet had attracted; and so the strangelet would cease attracting nuclei and therefore stop growing.

This is a theoretical claim because no strangelets have been observed, and it is inconclusive because of the absence of "first-principles theory of strange quark matter or strangelets" of which the authors spoke. But the LHC study bolsters its theoretical analysis with empirical evidence of several sorts. Two in particular are emphasized. One is that in RHIC's four years of operation, no strangelets have been detected.[117] This suggests that not only are strangelets unlikely to grow to disaster proportions, but they are unlikely to be created in the first place even in high-luminosity accelerators. The second type of evidence, which had figured in the RHIC risk assessments as well,[118] involves collisions of cosmic rays with each other rather than with the moon. Some cosmic rays consist not of individual particles (protons or muons, for example), but of iron nuclei, which, as I said, are heavy. The authors of the study believe that should such cosmic rays collide and form strangelets, the strangelets "will be eventually swept up in star formation and lead to the subsequent destruction of the star as it is converted into strange matter. This would be detectable as a supernova-like event,"[119] and supernovas are very rare. It was on the basis of the incidence of supernovas that Dar and his colleagues produced the upper-bound estimate for a strangelet disaster at RHIC of 1 in 500 million per year, to which I referred earlier.

Neither point is conclusive. It is true that before RHIC began operating, one didn't even know that it could go full blast for four years without precipitating a strangelet disaster. Now we know it can; and a subjective estimate, based purely on theory, is always subject to being modified by experience. To give an extreme example, one might predict that the probability that an innocuous-seeming object was a land mine that would explode when one stepped on it was 1 in 1,000. But if one then stepped on it once and it did not explode, one would no longer think that the risk of explosion if it were stepped on again would be 1 in 1,000; the risk would be reestimated downward, perhaps radically, because stepping on the object was in the nature of an experiment and yielded highly relevant information. But the situation with respect to RHIC is different. The fact that the first particle collision in RHIC, or the first four years of collisions, did not result in a strangelet disaster did not falsify the very low probabilities that the concerned scientists had assigned to such an event. If an aircraft engine were predicted to fail in only 1 out of 50,000 flight miles, the fact that the engine had run smoothly for the first 1,000 miles of flight would not require a reassessment of the odds that had been assigned beforehand.

The second piece of evidence against the possibility of a strangelet disaster is no more conclusive. Apart from and probably more important than the fact that iron nuclei are not as heavy as gold ones (iron has 56 protons and neutrons, gold 197), the authors of the LHC study acknowledge that the cosmic-ray evidence is not conclusive because the strangelet created by such a collision might decay in less "than the time it takes for it to be swept up into a protostellar nebula."[120] They are therefore able to offer no stronger conclusion than that "under plausible assumptions the cosmic-ray data exclude the possibility of dangerous processes in heavy-ion colliders like RHIC or the LHC."[121]

The difficulty facing the authors of both the RHIC and LHC risk assessments was twofold. First, it is almost impossible to prove—*really* prove—a negative. Second, the theory and evidence on which such studies rely cannot be made fully intelligible to a nonphysicist. Therefore, because of the apocalyptic consequences of a mistake, the studies leave an outsider with a slight, but uneliminable, residual disquiet.

Some might argue that because even Martin Rees thinks the likelihood of a strangelet catastrophe less than that of an asteroid collision that would also extinguish the human race,[122] we shouldn't worry about strangelets. That would be a poor argument, however, because the risks are, roughly, additive. In the formula $(1 - p)^n$, when p is very small the difference between $(1 - p)^n$ and $(1 - np)$ is also very small (notice how if p goes to zero, both expressions equal 1) unless n is immense (provided p is greater than zero, however slightly). Suppose that instead of being small, p were .33 and the question were the probability of surviving three disasters of that probability. If the probabilities of the events were additive, the survival probability would be only 1 percent. But when the formula is applied, the survival probability soars: $(1 - .33)^3 = .3$. It would soar much higher if p were small. (As in my other examples, independent probabilities are assumed.)

If (to use unrealistically large numbers for clarity) the risk next year of an asteroid collision that destroys the human race is .0001 and of a strangelet catastrophe .00005, the probability that there will be no asteroid collision is .9999 but the probability that there will be neither an asteroid collision nor a strangelet catastrophe—the probability computed by multiplying $1 - .0001$ by $1 - .00005$—is .99985005. The difference between these probabilities is only infinitesimally smaller than the probability of the strangelet catastrophe (.00004995 versus .00005). (The difference would be even smaller if realistically smaller probabilities of these disasters were used.) If a catastrophe having a probability of .00005 is worth preventing, so is one that is one ten-thousandth of that probability. The fact that prevention would be wasted if an asteroid of dinosaur-slaying dimensions hit first is a weak argument against prevention because the probability of such a hit is so small.

What is most remarkable about the handling of the RHIC controversy in this age of regulation—many believe, of overregulation—is that there is no regulatory review of the safety of Brookhaven's accelerator experiments. This may be because it is a government facility. Whatever the reason, although Brookhaven's staff makes safety assessments and issues safety directives, they are concerned with such things as fire and radiation hazards and ignore catastrophic risks. The RHIC risk assessment was ad hoc and informal rather than being a stage in a systematic safety evaluation.

And here is a good place to remind the reader that the catastrophic risks posed by current technology are only part of the catastrophic-risk problem. We shall almost certainly survive another six years of RHIC, and the Large Hadron Collider as well, but what is next? Many scientists are unsure about the future direction of such research.[123] And remember RHIC–II, which Brookhaven hopes to begin operating in 2010 and which will have 40 times the luminosity of RHIC. One hopes that before a decision is made on the funding request, the proposed upgrade will be subjected to a careful cost-benefit analysis by neutral experts. At this writing, there is no indication that it will be.

Summary

L et me try to summarize this rather complex chapter by offering my "bottom line" (necessarily tentative) on whether the catastrophic risks are really worth attending to by American and world policy makers or should be left to the science-fiction writers. Cost-benefit analysis is invaluable in cutting through the psychological and political fogs that surround and obscure the terrifying possibilities that I canvassed in the first chapter, but there are a host of obstacles to applying the conventional techniques of cost-benefit analysis to the catastrophic risks. The present chapter has been an inquiry into what can be done to overcome the obstacles. Enough, I think, to allow me to say, with some approach to objectivity, that the probable costs of the catastrophic risks, when compared with the probable costs of efforts to minimize them, indicate that we are not doing enough. The most dramatic example is the risk of a strangelet disaster. Although that risk is probably low enough to make the expected cost of such a disaster smaller than that of the other catastrophic risks, the costs of reducing the risk, for instance by terminating experiments in RHIC involving heavy-ion collisions or delaying the opening of the LHC or RHIC–II by a few years, may well be negative. If so, the risk, however small, simply is not worth running.

It is equally clear, I think, that greater investment in the detection and prevention of asteroid collisions would be cost justified. For we know a great deal not only about the costs, which seem modest, but also about the benefits, which seem great. The benefits are the costs of the collisions that defensive measures would prevent, discounted by the probabilities—which we know, at least within a range—that collisions of specified destructive force will occur unless defensive measures are taken.

The case for doing more than we are doing to arrest global warming—at present our total effort consists of an annual investment of some $2 billion, in research—is also compelling, once the focus is placed on abrupt global warming. (If the only risk were gradual global warming, the case for taking preventive action now would be greatly weakened.) We do not know what the risk is, but we know that it exists, that it is growing, that it can be checked by means of a system of emissions taxes (plus modest subsidies for research on climate science and carbon-sequestration techniques) less ambitious that envisaged by the drafters of the Kyoto Protocol, and that the system would have the collateral advantage, which would reduce its net cost, of being an efficient method of revenue raising until such time as its technology-forcing effects brought about a dramatic decline in emissions of greenhouse gases.

When we turn to the risks of catastrophic bioterrorism and catastrophic loss of biodiversity (which are related to each other), we encounter baffling questions about probability in the case of the former and about magnitude in the case of the latter. We cannot assess the probability of terrorist attacks, and we cannot either measure the effect of human activities on genetic diversity or assess the impact on human welfare of losses (within a very broad range) of such diversity.

Because a biological attack could be an extinction event or close to it, and because such an attack is, or will soon be, feasible, it behooves us to give serious consideration to increasing our efforts at prevention. We must be wary of throwing money at the problem, or in other words of neglecting the difference between total and marginal costs. But we shall see in the next chapter that additional measures may well be warranted, although their costs, which have mainly to do with a possible loss of civil liberties, are very difficult to assess. In the case of biodiversity loss, about all that can prudently be recommended at this time is continued efforts to preserve specimens of species or varieties that are verging on extinction and to conduct more research into the extent and likely consequences of further declines in genetic diversity.

Chapter 1 discussed a number of catastrophic risks that I have not attempted to subject to cost-benefit analysis, including nuclear terrorism, runaway nanomachines, natural pandemics, and conquest by super-intelligent robots. Careful assessment of the costs and benefits of responding to these risks remains a project for further research.

4

How to reduce the catastrophic risks

I have said that the risk of catastrophe is growing because science and technology are advancing at breakneck speed. Oddly, this is a source of modest comfort. We do not know what the cumulative risk of disaster is today, but we know that it will be greater several decades from now, so there is time to prepare measures against the truly terrifying dangers that loom ahead. But we must begin. And the formulation and implementation of the necessary measures cannot be left to scientists, as we know. The role of law and the social sciences is crucial. The law, however, is making little contribution to the control of catastrophic risks. Likewise the social sciences, with the partial exception of economics, which has produced a significant scholarly literature on global warming. The legal profession may even be increasing the probability of catastrophe by exaggerating the cost to civil liberties of vigorous responses to threats of terrorism. Improvement in the response to catastrophic risks may require both institutional reforms and changes in specific policies, procedures, and doctrines.

Toward a scientifically literate legal profession

The legal system cannot deal effectively with scientifically and technologically difficult questions unless lawyers and judges—not all, but more than at present—are comfortable with such questions. Comfortable not in the sense of knowing the answers to difficult scientific questions or being able to engage in scientific reasoning, but in the sense in which most antitrust lawyers today, few of whom are also economists, are comfortable in dealing with the economic issues that arise in antitrust cases. They know some economics, they work with economists, they understand that economics drives many outcomes of antitrust litigation, and as a result they can administer—not perfectly but satisfactorily— an economically sophisticated system of antitrust law.[1] Economics, however, although at least quasi-scientific in method and outlook, and increasingly mathematized, is easier for lawyers and judges to get comfortable with than the natural sciences are. Because it plays an important role in many fields of law, economics is taught in law schools, whether in special courses on economic analysis of law or more commonly as a component of substantive law courses, such as torts, antitrust, securities regulation, environmental law, and bankruptcy. It has been allowed to play that role because of the considerable isomorphism (which I have emphasized in my own work in economic analysis of law)[2] between law and economics. Much of law is intuitive economics.[3] And although economics has now moved far beyond the kind of simple verbal logic one finds in legal analysis, the most important principles of economics remain intuitive ones—such as the law of demand, cost as opportunity forgone, and equilibrium—that can be described in words. Little of importance in economics cannot be grasped by a person who knows high-school algebra and geometry and basic calculus and statistics, and even calculus and statistics may be dispensable. It isn't asking too much of modern law students to know that much; it is remarkable, and deplorable, how many students at leading law schools are terrified of high-school algebra. Yet they still manage to pick up at least the rudiments of those parts of economics that bear importantly on law.

The characteristics that have enabled economics to be integrated into legal education and practice are not found in the modern physical sciences (including computer science, a combination of mathematics and electrical engineering). The logic of the law may be economics, but it is certainly not any of the physical sciences. Apart from the lack of isomorphism between law and the physical sciences, the principles of those sciences are less intuitive than those of economics. (An exception is evolutionary biology, which, with its emphasis on competition, relative fitness, survivorship, and equilibrium, has a conceptual structure similar to that of economics.) Economics deals with human behavior, which is familiar, obviously, and lawyers can understand the intuitive versions of economic principles even when the principles themselves may have been derived from unrealistic premises by math-wielding economists—such premises as, in models of perfect competition, an infinite number of sellers having identical cost functions selling an identical product to perfectly informed consumers. The modern physical sciences concern phenomena of which ordinary people have no intuitive sense whatsoever, such as cell processes, the carbon cycle, and subatomic forces.

Economics, moreover, is a normative as well as a positive discipline, whereas the physical sciences are exclusively positive disciplines, though their findings, notably in human biology, may have normative relevance. Economics furnishes grounds for criticism and reform and thus can be employed in lawyers' advocacy and judges' decisions—which brings me to the deepest gulf between the legal and scientific cultures. The physical sciences are committed to a mode of inquiry in which propositions are accepted only if they survive confrontation with experimental data. "The principle of science, the definition, almost, is the following: *The test of all knowledge is experiment.* Experiment is the *sole judge* of scientific 'truth.'"[4] The idea of subjecting a legal proposition to a decisive experiment—an experiment that might refute it—horrifies the lawyer. His job is to win for his client. He cannot stake the client's all on the outcome of an experiment, when he might win his case by a moving narrative, carefully coached witnesses, and withering cross-examination designed to make even truthful testimony sound false.

Judges do not face the same pressure to make the worse appear the better cause. But they come from the same legal culture, the culture of advocacy and doctrinal manipulation. And when they are faced with uncertainty about the correct outcome, as they often are, they don't have the luxury of deferring decision until their uncertainty can be dispelled by patient study, however protracted. Instead they decide which party has the burden of proof, and if uncertainty as to the correct outcome persists, that party loses. And since the judge usually cannot defend his decision by scientific proof, he too must use rhetoric to provide a persuasive justification for the decision. In short, the lawyer's commitment is to his client, and the judge's to the need to decide; neither can make truth his priority, let alone the truths that science reveals by experimental methods.

A striking feature of law that is largely invisible to its practitioners and to most outsiders as well is that it has (except perhaps where it has embraced the economic approach) no theoretical core or empirical methodology. Law is more like a language than a science. It is important to know the rules of a language as codified in a grammar, lexicon, and textbook, but that knowledge is only the first step in learning how to *use* the language. From the standpoint of the practitioner law is not only, or even mainly, a set of rules, but a knack for bending the rules, for fitting them to goals. The rules are resources in much the same way that the formal rules of a language are resources. All this is remote from the physical sciences.

And here is a paradox: despite their much more powerful apparatus of inquiry, scientists are more tentative than lawyers. Scientists talk more in terms of "theory" and "hypothesis" and "data" and "belief" than of "fact" and "truth," which are terms that pervade legal discourse. Obviously there are many scientific facts and scientific truths, but they are not the focus of interest. In Karl Popper's influential theory of scientific inquiry, the march of science is a process of error correction, and truth its ever-receding goal. That way of thinking is alien to the legal profession. A lawyer says, "My client is innocent, and that's the truth." More than a rhetoric of certitude is involved. Lawyers inhabit a plane of inquiry where facts are salient, such as the date of an automobile accident or the date the plaintiff filed his case. Even in this age of science, their concern is mainly with the visible everyday world, the world navigable by common sense.

For present purposes, the deepest difference between law (and other social sciences) and the natural sciences may be that the orientation of the former is toward action and of the latter toward knowledge. That is one reason scientists cannot be entrusted with the defense of the nation and the human race, whether it is defense against the public enemy or (an overlapping category) against the catastrophic risks with which this book is concerned. This is not a criticism of science or scientists. To seekers after knowledge, measures of protection against dangerous knowledge, such as knowledge of how to use gene splicing to create a more lethal pathogen, are simply an impediment, and the value of astronomical skills in crafting a defense against asteroid collisions simply an irrelevance. Not that good scientists can't be hired to work on defense projects; think only of the Manhattan Project (though the motives were more patriotic than pecuniary). But building a bomb was not a *scientific* priority for atomic physicists.

These cultural and epistemic differences between law and science to one side, it would be infeasible to require law students to demonstrate competence in the physical sciences considered as a lump; those sciences are too diverse to be considered a single field like economics. But it would be entirely feasible to require that a substantial fraction of law students be able to demonstrate by the time they graduated from law school a basic competence in college-level math and statistics plus one science such as physics, chemistry, biology, computer science, medicine, public health, or geophysics. Usually they would have gained the required competence in college or graduate school before coming to law school, but if not they would be eligible to obtain remedial instruction elsewhere in the university at the same time that they were taking their law courses.

The goal would not be to channel scientifically literate law students into the particular area of law to which they could most easily apply their slice of scientific knowledge. It would be to assure that a nontrivial number of lawyers were comfortable with scientific methods, attitudes, usages, and vocabulary. Having surmounted the cultural barriers that separate law from the physical sciences, these lawyers would constitute the pool from which government agencies, universities (especially law schools and schools of public policy), and think tanks would recruit lawyers who could contribute to the regulation of catastrophic risks, as well as to the formulation of science policy, and the management of scientific and technological activities, more generally.

The most dramatic way to attain this goal would be for one or more of the elite law schools to announce that beginning in five years no students shall be admitted who lack the scientific competence specified above and will not commit to obtaining the remedial instruction necessary to equip them with the required competence by the time they graduate from law school. A less dramatic though still effective measure would be for law schools to give preference in admissions to students having the specified scientific competence or willing to commit to obtaining it.

The situation is not hopeless. According to statistics compiled by the Law School Admission Council and summarized in Table 4.1, 11 percent of students matriculating in the fall of 2002 at law schools accredited by the American Bar Association had majored in the natural sciences, engineering, computer science, or health professions (the boldfaced fields in the table). Almost half the natural-science majors were biology or biochemistry.

Notice how similar are the statistics for the seven elite law schools shown separately in the table, the only marked difference being the higher percentage of computer-science majors at the elite schools. Of minor interest is how few science majors Yale Law School attracts, confirming that school's head-in-the-clouds image.

My impression (I cannot find data) is that students who have a background in physics, chemistry, biology, or engineering tend to go into patent law, into copyright law if their background is computer science, into environmental law if they have a background in ecology (or, sometimes, in biology), and into medical malpractice or mass-tort law if their background is medicine or biology (the principal mass-tort cases have involved health issues, such as the tobacco, bendectin, Agent Orange, HIV, silicone-implant, and asbestos litigations), but otherwise to drop science altogether—the last being, I suspect, the most common choice. Apart from those science-friendly law school graduates who go into environmental law, where they might encounter issues of global warming (an environmental problem if ever there was one) or biodiversity loss, very few law school graduates are equipped or motivated to play a constructive role in dealing with catastrophic risks as defined in this book. Not that many are needed, barring a more ambitious expansion of the legal regulation of such risks than can prudently be recommended at this time; but more are needed than are available. This scarcity reflects in part the lack of interest in catastrophic risks on the part of law professors, few of whom have any interest in science. The dearth of regulatory, legislative, and other law-related activity, particularly court cases, concerning those risks is a factor as well. The American legal profession, especially its academic branch, is court-centric to an obsessive degree. Phenomena that are not the stuff of litigation rarely engage the professional interest of academic lawyers. Science has great prestige in the larger society, none in the academic legal community.

Table 4.2 reports the number of law teachers in different fields today and a decade ago as recorded by the Association of American Law Schools (AALS).[5] Notice how the field of jurisprudence, a notably unprogressive field, has grown almost as fast as law and science and is 6 times larger, while constitutional law, the most prestigious field of ac-

Table 4.1. Majors of Entering Law Students

	Columbia	Harv.	N.Y.U.	Stanford	U. Chi.	U. Mich.	Yale	Seven-school Total	Total all schools
Social sciences/ helping professions	161 (41%)	243 (44%)	189 (44%)	87 (48%)	71 (37%)	167 (41%)	120 (62%)	1,038 (44%)	19,220 (42%)
Arts & humanities	103 (26%)	119 (22%)	121 (28%)	38 (21%)	45 (23%)	110 (27%)	52 (27%)	588 (25%)	10,088 (22%)
Business & management	72 (18%)	93 (17%)	58 (14%)	27 (15%)	32 (16%)	69 (17%)	9 (5%)	360 (15%)	8,247 (18%)
Natural science	19 (5%)	47 (8%)	31 (7%)	12 (7%)	18 (9%)	33 (8%)	6 (3%)	166 (7%)	2,993 (7%)
Engineering	21 (5%)	21 (4%)	21 (2%)	21 (4%)	10 (5%)	19 (5%)	3 (2%)	91 (4%)	1,452 (3%)
Computer science	13 (3%)	16 (3%)	10 (2%)	7 (4%)	3 (2%)	7 (2%)	4 (2%)	60 (3%)	484 (1%)
Health professions	0 (0%)	1 (0%)	0 (0%)	1 (1%)	0 (0%)	1 (0%)	0 (0%)	3 (0%)	545 (1%)
Other/no major listed	5 (1%)	13 (2%)	9 (2%)	1 (1%)	15 (8%)	0 (0%)	1 (1%)	44 (2%)	2,963 (6%)

Note: "Helping professions" refers to such fields as guidance counseling, education, and social work.

Table 4.2. Size of Fields of Academic Law, 1992–1993 and 2002–2003

	1992–93	2002–03	Difference	Percentage increase
Jurisprudence	658	808	150	22.80%
Law and economics	123	209	86	69.92%
Law and science	107	136	29	27.10%
Constitutional law	1452	1679	227	15.63%

ademic law and one as little touched as any (except perhaps jurisprudence) by the scientific culture, is 12 times larger. The rapid growth of "law and economics" attests to the increasing receptivity of law to the social sciences but is not matched by increased receptivity to the physical sciences. The growth in the number of law and science professors has barely outpaced the growth in the number of professors of jurisprudence. Indeed, there is little perception of law and science as a subfield of legal studies. When several years ago I had occasion to list those subfields, it did not occur to me to include law and science.[6]

And what exactly are the law and science professors doing? I inquired of a random sample of 30 of them for the titles of their three most recent publications. Table 4.3 gives the breakdown of the 78 books and articles listed by the 26 professors who responded to my inquiry. (Actually, 27 responded, but one had just become an academic and had no publications.)

The "nonscientific" category is a bit of a misnomer, as it includes articles on the philosophy of science, which are not at the intersection of law and science. The "forensic" category refers to the use of expert scientific evidence. Of the 78 books and articles, only one deals with bioterrorism and none with any other of the catastrophic risks. A further straw in the wind is that almost all the articles in the promisingly named online *Yale Journal of Law and Technology* are about either intellectual property or computers (or both).

These tables provide further evidence that at present the legal profession has or at least is deploying few resources for contributing constructively to the management of the catastrophic risks. Especially the academic branch of the profession—for the science and technology section of the American Bar Association is the ABA's fastest-growing section, reflecting the increase in the number of scientific issues (primarily, I imagine, computer related) arising in legal cases. I should also mention the National Conference of Lawyers and Scientists,[7] jointly

Table 4.3. Recent Output of Law and Science Professors

Type of book or article	Number	Percentage
Forensic	16	21%
Intellectual property	14	18%
Biology and health	9	12%
Environmental	7	9%
Nonscientific	32	41%

sponsored by the ABA and the American Association for the Advancement of Science (AAAS). The conference assists lawyers in finding and working with scientific expert witnesses.

Like the academy, the judiciary is lagging badly. Only .2 percent of federal district judges have a Ph.D. in any field and only .75 percent have an M.S.—and M.S.'s are often awarded in nonscientific fields, such as journalism. Among federal court of appeals judges the percentages are 1.6 percent and .4 percent.[8]

In light of these statistics, it is no surprise that little attention has been paid to bridging the gap between law and science. But maybe that's as it should be. Maybe lawyers and judges and law professors, even if more of them were comfortable with science, would have nothing to contribute to the administration of science policy. But I doubt that. Unless the regulation of science and technology is to be left entirely to scientists and to the market, which would be perilous for the reasons explained in previous chapters, there is a role for experts in regulation. Not that lawyers are the only such experts. Cost-benefit analysis is central to the management of the catastrophic risks and is primarily the domain of economics rather than of law. But the inescapability of value judgments in cost-benefit analysis of the catastrophic risks, and the indispensability of neutrality in the conduct of such analysis, open up, even in doing cost-benefit analysis, a potentially important role for the legal profession.

At bottom, moreover, cost-benefit analysis is just a way of giving some structure to instrumental (means-end) reasoning. There is a goal, that of reducing catastrophic risks, and a need to decide what if any resources to devote to attaining that goal, and the answer depends on the value of the goal and of what has to be given up to attain it. Whatever responses are picked out by cost-benefit analysis and run the political gauntlet successfully have then to be implemented, and the legal system will inevitably be deeply involved at the implementation stage. The next section of this chapter considers a pair of possible institutional forms that might involve the legal profession more productively than at present in responding to the catastrophic risks.

Against my proposal for the reform of legal education it can be argued that I am being retrograde—that the gulf between law and science is the inevitable result of specialization and that specialization is the royal road to efficiency. But if we accept that the gulf is unbridgeable and that lawyers are condemned to be eternal scientific ignoramuses, we shall be forced to confide the regulation of catastrophic risks to scientists. And scientists, by virtue of the very specialization that has made science the powerful tool of inquiry that it is, are not competent to be regulators, quite apart from the conflicts of interest that beset them when they are regulating activities that are the lifeblood of their scientific careers. Few scientists have the time, the background, or the inclination to master the alien methods of public policy. They are oriented to the acquisition of scientific knowledge rather than to defense against scientific and other dangers.

The Large-aperture Synoptic Survey Telescope (LSST) would as we know be an ideal tool for identifying potentially hazardous near-earth objects. The principal advocates of the project, however, are academic astronomers who are interested not in near-earth objects, but in remote galaxies. Their goal is knowledge, not safety. The distinction is not the familiar one between science (basic) and engineering (applied). The skills and equipment required for a defense against asteroids are the same as those required for doing pure astronomical research. The question is not means but ends, and scientists and policy makers evaluate the ends of scientific research differently.

Policing the intersection between law and science is a more natural role for lawyers than for scientists to play—provided they are scientifically literate lawyers. Literate in the sense in which a good patent lawyer is literate. Just as a good patent lawyer can ask probing questions of an expert scientific witness and not be blown away by a blast of scientific jargon, so a good catastrophic-risk lawyer should be able to ask probing questions of a biologist who declares that it is impossible for a group of terrorists to fabricate and disseminate lethal pathogens or that any restriction of scientific publication would paralyze biological research.

These examples can help us see that the generalist-specialist dilemma is a false one. Only against the background of expectations formed by the list of existing specializations does a catastrophic-risk lawyer appear to be a generalist. There is no reason why catastrophic-risk law cannot evolve into its own interdisciplinary specialty, perhaps with subspecialties such as the legal control of bioterrorism. Economic analysis of law, once a venture of economists into law and lawyers into economics, is now a specialized interdisciplinary field of social science.

Not that the catastrophic risks necessarily supply the best organizing principle for the requisite specialization. There may be better joints at which to carve. For example, the relation between epidemiology in general and bioterrorism in particular is very close, and so one can imagine the emergence of a legal specialty in the social control of infectious disease. Other possibilities that come to mind are law and scientific terrorism, law and climate science, law and ecology, and law and physics. Such a pattern of specialization would resemble the division of the philosophy of science into subspecialties such as the philosophy of quantum theory and the philosophy of evolutionary biology. This book is a generalist work, but it is also a menu of specialized research.

A science court?

Suppose a safety board within the Department of Energy had ruled that RHIC was too dangerous to be permitted to operate. The ruling would have required the application of a legal standard to facts, and lawyers would doubtless have been involved in both the formulation and the application of the standard. But I want to focus on the next stage, which would be Brookhaven's appeal to a court to reverse the department's decision. (All this is hypothetical. There is no judicial review of safety determinations made by the Department of Energy because, as I said, the department does not make safety determinations regarding accelerator experiments.) Since Brookhaven is owned by the Department of Energy, it probably would not be allowed to litigate against it, but let me wave that issue aside and assume it would be. Its appeal of the safety board's decision would go to a federal court of appeals having a general jurisdiction and composed of generalist judges, few if any of whom would have a scientific background. So one question to consider is whether such appeals should go instead to a "science court," a court of specialists composed of lawyers with a substantial background in one of the physical sciences.[9]

The idea of a science court has been kicking around for many years, but has gotten nowhere.[10] The original proposal[11] had the bizarre feature of casting scientists in the roles—those of judges and advocates—ordinarily occupied by lawyers. They are not roles that scientists are accustomed to play, and giving the roles to scientists would merely underscore the cultural differences between them and lawyers.[12]

The only precedent known to me for an *appellate* court of science is the United States Court of Appeals for the Federal Circuit, which has exclusive jurisdiction of appeals in patent-infringement and other patent cases. Two decades of experience with this court have not yielded convincing evidence that it is doing a better job with patent cases than the generalist federal appeals courts did before the federal circuit was created.[13] But the experience is not decisive on the question whether to create a science court, if only because the federal circuit's jurisdiction is not limited to patent cases. The rest consists mainly of cases involving government contracts and employment disputes, which rarely involve scientific issues. Reflecting the diversity of the court's jurisdiction, only a minority of the court's judges have a patent-law background. Yet the three-judge panels that decide appeals (except in the rare case in which the court sits en banc, meaning that all the judges of the court participate in the decision) are composed randomly, so that a patent appeal may be decided by a panel that contains no judge who has even the limited technical background that a patent lawyer would have. Yet those judges who had pre-judicial patent experience have written most of the court's patent opinions,[14] despite which, as I have said, the court's performance in the patent area has not been demonstrably superior to that of the generalist courts that preceded it.

Notwithstanding the doubts engendered by the federal circuit's performance as a patent court, I would anticipate benefits from having cases dense with scientific issues reviewed by judges who are comfortable with such issues (which, by the way, not all patent lawyers are, especially those who litigate in court rather than preparing the actual patent applications and moving them through the review process in the Patent and Trademark Office). But there is a compelling practical objection to an appellate science court, and that is the difficulty verging on impossibility of configuring its jurisdiction intelligently. Whether its jurisdiction were defined as embracing cases that involve scientific issues, or (improbably) confined to cases that involve catastrophic risks, there would be endless haggling over whether the jurisdictional triggers were sufficiently important to the decision of a particular case to warrant channeling the appeal to the science court. The range of cases that may involve scientific issues is broad, encompassing environmental protection, medical malpractice, disability benefits, products liability, energy regulation, workplace safety, regulation of food and drugs, reproductive technology, and intellectual property in computer software and digitized products generally (such as music CDs). It would be infeasible to shunt all appeals in cases in these categories to a single court, impossible to devise readily applicable criteria for separating the "important" from the "unimportant," and exceedingly difficult to devise clear and readily applicable criteria for distinguishing catastrophic from subcatastrophic risks so as to confine the court's jurisdiction to the former— and there wouldn't be enough cases involving catastrophic risks to keep a court occupied.

I have been discussing appeals because the federal circuit, the nearest thing we have in the federal system (the significance of this qualification will become apparent momentarily) to a science court, is an appellate court and because my opening example was of a case that originated in an executive agency, the Department of Energy, rather than in a federal trial court, so that judicial intervention if any would be appellate in character. A science *trial* court would present fewer difficulties of the sort discussed in the preceding paragraph than a science appellate court would. There is a model for such a trial court in the new (as of January 1, 2003) Maryland Business and Technology Case Management Programs, which require each Maryland circuit court (a trial court having a general jurisdiction) to designate three specially trained judges for the business and technology track. Lawyers can request that their case be placed in that track; a court administrator decides whether to grant the request.[15]

It is too early to evaluate the success of this experiment. But it is a promising idea and one that federal district courts might well consider emulating on an experimental basis, as they could do without new legislation. Federal district judges could volunteer to take science-intensive cases, lawyers could request that their case be placed on the science-intensive track, and the chief judge of the court could decide whether the case really belonged there. The problem of uncertain appellate jurisdiction would then be solvable; a special court, or (as at the trial stage) perhaps volunteers from among the judges in the existing federal courts of appeals, would handle appeals from the cases that had been shunted to the science track. This approach would avoid the main objection that was made to the proposal of a science court: that it envisaged scientists as lawyers and judges. A problem would remain of what to do when only one of the parties to a litigation wanted to place the case on the science track. But that is secondary; the most serious problem is that at present there probably are too few federal judges who are scientifically literate to man the science track and thus to preside over the kind of debate envisaged by Calogero.[16] Hence the importance of my proposals regarding legal education.

I have reservations, however, concerning the implications of dubbing any legal tribunal a science *court*. The antiscientific culture of the legal profession is not just a matter of education or mindset; it is also embedded in procedures, which in turn affect the legal mindset. For good as well as bad reasons—the good having to do with the social benefits of making legal rights and duties reasonably predictable—the institutional as well as doctrinal structure of the law changes slowly. The modern American trial is essentially an eighteenth-century creation, and it is poorly adapted to resolving disputes in which scientific issues figure. The assignment of the adjudicative function to randomly selected jurors and generalist judges is only part of the problem. Another part is the trial procedure itself, with its reliance on direct and cross-examination as the main method of eliciting the facts of the case, its premise that a trial is a contest and the judge's role therefore an umpireal one, and the corollary that witnesses are adversarial and are coached by the lawyers to maximize their contribution to "the team." What this all too frequently means in practice, in a case involving scientific questions, is that the scientists who testify, having been hired by the competing litigants and prepped by the lawyers for "their" side, will on direct examination be reciting from a script prepared by a lawyer, while on cross-examination they will be in a defensive posture, refusing to make any concessions, giving nothing away. The rival scientific expert witnesses won't even be testifying in succession to each other, because the plaintiff gets to present all his witnesses before the defendant gets to present any witnesses. The trier of fact sees only one side of each scientific dispute at a time; the scientific dispute is never brought into sharp focus; the disputants never join issue clearly.

The procedure that I have outlined—the traditional Anglo-American adversarial procedure mechanically applied to cases in which scientific issues figure—is poorly calculated to elicit reliable scientific information. The more the judge knows about science, the better the procedure will work, but it will not work well. A better procedure, though difficult to reconcile with traditional assumptions about the operation of American courts and requiring (by virtue of the Seventh Amendment to the

U.S. Constitution) a constitutional amendment in order to eliminate or curtail the use of juries in federal cases, would dispense with juries and with the standard method of witness interrogation. It would instead have the judge—who would be the sole trier of fact and would be expected to have some minimum competence in the relevant science—sitting at a round table with scientists selected by some neutral procedure (for example by agreement between the parties or from lists maintained by professional associations, such as the National Conference of Lawyers and Scientists that I mentioned earlier) and discussing the scientific issues in the case with them. The lawyers would be sitting in the back of the room and could interject their own questions at appropriate times.

Such an informal approach is more congenial to the continental European ("inquisitorial") than to the Anglo-American ("adversarial") adjudicative tradition. (I call it "continental European," but it has spread to most of the world outside the Anglo-American sphere.) This provides a ray of hope. The institutional mechanisms for dealing with catastrophic risks are likely to be international, to a degree anyway, which may force American lawyers to think hard about alternatives to conventional American trial procedure. Europe (even including the United Kingdom) and Japan also provide more numerous precedents for a science court than anything in U.S. legal experience. The United Kingdom has a specialized patent trial court; Japan has court divisions that specialize in intellectual property cases and are assisted by technical advisors, while France delegates powers that in the United States are exercised mostly by courts to "technocrats," who are civil servants with extensive scientific training. European and Japanese courts also use more flexible procedures in technical cases than we do.[17] These adaptations to modernity are easier to make in the continental system than in our system, not only because of the differences between inquisitorial and adversarial procedure but also because specialization is much more common in foreign judiciaries than in our own. It is easier to create and staff a science court—a court of specialists—when specialized judging is already the norm.

A center for catastrophic-risk assessment and response

Another way to draw law and science together in responding to the problem of catastrophic risks would be to establish a Center for Catastrophic-Risk Assessment and Response. Such a center would provide a meeting place for the different disciplines, primarily the various physical sciences along with economics and law (also political science and perhaps philosophy), that have contributions to make to dealing with the problem of catastrophic risks. The center would not have to be governmental; indeed it would probably work better as a consortium of universities. One model might be the recently authorized Regional Centers of Excellence for Biodefense and Emerging Infectious Disease Research. These are federally funded university consortia whose mission is "not only to increase quick response to terrorist attacks, but also to develop drug treatments and vaccines against germs that can be readily transported around the world and take hold in a community within days."[18]

A Center for Catastrophic-Risk Assessment and Response would concentrate the intellectual resources upon which generalist courts (as well as a federal science court or track, if one were to be created) could draw when faced with cases involving the regulation of those risks. Members of the center's staff could appear as expert witnesses or be appointed as ad hoc advisors to the judges. The center would also provide training for lawyers and scientists involved in the making or administering of government science policy. Additional precedents are such university centers as Harvard's Belfer Center for Science and International Affairs, M.I.T.'s Security Studies Program, and Stanford's Center for International Security and Cooperation. These are among the organizations receiving grants from the Science, Technology, and Security Initiative of the John D. and Catherine T. MacArthur Foundation. A related program, joint between the MacArthur Foundation and the Carnegie Corporation—the U.S. State Department's Thomas Jefferson Science Foundation Program—will, as explained in an October 8, 2003, press release by the MacArthur Foundation, "annually bring five tenured research scientists and engineers from the U.S. academic community into the State Department for one-year assignments in Washington, D.C., or at U.S. embassies and missions abroad." This seems a worthwhile step toward narrowing the culture gap between science and policy.

The need for the kind of center I am proposing is underscored by the sheer variety of analytic tools and policy instruments that are relevant to dealing with the catastrophic risks. For example, population policy may be critical to dealing with global warming and loss of biodiversity, police measures to dealing with nuclear and biological terrorism, administrative law to regulating the safety of particle accelerators, and foreign policy and international law to coping with all the catastrophic risks because all are global. Difficult mathematical techniques not discussed in this book, such as catastrophe theory and reliability theory, must be evaluated for their potential contribution to the understanding and reduction of the catastrophic risks, as must principles of judicial administration, methods of legal education, and techniques of intelligence gathering and threat assessment. Civil-liberties issues must also be considered. And all these things must be integrated with the politics, the law, the psychology, the statistics, and the economics of science policy and catastrophic risk. Managing the catastrophic risks is quintessentially an interdisciplinary challenge. There would be plenty of work for such a center. Not least would be the identification of catastrophic risks that I have not identified—I fear there may be many.

Fiscal tools: a recap

In the last chapter I pointed out several methods of catastrophic-risk response that would employ the tools of fiscal policy: taxation, tradable emissions limits, subsidies for R & D, and curtailing the subsidies for high-energy particle physics. There is no need to repeat that discussion. But I do want to point out that fiscal tools appear to be the best tools for dealing with global warming and the strangelet scenario, the first by coupling an emissions tax with a subsidy for forms of carbon sequestration that confer public goods (such as removal of carbon dioxide from the atmosphere, as distinct from preventing it from getting into the atmosphere in the first place), the second by withholding subsidy from RHIC-II in order to delay its opening for several years. Yet even in these two cases, fiscal tools alone are not enough. I argued that RHIC-like experimentation should be subjected to cost-benefit analysis conducted by neutrals; and in the next section of this chapter I argue for the creation of an international environmental protection agency to enforce (among other treaty measures) a modified Kyoto Protocol.

Fiscal tools may have a role to play with respect to other catastrophic risks as well. For example, there is a case for subsidizing research on biodiversity depletion and a case for devoting a portion of the current heavy federal subsidy for nanotechnology to defenses against the technology's getting out of hand with disastrous consequences. We should continue subsidizing, quite possibly more generously than we are doing, the destruction or sequestration of Russia's abundant, scattered, and perhaps poorly guarded fissile material.

Some hypothetical regulatory policies

With the institutional framework for dealing with catastrophic risks largely nonexistent, the risks themselves understudied, and my own expertise limited, it would be premature for me to attempt to offer a laundry list of specific risk-reduction measures. But it is important to recognize that such measures, not limited to the fiscal measures, are feasible; they might supply the agenda of a center for catastrophic-risk assessment and response. The examples that follow are deliberately provocative, highly tentative, and intended for discussion rather than for immediate action.

An international EPA

My first tentative suggestion is that the nations of the world create an international environmental protection agency, presumably under the aegis of the United Nations. The agency would enforce environmental norms created by treaty, such as the ban on chlorofluorocarbons that is designed to preserve the ozone layer in the stratosphere, an improved version of the Kyoto Protocol,[19] and limitations on overfishing and perhaps on depletion of biodiversity generally. There are many environmental treaties[20] but very little in the way of enforcement machinery.[21] The creation of an agency to enforce them would involve a significant surrender of sovereign powers on the part of the nations of the world—which is probably why there is no such agency. It would also raise issues of political legitimacy. Democratic countries such as the United States would be surrendering a part of their sovereignty to an institution that, like the United Nations itself, lacks a democratic pedigree.[22] For while most countries pay lip service to democracy, only a minority are actually functioning democracies.[23] This is an objection to our surrendering a part of our sovereignty to the UN.

But there may be no feasible alternative means of curbing highly destructive global negative externalities; and it has been a commonplace since Thomas Hobbes wrote *Leviathan* that trading independence for security can be a profitable swap. The disorder, the chaos, that he feared was civil war—disorder internal to a nation and requiring in his view an all-powerful government. Today the greatest threats of chaos are global, which requires us to rethink the assumption, powerfully embedded in the psyche of the U.S. population (and of that of China and many other countries as well), that the proper locus of strong sovereignty is national.

It is no accident that our Environmental Protection Agency has not been authorized to classify carbon dioxide as a pollutant required to be regulated under the Clean Air Act. Most of the benefits of regulating U.S. emissions of carbon dioxide would accrue to other nations, except insofar as such regulation might reduce the likelihood of an abrupt global warming that would produce a global catastrophe. Barring that possibility, such a regulation would be a classic case of the conferral of external benefits, and American taxpayers, commuters, automobile manufacturers, and energy producers would all howl. Internationalizing emissions control would internalize the benefits of such control, though imperfectly because the costs of global warming are not uniform across the globe. When the focus of concern shifts from gradual to abrupt global warming and from inducing substitution of products made by processes that emit greenhouse gases to forcing novel technological solutions to global warming, the need for international cooperation is lessened; unilateral national action can achieve much. But not all.

Conservatives worry that international agencies place the United States at the mercy of other nations, many of them unfriendly to the United States. The worry probably is groundless.[24] It may *seem* that because the United States is the world's most powerful nation it has more to lose than other nations from surrendering a part of its sovereignty to an international organization—that it would be a Gulliver tied down by Lilliputians. Hope for precisely this result motivates the support for international organizations by many on the left, especially in Europe. The hostility of the Bush administration to international organizations may be a reaction to that hope; your ill-wishers' hope is your fear. But both the hope and the fear (the two being based on the same expectation) are exaggerated. As the world's most powerful nation, the United States tends to dominate international organizations, and, when it does not, it ignores them with impunity. For example, because the International Criminal Court would tend to inhibit the use of violence by the United States, which as the world's foremost policeman insists on being allowed a broad latitude to threaten and if necessary use violence, we have refused to submit to the court's jurisdiction. In contrast, the Hobbesian trade involved in subjecting environmental policy to international control might not be a painful and one-sided one for the United States.

More troublesome is the exceedingly mixed record of international agencies in general and United Nations agencies in particular. An initial research task, therefore, is to identify those agencies that have performed badly and those that have performed well,[25] with a view to determining whether there is a realistic prospect that an international environmental protection agency would be successful and how it might be configured to maximize the chances of its succeeding. I don't want to prejudge the results of such a study. But I do want to draw attention to one of the relevant advantages, distinct from internalizing global costs and benefits, of regulating catastrophic risks by treaty rather than by purely domestic legislation. Like a difficult-to-amend constitution,[26] a treaty is a technique for lengthening politicians' time horizons,[27] which, as we know, are particularly short in relation to the catastrophic risks. When the stars are aligned just right, a politician may see a political advantage in the adoption of regulatory controls over a risk that is not likely to materialize before his term of office expires. If he can get the controls adopted by means of a treaty (perhaps in the form of an international convention, like the biological-warfare convention of 1972), this will tend to bind his successors. Only loosely, to be sure, because a treaty can be rescinded more easily than the federal Constitution can be amended. (The president may be able to rescind it unilaterally, though the Supreme Court has never decided this question.) Still, the United States is somewhat reluctant to abandon or violate its treaties. This reluctance is an argument for trying to deal with the catastrophic risks, in part anyway, by treaty or international convention.

An international bioweaponry agency?

There might appear to be an even stronger argument for conferring legal authority on the World Health Organization to enforce worldwide security against the development of bioweaponry, since, after all, the WHO already exists. Actually the argument is weaker than the argument for an international EPA, mainly because of the tension between a health agency and a police agency. The dual-use character of biotech research makes that tension acute. Access to lethal pathogens for conducting experiments in recombinant DNA, and the publication of the results of such experiments with a level of detail enabling the experiments to be replicated, are at once risk factors for bioterrorism and key steps in defending against epidemics, whether natural or man-made. A health agency would be particularly reluctant, therefore, to curtail or conceal such experimentation.

A police agency, perhaps a greatly strengthened Interpol (Interpol's annual budget is less than $50 million), is needed to deal with bioterrorism, precisely because it is a police problem as well as a scientific and medical one.[28] International cooperation is required in the investigation and apprehension not only of bioterrorists but also of innocent scientists who by failing to observe security precautions may become unwitting accomplices of bioterrorists. A great many countries are active in gene-splicing research, and, as I explained in chapter 2, unilateral regulation of dual-use biotechnology, even by the world's leader in biotechnological research, which is the United States, would be of limited efficacy. Some countries, such as the United States, the United Kingdom, and Japan, have imposed controls designed to prevent biotechnology from being used to create bioweaponry. But there are no uniform safety standards in biotechnical research, development, and production, no international regime for monitoring or enforcing compliance with such standards, and a growing number of Third World countries engaged in biotech research that has weapon possibilities.

The current U.S. practice regarding the international control of bioterrorism is to counsel nations on how to strengthen their controls over access to and research on lethal pathogens and toxins and to encourage them to adopt the strengthened controls. No doubt there are also covert activities by both U.S. and foreign security services aimed at detecting and disrupting terrorist plans to acquire biological weaponry. These efforts could probably be enhanced uncontroversially and at low cost by giving Interpol a modest capability for investigating and exchanging information relevant to detecting and apprehending bioterrorists. But police and intelligence officers are not enough, just as they are not enough to prevent nuclear proliferation. An agency is needed that will reduce the risk of bioterrorism not by detecting and apprehending bioterrorists (the task of police, customs, and intelligence services), guarding facilities in which lethal pathogens are stored, conducting background investigations of persons having or seeking access to such facilities, or developing and administering vaccines and treatments (the World Health Organization and the Centers for Disease Control, for example), but instead by establishing, and verifying compliance with, standards for (1) securing such facilities, (2) denying access by dangerous people to lethal pathogens and to the training, facilities, and knowledge required to create bioweaponry, and (3) regulating the publication of research involving such substances.

This is provided that such an agency would be *effective* as a standard-setter and monitor. Were it ineffective in these respects, it would be worse than useless because it would deflect resources from alternative methods of preventing bioterrorism and might lull the world into thinking that the problem was under control when it was not. The International Atomic Energy Agency, the major mission of which is preventing nuclear proliferation, would be the natural template for an international bioterrorism agency—and it has been much criticized. Not only for its failures to detect nuclear-weapons programs, but also and more fundamentally for using a carrot-and-stick approach whereby to induce cooperation the agency offers nations assistance with civil nuclear energy projects in exchange for the nations' abandoning efforts to become nuclear powers. Because civilian and military nuclear technologies are similar, the IAEA's assistance with civilian technologies makes it easier for recipients of the assistance to manufacture nuclear weapons, though this concern may be exaggerated.[29] Adoption of the carrot-and-stick approach by an international bioterrorism agency would be at once tempting, because nations have to be given an inducement to surrender sovereignty unless it is feasible to coerce them, and potentially disastrous, because the beneficial and the destructive bioengineering technologies are not merely similar but identical.

The argument for giving enforcement powers to an international organization may seem weaker in the case of bioterrorism than in the case of global warming and other environmental threats, for two reasons: the threat of bioterrorism is immediate and has galvanized our politicians into action despite their limited terms of office; and the threat is more nearly (though not completely) symmetrical across countries. Symmetrical threats invite voluntary international cooperation, while asymmetrical threats may require coercion or compensation to induce cooperation. But these considerations are overwhelmed by the magnitude of the bioterrorist threat and the limited institutional and other resources for controlling it in a number of the countries in which biological weapons might be produced. Unless the international biotech industry is tightly regulated, efforts by individual countries such as the United States to rein in their own biotech research may be fruitless, their principal effect being to drive such research abroad. And as I explained earlier, the United States need not fear that it would be surrendering a vital component of national sovereignty by joining an international organization for the regulation of biotechnology.

All this is not to gainsay the well-documented failures, political deformities, unintended adverse consequences, wastefulness, and economic perversity of much government regulation. But these are merely costs to be balanced against the benefits of regulation. If the catastrophic risks are as serious as I fear they may be, and are manageable only by some form of international regulation, the costs may be worth bearing.

Catastrophic-risk review of new projects

Congress should consider enacting a law that would require all scientific research projects in specified areas, such as nanotechnology and experimental high-energy physics, to be reviewed by a federal catastrophic-risks assessment board and forbidden if the board found that the project would create an undue risk to human survival. Other technologically advanced nations would have to be brought around to create similar boards, however, lest the effect of the legislation be merely to divert high-risk projects overseas. In time the responsibility for assessment might be given to a United Nations agency, such as the biotech regulatory agency suggested in the preceding section.

At present our government is largely oblivious to catastrophic risks as I am defining them, other than those created by the threat of nuclear or biological terrorism. For example, the Environment, Safety, and Health Division of the Department of Energy states that "hazards at [particle] accelerators are magnitudes below those of nuclear reactors."[30] Yet as the department owns both Brookhaven, with its RHIC, and Fermilab and the Stanford Linear Accelerator Center, the other two major U.S. research accelerators, it ought to be aware of the potential dangers. Current federal policy toward asteroid collisions, global warming, biodiversity loss, and the other accidental doomsday dangers is, with the exception of natural pandemics and the partial exception of global warming, essentially one of ignoring them.

The need for safety regulation respecting catastrophic risks is occasionally recognized. But concrete proposals are rare and when offered disappointingly vague.[31]

Limiting science study by foreigners

My next example of a measure for reducing catastrophic risks is a restriction on advanced study of science by foreigners. The restriction should not be absolute. But it is arguable—no stronger word is possible, and I present the counterargument below—that citizens of foreign countries that are hostile to the United States, and citizens of countries (mainly Muslim) in which a significant fraction of the population is deeply hostile to the United States even if the government is friendly, should not be admitted to advanced study of dangerous technologies, such as nuclear engineering, nanotechnology, molecular biology, computer science, and artificial intelligence. Other nations that have programs in these areas would have to be induced to participate in the ban (so again one can imagine a role for international organizations) because purely unilateral restrictions on scientific research and training would probably be ineffective, certainly in the long run. Foreign students denied admission to U.S. universities to study sensitive scientific fields would go to universities in other countries to study them unless those countries imposed comparable restrictions, and not all would do so in the absence of an international regulatory regime with sharp teeth. The United States is the world's scientific leader, but it has no monopoly on scientific knowledge or technical know-how, especially the knowledge and know-how required for the creation of catastrophically destructive biological weapons. The principal effect of making it more difficult for foreigners to study science in the United States may be to strengthen science in countries unwilling to engage in careful screening of foreign scientists and science students.[42]

In the wake of the 9/11 terrorist attacks on the United States, foreigners' opportunities to study science in our universities are already being restricted—though only to a limited extent and only with respect to study that involves access to specified lethal pathogens and toxins—as part of a general tightening of standards for granting visas to foreigners for travel and study in the United States.[43] Even as so limited, the denial to foreign students of access to the full range of study activities available at the university that admitted them, on inherently speculative grounds of national security, is anathema to universities for both financial and ideological reasons, as we glimpsed in the discussion in chapter 2 of the article by Barry Bloom. Broadened to the full range of potentially dangerous technologies, such a restriction would damage our foreign relations and weaken our science and our universities.

In light of these concerns it would probably be unsound as well as unrealistic to expand the restriction beyond its current scope, which is limited to the denial of access to the most dangerous pathogens and toxins. Something to consider in the interest of further accommodating the universities' concerns and minimizing the insult to foreign students, as well as reducing the flow of information facilitative of bioterrorism, is shifting research that requires access to dangerous substances to classified facilities off campus. The model is Lincoln Labs (formally, the M.I.T. Lincoln Laboratory), which, though owned by the Massachusetts Institute of Technology, is a separate entity with its own technical staff, which conducts classified research. Universities can retain ownership of classified facilities, as M.I.T. has done, and foreign students do not expect to have access to such facilities. As there are plenty of opportunities in the United States for studying biology and related fields that do not require access to lethal pathogens or toxins, our universities are unlikely to lose a great many foreign students by shifting that research to facilities unavailable to them—and not to all foreign students but only to whose who come from nations believed to sponsor, nourish, or condone terrorism.

Classifying sensitive biological research is not a costless solution to the security problems created by such research, because classified research doesn't circulate as freely throughout the scientific community as unclassified research does. If as I suggested in chapter 2 the best theory of technological progress is modeled on the theory of natural selection, then progress is optimized by free exchange of scientific ideas among the broadest possible community of scientists. Such exchange maximizes the field of selection—the range of ideas from which the best ones will be selected by a competitive process. (The more mutants, the faster evolution proceeds.) The field of selection would be narrowed if many qualified scientists were kept in the dark about the latest developments and so were in effect expelled from the relevant community. But trade-offs are inescapable. If a risk to the safety of the nation and indeed of the entire world is great enough, some retardation in the rate of scientific progress may be a price worth paying for reducing the risk. That is true even though in the case of biological research such retardation may expose humanity to heightened danger from natural pandemics. Natural pandemics, as we know, pose a smaller risk of truly catastrophic consequences than bioterrorism utilizing the latest bioengineering techniques does. And how great would the retardation be, anyway? That question will not even be asked until the existence of the trade-offs is acknowledged and analysts endeavor to measure them. One would like to know, as bearing on the answer, such things as whether progress in atomic physics has been significantly hampered by the fact that atomic research having military potential is classified, though a difference is that what is mainly classified in the atomic realm is engineering know-how rather than basic research.

But I repeat that unless the other scientifically progressive nations of the world join the United States in limiting the access of potentially hostile foreigners to lethal pathogens and toxins, our efforts in that regard are likely to prove futile. The scientific community is international, and there is almost complete mobility within it. That is one of the things that make science so dangerous.

Police measures

This subsection and the next consider a variety of measures for reducing catastrophic risk that have even more of a "police" flavor, and will therefore be even more resented by members of the scientific community and civil libertarians, than limiting the study opportunities of foreign students. An example of such a measure would be screening, for psychological traits or political beliefs that may predispose scientists to use their knowledge in highly destructive ways, those scientists, American as well as foreign, who are working on highly dangerous technologies. Scientists involved in weapons programs are already screened for loyalty, discretion, and basic psychological stability. But that may not be enough; scientists exploring technologies that *can* be used for destructive purposes are potential security risks even if they were not hired to make weapons. We should not go to the extreme of treating every citizen as a potential terrorist, and yet—to put the matter bluntly, at the risk of offense—it might be prudent to treat thousands of American scientists and technicians as potential terrorists, in much the same way that all airline passengers are treated as potential terrorists.

Although the threat of bioterrorism is recognized and measures to combat it are being taken, they mostly are passive, such as improving early detection of incipient epidemics and developing vaccines and cures.[34] But as we have just seen,[35] some attention is being paid to police measures for heading off bioattacks in the first place, as distinct from measures for merely minimizing their severity.[36]

In evaluating police measures, we must distinguish between ex post and ex ante regulation.[37] In general, the law—both tort law and criminal law—relies on the threat of punishment or of other sanctions, such as damages judgments in tort cases, to deter harmful conduct. From an economic standpoint the imposition of a sanction ex post as distinct from the ex ante threat to impose the sanction has no curative effect, even if it takes the form of restoring to the victim what the defendant took from him. The economic damage, which is the diminution in the total value of society's goods and services, tangible and intangible, will have occurred when the defendant incurred costs to commit the harmful act and, at the same time, the victim suffered injury or incurred costs to resist the defendant's aggression. The injury can be compensated, and perhaps rendered temporary by treatment, but it cannot be undone completely even when compensation is full.

Suppose a burglar breaks a window to get into a house and steals $100 that he finds there. He is caught and forced to return the $100 to the owner of the house and in addition to reimburse the owner for the $20 cost of replacing the window. Although compensation is complete, the total value of goods and services will have been irrevocably diminished by one window. This is apart from other unrecoverable costs, such as police and judicial costs, burglary tools and alarms, and the loss of the value of the output that the burglar would have produced had he devoted his time to productive labor rather than to stealing. The imposition of the sanction (restitution, in the example) means that deterrence, which would have averted the costs created by the burglary, has failed. The only economic function of that imposition, therefore, unless it takes a form such as imprisonment or capital punishment that prevents the defendant from committing further bad acts either for a period of time or forever, or unless the emotional satisfaction associated with retribution is deemed an economic value, is to maintain the credibility of the threat to impose the sanction on other wrongdoers in the future. That credibility is the condition of effective deterrence.

The threat of punishment cannot be relied upon to prevent bioterrorism, at least on the scale at which bioterrorism creates catastrophic harm. That is why in the last chapter I derided the idea of using international criminal law to prevent such terrorism. Someone bent on destruction on the scale with which this book is concerned is unlikely to be deterrable by the threat of sanctions. Not that sanctions have no place in a program to combat bioterrorism. They may be effective against some would-be terrorists and even more so against their accomplices. Indeed, the net of criminal liability should be cast wide enough to catch the suppliers of pathogens and toxins to unauthorized users. The suppliers might also be amenable to tort sanctions. Either way they are deterrable. Even reprisals against family members of terrorists, and other forms of collective punishment, although distasteful, should be considered, though obviously they would be ineffectual against someone intending, or willing to risk, the destruction of the entire human race.

When a system of punishment after the fact will be largely ineffectual because of the size of the harm, the difficulty of tracing causation, the number of victims, the difficulty of quantifying the harm or apportioning it among the victims, or—the particular concern here—the unresponsiveness of the potential wrongdoer to the incentives that the sanctions imposed pursuant to tort law and criminal law create, the law adds to the usual ex post sanctions regulatory measures designed to prevent the wrongful act from being committed in the first place. It shifts, in other words, from an exclusively deterrent strategy to a mixed deterrent-prophylactic strategy. That is why recidivists, who may by their repeated criminal acts have demonstrated that they are undeterrable, are given long prison terms anyway. This is done not to deter them but to prevent their committing further crimes for a period of time measured by the duration of their confinement.

Minimizing the threat of bioterrorism is likely to require a heavy dose of prophylactic measures, possibly including some curtailment of the civil liberties to which Americans have grown accustomed.[38] Already the immigration authorities are operating a Student and Exchange Visitor Information System designed to keep track of foreigners studying in the United States.[39] The Public Health Security and Bioterrorism Preparedness and Response Act of 2002, in further response to concerns created by the 9/11 attacks and the anthrax mailings that followed quickly upon them and killed five persons, directs the FBI to conduct background investigations of scientists and others who have access to items on a list of pathogens and toxins and requires these persons to register with the Department of Health and Human Services.[40] And the USA PATRIOT Act forbids access to the listed items ("select agents," they are called) by drug abusers, the insane, illegal aliens, felons, fugitives from justice, persons who have been dishonorably discharged from the U.S. armed forces, and—the particular concern of Barry Bloom—"an alien who is a national of a country that is currently designated by the Secretary of State as a supporter of terrorism."[41] Currently 25 countries are so designated.[42]

Preventive as distinct from merely punitive measures for dealing with wrongful conduct trouble civil libertarians because of the reach and scope of such measures. It is one thing to punish someone who has been proved beyond a reasonable doubt to have committed a crime; barring the occasional mistaken conviction, the likelihood of which is diminished by the requirement of proof of guilt beyond a reasonable doubt, the sanction will be confined to criminals. Preventive measures sweep more broadly, though usually more gently as well. Just think of the number of government employees—including, by the way, federal judges—and employees of federal contractors, who undergo background investigations without believing that their liberty or privacy is being seriously compromised. In principle, though, preventive measures could be as severe as punitive ones, as where persons detained on suspicion are held in a jail or other detention facility indefinitely, without trial or even without formal charges being lodged against them and without access to a judge via habeas corpus.

From the standpoint of this book, the most important question concerning draconian preventive measures is whether reducing civil liberties should be part of law's contribution to the struggle against catastrophic forms of terrorism, principally bioterrorism and nuclear terrorism. Remember the Australian mousepox experiment? The editors of the *Journal of Virology* had qualms about publishing the article describing the experiment. But eventually of course they decided to publish it, "materials and methods" section and all. Their decision has been defended by a committee of (our) National Research Council on the ground that the article contained few surprises, the biggest being that even vaccinated mice were killed; and that anyway "it was important to publicize that this strategy could overcome vaccination because it alerted the scientific community to such a possibility, occurring either intentionally or spontaneously."[43] Maybe so; and the committee may also be correct that the sheer scale of biological research and the large number of biology journals may make effective controls over the publication of such articles infeasible,[44] a question I return to in the next section of this chapter. At least the committee did not invoke bromides about free speech. It summarized noncommittally the police measures that I listed earlier for combating bioterrorism. But we know that many scientists would like to see them relaxed, and the committee did not recommend that they be extended.

Only two of the committee's 18 members were lawyers, and this may explain why it didn't recommend a rollback of existing security measures. Many lawyers, other than prosecutors, think it their role to defend civil liberties against all comers on the ground that law's function is to limit the control of antisocial behavior rather than to promote or facilitate such control. This may be why environmental lawyers, though concerned about genetically modified crops, have not, to my knowledge, expressed concern about bioterrorism, the most ominous form of which depends on the same technology (recombinant DNA). Bioterrorism is a problem of security, and most lawyers conceive of their role in relation to security to be an oppositional one.[45] That is a misconception of the law's social role, and indeed a symptom, it seems to me, of a warped legal culture. The social role of law has always included the protection of person and property against private as well as state invasions—how else to describe the enforcement of property rights, or tort law's provision of remedies against negligent or deliberate personal injuries? Environmental law itself is mainly concerned with policing private actions. Law's function of protecting society against criminals and other predators, including terrorists aspiring to the possession of weapons of mass destruction and suicidal scientists who may want to take the world with them when they go, is as important as law's function of protecting society against its protectors (the police, etc.). Call the first function security, and the second liberty. The set of rights that we call "civil liberties" is then the point of balance between security and liberty, with neither entitled to priority. When the threat to security increases, the protection of civil liberties may properly be reduced if that is the most effective way of meeting the threat.[46]

In economic terms, "after the 9/11 terrorist attack, society's expectations of terrorism losses associated with any given level of civil liberties changed dramatically. Perceived risks rose for any level of civil liberties, and the marginal cost of civil liberties increased dramatically."[47] (The authors make no effort, however, to estimate the cost of reducing civil liberties.) In statistical terms, 9/11 altered the relative costs of false positives and false negatives (type I and type II errors). A false positive would be apprehending a person mistakenly suspected of being a terrorist, a false negative failing to apprehend an actual terrorist. After 9/11 the ratio of these costs fell; the false negative was now more costly to society, relative to the false positive, than had been the case previously, because the aims and capabilities of terrorists were revealed as more ominous than had been thought previously.

But this way of describing the balancing process that determines the optimal level of civil liberties suggests a potentially important qualification. Type I and type II errors in sampling can be reduced simultaneously by increasing the sample size. Similarly, both type I and type II errors in applying police measures to terrorism can be reduced by devoting greater resources to those measures, and overall social costs may be minimized by doing so. A roadblock is a cheaper method of apprehending likely violators of the drug laws than a system that requires individualized suspicion before a car can be inspected. But the roadblock imposes inconvenience on innocent drivers and if that inconvenience is weighted heavily enough the seemingly more costly system may actually be cheaper from an overall social standpoint. To put this differently, in a roadblock system innocent people are inputs into criminal law enforcement, and there may be cheaper inputs.

This point deserves more consideration than it is receiving, as there happens to be a very large pool of resources that could, were it not for political obstacles, readily be diverted to police measures against terrorism, and at little—and maybe actually at negative—social cost. I am referring to the resources that the nation continues to pour into the war on drugs. Because the drug trade is organized and clandestine, the methods employed by law enforcement agencies against it (increasingly with the aid of the military) are similar to those employed against international terrorism. The resources, or many of them, that are being used in the war on drugs could be reallocated to the war on international terrorism at modest costs in reorganization and retraining of the personnel involved in the reallocation.[48]

The principal costs would not be those incident to the redeployment of resources (transition costs), but those resulting from increased consumption of illegal drugs as a result of the reduction in the resources devoted to the enforcement of the drug laws. Those costs would be greater the greater the diversion of effort from the drug war to the terrorism war, yet at most might be slight or even negative, depending on the value that society assigns, or should assign, to reducing the consumption of those drugs. This is not the place to attempt a cost-benefit analysis of the war on drugs. Suffice it to say that throwing hundreds of thousands of people into prison, inciting gang warfare, and complicating our foreign relations—all in order just to raise somewhat the price of an arbitrary subset of mind-altering substances—may well be measures that cost more than they are worth. This is apart from the opportunity costs of the resources that the measures consume—which is to say the value the resources would have in other uses, specifically in fighting terrorism.

Civil libertarians might be more effective in opposing any relaxation of civil liberties to fight terrorism if they considered the sort of trade-offs that I've been discussing. Instead they are wont to say such things as that life would not be worth living if to combat terrorism we curtailed however minutely the civil liberties to which we have become accustomed. Such hyperbole, the secular equivalent of religious fundamentalism and an echo of the right-wing 1950s slogan "better dead than red," which I found no more persuasive then than I find its left-wing counterpart now, will not impress pragmatists. And speaking of the 1950s, Americans had fewer liberties back then, before the Warren Court hit its stride, but most Americans thought life quite worth living nonetheless. To sacrifice some of our currently much enlarged liberty for greater security against catastrophic terrorist attacks is a trade that should not be rejected out of hand.

In wartime we tolerate all sorts of curtailments of our normal liberties, whether in the form of conscription, censorship, disinformation, intrusive surveillance, or suspension of habeas corpus. A lawyer might say that this is because war is a legal status that authorizes such curtailments. But to a realist it is not war as such, but danger to the unusual degree associated with war, that justifies the curtailments. The headlong rush of science and technology has brought us to the point at which a handful of terrorists may be more dangerous than an enemy nation because the terrorists (unlike an enemy nation) may be undeterrable, may have both the desire and the ability to cause a global catastrophe, and may be able to conceal not only their plans and their whereabouts but their very existence from the world's intelligence services.

The trading off of liberty against security is already implicit in the law, which has more play in its joints than many civil libertarians will acknowledge. Even the right of free speech—that touchstone of civil libertarianism—is not absolute. Constitutionally permitted restrictions of speech and other expressive activity abound. They include laws against defamation, invasion of privacy, trespass, criminal solicitation, the disclosure of trade secrets, child pornography, adult hard-core pornography, false advertising, the disclosure of military secrets, advice on committing violent acts, unauthorized publication of copyrighted materials, publicizing sealed court records, hate speech, obscene advertisements, nude dancing, burning one's draft-registration card, loud soundtrucks, parading without a permit, unlimited donations to political campaigns, and indecent speech on radio and television. The Supreme Court has held that the government may prevent "the publication of the sailing dates of transports or the number and location of troops" in time of war.[49] *Progressive* magazine once was enjoined from publishing an article that contained classified information about the design of the hydrogen bomb;[50] the scientific character of the information did not immunize it from regulation. More recently the publisher of *Hit Man: A Technical Manual for Independent Contractors* was held liable in damages, over the publisher's First Amendment objections, to the family of a man murdered by a hit man who had followed the instructions in the book.[51] These cases, especially the last, are persuasive legal authority for suppressing the publication of recipes for creating bioweapons. Many perpetrators of past biological attacks "relied on widely available medical and scientific publications. In a considerable number of cases, perpetrators have also used 'how-to' manuals, including *The Poisoner's Handbook* and *Silent Death*."[52] The publication of such manuals is not privileged by the First Amendment.

Of particular pertinence to this book is the long list of visa restrictions and export controls designed, albeit often ineptly, to restrict the communication of scientific information to potential foreign enemies. Under the International Trade in Arms Regulations,[53] for example—a prize example of an inept attempt to bottle up sensitive information—"a foreign student could be prevented from working in a research laboratory to learn about microprocessor development that has application in high speed computation, but would have access to any information on the subject found in the public domain, i.e., a scholarly journal."[54] My point, however, is only that the restrictions that concern biologists are merely an extension of existing restrictions to an area of science that poses a growing threat to public safety.

The issue presented by such restrictions is not their constitutionality but, as just suggested, their efficacy. The methods and materials for making bioweapons have been so widely publicized that it may be futile to suppress the further dissemination of research findings that could facilitate the creation of new, more potent bioweapons. That is not certain,[55] however, although undoubtedly it is late in the day; the lawsuit against the *Progressive* became moot when the article was published elsewhere.[56] Not all terrorists and potential terrorists have ready access to the *Journal of Virology* or even the *New York Times*. And science is bound to come up with more deadly pathogens, easier ways to manufacture them, more efficacious means of dissemination, and more ways to defeat vaccines, but also better means of defense. It is arguable that the results of such research should be classified.

It is doubtful, moreover, that we should positively *invite* to our biological laboratories students from nations that sponsor or harbor terrorism, on the theory, propounded to me in all seriousness by a distinguished biochemist, that they will remain in the United States, absorb

American values, and cease to pose a danger to the nation. Many individuals admitted to the United States on student visas do remain in the United States, but many do not; of foreign students who received Ph.D.s from American universities in the period 1994–1995, 49 percent were no longer in the United States in 1999.[57] It is doubtful that all of those who returned home had, by virtue of their sojourn in the United States, become inoculated against rabid anti-Americanism.

Turning from censorship to surveillance, I note that the Fourth Amendment prohibits searches, including wiretapping and other forms of electronic surveillance, and seizures (including arrests), only if they are "unreasonable." The conventional lawyer's view is that arrests and searches, both physical and electronic, violate the Fourth Amendment unless they are supported by probable cause (reasonable probability) to believe that the person arrested has committed a crime or that the search will turn up either contraband or evidence of crime, which can then be lawfully seized. But the word "unreasonable" invites and increasingly is receiving an interpretation that requires comparison of the benefits with the costs of the search or seizure. For example, the less costly the search is to the person searched, the less likely it is to be found unreasonable. And because a brief stop of a suspect for minimum questioning and a pat-down search is less intrusive than a full arrest, such stops are permissible upon reasonable suspicion, a less demanding requirement than probable cause.[58]

Realistically, a stop is an arrest, and so the legal treatment of stops shows that the requirement of probable cause to make an arrest or conduct a search is not considered absolute even under existing law (and law can change). This is also shown by the Foreign Intelligence Surveillance Act.[59] That statute, which long predates the 9/11 attacks, authorizes electronic surveillance on the basis of less suspicion than is required in ordinary criminal investigations, when the goal of the surveillance is to obtain information about threats to national security posed by a foreign state—or foreign terrorist group. The rationale for the relaxed standard is that threats to national security are more dangerous than those posed by ordinary criminals.

Generalizing from the FISA, we may say that if the cost of a search or seizure to the person searched or seized is held constant, the level of suspicion required to justify it should fall as the potential harm from the conduct under investigation rises. If C_s is the cost of the search (or seizure) to the person searched, P the probability that the cost will turn up contraband or evidence of crime, and H the harm that the search will avert if successful, so that PH is the expected benefit of the search, the search should be allowed if $C_s < PH$. Thus an increase in H can offset a reduction in P and enable the inequality to be satisfied even though P is now smaller. As my court said in a pre-9/11 opinion, "If the Indianapolis police had a credible tip that a car loaded with dynamite and driven by an unidentified terrorist was en route to downtown Indianapolis, they would not be violating the Constitution if they blocked all the roads to the downtown area even though this would amount to stopping thousands of drivers without suspecting any one of them of criminal activity."[60] Agreeing, the Supreme Court remarked that "the Fourth Amendment would almost certainly permit an appropriately tailored roadblock set up to thwart an imminent terrorist attack."[61] And what I am concerned with in this book is not dynamite but weapons of catastrophic potential, manufactured in laboratories indistinguishable from those used to produce lawful drugs, easily concealed, and wielded by fanatics who may be undeterrable by threat of punishment.

The Foreign Intelligence Surveillance Act allows a curtailment of civil liberties when there is merely a threat to national security. When such a threat becomes actualized in a state of war, further curtailments have traditionally been allowed. Enemy combatants are denied the protection of the First and Fourth Amendments, for example. The reason is not some magic in the word "war." The reason is twofold: the greater menace of war than of crime and the lack of regard that a nation has for foreigners who are warring against it. These reasons apply to international terrorist organizations such as Al Qaeda that are eager to deploy weapons of mass destruction. Organizations of that character are as dangerous as some of the foreign nations that we have warred against. More to the point, a state of war justifies a nation in imposing restrictions on its own citizens that would be excessive in a peacetime setting. It is the same kind of rebalancing of safety and liberty that Congress undertook in the FISA.

Against this doctrinal and historical background, the monitoring of biologists and biological research facilities seems a minimum measure and can readily be squared with constitutional norms. One reason that many civil libertarians will not agree returns us to the opening section of this chapter. The expertise of civil libertarians is in constitutional law, a field innocent of science. The civil libertarian is not expected to know anything about science. But his ignorance injects bias. If he can't evaluate the threat of bioterrorism because evaluation requires a knowledge of biotechnology, he can't balance the liberty interest and the security interest. He is flying on one wing.

Extreme police measures

The measures discussed above, although offensive to doctrinaire civil libertarians as well as to many biologists, stretch but do not break constitutional norms. I think this is probably also true of the various innovations in law enforcement found in the USA PATRIOT Act, only one of which (the limitation on access to lethal pathogens and toxins) I have mentioned. The others include a relaxed standard for eavesdropping on conversations between a criminal defendant and his lawyer, the detention of noncitizens on secret charges, increased power to monitor email traffic, easier access to certain private records, and liberalized use of secret warrants. Taken together, the powers conferred by the act are somewhat ominous, but relatively few people are affected, and it would require a more free-wheeling use of the conferred powers than yet attempted by the Department of Justice to return civil liberties to where they were in, say, the 1950s. I grew up in the 1950s, in a left-wing family, and know all about the harassment to which persons suspected of being communists or fellow-travelers were subjected in that era. My mother lost her job as a New York public school teacher because she refused to swear that she had never been a member of the Communist Party. A number of my parents' friends also lost their jobs because of actual or suspected communist activities.

But the relatively mild measures authorized by the USA PATRIOT Act, and the measures that I discussed in the preceding section of this chapter, may not be adequate to deal with so great a threat as that of bioterrorism or with such lesser but still enormous threats as that of a suitcase nuclear bomb—perhaps a suitcase full of orange-sized nuclear bombs (see chapter 1)—or a dirty bomb (a conventional bomb coated with radioactive material). Understandably in the wake of 9/11, there is growing interest in extreme police measures as a response to extreme risks.[62] These measures might include reprisals against family members of bioterrorists (Israel punishes families of suicide bombers, and Pakistan is beginning to punish tribes that fail to inform on members of Al Qaeda) and also coercive interrogation, verging on or maybe even crossing over into torture, of suspected terrorists believed to have information concerning an impending attack; recently we have learned that coercive interrogation, and worse, have been used against suspected members of Al Qaeda, and others, as part of our global war against terrorism. The rationale for using coercion to extract information is obvious. The rationale for reprisals against family members is less so, but there are grounds for such reprisals. Even would-be mass murderers may be altruistic toward the members of their own family and if so may be deterrable by the threat of punitive measures applied to their family members, although this rationale fails in the case of a terrorist who either has no family or intends or is prepared to destroy the entire human race. A second ground of collective punishment is that the threat of reprisals imparts an incentive to the members of the terrorist's family to try to prevent him from carrying out an attack. Family members become auxiliary police. The analogy is to the common-law principle of respondeat superior, which makes an employer strictly liable for torts committed by his employees in the course of their employment (even for intentional torts, provided they are committed to further, however misguidedly, the employer's business), and by doing so gives the employer an incentive to monitor his employees' conduct.[63]

Forms of collective punishment far more severe than respondeat superior are not alien to our traditions.[64] The economic sanctions that we imposed on Iraq between the 1991 and 2003 wars were a form of collective punishment and caused many innocent people to die, as did our bombing of German and Japanese cities in World War II.

Civil libertarians raise the following objections to resorting to torture to extract information no matter how urgently the information is needed in order to prevent a catastrophe. (They have similar objections to other extreme measures, but I will confine my discussion to torture.) The first is that torture, like slavery, is always and everywhere wrong. Maybe so, but there are lesser and greater wrongs and most people think that a lesser wrong should sometimes be committed to avoid a greater one. "Fighting fire with fire" is an apt metaphor for the use of torture when nothing else will avert catastrophe. And while "the end justifies the means" is a dangerous slogan too, it is dangerous because it ignores the possibility that the end does *not* justify the means. The end may be a good one, yet not as valuable as the means are costly. That is a danger that a balancing test, which compares the value of the end with the cost of the means, avoids.

The second objection is that torture is an ineffectual method of interrogation. This is not so much an objection, however, as a plea in avoidance, since if it is true that torture is always ineffectual it will always flunk a cost-benefit test. Torture may well be a clumsy and inefficient method of interrogation, as well as a method that should be reserved for the gravest of emergencies because of its repulsiveness and frequent inefficacy. Any doubts on this score have been dispelled by the recent revelations concerning the interrogations by American military and civilian personnel at Abu Ghraib prison in Iraq. But it is unrealistic to suppose torture always and everywhere ineffectual; if it were, one wouldn't have to spend so much time debating it.

The insistence of civil libertarians that torture is ineffectual is of a piece with their insistence that the threat of terrorism is exaggerated, and what these insistences reflect is less insight or knowledge than a reluctance to confront difficult choices. Jeffrey Rosen intimates that because people often exaggerate risks, they must be exaggerating the risk of future terrorist attacks.[65] That is a non sequitur. It is especially difficult to see how people can be exaggerating a risk too uncertain to be quantified in even the loosest terms. How could one know whether the risk was being exaggerated? Rosen has no idea; he is whistling in the dark. He is not alone. When the distinguished scientific journal *Nature* uncritically states that "some researchers fear that [research on defenses against bioterrorism] will distort priorities in infectious-disease research, sucking money away from work to understand and counter *natural disease outbreaks that ultimately pose a greater threat to public health*,"[66] one has to ask—how do those researchers know that natural disease outbreaks pose a greater threat to public health than bioterrorism does? In fact nobody knows. In the same article, a Stanford University microbiologist is reported as arguing "that diseases such as influenza and other respiratory-tract infections routinely kill more people than would die in a bioterrorist attack."[67] Again, how does he know? Notice the lack of qualification: not "would probably die," or "might die," but "would die." This is further evidence that the scientific community cannot be trusted to formulate responsible policies regarding the catastrophic risks.

A separate question about the efficacy of torture is its *incremental* effectiveness, given that there are methods of interrogation that, though coercive and even harsh—even cruel—do not rise to the level of "torture,"[68] at least in an unambiguous sense of that word (an important qualification, since the word has in fact no definite extension). It may be enough to go near the borderline without having actually to cross it.[69]

Extracting accurate information is not the only motive for torture. Other motives include extracting false confessions to otherwise unprovable crimes (such as sorcery, for which a confession is likely to be the only type of evidence that has any persuasive force), framing the innocent, intimidating the population or particular subgroups, and sheer sadism. Given the existence of these despicable motives—which go far to explain the abhorrence, and the terrible historical record, of the practice (think of the Inquisition, and of Stalin's show trials—and now of Abu Ghraib)—it is *conceivable* that torture, though resorted to frequently, is a completely inefficacious method of obtaining information. But it is unlikely; the practice is too common, and there is evidence of its efficacy. Alan Dershowitz cites a federal court opinion that approved a police officer's choking a kidnapping suspect until the suspect revealed where the kidnap victim was. Dershowitz also reports the telling example of the Philippine authorities who in 1995 "tortured a terrorist into disclosing information that may have foiled plots to assassinate the pope and to crash eleven commercial airliners carrying approximately four thousand passengers into the Pacific Ocean."[70] Alternative methods of interrogation might not have worked in these cases; in the first, there probably was no time. And Dershowitz asks: "What moral principle could justify the death penalty for past individual murders and at the same time condemn nonlethal torture to prevent future mass murders?"[71]

The third civil-libertarian objection to torture is that recourse to it so degrades a society that it should be forsworn even if the death of many innocents is certain to follow.[72] That proposition can have little appeal to common sense when the survival of the human race is at stake, as it may be in the war against bioterrorism, and even when the stakes are a good deal smaller. It is moral preening. And it is falsified by history. In very recent times, France (in Algeria), the United Kingdom (in its struggle with the Irish Republican Army), and Israel (in combating the Palestinian uprising) have all used torture to extract information, and yet none of these countries has "sunk . . . into barbarism."[73] The use of quasi-torture in the form of the "third degree" to extract information from criminal suspects was common in the United States throughout the first half of the twentieth century and has cropped up occasionally since, and the United States has not sunk into barbarism either. Torture is uncivilized, but civilized nations are able to employ uncivilized means, especially in situations of or closely resembling war, without becoming uncivilized in the process. This may be especially true when the torture is being administered by military personnel operating not in their own country against a domestic enemy but overseas, against foreign troops or terrorists. *Inter armes silent leges.* Nothing is more common than the double standard of cruelty to one's foreign enemies and kindness to one's fellow citizens.

How to reduce the catastrophic risks

Fourth, and most interesting from the perspective of this book, is the implicit argument of some civil libertarians that curtailing civil liberties is itself a catastrophic risk. On this view, the fabric of civilized society, like the fabric of the physical universe according to some scientific theories (recall from chapter 1 the speculation that space may be merely metastable and therefore vulnerable to a disastrous phase transition), is delicate and easily rent, and vulnerable therefore to political disasters fully comparable to natural ones. This is not impossible, and so it should be a consideration included in a cost-benefit analysis of extreme measures for combating bioterrorism. But civil libertarians have not tried to estimate the costs associated with particular curtailments, actual or proposed, of civil liberties. They have been content with uttering extravagant denunciations of any measure, however limited, that cuts back on the current scope of these liberties. Maybe they are science-shy and therefore incapable of evaluating the technological dangers that might make a reduction in civil liberties beneficial to society. Or maybe, like many environmentalists, they believe that the battle for the values they cherish is half lost as soon as those values are subjected to cost-benefit analysis.

Or maybe they just lack confidence that the result of cost-benefit analysis would support their position. After all, given the history of civil liberties in this country, it is highly unlikely that any measures for combating terrorism that are under consideration threaten, whether singly or in combination, to push the country to the brink of a meltdown of liberty and democracy. Americans' civil liberties were less extensive during most of the nation's history, including the Civil War, the two world wars, and the Cold War, than they are today (even after the USA PATRIOT Act and the other legislative and executive responses to 9/11) and no catastrophic political consequences ensued. There must be *some* room for curtailing the current, historically unprecedented extent of those liberties without precipitating a political catastrophe. We are many notches below the trigger point at which the slightest further curtailment of civil liberties would precipitate political catastrophe.

Assuming that constitutional norms cannot be stretched by judicial interpretation far enough to accommodate what I am calling extreme measures, we must ask what the best institutional framework would be for making the trade-off between constitutional rights and public safety. There are two basic alternatives. The first would be a constitutional amendment authorizing the president to suspend normal civil liberties in "emergency" situations. Already the Constitution authorizes the suspension, though only by Congress,[74] of habeas corpus in times of war or rebellion; and the terms "war" and "rebellion" can be stretched, in accordance with the dominant loose-construction approach to the Constitution, to cover a situation in which a terrorist group or a deranged scientist is suspected of being about to launch a biological attack. But Congress might not be able to act in time; suspension of habeas corpus would permit only detentions and not other extreme measures; and extreme measures may be justified on the basis of activities that while dangerous are insufficiently organized to be plausibly described as acts of war or rebellion. When terrorists killed more Americans on September 11, 2001, than had been killed by the Japanese at Pearl Harbor, was that war? It was not rebellion. A broader power to suspend civil liberties, lodged in the president, might thus be necessary to enable measures necessary to prevent catastrophic risks from materializing to be carried out.

But how to define the occasions on which the exercise of such authority would be proper? Catastrophic risks are risks of low or unknown probability though cataclysmic potential. Should the mere existence of such a risk give the president carte blanche to suspend civil liberties? That would be an extreme position. But at the same time, when the issue is how to define the occasions on which it is appropriate to suspend civil liberties, the definition of catastrophic risk in this book is too narrow. It would be unacceptable to have a rule that the president can suspend civil liberties if such suspension is necessary to prevent the extinction of the human race, but not if it is necessary "merely" to prevent the killing of a million Americans. But where to draw the line? And if the line is left fuzzy, as it is bound to be, officials will be tempted to investigate its location by aggressive assertion of the suspension power.

A better alternative might be to give the president no legal authority to suspend civil liberties, instead trusting to his doing so extralegally should the occasion imperatively demand it. The fact that he would be acting extralegally, as Lincoln frequently did during the Civil War, would act as a brake on the irresponsible exercise of his power. So would the fact that his subordinate officers who implemented a directive to disregard the constitutional rights of suspects could be sued and made to pay damages to the persons whose rights they had violated.

Alan Dershowitz proposes "torture warrants"[75] as a means of bringing the use of torture under judicial control so as to minimize abuses. It is unclear whether that would be the effect. The significance of warrants as a check on executive discretion is exaggerated. A warrant is issued in an ex parte proceeding, and usually the police officer seeking the warrant has a choice of judges or magistrates from whom to seek it. So there isn't much actual screening in most cases. And it is probably inevitable that in national-security cases the judicial officers authorized to issue such warrants will be chosen in part for their sensitivity to security concerns. Moreover, the warrants and supporting affidavits, as well as the judges' reasons for granting the warrants, would be likely to remain secret. The requirement of a warrant would make the officers seeking authority to conduct coercive interrogations a little more careful, but perhaps not much more truthful or candid given the secrecy of the proceeding. The main effects of requiring a warrant in cases of coercive interrogation might be to provide legal immunity for the officers executing the warrants[76] (the judges or magistrates who issued the warrants would enjoy the usual absolute judicial immunity from damages suits) and to whitewash questionable practices by making people think there was firm judicial control over such interrogations.

Historically, warrants were feared because they gave searching and arresting officers immunity from being sued for violating property rights. Contrary to its modern interpretation, the Fourth Amendment does not favor warrants. Rather, as is apparent from its text ("The right of the people to be secure in their persons, houses, papers, and effects, against unreasonable searches and seizures, shall not be violated, and no Warrants shall issue, but upon probable cause, supported by Oath or affirmation, and particularly describing the place to be searched, and the persons or things to be seized"), it disfavors them. It limits their use by authorizing them only upon probable cause and particular description of the place to be searched (or the person or thing to be seized), whereas searches and seizures not made pursuant to warrant are allowed as long as they are not "unreasonable," a word that the amendment does not define.

Moreover, to amplify an earlier point, if legal rules are promulgated that permit torture in (though only in) defined circumstances, officials will want to explore the outer bounds of the permission; and the practice of torture, once it was thus regularized by judicial demarcation of those bounds, would be likely to become regular within them, ceasing to be an exceptional practice and setting the stage for further extensions. It is a valid worry of civil libertarians that once one starts down the balancing path, the protection of civil liberties can quickly erode. One begins with the extreme case—the terrorist with plague germs or an A-bomb the size of an orange in his Dopp kit, or the kidnapper who alone can save his victim's life by revealing the victim's location. So far, so good; but then the following reflections are invited: if torture is legally justifiable when the lives of thousands are threatened, what about when the lives of hundreds are threatened, or tens? And the kidnap victim is only one. By such a chain of reflections one might be persuaded to endorse a rule that torture is justified if, all things considered, the benefits, which will often be tangible (lives, or a life, saved), exceed the costs, which will often be nebulous.

A related objection to torture warrants is the difficulty of defining in advance the occasions that would justify such extreme measures (what exactly would a statute authorizing such warrants say?), which may lead to embarrassment if an unforeseen situation arises in which the case for allowing torture is compelling but the situation happens to fall outside the boundaries that had been fixed in advance. It may be better to stick with our rather strict rules (though they are not as strict as many civil libertarians believe they are or should be), trusting executive officials to break them when the stakes are high enough to enable the officials to obtain political absolution for their illegal conduct, rather than giving officials legal immunity. This is a case where we may not want judges to engage in cost-benefit analysis.

I fear that I will be misunderstood as advocating the use of torture to combat the threat posed by bioterrorism or other deliberate catastrophic acts. I do not advocate it. I have no idea whether it is necessary, given the availability of methods of coercive interrogation that are not torture, or at least not quite torture, or at least not torture in the strongest sense, yet that appear to be effective, at least given time (a potentially significant qualification, obviously). I have in mind such things as isolation, bright lights (the old "third degree"), shouting, threats, truth serums, and lies. These are not pretty methods of extracting information, but neither are they *necessarily* to be regarded as "torture." The word has no settled meaning. It is the label we pin on forms of coercion that we consider especially abhorrent. It has therefore a flexible denotation. The methods of coercive interrogation that I have listed do not involve the infliction of physical pain or extreme humiliation, yet even so are appropriate only when there is a solid basis for supposing that vital information can be obtained only by that route, and not by alternative means.

My reason for bringing "real" torture into the picture was, I repeat, not to propose its use (the prudential arguments against it have been greatly strengthened by the Abu Ghraib scandal) but to demonstrate that even curtailing civil liberties to the point of authorizing the use of torture against suspected terrorists would not pose a *catastrophic* political risk. Its use in this setting therefore cannot be opposed on the ground that it would create a risk, such as that of military dictatorship, that might be considered comparable (weighting probability by consequences) to the risk of a catastrophic bioterrorist attack. Ugly as the Abu Ghraib scandal is, no one supposes that it threatens to unravel our liberal democratic society.

What civil libertarians should be worrying about is what will happen to civil liberties if there is *another* attack comparable to that of 9/11. Most Americans put safety ahead of civil liberties. If moderate curtailment of those liberties today will prevent terrorist attacks tomorrow, the total curtailment may be much less than if a no-curtailment policy allows such an attack to occur.⁷⁷ The civil libertarian who treats the Bill of Rights as a suicide pact does less damage to national security than he does to the Bill of Rights. Before 9/11, the American Civil Liberties Union opposed the screening of airline passengers who traveled to countries that sponsored terrorism.⁷⁸ It is conceivable that such screening would have prevented the 9/11 attacks—and the restrictions on civil liberties that ensued in reaction to those attacks.

Another way in which civil libertarians exhibit, as it seems to me at any rate, a blinkered perspective is by taking a purely legalistic approach to the civil-libertarian implications of efforts to deal with the danger of catastrophic terrorism, and, specifically, by being fixated on constitutional law. Censorship, searches, and torture are all matters regulated by constitutional law. There would be no constitutional violation if the government, without using any such methods, but simply by pooling the information contained in databases to which it lawfully has access, created detailed dossiers on every person in the United States, and as I suggested in the last section of chapter 1, this is rapidly becoming feasible. Although some civil libertarians are alert to this danger,⁷⁹ they have no constructive suggestions for averting or even evaluating it, because it doesn't present a question of constitutional law. A closely related point is the failure of most civil libertarians⁸⁰ to connect the surveillance involved in trying to prevent terrorism to those "innocent," often private, forms of surveillance and data discussed in the earlier chapter. The danger may be less that the government will get its hands on additional personal data for use against terrorism than that the enhanced activities of surveillance and digitization associated with defending the nation against international terrorism will move us closer to the day in which personal privacy is completely extinguished as a result of the growth and linkage of electronic databases. That is a prospect well worth worrying about.

Punishing hackers

My final example of a specific policy that merits consideration concerns the punishment of people who deliberately "infect" computers with computer viruses.[81] (This is actually a subset of computer hackers, others being engaged in such relatively—I stress relatively—innocuous activities as facilitating the violation of copyright law. The term is also used, by those within the computer community, to refer to the virtuous activity of deriving ingenious and unconventional solutions to difficult computer problems.) Here I speak with greater confidence: they should be subjected to severe criminal punishments, such as a mandatory prison sentence of five years. The heavier the punishment, the greater the deterrence and also the less that needs to be spent on trying to catch violators, though if punishment is too heavy juries may be reluctant to convict.

There are four objections to severe prison sentences, but none is applicable to the hacker case. The first, which is ethical in character, resting on notions of retribution rather than of deterrence, is that severe punishment for a particular crime may be disproportionate to the gravity of that crime. That objection is answered here by the potential dangers that computer viruses pose not merely to the economic health of the nation but also to its physical safety, when one considers the havoc that computer viruses might wreak on military and other security-related computer operations and how, specifically, such viruses might interact with acts of physical terrorism to increase the damage caused by such acts. Think of the hacker who by hacking into a truck company's computer network pinpoints the location of a shipment of fissile materials or lethal pathogens and conveys the information to a terrorist group.

The second objection is that heavy sentences enlarge the prison population and it is expensive to imprison people—the direct expenses are great and in addition society is deprived of the benefits of the prisoner's engaging in lawful employment. A worker who cannot capture the full social value of his work in the compensation he receives—and that is the usual case—confers a net benefit on the rest of society. A prisoner confers no benefit. The objection depends, however, on a tacit assumption that the elasticity of crime to punishment is less than 1. If a 1 percent increase in the length of the prison sentence for some crime resulted via deterrence in a 1 percent reduction in the number of crimes, the prison population would be unchanged.[82] The length of time each prisoner would spend in prison would rise by 1 percent but this would be offset by the fact that there would be 1 percent fewer prisoners. If instead of being −1 (negative because the increase in punishment reduces the amount of crime and hence the number of prisoners) the elasticity were −2, the total number of prisoners and hence the total costs of imprisonment would fall, while if it were −½ the prison population would increase because the increase in the length of imprisonment would be double the decrease in the number of prisoners.

In the case of hackers the elasticity of crime to punishment is likely to be greater than −1 in absolute terms (that is, to be a larger negative number) because they are intelligent people with good lawful alternative uses of their time. They will be quick to learn about the heavier penalties, to assess the significance of such penalties, and to search and find alternative uses for their computer skills. Some of them are unbalanced but few are the kind of political or religious fanatic who cannot be deterred by threat of punishment.

Third, for people who have high discount rates, increasing the length of prison sentences has only a limited deterrent effect because the increase is tacked on at the end of the sentence and as a result may have little weight in the decision whether to commit the crime. This should not be a problem with hackers. They are for the most part educated people, and people who bother to obtain an education generally have low discount rates because the costs of education are incurred in the present but the benefits, in the form of the higher income that an education enables a person to obtain, are deferred to the future.

Finally, heavy punishments can impair marginal deterrence, which is the policy of maintaining heavier punishments for more serious crimes in order to deter substitution of more for less serious crimes. If robbery were punished as heavily as murder, robbers would have an increased incentive to murder their victims because that would reduce the probability of punishment (by eliminating witnesses) without increasing its severity. This is not a danger with hackers. If deterred from creating and spreading computer viruses, they will not become rapists and murderers; they will become lawful computer programmers—perhaps specializing in making computers more secure against viruses!

Conclusion

To summarize *very* briefly:

The risks of global catastrophe are greater and more numerous than is commonly supposed, and they are growing, probably rapidly. They are growing for several reasons: the increasing rate of technological advance—for a number of the catastrophic risks are created or exacerbated by science and its technological and industrial applications (including such humble ones as the internal combustion engine); the growth of the world economy and world population (both, in part, moreover, indirect consequences of technological progress); and the rise of apocalyptic global terrorism. And the risks are, to a degree, convergent or mutually reinforcing. For example, global warming contributes to loss of biodiversity, an asteroid collision could precipitate catastrophic global warming and cause mass extinctions, and cyberterrorism could be employed to facilitate terrorist attacks with weapons of mass destruction.

Each catastrophic risk, being slight in a probabilistic sense (or *seeming* slight, because often the probability cannot be estimated even roughly) when the probability is computed over a relatively short time span, such as a year or even a decade, is difficult for people to take seriously. Apart from the psychological difficulty that people have in thinking in terms of probabilities rather than frequencies, frequencies normally provide a better grounding for estimating probabilities than theory does; frequent events generate information that enables probabilities to be confirmed or updated. The fact that there have been both nuclear attacks and, albeit on a very limited scale, bioterrorist attacks—which, however, resemble natural disease episodes, of which the human race has a long experience—has enabled the public to take these particular risks seriously. The general tendency, however, is to ignore the catastrophic risks, both individually and in the aggregate. Economic, political, and cultural factors, including the religious beliefs prevalent in the United States, reinforce the effect of cognitive factors (including information costs) in inducing neglect of such risks. The neglect is misguided. The expected costs of even very-low-probability events can be huge if the adverse consequences should the probability materialize are huge, or if the interval over which the probability is estimated is enlarged; the risk of a catastrophic collision with an asteroid is slight in the time span of a year, but not so slight in the time span of a hundred years.

As my reference to "expected costs" suggests, the tools of economic analysis—in particular, cost-benefit analysis—are indispensable to evaluating the possible responses to the catastrophic risks. This is so despite great difficulties in quantifying the essential elements of such analysis, including value of life and discount rates, and a variety of subtle and impalpable, but potentially substantial, costs and benefits. Through such techniques discussed in chapter 3 as "time horizons," "tolerable windows," and "inverse cost-benefit analysis," it may be possible to adapt cost-benefit analysis to the major challenges that the catastrophic risks present to such analysis.

Sadly, some of the measures that may be essential to responding effectively to the most serious of the catastrophic risks are likely to involve heavy economic costs, as in the case of global warming; or substantial interference with civil liberties and our accustomed way of life generally, as in the case of bioterrorism; or, as in both cases, a significant surrender of national sovereignty to international organizations. Other measures, however, such as shifting the focus of both general and professional education in the direction of a greater understanding of science, and improving our domestic arrangements (judicial and otherwise) for dealing with catastrophic risks, seem relatively unproblematic, although they are neither costless nor sufficient.

In an attempt to put a little flesh on the foregoing very skeletal summary, I shall revisit a number of the doomsday scenarios described in chapter 1, pointing out the distinctive features bearing on assessment and response that each presents. The first was a natural disease pandemic that might cause even more deaths than the Spanish flu pandemic of 1918–1919. It is the least problematic of the doomsday scenarios, not because it is less probable than the others (it is less probable than some, more probable than others, so far as one can estimate the probabilities) but because it is being addressed in a rational way. The reason is that it is so familiar. Not only is there a very long history of pandemics—one of which, the Black Death that wiped out a substantial fraction of the European population during the Middle Ages, remains seared into historical memory—but there have been a number of recent pandemics, such as AIDS and SARS, that have kept the problem in the public eye. There is nothing *novel* about a pandemic to fog thinking about it. The Centers for Disease Control, and similar institutions in other nations, along with the World Health Organization, constitute a network of experienced public health officials and workers, physicians, epidemiologists, and biologists who are alert to new diseases and ways of containing them. There is always the possibility that the entire global public health infrastructure might be overwhelmed by a disease of unprecedented lethality and contagiousness; and maybe more resources ought to be devoted to preventing such an eventuality. But I am unaware of any serious analytical deficiencies or political distortions in the global response to the risk of natural pandemics.

I have a similar though not identical view regarding measures being taken against nuclear war, nuclear proliferation, and nuclear terrorism. It is not identical because additional police measures may be needed to deal with the efforts of terrorist groups to obtain weapons of mass destruction. Probably the United States and other wealthy countries should be devoting even more resources to helping a still-impoverished Russia secure its enormous stocks of fissile material; but I am not competent to assess the adequacy of the measures that we are taking to restrict the nuclear programs of North Korea and Iran and to prevent North Korea and Pakistan from assisting other nations to obtain nuclear weapons.

Nuclear threats are familiar and feared, like the threat of pandemics. It is otherwise when attention shifts to the second natural catastrophe that I emphasized—a major asteroid collision. The number of expected human deaths from asteroid collisions follows a catastrophic risk distribution, meaning that the most serious collision in the range of possibilities considered would account for most of the deaths. Although a collision of that magnitude is highly unlikely if its probability is computed over the span of a few decades (a probability is greater the longer the interval being considered—the probability that one will be involved in an automobile accident is greater in the next 10 years than in the next month), its expected cost is not negligible, because a very low probability is being multiplied by a very great loss if the risk materializes. That conjunction defines "catastrophic risk" as I am using the term, but with the further proviso that the loss must be cataclysmic.

The very low probability associated with a catastrophic risk distribution causes two problems from the point of view of rational policy responses. The first is that for reasons evolutionary biology illuminates, most people have, as I have already noted, difficulty in thinking sensibly either about probabilities in the abstract, as distinct from experienced frequencies, or, the same point viewed differently, about events that could occur but haven't yet. In economic terms, they incur a high imagination cost when they try to think about new situations—situations that have no history—especially if the new situation is unlike any found in the environment to which the ancestors of modern human beings became adapted tens of thousands of years ago as a result of the operation of natural selection. Being able to cope with very-low-probability events would not have had survival value in that environment; hence the difficulty most of us have working with statistics. People tend either to ignore very small probabilities altogether or to exaggerate them.

It is not just small probabilities that people have difficulty with; it is also unmemorable events. A remarkable fact is how unafraid people are of influenza, even though the 1918–1919 pandemic killed upwards of 20 million people in a short period of time, a similar pandemic could recur, there is still no cure for the disease, and flu vaccines are unreliable because of the mutability of the virus. Because influenza is not disfiguring and even in the 1918–1919 pandemic the mortality rate was low, although total mortality can be very great and was then, and most curiously of all because no famous people died in the pandemic, its victims being almost all young adults, the pandemic has faded from our historical memory.[1] This doesn't show that people are dopes or are irrational, only that human mental capacity is limited and the mind uses various triggers to direct its attention. At present those triggers are lacking not only for influenza but also for asteroid collisions, even though many people are fearful of much lesser threats, such as low-level radiation and ambient cigarette smoke. There is no historical memory of asteroids colliding with the earth and so we find it hard to take the threat of such collisions seriously even if we accept that it exists. This is an example of the distinction that I pointed out in the introduction between notional and motivational beliefs.

A further problem arising from the low-probability character of the catastrophic risks concerns estimates of the value of life, which play so central a role in cost-benefit analyses of measures for dealing with lethal risks. These estimates turn unreliable, even indeterminate, when, however cataclysmic the consequences should the risk materialize, the probability of its materializing is very slight. Recall that value of life is estimated by dividing the cost that people incur to avoid a risk by the risk itself, so that if a person will pay $30 or its equivalent to avert a 1 in 100,000 risk of death, his or her value of life will be estimated at $3 million. Observation of people's behavior with respect to the risk of death from crossing a street against the light suggests that when a risk is very small, people will not incur even a trivial cost to avert it even though they are likely to be risk averse—they're just not *that* risk averse. More generally, the function that relates value of life to risk is asymptotic, so that while no amount of money will compensate the average person for assuming a very high risk of death (because if the risk materializes he will have derived no benefit from the compensation), very little if any money may be required to compensate him fully for assuming a minute risk, such as a one-in-a-million or one-in-a-billion probability of being killed. Whether this reaction should be considered a matter of preference or an inability to handle very small probabilities is relevant from a policy standpoint because if it is the former, government intervention would be paternalistic in a strong sense—would be a matter of protecting people (at some cost) against risks they don't want to be protected against, rather than just of correcting a cognitive defect.

Even if our insouciant reaction to small probabilities of great losses is accepted as an authentic basis for estimating the value of life in most such situations, the reaction may not generalize to ones in which the loss, should it materialize, would be the near or total extinction of the human race. If the annual probability of an asteroid collision that would kill 6 billion people is only 1 in 75 million, the expected number of deaths worldwide is only 80 per year, which may not seem a

Conclusion

large enough number to justify the expense of an effective defense against an asteroid collision. (This of course ignores smaller but still lethal collisions; but read on.) But if there is a minute chance that the entire human race, both current and future, would be wiped out, together with all or most of the world's animal population, we (the ambiguous "we" of policy analysis, but here it may represent dominant public opinion) may think that *something* should be done to eliminate or reduce the risk, slight as it is, beyond what a standard cost-benefit analysis would imply; may be willing, if the risk and the possible responses are explained carefully, to incur some cost in higher taxes or otherwise to reduce the risk.

So there is a conundrum. We don't know how to value life for purposes of conducting a cost-benefit analysis of asteroid defense because we don't know whether we should be discounting or escalating the conventional value of life estimates or, if we should be doing both, whether the adjustments would be offsetting. But what we can do is generate a range of estimates of the expected costs of asteroid collisions to human life and compare it with the amount of money currently being spent on asteroid defense. If that amount is below the lowest point on the range, we know that we're spending too little—which appears to be the case, as we saw in chapter 3. We can also, as we did there as well, divide the amount being spent on asteroid defense by the range of estimates of the expected costs of asteroid collisions to obtain the probability range that would make the expenditure optimal. When we did this, we discovered that the risk is being underestimated. (This is an application of what I have called "inverse cost-benefit analysis.")

The next analytical step is to try to discover *why* the risk is being underestimated. In the case of the asteroid menace the answer may lie in a combination of the science-fiction label that has become attached to the menace, the lack of any history of casualties being caused by asteroids (in contrast to the history of natural disease pandemics), and the sense that concern with such low-probability dangers would be a distraction from the struggle against international terrorism. I am not satisfied with the answer, and not only because of its spongy and speculative character. NASA should be eager to shift some of its emphasis from manned space flight, with all the controversy that manned space flight has engendered—increasingly both the monetary and the safety costs seem disproportionate to the benefits—to combating the asteroid menace. A practical obstacle to such a shift may be that the asteroid defense itself, as distinct from the system of detecting approaching asteroids, would be a project for the Air Force. And the Air Force may not wish to be deflected from preparing for and conducting wars, or from the greater technological challenge posed by the ABM defense— while NASA may wish to keep the Air Force, a more influential institution, out of space, where at present NASA reigns supreme except for a handful of military satellites. But all this is just conjecture.

The first of the man-made but accidental catastrophes that I discussed was the threat of an earth-destroying strangelet disaster resulting from experiments conducted in high-energy particle accelerators, beginning with Brookhaven's new (in 2000) Relativistic Heavy Ion Collider. That disaster threat shares with the threat of asteroid collisions all the problems for cost-benefit analysis created by the combination of an extremely low probability of disaster with an extremely high cost if disaster occurs. But these problems are even more acute in the case of a possible strangelet disaster. Not only would such a disaster involve the destruction of the earth, together with *all* its inhabitants, human and nonhuman alike, but the probability of such a disaster, although it appears to be even lower than that of an asteroid collision that would wipe out the human race and most other species, cannot be estimated. That is why no stronger statement is possible than that the probability of a strangelet disaster "appears" to be lower than that of a catastrophic asteroid collision. So estimating the safety costs of RHIC, or of future accelerators such as CERN's Large Hadron Collider or (if it is funded) RHIC–II, is even more difficult than in the case of asteroid collisions— and for the further reason that the benefits of the experiments conducted in such facilities cannot be quantified or even, it seems, estimated, whether by the method of contingent valuation or otherwise. Those benefits are the incremental value to human welfare (in its broadest sense) of the experiments, and are unknown and cannot be presumed to be great. Because research accelerators are costly both to build and to operate, the net benefits of these new accelerators may actually be negative quite apart from safety costs.

There is an argument, which if accepted would help resolve the safety issue, for leaving the financing of such experiments, and of the facilities in which they are conducted, to the private sector. It is not obvious why particle research is being financed by government, or why it should be. There are no military benefits or, so far as appears, any other public benefits, unless quenching abstract scientific curiosity is reckoned a benefit to the public as a whole. High-energy physics research is costly, but it is also collaborative, and universities the world over could pool their resources to operate the limited number of cutting-edge research accelerators. If that were done and the requisite financing were found, the issue of safety would remain. But because the danger would no longer be one created by a government project, we could expect greater regulatory attention to safety concerns. Stated differently, the privatization of accelerator research would pave the way for a better institutional framework for making decisions about the catastrophic risks that such research may create. The existing framework is unsatisfactory. Brookhaven's director appointed an ad hoc committee to evaluate the catastrophic risks created by RHIC, for which he is to be commended because he was under no legal duty to do so. (As a practical matter, however, he may have had no choice because of Brookhaven's famously poor safety record.) But the committee was not balanced and could not be considered completely neutral and disinterested.

Whoever owns the research accelerators, we know that if a project's margin of expected benefits over expected costs, ignoring safety, is small, bringing safety into the picture might well tip the balance against the experiments and hence the facilities in which they are conducted, since they are so expensive to build and operate. Hence the importance of careful cost-benefit analysis conducted by neutral experts. But would it have been *possible* to constitute a balanced, neutral, disinterested—but informed—committee to determine the safety of allowing RHIC to go into operation? This is part of the larger question of the social control of science and technology, and in turn the question of the legal profession's scientific literacy. The rapid advance of science, and the concomitant increase in the complexity and opacity of scientific knowledge, have widened the gap between expert and lay understandings of science. Social control of science cannot be left to scientists, but neither can it be consigned to scientific ignoramuses.

The problem is not solely one of a knowledge or skills gap. There is also an attitude gap created by the different goals, and resulting different mindsets, of science on the one hand and public policy on the other. The scientist qua scientist wants to increase scientific knowledge, not make the world safer—especially from science. But if science policy therefore cannot be left to scientists, then, given the centrality of lawyers in the administration of public policy in this country, a reform of legal education that stresses the need for a greater number of lawyers to understand science than do at present should be a priority. It would not be a very costly reform. Only the will is wanting.

When we turn to the next of the disaster scenarios, runaway nano-technology, the new wrinkle is that the threat is safely, as it were, in the future. An asteroid collision or an earth-destroying particle-accelerator accident could happen at any time, although because of its low probability such an event is unlikely to happen soon. The *cumulative* probability of such a disaster is much greater. That is one reason discounting to present value is such a fraught issue in evaluating proposed responses to catastrophic risks. The longer the interval, the higher the probability of catastrophe but the further the expected costs of the catastrophe lie in the future—and we don't have a good idea of how to weight future losses. That situation is to be distinguished from one in which we *know* that the risk is not imminent, provided that a failure to take precautions now will not prevent us from dealing effectively and economically with the risk when and if it does materialize. There won't be a danger of runaway nanotechnology until general-purpose molecular assemblers are created; and it is not even certain that they ever will be created, although it would be reckless to assume they won't be. The same is true of the threat (which is real, despite its being a staple of science-fiction cinema) posed by the development of superintelligent robots as a result of advances in nanotechnology, molecular biology, artificial intelligence, robotics, and computerization. In both cases—the nanotech "gray goo" threat and the threat of conquest by super-intelligent robots—we can wait a few years, meanwhile gathering information that will help us to anticipate and head off any disasters that may emerge from these threats. (But is anyone actually trying to gather that information?) The closely related though probably much slighter danger posed by genetically modified crops is imminent, however. It is closely related because the nanomachines feared by Martin Rees would be a kind of superweed, and genetically modified crops are modified in part to give them a weedlike robustness. The process could conceivably get out of hand, generating voracious GMCs that would squeeze out other crops and natural flora, though at present this seems highly unlikely. Unfortunately, serious thinking about the dangers posed by GMCs has been retarded by what appears to be a completely unfounded, and therefore easily ridiculed, fear that genetically modified foods are not safe to eat.

Turning to global warming, we again confront a danger that seems to lie comfortably in the future. But in this case a wait-and-see policy would be perilous. We cannot assume continued *gradual* warming that will not reach a critical level for a century or more. We probably can assume that it will be decades before rising global temperatures reach a level at which catastrophe, in the form of abrupt global warming such as occurred at the end of the Younger Dryas period more than 10,000 years ago, becomes a live possibility. But during this period the level of greenhouse gases in the atmosphere will probably be increasing rapidly. The burning of fossil fuels, and of Third World forests, will be continuing unabated, and because once emitted into the atmosphere carbon dioxide takes a long time to be removed from it by being absorbed by the oceans, the continued emissions will have a cumulative effect on the amount of carbon dioxide in the atmosphere. Even if the annual level of emissions falls, which is unlikely without costly public intervention in the form of emissions taxes or a cap-and-trade regime, atmospheric concentrations of carbon dioxide and other greenhouse gases will continue increasing as long as emissions are positive. Eventually, and perhaps sooner rather than later, the atmospheric concentrations may reach a level that triggers abrupt, catastrophic global warming—the kind of global temperature spike that ended the Younger Dryas. No one knows what that trigger point is or when it will be reached (if ever), but it will be reached sooner if we do nothing, starting now, to reduce emissions.

There is a seductive argument (seductive because emissions controls, even in the moderate form that I suggested in chapter 3, would be very costly) that we can ignore global warming because *surely* by the middle of the century clean energy technologies, such as wind, sun, and hydrogen, and technologies for removing carbon dioxide from the atmosphere, such as nanotech scrubbers, will be feasible and economical, and will come on line either without governmental prodding or with just modest subsidies for R & D. This is possible, but it is far from certain—and anyway the trigger point that I mentioned may be reached before midcentury, though this is still another thing that no one knows. It may not even be highly probable, unless the pace of technological change is forced by subsidization, or (my preference) by emissions taxes that raise the cost of fossil fuels dramatically. It is not easy to foresee automobiles or airplanes powered by wind or sunlight; current methods of producing hydrogen use large amounts of fossil fuels; and nuclear energy, though clean, is likely to remain marginal for a combination of political and safety reasons, including the risk of nuclear terrorism, which is greater the more nuclear reactors there are in the world.

Speaking of clean fuels and carbon sequestration—cars powered by hydrogen generated without burning fossil fuels and nanomachines that float through the air gobbling the molecules of carbon dioxide dissolved in it—we can't responsibly assume that technology will bail us out, courtesy of the free market. Policy based on best-case scenarios is sensible only for ostriches. Headlong as the pace of scientific advance has been and will doubtless continue to be, there are plenty of recent examples of technologies that stagnated. Think of how little the technology of civilian aircraft and of automobiles has changed in the last half century (since the introduction of jet airliners). All this time they have been guzzling gasoline, and they may still be doing so in fifty years. What may be more promising, though as yet hypothetical, is the development of technologies for removing carbon dioxide from the atmosphere or preventing it from entering the atmosphere in the first place. But the market cannot be relied on to adopt such technologies, because they would not reduce private costs. A device installed in automobiles for removing carbon dioxide would confer no measurable benefit on the manufacturer or owner of the automobile and so would lack a market.

Although there is a strong case for taking measures against global warming now rather than waiting decades to do so, the question remains what measures to take—how much cost to incur—and the answer depends in part on the weight to be given the welfare of future generations, since it is most likely that the costs of global warming will be borne primarily by them. That weight depends on the discount rate used to translate future into present costs, and there is no objective guide to the choice of that rate when the costs to be discounted will be borne primarily by remote future generations. At any significant discount rate, even one as low as 2 or 3 percent, the distant future receives almost no consideration, while at a zero discount rate, proposed by some philosophers, the cost of a risk that will affect an indefinite number of future generations will approach infinity. So again, as with valuing extinction events, we have an enormous range of possibilities and no obvious way of selecting among them. However, the "time horizons" method of restating the outcome of discounting seems to me helpful in thinking about the problem. That ingenious method involves partitioning the future into a near term in which the future is weighted equally with the present and a far term in which the future is given no weight. The length of the near term is obtained simply by dividing 1 by the discount rate. So if the discount rate is 2 percent, the near term is 50 years, and the costs expected to be borne in that period are taken into the cost-benefit analysis without discounting, while any costs borne after that term are ignored. If we are willing to weight costs incurred by others, and ourselves if we live so long, 50 years hence as heavily as we would weight a cost incurred today, but are not willing to weight more remote costs, then 2 percent is indeed the right discount rate. If we are more future-regarding, and would be willing to weight costs incurred 100 years hence as heavily as those incurred today, the right discount rate to use would be 1 percent.

It may even be possible to dispense with explicit discounting altogether when the focus is on the risk of abrupt rather than gradual global warming; and that is my focus. Abrupt global warming could happen soon enough to make discounting unimportant in deciding whether we should take steps to avert it.

A further complication, both in choosing a discount rate and in organizing international cooperation on measures to retard global warming, is that the poor countries bear the primary risk from global warming while the rich countries would bear the primary cost of measures to control it, and the poor countries aren't able to compensate the rich for taking those measures. Another complication is that to arrest global warming is thought to require limitations on greenhouse-gas emissions by developing countries, and the steep costs of those measures would be borne by the inhabitants of those countries, who are already poor. But these problems, too, can be elided by shifting the focus to abrupt global warming, which could be catastrophic for the wealthy as well as for the poor countries and cannot be assumed to threaten merely in the distant future, and by emphasizing the technology-forcing effects of emissions controls. Even if just the wealthy countries limit their emissions, the resulting increase in the price of fossil fuels would create strong market incentives to develop new technologies, whether cheap and effective methods of carbon sequestration or cheap clean fuels (that is, either taking carbon dioxide out of the atmosphere or preventing it from entering the atmosphere in the first place).

With global warming we have our first taste of sharp scientific disagreement. This statement may seem surprising in view of the controversy that swirled around RHIC. But actually there wasn't a great deal of controversy over the basic *scientific* question, which was whether a strangelet disaster could occur. All the scientists agreed both that the probability of such a disaster was greater than zero and that it was very small. The disagreements, flagged with particular clarity in the articles by Kent and Calogero that I cited in chapter 3, had mainly to do with attitude toward risk and estimations of the cost if the risk materialized, though there was also disagreement about the robustness of the empirical evidence used to bolster the theoretical argument against the likelihood of a strangelet disaster. Similarly, while there is disagreement regarding the probability and consequences of asteroid collisions, the disagreement occupies a relatively narrow range, so far as bears on policy. The fiercest controversy is over the Alvarezes' hypothesis that the asteroid that hit what is now Mexico 65 million years ago was the sole cause of the extinction of the dinosaurs. The difference is not important to evaluating the consequences of such a collision for the human race today—it is certain that they would be catastrophic and quite possible that they would be terminal. A collision with a much smaller asteroid could be catastrophic as well, and is much more likely.

But in contrast to the broad area of scientific agreement regarding experiments in RHIC and asteroid collisions, there are reputable scientists who do not believe that the burning of fossil fuels, or other human activities, such as deforestation, are a significant factor in global warming, or who believe that global warming will almost certainly not reach a level that will impose significant costs. The skeptics are in a distinct minority, however, and the most sensible response is to use their doubts as a basis for adjusting one's estimate of the mean probability of specific consequences of continued greenhouse-gas emissions and the confidence intervals surrounding those means, rather than for dismissing the dangers presented by global warming as unproven. It would be a mistake either to ignore the doubters, which is the tendency of environmentalists, or to ignore majority opinion, which is the tendency of conservatives. The tendency to go with a doubt, however slight, when it coincides with one's preferences is a conspicuous example of wishful thinking. And to the extent that doubts about the gravity of global warming rest, as they largely do, on sheer uncertainty about the causality of climate change, they may, by broadening the confidence interval around whatever mean probability is picked, actually point to the desirability of *greater* efforts to control global warming, because variance imposes disutility on the risk averse. Alternatively, if the nature of the scientific disagreement is such that splitting the difference, as it were, would be irrational—as it would be if one scientist said that restricting emissions would not affect global warming and another said it would but only if emissions were cut by at least half—then we have an either-or choice, and if we are risk averse we'll be inclined to choose the safe option. But this will depend in part on the option's cost. In the example just given, it would make no sense to try to split the difference of opinion by cutting emissions by one-quarter.

Though analytically appealing, the suggested methods of adjusting cost-benefit analysis to take account of scientific uncertainty are politically naive, at least with respect to global warming. Because the costs of an effective response to global warming are very great and are concentrated on politically influential industries and their customers (think of the fate of President Clinton's proposed B.T.U. tax in his first term of office and the subsequent disappearance of such proposals from the political agenda), doubt about the necessity for a response becomes a powerful talking point against having to respond. It is difficult to ask people to lower their standard of living in order to avoid a harm that reputable experts tell them is a fantasy, even if those experts are in the minority.

Indeed, what most distinguishes global warming from the other doomsday scenarios is the seemingly enormous cost of controlling it—hundreds of billions, probably trillions, of dollars, to roll back emissions levels to where they were just a few years ago. That cost interacts with the possibility of a market solution (clean fuels) or of developing technologies for atmospheric cleansing, and with uncertainty concerning not the fact of global warming or the causal role of greenhouse-gas emissions in it but the precise future consequences of it, to create doubt whether anything should be done at this time. It is tempting to take a leap in the dark and hope that in a few years climate science will develop to the point at which precise predictions about the course and consequences of global warming are possible, and that the relevant technologies will have developed to the point at which a cheap cure for global warming is possible even though the atmospheric concentrations of greenhouse gases are likely to be much greater than at present.

The danger of wait and see (and hope) lies in the fact that atmospheric concentrations of those gases will continue to rise even if the emissions rate does not increase (but probably it will increase, as world population and output grow). Given the unknown trigger point at which catastrophically abrupt global warming might occur, a better solution than wait and hope and meanwhile study might be to place a moderate tax on carbon dioxide emissions—a tax calibrated not to roll back emissions in the short run, which would require both a very heavy tax and full international cooperation, but instead to induce industry to invest more in the quest for clean fuels and economical methods of carbon sequestration.

It would not matter critically whether other countries imposed similar taxes or whether the tax reduced emissions by causing a substitution of different activities for those in which emissions are produced—walking for driving, to choose a banal example. By increasing the cost of emissions-producing activities, the tax would create market incentives to develop clean fuels and effective methods of carbon sequestration. The tax would (with a qualification noted below) take the place of a public subsidy program, which would require increases in less efficient taxes to finance and would place the government in the uncomfortable position of trying to determine the most deserving projects for the subsidy.

The emissions tax would not be a panacea. Besides being costly to administer compared to a tax on the fossil fuels themselves, it would not encourage producers of electric power to remove emissions already in the atmosphere, because the producers would already have paid the tax on them. Nor would anyone else have such an incentive, because there would be no market for such a service. For this type of carbon sequestration to be developed, a government subsidy may be necessary, either directly or in the form of emissions-tax credits for removing carbon dioxide from the atmosphere.

The appeal to scientific doubt not to justify inaction but merely to adjust one's estimate of the probability of catastrophe—the approach that I've suggested for global warming—won't work with respect to another catastrophic risk, that of loss of biodiversity, even though that risk is entwined with that of global warming. Global warming is bad for species because they are adapted to current temperatures, and deforestation is both causing extinctions directly by destroying habitats and indirectly by contributing to global warming by releasing carbon dioxide from the forests as they burn and reducing the forests' capture of atmospheric carbon dioxide. Genetic modification of crops may also be contributing to extinctions.

And there is more: environmentalists are correct that burgeoning human population and economic activity are stressing the environment in a variety of ways that may be interacting ominously to cause biodiversity loss and other social harms. But stressing the environment is not the only thing that growth of population is doing. On the plus side, among other things, because the principal costs of innovation are fixed (that is, upfront) rather than variable (that is, varying with output), the larger the market, the likelier the innovator is to be able to cover his costs by increasing his output; increased output will produce revenue disproportionately greater than the increased cost of production because that cost will increase more slowly than output. But on the minus side, with specific reference to the concerns of this book, (1) if there is some more or less fixed, and undoubtedly minute, percentage of people who have the skills and motivations to launch, say, bioterrorist attacks, then the larger the population is, the greater is the number of such people; (2) if increased population is a source of increased global warming, then population increase is imposing a negative externality; and (3) if technology is a source or enhancer of catastrophic risk as well as a source of immense social benefits, then increasing the rate of technological advance (as an indirect result of greater population) could increase the risk of catastrophe. The last point is uncertain because of the dual-use phenomenon. Technological progress can reduce catastrophic risks, for example by enabling the development of an effective defense against asteroid collisions, as well as create or exacerbate such risks.

The purely scientific doubts concerning the extent and gravity of biodiversity loss are far more serious than the corresponding doubts concerning global warming. The precise course and consequences of global warming are unclear, but at least the direction is pretty clear, and pretty definitely negative. The extinction picture is different. No one knows how many species there are, what the natural background rate of extinction is, how the extinction rate is being affected by human activities, and what the consequences of extinctions are for human welfare. Moreover, number of species and genetic diversity are only roughly correlated, and it is the latter, not the former, that is important. About all that can be said with any confidence is that continued rapid growth of the human population and the changes in land use that such growth portends are likely, in combination with continued global warming, to increase the rate of biodiversity loss, but by how much and with what consequences for human welfare is entirely unclear.

That is merely my judgment, however, and I am not a scientist, and so the controversy over loss of biodiversity raises in acute form the question of how nonscientists can and should respond to deep divisions in scientific opinion. (The problem exists in the small when judges or jurors are called upon to resolve conflicts in the testimony of equally reputable scientific expert witnesses. The problem has not been solved in that context either.) There is no obvious way to adjust the estimates of ecologists such as Robert May or Edward O. Wilson so as to weight the views of the doubters properly. The choices are, as in the example of radical scientific disagreement that I gave when discussing global warming, too stark. Whether the best estimate of the annual number of extinctions being caused by human activity is 0, 10,000, 40,000, or 80,000 is not something on which the scientific literature enables a nonscientist to opine. It would be reckless for the U.S. government to start paying Brazil hundreds of billions of dollars to stop clear-cutting the Amazonian rain forest, or to try to organize a coalition of nations to use economic sanctions to force Brazil to stop doing so, on the basis of hopelessly divided scientific opinion, especially when not only the amount but also the consequences of current biodiversity loss are so uncertain. The only responsible governmental activity at this stage would be to subsidize efforts to resolve the scientific controversy through additional theoretical and empirical work in paleontology, ecology, botany, and related fields, meanwhile continuing with efforts to preserve specimens of endangered species and varieties of plants and animals.

When we turn from accidental to intended catastrophes, such as nuclear attacks, bioterrorism, and cyberterrorism, we enter the realm of strategic behavior, where the potential catastrophists' concealment of their motives, intentions, plans, number, methods, and capabilities makes estimating probabilities particularly difficult and maybe impossible and in any event not a task primarily for scientists. About all that is clear with respect to such menaces is that a purely passive defense, as if the threat were of the same nature as that, say, of an asteroid collision, is unlikely to be sufficient. In the case of accidental man-made catastrophes, such as global warming, it is understood that the response must include measures to alter incentives, such as emissions taxes or research subsidies, and not just passive defenses such as efforts to remove carbon dioxide from the atmosphere. Nevertheless there is no question of having to deal with a deliberately concealed menace. Natural pandemics provide an interesting mixed case because an effect of natural selection is that life forms that have no capacity to form plans, such as bacteria, nevertheless behave as if they did have such a capacity. Antibiotics, pesticides, herbicides, and other defense measures induce bacteria and other pathogens to "choose" to mutate into resistant forms, and so one possible measure of defense is, by reducing the use of antibiotics, to affect the pathogen's "choices."

Conclusion

In considering deliberate catastrophes, if we set to one side the case of state aggression we confront criminal behavior on a grand scale and the need for police measures is evident, though strongly resisted by scientists and universities. Cost-benefit analysis of such measures is exquisitely difficult. On the one hand, we cannot estimate the probability of terrorist acts, whether they take the form of detonating nuclear or dirty bombs, mounting biological attacks, or disrupting vital computer networks, or derive meaningful estimates from "information markets" or insurance premium rates. On the other hand, we cannot estimate (or at least no one has tried to estimate) the principal costs of police and military measures to combat terrorism, which are not the salary expense of additional security personnel but the adverse effects—summed up in the expression "police state"—on personal and political liberty, privacy, and, potentially, even political stability. There is overlap with another potential catastrophe: the exploitation of modern technology to create an apparatus of surveillance so pervasive that it would extinguish privacy, which apart from its psychological importance (possibly exaggerated) serves an essential political function by enabling dissenting thought to be nurtured and expressed. So police measures might be catastrophically costly, but we do not know at what point they would become so, and until that point is reached their efficacy in combating the catastrophic risks that terrorism can create is likely to be decisive on the question whether to employ such measures.

The strategy of civil libertarians is to oppose the slightest curtailment of traditional liberties. The strategy may serve their fund-raising and other organizational goals, but it is questionable from an overall social-welfare standpoint. There is nothing sacrosanct about the specific level of protection of civil liberties that has been established by Supreme Court justices interpreting, under the influence of their personal values and temperaments, the plastic phrases of the Constitution. Civil liberties are the point of balance between liberty and security, and the balance can and, in my opinion, should shift in accordance with shifts in the relative weight of the two values. Modern technology, conjoined with the emergence of terrorist groups harboring unlimited destructive ambitions, has made the world less secure than at any time since the height of the Cold War (when civil liberties *were* curtailed), which argues for some curtailment of our expansive personal liberties.

Adjusting the balance between liberty and security is a task that obviously requires the participation of lawyers, but not just lawyers who are Johnny-one-note civil libertarians uttering fallacious slogans, such as that one must never fight fire with fire, that police measures are bound to be totally ineffective against terrorism, and that any reduction in Americans' civil liberties would be too high a price to pay for national or even world survival. But what is particularly required, besides some common sense, capacity for logical thought, abstention from moral preening, and realism about the terrorist mentality, is familiarity with the relevant science and technology. Without that, the participation of lawyers in the response to technological terrorism, as in the response to the other catastrophic risks discussed in this book, will be stunted. The culture and customs of legal education and the legal profession must change before the profession can carry its weight in the response to the catastrophic risks. Civil libertarians think it their business to know legal doctrine, not scientific reality. It is natural to think that what one doesn't know is not knowledge, or at least not relevant knowledge. Because law students are not taught that civil libertarians should know science, civil libertarians, almost all of whom are lawyers, don't think science relevant to determining how expansive our civil liberties should be. It is not merely relevant; it is central.

It is not only civil libertarians and other liberals who should be rethinking their politics in the face of technological terrorism. Conservatives should be rethinking their politics in the face of other catastrophic risks, notably global warming, about which conservatives are in a state of denial. Global warming is to a significant degree a byproduct of the success of capitalism in enormously increasing the amount of world economic activity (it is telling that the U.S. per capita emissions of carbon dioxide are five times the world average)[2] and expressions of concern about global warming are interpreted as attacks on capitalism. As often they are; global warming has been embraced by anticapitalists as a symbol of the consequences of capitalism. A further reason that fear of global warming has become a conservative bête noire is that arresting global warming is assumed to require collective international action, though I have expressed doubt about this. Still, it will require new taxes and (modest) subsidies, and that is bad enough in conservatives' eyes, although new taxes could of course be offset by reductions in existing taxes.

That attitudes toward global warming have become a political litmus test is unfortunate because global warming is a great and growing threat to anyone's idea of human welfare. And conservatives' fear of international organizations is exaggerated. Not only does the United States tend to dominate those organizations or render them impotent by refusing to join when it cannot dominate them, but it was Hobbes—no lefty—who taught that swapping independence for physical security can be a rational response to danger. Life may indeed become solitary, poor, nasty, brutish, and short if the chimera of international control of American policy is allowed to deter us from fashioning global weapons against catastrophic risks.

The issue of international cooperation is not limited to global warming. Most of the catastrophic risks are global in cause as well as (by definition) in consequence and so either cannot, or because of the erosive effects of free riding and other collective-action problems will not, be dealt with effectively at the purely national level. Which shows by the way that responding effectively to the catastrophic risks poses institutional as well as technical and analytical challenges; this opens still another potential role for lawyers, but again one that they cannot play well without becoming intimate with science and technology.

The point about catastrophic risk as political litmus paper is not limited to global warming. It is general, reflecting the scientific illiteracy of most nonscientists. The nonscientist, not being in a position to evaluate the significance of scientific disagreement, will unless there is unanimity of scientific opinion be sorely tempted to adopt the scientific position that fits his own political outlook. So liberals oppose the ABM defense and controls on biotechnology, and conservatives oppose taxes on carbon dioxide emissions and measures to preserve genetic diversity. The scientific ignorance not of the public at large, but of the people who count in making and implementing policy, is perhaps remediable. More stubborn are the obstacles that interest-group politics, as illuminated by the theory of public choice, and politics more broadly, strew in the path of responding to the catastrophic risks. Perhaps the greatest of these obstacles is that politicians are unlikely to earn any gratitude from the electorate for minimizing risks that are unlikely in any event to occur, no matter how great the consequences if they do occur, when to deal with such risks a politician might have to forgo responding to risks of losses that, though much smaller, are also much more likely to occur before the politician leaves office. The person who wants his health insurance restored is unlikely to be impressed by being told that the government has decided that an asteroid defense is a more urgent priority than universal health insurance.

The critical analytical technique for evaluating and ameliorating the catastrophic risks is cost-benefit analysis. It remains a usable tool despite the pervasive uncertainties, ethical and conceptual as well as factual, concerning those risks—that is one of the most important points that I have tried to make in this book. But cost-benefit analysis of catastrophic risks must be enriched with recognition of the cognitive difficulty that people encounter in dealing with very small probabilities and very large magnitudes. And the uncertainties arising from the peculiar character of the catastrophic risks create an inescapable need for value judgments concerning such matters as the proper weight to be given the interests of remote future generations, the nonmonetizable social benefits to be ascribed to basic scientific research, and the degree of risk aversion appropriate in responding to the catastrophic risks. Bridging the gap between a purely economic analysis of these responses and the ultimate decision that answers the question "what is to be done?" is another project in which properly informed lawyers can play a critical role. But emphasis must fall on "properly informed," as yet merely an aspiration.

A final point is that cost-benefit analysis should not be thought of as purely normative or public-choice theory as purely positive. The political process may not be dominated by costs and benefits, but it is influenced by them. Inverse cost-benefit analysis, in which the expected costs of a disaster are divided by the current government expenditures on preventing the disaster from occurring to yield the probability of disaster implied by the expenditures, can be a wake-up call for politicians and the public. We have seen that the levels of current expenditure to combat the major catastrophic risks, even bioterrorism, the one that has managed to thrust itself into the public consciousness, assume that the risks are much smaller than they probably are. We have also seen that there are many possibilities, ranging from detection and interception systems for averting asteroid collisions to additional police measures for averting bioterror attacks, for responding to the catastrophic risks without breaking the bank. Were the dangers posed by the catastrophic risks *and* the opportunities for minimizing those dangers at reasonable cost more generally recognized, the United States and the world would rouse themselves to effective action, and the world would be a safer place.

Notes

Preface

1. For a good discussion, see J. Barkley Rosser Jr., "On the Complexities of Complex Economic Dynamics," *Journal of Economic Perspectives*, Fall 1999, pp. 169, 171–173.

2. See, for example, Garnett P. Williams, *Chaos Theory Tamed* (1997).

3. Igor Ushakov, "Reliability: Past, Present, Future," in *Recent Advances in Reliability Theory: Methodology, Practice, and Inference* 3, 13 (N. Limnios and M. Nikulin eds. 2000).

4. A variety of analytical techniques for dealing with unexpected adversity is discussed in Stephen H. Schneider, B. L. Turner II, and Holly Morehouse Garriga, "Imaginable Surprise in Global Change Science," 1 *Journal of Risk Research* 165, 167–171 (1998).

5. Richard A. Posner, "The End Is Near," *New Republic*, Sept. 22, 2003, p. 31.

6. SmithKline Beecham Corp. v. Apotex Corp., 247 F. Supp. 2d 1011, 1032–1033 (N.D. Ill. 2003), affirmed, 365 F.3d 1306 (Fed. Cir. 2004).

Introduction

1. See, for example, Philip D. Bougen, "Catastrophic Risk," 32 *Economy and Society* 253 (2003).

2. See, for example, Patricia Grossi and Howard Kunreuther, *Catastrophe Modeling: A New Approach to Managing Risk* (University of Pennsylvania, unpublished, Dec. 2003); Neil A. Doherty, "Innovations in Managing Catastrophe Risk," 64 *Journal of Risk and Insurance* 713 (1997); Stephen P. D'Arcy, Virginia Grace France, and Richard W. Gorvett, "Pricing Catastrophe Risk: Could CAT Futures Have Coped with Andrew?" (1999 Casualty Actuarial Society "Secularization of Risk" Discussion Paper Program).

3. Alfred W. Crosby, *America's Forgotten Pandemic: The Influenza of 1918* 207 (1989).

4. Jennifer Brower and Peter Chalk, *The Global Threat of New and Reemerging Infectious Diseases: Reconciling U.S. National Security and Public Health Policy* 26 (2003).

5. Leon R. Kass, "Introduction: The Problem of Technology," in *Technology in the Western Political Tradition* 1, 20 (Arthur M. Melzer, Jerry Weinberger, and M. Richard Zinman eds. 1993). See also Kass, "The New Biology: What Price Relieving Man's Estate?" in *Science, Technology, and Public Policy* 134 (Richard Barke ed. 1986); Kass, "The Wisdom of Repugnance," in Leon R. Kass and James Q. Wilson, *The Ethics of Human Cloning* 3 (1998); Michael J. Sandel, "The Case against Perfection: What's Wrong with Designer Children, Bionic Athletes, and Genetic Engineering," *Atlantic Monthly*, April 2004, p. 51. For a popular version of the kind of technological pessimism articulated by Kass and Sandel, see Bill Mckibben, *Enough: Staying Human in an Engineered Age* (2003). And for criticism, see Arthur Caplan, "Is Biomedical Research Too Dangerous to Pursue?" 303 *Science* 1142 (2004).

6. *Beyond Therapy: Biotechnology and the Pursuit of Happiness—A Report by the President's Council on Bioethics* 302 (2003).

7. The trade name is Mifeprex, manufactured by Danco Laboratories; the active ingredient is mifepristone. Stanley K. Henshaw and Lawrence B. Finer, "The Accessibility of Abortion Services in the United States, 2001," 35 *Perspectives on Sexual and Reproductive Health* 16, 20 (2003). I am being overemphatic, since some women will not take the pills, either through inadvertence or because they want to become pregnant and only later decide to terminate the pregnancy, maybe because the fetus is seriously deformed or because the pregnancy is endangering the woman's health or imposing unanticipated costs on her.

8. James M. Redfield, *The Locrian Maidens: Love and Death in Greek Italy* 12 (2003).

9. Susan Greenfield, *Tomorrow's People: How 21st-Century Technology Is Changing the Way We Think and Feel* (2003). For brilliant speculations on a world made male-free by technology, see Redfield, note 8 above, at 5–8.

10. On the scope and problems of public policy toward science, see, for example, Harvey A. Averch, *A Strategic Analysis of Science and Technology Policy* (1985); *Science, Technology, and Public Policy*, note 5 above; Bruce L. R. Smith, *American Science Policy since World War II* (1990); Daniel Sarewitz, *Frontiers of Illusion: Science, Technology, and the Politics of Progress* (1996).

11. I use the words "science" and "technology" pretty interchangeably, though mindful that while "technology" usually connotes applications of science, some important technologies, such as the wheel, owe nothing to scientific research.

12. On which see, for example, David L. Faigman et al., *Science in the Law: Standards, Statistics and Research Issues* (2002); Victoria Sutton, *Law and Science: Cases and Materials* (2001); "Science in the Regulatory Process," *Law and Contemporary Problems*, Autumn 2003, p. 1; David E. Adelman, "Scientific Activism and Restraint: The Interplay of Statistics, Judgment, and Procedure in Environmental Law," 79 *Notre Dame Law Review* 497 (2004); David Friedman, "Does Technology Require New Law?" 25 *Harvard Journal of Law and Public Policy* 71 (2001); David S. Caudill and Lewis H. LaRue, "Why Judges Applying the Daubert Triology Need to Know about the Social, Institutional, and Rhetorical—and Not Just the Methodological—Aspects of Science," 45 *Boston College Law Review* 1 (2003); Laurence H. Tribe, *Channeling Technology through Law* (1973). Friedman's on-line book, *Future Imperfect*, http://patrifriedman .com/prose-others/fi/commented/Future_Imperfect.html (visited Jan. 26, 2004), discusses several doomsday scenarios briefly, though they are not its focus.

13. "How long we shall continue to blunder along without the aid of unpartisan and authoritative scientific assistance in the administration of justice, no one knows; but all fair persons not conventionalized by provincial legal habits of mind ought, I should think, unite to effect some such advance." Parke-Davis & Co. v. H. K. Mulford Co., 189 Fed. 95, 115 (Cir. Ct. S.D.N.Y 1911) (L. Hand, J.).

14. William M. Landes and Richard A. Posner, *The Economic Structure of Tort Law*, ch. 9 (1987). For a bizarre judicial response to such a case, see Kennedy v. Southern California Edison Co., 219 F.3d 988, 999 (9th Cir. 2000), discussed in Sutton, note 12 above, at 256–261.

15. 21 U.S.C. § 348(c)(3)(A); John Wargo, *Our Children's Toxic Legacy: How Science and Law Fail to Protect Us from Pesticides*, ch. 6 (1996).

16. Food Quality Protection Act of 1996, Public Law 104–170, 110 Stat. 1489 (Aug. 3, 1996).

17. See, for example, SmithKline Beecham Corp. v. Apotex Corp., 247 F. Supp. 2d 1011, 1032–1033 (N.D. Ill. 2003), affirmed, 365 F.3d 1306 (Fed. Cir. 2004).

18. Sheila Jasanoff and Dorothy Nelkin, "Science, Technology, and the Limits of Judicial Competence," in *Science, Technology, and Society: Emerging Relationships* 196 (Rosemary Chalk ed. 1988).

19. Gary S. Becker, *Accounting for Tastes* 11–12 (1996); Becker and Casey B. Mulligan, "The Endogenous Determination of Time Preference," 112 *Quarterly Journal of Economics* 729 (1997). On the difficulty, central to this book, that people have in evaluating and responding to low-probability risks, see, for example, Howard Kunreuther and Mark Pauly, "Neglecting Disaster: Why Don't People Insure against Large Losses?" 28 *Journal of Risk and Uncertainty* 5 (2004); W. Kip Viscusi, "Economic and Psychological Aspects of Valuing Risk Reduction," in *Determining the Value of Non-Marketed Goods: Economic, Psychological, and Policy Relevant Aspects of Contingent Valuation Methods* 83 (R. J. Kopp, W. W. Pommerehne, and N. Schwarz eds. 1997).

20. Gerd Gigerenzer and Ulrich Hoffrage, "How to Improve Bayesian Reasoning without Instruction: Frequency Formats," 102 *Psychological Review* 684 (1995); Gigerenzer and Adrian Edwards, "Simple Tools for Understanding Risks: From Innumeracy to Insight," 327 *British Medical Journal* 741 (2003); Ralph Hertwig and Ulrich Hoffrage, "Technology Needs Psychology: How Natural Frequencies Foster Insight in Medical and Legal Experts," in *Etc. Frequency Processing and Cognition* 285 (Peter Sedlmeier and Tilmann Betsch eds. 2002).

21. For a lively discussion, see Deborah J. Bennett, *Randomness* 72–82 (1998).

22. Daniel Kahneman, "Maps of Bounded Rationality: Psychology for Behavioral Economics," 93 *American Economic Review* 1449, 1457, 1460–1461 (2003).

23. Cf. Herbert A. Simon, *Reason in Human Affairs* 79–83 (1983) ("limits of attention").

24. "Last" as calculated from the predicted date, not the predicting date. Someone who in the year 1 A.D. predicted the end of the world in the year 3000 would be in my sense the last predicter if the world ended then, even though someone in the year 2000 might have predicted that the world would end in 2001.

25. For a recent discussion, see Cass R. Sunstein, "Are Poor People Worth Less Than Rich People? Disaggregating the Value of Statistical Lives" (AEI-Brookings Joint Center for Regulatory Studies, Working Paper 04–05, Jan. 2004).

26. Criticisms of cost-benefit analysis are legion. For a vivid statement, see Frank Ackerman and Lisa Heinzerling, *Priceless: On Knowing the Price of Everything and the Value of Nothing* (2004).

27. This estimate is from Averch, note 10 above, at 40.

28. Gross Domestic Product, now more frequently used as a measure of aggregate economic activity than Gross National Product. GDP refers to production in the United States by both citizens and foreigners, GNP to production by U.S. citizens either in the United States or abroad. The difference in amounts is very slight, however. According to the U.S. Bureau of Economic Analysis, U.S. GNP in 2002 was $10.50 trillion, GDP $10.48 trillion.

29. Kevin M. Murphy and Robert H. Topel, "The Economic Value of Medical Research," in *Measuring the Gains from Medical Research: An Economic Approach* 41 (Murphy and Topel eds. 2003).

30. Leon Golub and Jay M. Pasachoff, *Nearest Star: The Surprising Science of Our Sun*, ch. 2 (2001).

31. Brian Greene, *The Elegant Universe: Superstrings, Hidden Dimensions, and the Quest for the Ultimate Theory* 130, 136, 141 (1999).

32. From an email communication to me in August 2003. Quoted with Friedman's permission.

33. For different estimates of the number of galaxies, compare Eric Chiasson and Steve McMillan, *Astronomy: A Beginner's Guide to the Universe* 406 (3d ed. 2001) (100 billion), with Michael A. Seeds, *Foundations of Astronomy* 331 (1999) (30 billion). However, in another book Chiasson and McMillan estimate the number at only 40 billion. Chassion and McMillan, *Astronomy Today* 554 (3d ed. 1999).

34. John Leslie, *The End of the World: The Science and Ethics of Human Extinction* 9 (1996).

Chapter 1

1. Alfred W. Crosby, *America's Forgotten Pandemic: The Influenza of 1918* 62 (1989). For a recent popular treatment of the pandemic, see John M. Barry, *The Great Influenza: The Epic Story of the Deadliest Plague in History* (2004).

2. On structure, see James Stevens et al., "Structure of the Uncleaved Human H1 Hemagglutinin from the Extinct 1918 Influenza Virus," 303 *Science* 1866 (2004). On contagion, see Paul W. Ewald, *Evolution of Infectious Disease* 110–113 (1994).

3. Richard A. Goldsby et al., *Immunology* 393–394 (5th ed. 2003).

4. Ibid., 441 (fig. 19–7). Almost 40 million living people have AIDS. Ibid.

5. William A. Blattner, "Comparative Epidemiology of Human Retroviruses," in *Immunobiology and Pathogenesis of Persistent Virus Infections* 51, 79 (Brian W. J. Mahy and Richard W. Compans eds. 1996).

6. Ewald, note 2 above, at 143.

7. Blattner, note 5 above, at 90.

8. Goldsby et al., note 3 above, at 454–455.

9. Ibid., 410.

10. Ibid., 406–410. See generally Jim Bull and Dan Dykhuizen, "Epidemics-in-Waiting," 426 *Nature* 609 (2003).

11. See, for example, David M. Livermore, "Bacterial Resistance: Origins, Epidemiology, and Impact," 36 *Clinical Infectious Diseases* S11, S12 (2003); Helen Pearson, "'Superbug' Hurdles Key Drug Barrier," 418 *Nature* 469 (2002); Richard Bax, Noel Mullan, and Jan Verhoef, "The Millennium Bugs—The Need for and Development of New Antibacterials," 16 *International Journal of Antimicrobial Agents* 51 (2000).

12. See generally *Battling Resistance to Antibiotics and Pesticides: An Economic Approach* (Ramanan Laxminarayan ed. 2003).

13. United Nations Secretariat, Population Division, Department of Economic and Social Affairs, "The Components of Urban Growth in Developing Countries" (ESA/P/WP.169 Sept. 2001).

14. D. Gale Johnson, "Population, Food, and Knowledge," 90 *American Economic Review* 1 (2000).

15. Rustom Antia et al., "The Role of Evolution in the Emergence of Infectious Diseases," 426 *Nature* 658, 660 (2003).

16. For lucid descriptions of the danger, see *Report of the [U.K.] Task Force on Potentially Hazardous Near Earth Objects* (Sept. 2000); Clark R. Chapman, "The Hazard of Near-Earth Asteroid Impacts on Earth," 222 *Earth and Planetary Science Letters* 1 (2004); Clark R. Chapman, Daniel D. Durda, and Robert E. Gold, "The Comet/Asteroid Impact Hazard: A Systems Approach" (SwRI White Paper, Feb. 24, 2001), http://www.internationalspace.com/pdf. For excellent popular accounts, see Bill Bryson, *A Short History of Nearly Everything*, ch. 13 (2003); Marcelo Gleiser, *The Prophet and the Astronomer: A Scientific Journey to the End of Time*, ch. 4 (2001).

17. Near-Earth Object Science Definition Team, *Study to Determine the Feasibility of Extending the Search for Near-Earth Objects to Smaller Limiting Diameters* 14–17, 31–33 (NASA Aug. 22, 2003).

18. Don Yeomans, "Small Bodies of the Solar System," 404 *Nature* 829 (2000).

19. Chapman, Durda, and Gold, note 16 above, at 5.

20. Ibid., 19. *Report of the [U.K.] Task Force on Potentially Hazardous Near Earth Objects*, note 16 above, at 39–42, contains useful tables of major impacts of asteroids and comets, documented collisions with the earth in the 1990s, and recent and predicted close approaches (defined as coming within twice the distance between the earth and the moon). The damage caused by a collision with a 1-kilometer asteroid would be very great, though short of being an extinction event. "Because of the orbital velocities involved, impact on Earth of an asteroid of this size would instantly release energies calculated to be equivalent to the detonation of almost a 100,000 megaton nuclear device, i.e., more than all the world's nuclear arsenals detonated at the same time. Not only would the continent or ocean where the impact occurs be utterly devastated, but the effects of the super-heated fragments of Earth's crust and water vapor thrown into the atmosphere and around the world would adversely affect the global weather for months to years after the event. Such an event could well disrupt human civilization anywhere from decades to a century after an impact." Testimony of Dr. Lindley Johnson at a Science, Technology, and Space Hearing on Near Earth Objects (NEO) before S. Comm. on Commerce, Science & Transportation, Apr. 7, 2004, http://commerce.senate.gov/hearings/testimony .cfm?id=1147&wit_id=3241.

21. Luis W. Alvarez et al., "Extraterrestrial Cause for the Cretaceous-Tertiary Extinction: Experimental Results and Theoretical Interpretation," 208 *Science* 1095 (1980); Lee R. Kump, James F. Kasting, and Robert G. Crane, *The Earth System* 256–263 (2d ed. 2004); David M. Raup, *Extinction: Bad Genes or Bad Luck?* 66–72 (1991); David E. Fastovsky and David B. Weishampel, *The Evolution and Extinction of the Dinosaurs*, ch. 17 (1996); Kevin O. Pope, Steven L. D'Hondt, and Charles R. Marshall, "Meteorite Impact and the Mass Extinction of Species at the Cretaceous/Tertiary Boundary," 95 *Proceedings of the National Academy of Sciences* 11028 (1998).

22. Richard A. Kerr, "Evidence of Huge, Deadly Impact Found off Australian Coast?" 304 *Science* 941 (2004); L. Becker et al., "Bedout: A Possible End-Permian Impact Crater Offshore of Northwestern Australia," *Scienceexpress/* www.scienceexpress.org/13 May 2004/ page 1/ 10.1126/science.1093925; Asish R. Basu et al., "Chondritic Meteorite Fragments Associated with the Permian-Triassic Boundary in Antarctica," 302 *Science* 1388, 1391 (2003); Kenneth Chang, "Meteorite That Killed 90% of Species May Have Hit Tropics," *New York Times* (late edition), Dec. 16, 2003, p. F4.

23. See, for example, G. Keller et al., "Multiple Impacts across the Cretaceous-Tertiary Boundary: Year 2000 Assessment," 62 *Earth-Science Reviews* 327 (2003); Gerta Keller, "The End-Cretaceous Mass Extinction in the Marine Realm," 49 *Planetary and Space Science* 817 (2001). See generally *Cretaceous-Tertiary Mass Extinctions: Biotic and Environmental Changes* (Norman MacLeod and Gerta Keller eds. 1996). And for a good popular treat-

ment of the debate, see "Mass Extinctions: Making an End of It," *Economist*, Nov. 8, 2003, p. 77.

24. Kevin O. Pope, "Impact Dust Not the Cause of the Cretaceous-Tertiary Mass Extinction," 30 *Geology* 99 (2002).

25. Ibid., 101–102.

26. Near-Earth Object Science Definition Team, note 17 above, at 29.

27. Or might not, if Pope is correct. See note 24 above and accompanying text; also Owen B. Toon, Richard P. Turco, and Curt Covey, "Environmental Perturbations Caused by the Impacts of Asteroids and Comets," 35 *Reviews of Geophysics* 41 (1997).

28. Near-Earth Object Science Definition Team, note 17 above, at 20. See also Clark R. Chapman and David Morrison, "Impacts on the Earth by Asteroids and Comets: Assessing the Hazard," 367 *Nature* 33, 36 (1994); Clark R. Chapman, "The Asteroid/Comet Impact Hazard: Homo Sapiens as Dinosaur?" in *Prediction: Science, Decision Making, and the Future of Nature* 107 (Daniel Sarewitz, Roger A. Pielke, Jr., and Radford Byerly, Jr., eds. 2000).

29. *Report of the [U.K.] Task Force on Potentially Hazardous Near Earth Objects*, note 16 above, at 16, 20; Table 1.1 below.

30. As shown in Table 1.1, the actual estimate is not of an annual probability, but of the average interval, estimated at 250,000 years, between collisions of this magnitude. That translates into a 1 in 360,000 probability, however.

31. Chapman and Morrison, note 28 above, at 36; Martin Rees, *Our Final Hour: A Scientist's Warning: How Terror, Error, and Environmental Disaster Threaten Humankind's Future in This Century—On Earth and Beyond* 90–91 (2003).

32. Near-Earth Object Science Definition Team, note 17 above, at 12, 19, 21. The sizes of asteroids cannot be determined by direct measurement, but instead are inferred from their brightness. The number of identified NEOs of 1 kilometer and larger had by the spring of 2004 risen above 700. Johnson, note 20 above.

33. *Report of the [U.K.] Task Force on Potentially Hazardous Near Earth Objects*, note 16 above, at 14. For somewhat different estimates, see Jenifer B. Evans, Frank C. Shelly, and Grant H. Stokes, "Detection and Discovery of Near-Earth Asteroids by the LINEAR Program," 14 *Lincoln Laboratory Journal* 199, 201 (2003).

34. *Report of the [U.K.] Task Force on Potentially Hazardous Near Earth Objects*, note 16 above, at 17; Near-Earth Object Science Definition Team, note 17 above, at 140–142; Rees, note 31 above, at 95 (2003); John S. Lewis, *Comet and Asteroid Impact Hazards on a Populated Earth: Computer Modeling* 7 (1999).

35. Rees, note 31 above, at 91. This is not a surprising speed for a planetary object; the earth's orbital speed is 18 miles per second. It might seem that the asteroid's terminal velocity would depend on the direction from which the asteroid hit the earth compared to the earth's orbit—whether head on, or from the back, or from a side. To some extent this is true, but regardless of the initial closing speed, as soon as the asteroid gets close enough to the earth for the earth's gravitational pull to be strong, the asteroid will accelerate, reaching a speed of at least 15 miles per second when it hits.

36. *Report of the [U.K.] Task Force on Potentially Hazardous Near Earth Objects*, note 16 above, at 11, 28.

37. Testimony of Dr. Ed Lu at a Science, Technology, and Space Hearing on Near Earth Objects (NEO) before S. Comm. on Commerce, Science & Transportation, Apr. 7, 2004, http://commerce.senate.gov/hearings/testimony.cfm?id=1147&wit_id=3245; Testimony of Dr. Michael Griffin, in Ibid., 3243. Techniques of deflection are also discussed in Chapman, Durda, and Gold, note 16 above, at 13–14.

38. Rees, note 31 above, at 94.

39. Near-Earth Object Science Definition Team, note 17 above, at 23.

40. Chapman and Morrison, note 28 above, at 37.

41. Lewis, note 34 above, at 131–132.

42. Ibid., 115.

43. U.S. Geological Survey, "Mount St. Helens: From the 1980 Eruption to 2000" (U.S. Geological Survey Fact Sheet 036–00, 2000).

44. E. L. Jones, *The European Miracle: Environments, Economies, and Geopolitics in the History of Europe and Asia* 27 (2d ed. 1987) (tab. 2.2).

45. Rees, note 31 above, at 120–121. See also Ibid., 123–124; Francesco Calogero, "Might a Laboratory Experiment Destroy Planet Earth?" 25 *Interdisciplinary Science Reviews* 191 (2000); John Leslie, *The End of the World: The Science and Ethics of Human Extinction* 108–131 (1996). Thomas D. Gutierrez, "Doomsday Fears at RHIC," *Skeptical Inquirer*, May/June 2000, p. 29, implies incorrectly that only irresponsible journalists raised questions about RHIC's safety.

46. Ivan Carvalho, "Dr. Strangelet or: How I Learned to Stop Worrying and Love the Big Bang," *Wired Magazine*, May 2000, p. 254. One factor behind the director's decision may have been that Brookhaven had a history of mishaps, including leaks of radioactivity, though of course nothing of disaster proportions. David Voss, "RHIC Physicists Go to Media School," 285 *Science* 1196 (1999). The revised and published version of the assessment commissioned by the director is R. L. Jaffe et al., "Review of Speculative 'Disaster Scenarios' at RHIC," 72 *Reviews of Modern Physics* 1125, 1126 (2000).

47. John Marburger, "Synopsis of Committee Report," Oct. 6, 1999, http://www.phys.utk.edu/rhip/RHICNews/BNL_rhicreport.html.

48. Rees, note 31 above, at 121. See also Piet Hut, "Is It Safe to Disturb the Vacuum?" A418 *Nuclear Physics* 301c (1984); Jaffe et al., note 46 above, at 1126; Mark Yasin, "Space and the Universal Laws of Physics," 1998, www.markyasin.com (visited Nov. 7, 2003).

49. Jaffe et al., note 46 above, at 1126.

50. T. Ludlam, "Plans for the Future of RHIC," Sept. 21, 2002, p. 7, http://www4.rcf.bnl/gov/STAR/upgrades/future-plans.pdf.

51. See, for example, Richard Ellis, *Monsters of the Sea* 17–36 (1994).

52. The British Broadcasting Corporation claims to have conducted a thorough search of the lake, using sonar and satellites, but, so far as I have been able to discover, its results have been reported only in a television program. "BBC 'Proves' Nessie Does Not Exist: A BBC Team Says It Has Shown There Is No Such Thing as the Loch Ness Monster," *BBC News, UK Edition*, July 27, 2003, http://news.bbc.co.uk/1/hi/sci/tech/3095839.stm.

53. Jaffe et al., note 46 above, at 1126; Calogero, note 45 above, at 194.

54. Jaffe et al., note 46 above, at 1127–1139. See also Arnon Dar, A. De Rújula, and Ulrich Heinz, "Will Relativistic Heavy-Ion Colliders Destroy Our Planet?" 470 *Physics Letters B* 142 (1999). (Dar and his colleagues are physicists at CERN.) Remarkably, *Nature* declined to publish their article on the ground that the topic was not of general interest. Calogero, note 45 above, at 202 n. 3.

55. Stephen R. Byrn, Ralph R. Pfeiffer, and Joseph G. Stowell, *Solid-State Chemistry of Drugs* 16, 18–19, 225, 463 (2d ed. 1999).

56. Joel Bernstein, *Polymorphism in Molecular Crystals* 90–91 (2002).

57. Sherry L. Morissette et al, "Elucidation of Crystal Form Diversity of the HIV Protease Inhibitor Ritonavir by High-Throughput Crystallization," 100 *Proceedings of the National Academy of Sciences* 2180 (2003); John Bauer et al., "Ritonavir: An Extraordinary Example of Conformational Polymorphism," 18 *Pharmaceutical Research* 859 (2001); Sanjay R. Chemburkar et al., "Dealing with the Impact of Ritonavir Polymorphs on the Late Stages of Bulk Drug Process Development," 4 *Organic Process Research and Development* 413 (2000).

58. Byrn, Pfeiffer, and Stowell, note 55 above, at 17–18, 463; Bernstein, note 56 above, at 67; Jack D. Dunitz and Joel Bernstein, "Disappearing Polymorphs," 28 *Accounts of Chemical Research* 193, 194 (1995); and discussion in SmithKline Beecham Corp. v. Apotex Corp., 247 F. Supp. 2d 1011, 1020 (N.D. Ill. 2003), affirmed, 365 F.3d 1306 (Fed. Cir. 2004).

59. Compare David W. Oxtoby and Norman H. Nachtrieb, *Principles of Modern Chemistry* 531–533 (3d ed 1996), with David Halliday, Robert Resnick, and Jearl Walker, *Fundamentals of Physics*, vol. 2, pp. 1100–1101 (5th ed 1997).

60. Ibid., 1099.

61. I am using the term "minimum crystal" to acknowledge that as one breaks up a crystal into smaller and smaller chips, eventually the chips contain too few atoms for the atomic forces to maintain the crystalline structure. But the smallest chip that would retain the crystalline structure could consist of only a handful of atoms.

62. Don Brownlee, "A Walk to the Gallows: Could Scientific Advances Be Hastening the End of the World?" 423 *Nature* 803 (2003); Roger A. Pielke, Jr., "Which Future for Humanity" 301 *Science* 1483 (2003); Dennis Overbye, "It Was Fun While It Lasted," *New York Times*, May 18, 2003, § 7, p. 13. The title of the original British edition of Rees's book *Our Final Hour* was a less-alarmist-sounding *Our Final Century*.

63. K. Eric Drexler, "Molecular Nanomachines: Physical Principles and Implementation Strategies," 23 *Annual Review of Biophysics and Biomolecular Structures* 377 (1994); Drexler, *Nanosystems: Molecular Machinery, Manufacturing, and Computation* (1992); George M. Whitesides, "The Once and Future Nanomachine: Biology Outmatches Futurists' Most Elaborate Fantasies for Molecular Robots," *Scientific American*, Sept. 2001, p. 78.

64. Kaili Jiang, Qunqing Li, and Shoushan Fan, "Spinning Continuous Carbon Nanotube Yarns: Carbon Nanotubes Weave Their Way into a Range of Imaginative Macroscopic Applications," 419 *Nature* 801 (2002); Samuel Brauer, "The Carbon Nanotube Industry: These Revolutionary New Materials Have Some Unique Properties Not Previously Observed," *Nanoparticle News*, June 2003, p. 8.

65. Robert F. Service, "Nanodevices Make Fresh Strides toward Reality," 302 *Science* 1310 (2003); Kinneret Keren et al., "DNA-Templated Carbon Nanotube Field-Effect Transistor," 302 *Science* 1380 (2003); Kenneth Chang, "Smaller Computer Chips Built Using DNA as Template," *New York Times* (late ed.), Nov. 21, 2003, p. A20. For a good general introduction to nanotechnology, see Douglas Mulhall, *Our Molecular Future: How Nanotechnology, Robotics, Genetics, and Artificial Intelligence Will Transform Our World*, ch. 2 (2002).

66. George M. Whitesides and Mila Boncheva, "Beyond Molecules: Self-Assembly of Mesoscopic and Macroscopic Components," 99 *Proceedings of the National Academy of Sciences* 4769 (2002).

67. Mulhall, note 65 above, at 33 (fig. 2); H. J. Lee and W. Ho, "Single-Bond Formation and Characterization with a Scanning Tunneling Microscope," 286 *Science* 1719 (1999).

68. National Science and Technology Council, Committee on Technology, Interagency Working Group on Nanoscience, Engineering, and Technology, *Nanotechnology Research Directions: IWGN Workshop Report: Vision for Nanotechnology R&D in the Next Decade* xxxvi (M. C. Rico, R. S. Williams, and P. Alivisatos eds. 2001). This report is a comprehensive discussion of current research in nanotechnology. See also National Science and Technology Council, *National Nanotechnology Initiative: Research and Development Supporting the Next Revolution* (Supplement to the President's FY 2004 Budget, 2003); *Societal Implications of Nanoscience and Nanotechnology* (Mihail C. Roco and Williams Sims Bainbridge eds. 2001).

69. National Science and Technology Council, *Nanotechnology Research Directions*, note 68 above, at 14–15.

70. Thomas Scheibel et al., "Conducting Nanowires Built by Controlled Self-Assembly of Amyloid Fibers and Selective Metal Deposition," 100 *Proceedings of the National Academy of Sciences* 4527 (2003); Chang, note 65 above.

71. Peter Turney, Arnold Smith, and Robert Ewaschuk, "Self-Replicating Machines in Continuous Space with Virtual Physics," 9 *Artificial Life* 21, 38 (2003). On the prospects for artificial life generally, see Steen Rasmussen et al., "Transitions from Nonliving to Living Matter," 303 *Science* 963 (2004).

72. Rees, note 31 above, at 58. See also Center for Responsible Nanotechnology, "Dangers of Molecular Nanotechnology," http://www.crnano.org/dangers.htm (visited Jan. 27, 2004). For an early warning of the danger, see K. Eric Drexler, *Engines of Creation: The Coming Era of Technology*, chs. 11–12 (1986). Freeman Dyson argues that nanomachines could never move as fast as Rees envisions; but the argument appears to be incorrect, as I explain in the next chapter.

73. "Foresight Guidelines on Molecular Nanotechnology," http://www.foresight .org/guidelines/current.html (June 4, 2000).

74. Richard E. Smalley, "Of Chemistry, Love and Nanorobots," *Scientific American*, Sept. 2001, p. 76. For a lively debate on the question between him and Eric Drexler, see Rudy Baum, "Nanotechnology: Drexler and Smalley Make the Case for and against 'Molecular Assemblers,'" *Chemical and Engineering News*, Dec. 1, 2003, p. 37. For a recent, balanced discussion of the dangers of and obstacles to the creation of self-replicating nanomachines, and an argument that self-replication is unnecessary for the creation of efficient molecular

manufacturing systems, see Chris Phoenix and K. Eric Drexler, "Safe Exponential Manufacturing," 15 *Nanotechnology* 869 (2004). See also Drexler's Web site, http://e-drexler.com. Just recently, marked progress toward developing self-replicating nanotechnology has been reported. NASA Insitute for Advanced Concepts, *Modeling Kinematic Cellular Automata: Final Report*, Apr. 30, 2004, http://www.niac.usra.edu/files/studies/final_report/pdf/883Toth-Fejel.pdf. And for an amusing list of falsified predictions of scientific impossibility by reputable scientists, see Arthur C. Clarke, *Profiles of the Future: An Inquiry into the Limits of the Possible*, ch. 1 (1984).

75. *President's FY04 Budget Submission to Congress: Analytical Perspectives: Budget of the United States Government Fiscal Year 2004*, ch. 8, p. 185 (2003) (tab. 8–4), http://www.whitehouse.gov/omb/budget/fy2004/pdf/spec.pdf (visited Jan. 27, 2004).

76. On the potential—and the dangers—of autoproduction, see Phoenix and Drexler, note 74 above. On the potential role of nanotechnology in alleviating environmental problems, see National Science and Technology Council, *National Nanotechnology Initiative*, note 68 above, at 32.

77. Clyde F. Herreid II, *Biology* 85 (1977).

78. Neil A. Campbell, Lawrence G. Mitchell, and Jane B. Reece, *Biology: Concepts and Connections* 190 (1997). Viruses thus are "intracellular parasites." Goldsby et al., note 3 above, at 287.

79. National Research Council of the National Academies, *Biological Confinement of Genetically Engineered Organisms* (2004); Norman C. Ellstrand and Carol A. Hoffman, "Hybridization as an Avenue of Escape for Engineered Genes," 40 *BioScience* 438 (1990); P. J. Tranel et al., "Transmission of Herbicide Resistance from a Monoecious to a Dioecious Weedy *Amaranthus* Species," 105 *Theoretical and Applied Genetics* 674 (2002). Concerns about genetically modified crops are summarized in Abby Munson, "Risk Associated with and Liability Arising from Releases of Genetically Manipulated Organisms into the Environment," 22 *Science and Public Policy* 51, 52–57 (1995). See also Virginia Gewin, "Genetically Modified Corn—Environmental Benefits and Risks," 1 *PLoS [Public Library of Science], Biology* 15 (2003). Canada is one of the world's largest exporters of genetically modified crops. For strong criticism of Canada's standards and procedures for determining whether they are safe, see Katherine Barrett and Elisabeth Abergel, "Safety of GM Crops: Defining a Safe Genetically Modified Organism: Boundaries of Scientific Risk Assessment," 29 *Science and Public Policy* 47 (2002).

80. See, for example Erik Stokstad, "Genetically Modified Organisms: Experts Recommend a Cautious Approach," 303 *Science* 449 (2004).

81. Indur M. Goklany, *The Precautionary Principle: A Critical Appraisal of Environmental Risk Assessment* 41–46 (2001).

82. See, for example, Alan McHughen, *Pandora's Picnic Basket: The Potential and Hazards of Genetically Modified Foods* (2000).

83. Goklany, note 81 above, at 47.

84. Ibid., ch. 4.

85. Jay Lyman, "Computers Think Strategically in RoboCup," *NewsFactor SciTech*, June 11, 2002, http://sci.newsfactor.com/perl/story/18153.html (visited Sept. 12, 2003). For a lively treatment of advances current and foreseeable

in artificial intelligence, see Susan Greenfield, *Tomorrow's People: How 21st-Century Technology Is Changing the Way We Think and Feel*, ch. 3 (2003).

86. Jose M. Carmena et al., "Learning to Control a Brain-Machine Interface for Reaching and Grasping by Primates," 1 *PLoS [Public Library of Science]*, *Biology* 193 (2003). See also Miguel A. L. Nicolelis, "Actions from Thoughts," 409 *Nature* 403 (2001).

87. The debate is well summarized in Steven Goldberg, *Culture Clash: Law and Science in America*, ch. 9 (1994).

88. Ray Kurzweil, *The Age of Spiritual Machines: When Computers Exceed Human Intelligence*, ch. 12 and p. 180 (1999).

89. Donald Goldsmith and Tobias Owen, *The Search for Life in the Universe* 106, 386 (3d ed. 2001). See also ibid., 504.

90. Ibid., 449–452. The authors acknowledge the extraordinary roughness of their estimate, which they offer as the upper bound of a range the lower bound of which is only two.

91. Ibid., 451–452.

92. Kurzweil, note 88 above, at 3.

93. National Science and Technology Council, *National Research Directions*, note 68 above, at 22. "Whereas a digital bit may only store information in the form of a sequence of '0s' and '1s,' a quantum bit may be in a superposition state of '0' and '1,' that is, representing both values simultaneously until a measurement is made. A sequence of N digital bits can represent a single number between 0 and $(2^N)-1$, while N quantum bits can represent all 2^N numbers simultaneously." Ibid., 22–23.

94. Kurzweil, note 88 above, at 3.

95. Jim Garamone, "Unmanned Aerial Vehicles Proving Their Worth over Afghanistan," April 16, 2002, http://www.defenselink.mil/news/Apr2002/n04162002_200204162.html.

96. Louis Knapp, "SlugBot: Enemy of Slugs," Oct. 8, 2001, http://www.wired.com/news/gizmos/0,1452,47156,00.html.

97. Lauren Clement, "Self-Repairing Technologies," http://swiss.csail.mit.edu/projects/amorphous/6.978/final-papers/lclement-final.pdf (visited Feb. 4, 2004).

98. Sunny Bains, "Xerox Studies Self-Assembling Modular Robots," Jan. 10, 2000, http://www.eetimes.com/story/OEG20000110S0070.

99. Ross D. King et al., "Functional Genomic Hypothesis Generation and Experimentation by a Robot Scientist," 427 *Nature* 247, 247–248 (2004).

100. Bjørn Lomborg, *The Skeptical Environmentalist: Measuring the Real State of the World* 318 (1998).

101. Mostafa K. Tolba and Iwona Rummel-Bulska, *Global Environmental Diplomacy: Negotiating Environmental Agreements for the World, 1973–1992*, ch. 5 (1998).

102. Rees, note 31 above, at 108. The "success story" may be misleading in another way, as well, as we'll see in the next chapter.

103. Ibid., 109.

104. Stephen Schneider, "Global Warming: Neglecting the Complexities," *Scientific American*, Jan. 2002, p. 62.

105. Lomborg, note 100 above, at 310, 317–318. Indur Goklany is another environmental skeptic who concedes that global warming is a serious problem. See note 81 above.

106. William D. Nordhaus and Joseph Boyer, *Warming the World: Economic Models of Global Warming* 130–132 (and tab. 7.3), 163, 178 (2000). The economic literature on global warming is extensive. See, for example, references in Richard S. J. Tol, "Estimates of the Damage Costs of Climate Change: Part I: Benchmark Estimates," 21 *Environmental and Resource Economics* 47 (2002). I cite additional economic studies of global warming in chapter 3.

107. John F. B. Mitchell, "General Circulation Modeling of the Atmosphere," in *Climate-Ocean Interaction* 67, 80 (M. E. Schlesinger ed. 1990).

108. Lomborg, note 100 above, at 288–290; Samuel Fankhauser, *Valuing Climate Change: The Economics of the Greenhouse*, ch. 3 (1995).

109. For an especially lucid presentation of the relevant science, see Kump, Kasting, and Crane, note 21 above, esp. chs. 3, 12, 15–16. And see generally *Climate Change Policy: A Survey* (Stephen H. Schneider, Armin Rosencranz, and John O. Niles eds. 2002).

110. William R. Cotton and Roger A. Pielke, *Human Impacts on Weather and Climate* 121 (1995).

111. James Hansen and Larissa Nazarenko, "Soot Climate Forcing via Snow and Ice Albedoes," 101 *Proceedings of the National Academy of Sciences* 423 (2004).

112. K. Chatterjee, "Causes of Greenhouse Gas Emissions," in *Climate Change: An Integrated Perspective* 143 (Pim Martens and Jan Rotmans eds. 1999); Laurence Pringle, *Global Warming: The Threat of Earth's Changing Climate* 13 (2001).

113. D. W. Lawlor, *Photosynthesis: Metabolism, Control and Physiology* 170 (1987).

114. Kump, Kasting, and Crane, note 21 above, at 149, 154.

115. Klaus Keller et al., "Preserving the Ocean Circulation: Implications for Climate Policy," 47 *Climatic Change* 17, 32–34 (2000); National Research Council of the National Academies, *Abrupt Climate Change: Inevitable Surprises*, ch. 4 (2002); R. B. Alley et al., "Abrupt Climate Change," 299 *Science* 2005 (2003); Fankhauser, note 108 above, at 23–24. A lucid discussion of how to factor the possibility of catastrophic loss into cost-benefit analysis is Jan Gjerde, Sverre Grepperud, and Snorre Kverndokk, "Optimal Climate Policy under the Possibility of a Catastrophe," 21 *Resource and Energy Economics* 289 (1999).

116. Margaret Atwood, *Oryx and Crake: A Novel* 24 (2003).

117. William D. Nordhaus, *Managing the Global Commons: The Economics of Climate Change* 114 (1994). The words "recent evidence of" appear before "very rapid shifts in temperature and sea levels" in the quoted passage, but I assume that's a typographical error, since "evidence" could not be a "potential impact." For a recent discussion of the possibility of catastrophic global warming, see German Advisory Council on Global Change, *Climate Protection Strategies for the 21st Century: Kyoto and Beyond* 19–21 (2003).

118. In his book *Climate of Fear: Why We Shouldn't Worry about Global Warming* (1998). The superstitious reader of Moore's book may be worried

by his effusive thanks in his acknowledgments to his wife—she is named Cassandra.

119. National Research Council, note 115 above, at 107. See also Stephen H. Schneider, B. L. Turner II, and Holly Morehouse Garriga, "Imaginable Surprise in Global Change Science," 1 *Journal of Risk Research* 165 (1998); Evelyn L. Wright, *Catastrophe, Uncertainty, and the Costs of Climate Change Damages*, ch. 3 (Ph.D. thesis, Rensselaer Polytechnic Institute, Oct. 2000).

120. Alley et al., note 115 above, at 2006.

121. Spencer R. Weart, *The Discovery of Global Warming* 185–187 (2003); Raymond T. Pierrehumbert, "Subtropical Water Vapor as a Mediator of Rapid Global Climate Change," in *Mechanisms of Global Change at Millennial Time-scales* 339 (Peter U. Clark, Robert S. Webb, and Lloyd D. Keigwin eds. 1999); Nordhaus and Boyer, note 106 above, at 88; David Stipp, "The Pentagon's Weather Nightmare," *Fortune*, Feb. 9, 2004, p. 100. Cf. Nordhaus, note 117 above, at 114.

122. On the melting of the Antarctic ice sheet, see, for example, Andrew Shepherd et al., "Larsen Ice Shelf Has Progressively Thinned," 302 *Science* 856 (2003).

123. Alexander E. MacDonald, "The Wild Card in the Climate Change Debate," *Issues in Science and Technology*, summer 2001, p. 51; Rees, note 31 above, at 111.

124. R. J. Stouffer and S. Manabe, "Equilibrium Response of Thermohaline Circulation to Large Changes in Atmospheric CO_2 Concentration," 20 *Climate Dynamics* 759 (2003). The term "thermohaline circulation" refers to the effect of temperature and salt on ocean circulation.

125. Cf. Rees, note 31 above, at 111–112.

126. Mark Maslin et al., "Linking Continental-Slope Failures and Climate Change: Testing the Cathrate Gun Hypothesis," 32 *Geology* 53 (2004).

127. Bryson, note 16 above, at 431. Cf. Kump, Kasting, and Crane, note 21 above, at 240–244; Paul F. Hoffman and Daniel P. Schrag, "Snowball Earth," *Scientific American*, Jan. 2000, p. 68; Schrag et al., "On the Initiation of a Snowball Earth," *Geochemistry Geophysics Geosystems: G^3* 10.1029/2001GC000219 (June 27, 2002).

128. National Research Council, note 115 above, at 88–89.

129. Christopher J. Poulsen, Raymond T. Pierrehumbert, and Robert L. Jacob, "Impact of Ocean Dynamics on the Simulation of the Neoprotozoic 'Snowball Earth,'" 28 *Geophysical Research Letters* 1575 (2001).

130. Garnett P. Williams, *Chaos Theory Tamed* 4 (1997).

131. Nordhaus, note 117 above, at 114–115 and ch. 7.

132. Nordhaus and Boyer, note 106 above, at 90 (tab. 4.9).

133. Ibid. (tab 4.9 notes).

134. Ibid., 87.

135. Ibid., 91 (tab. 4.10).

136. Alley et al., note 115 above, at 2008. See also ibid., 2007. Nordhaus was one of the coauthors of the article. What appears to be meant by the quoted phrase is that there is virtually no economic analysis of global warming that is based on the scientific evidence concerning the likelihood and possible consequences of abrupt global warming.

137. Pringle, note 112 above, at 21–22.

138. For an excellent discussion, see Cotton and Pielke, note 110 above, ch. 11.

139. For a lucid discussion, see S. George Philander, *Is the Temperature Rising? The Uncertain Science of Global Warming*, ch. 13 (1998). Despite the skeptical note sounded in the subtitle, Philander concludes: "We are increasing the atmospheric concentrations of several greenhouse gases, not by a small percentage, but by factors of two and more. Particularly disquieting is the rapid rate of increase; the growth is exponential, a dangerous situation that calls for action long before there is clear evidence of impending trouble." Ibid., 204.

140. Ramakrishna R. Nemani et al., "Climate-Driven Increase in Global Terrestrial Net Primary Production from 1982 to 1999," 300 *Science* 1560 (2003).

141. For a comprehensive assessment, see P. D. Jones et al., "Surface Air Temperature and Its Changes over the Past 150 Years," 37 *Reviews of Geophysics* 173 (1999). The warming of Europe since the late twentieth century has no precedent in the previous 500 years of European climate history. Jürg Luterbacher et al., "European Seasonal and Annual Temperature Variability, Trends, and Extremes since 1500," 303 *Science* 1499 (2004).

142. Intergovernmental Panel on Climate Change (IPCC), *Climate Change 2001* 44 (2001).

143. Gregg Morland, Tom Boden, and Robert J. Andres, "Global CO_2 Emissions from Fossil-Fuel Burning, Cement Manufacture, and Gas Flaring: 1751–2000" (Aug. 27, 2003), http://cdiac.esd.ornl.gov/ftp/fossilfuel-co2-emissions/global 00.ems.

144. See, for example, Shepherd et al., note 122 above; Derek R. Mueller, Warwick F. Vincent, and Martin O. Jeffries, "Break-Up of the Largest Arctic Ice Shelf and Associated Loss of an Epishelf Lake," 30 *Geophysical Research Letters* 10.1029/2003GL017931 (2003); Xuanji Wang and Jeffrey R. Key, "Recent Trends in Arctic Surface, Cloud, and Radiation Properties from Space," 299 *Science* 1725 (2003).

145. Intergovernmental Panel on Climate Change, note 142 above, *Technical Summary* B.2.

146. David G. Victor, *The Collapse of the Kyoto Protocol and the Struggle to Slow Global Warming* 120 (2001).

147. Peter Ciborowski, "Sources, Sinks, Trends, and Opportunities," in *The Challenge of Global Warming* 213, 226–228 (Dean Edwin Abrahamson ed. 1989).

148. Intergovernmental Panel on Climate Change (IPCC), note 142 above, ch. 11.

149. Ibid., *Working Group II: Impacts, Adaptation and Vulnerability*, ch. 1.

150. Lomborg, note 100 above, at 278–287.

151. *Renewable Energy: Power for a Sustainable Future* (Godfrey Boyle ed. 1996).

152. This may change, though. David W. Keith and Alexander E. Farrell, "Rethinking Hydrogen Cars," 301 *Science* 315 (2003).

153. *The Future of Nuclear Power: An Interdisciplinary MIT Study* 67 (2003). The least of the concerns about nuclear energy is or should be the risk of an accidental meltdown, which is minute with respect to new reactors. And no previous meltdown, not even Chernobyl, has had truly catastrophic consequences.

154. Kump, Kasting, and Crane, note 21 above, at 293–296; National Research Council, note 115 above, at 14–15, 24–36; John Houghton, *Global Warming: The Complete Briefing* 54–55 (1994).

155. National Research Council, note 115 above, at 27; Steven Mithen, *After the Ice: A Global Human History, 20,000–5,000 BC* 12–13 (2003).

156. As strongly argued by Mithen. Ibid., 622 (index references to "Younger Dryas").

157. Alley et al., note 115 above, at 2006. See also Bruce E. Johansen, *The Global Warming Desk Reference* 138–139 (2002); Wallace S. Broecker, "Greenhouse Surprises," in *The Challenge of Global Warming*, note 147 above, at 196, 200–202.

158. Kump, Kasting, and Crane, note 21 above, at 294.

159. Patrick J. Michaels and Robert C. Balling, Jr., *The Satanic Gases: Clearing the Air about Global Warming*, ch. 11 (2000).

160. Johansen, note 157 above, at 22.

161. Ibid., ch. 3.

162. Ross Gelbspan, *The Heat Is On: The High Stakes Battle over Earth's Threatened Climate* 53 (1997). Gelbspan summarizes the scientific rebuttals to the skeptics in ibid., 197–237.

163. Weart, note 121 above, at 166–167.

164. "Natural Catastrophes and Man-Made Disasters in 2003: Many Fatalities, Comparatively Few Insured Losses," *Sigma*, No. 1, 2004, pp. 10–13 (*Sigma* is published by Swiss Reinsurance Company); Andrew Dlugolecki and Thomas Loster, "Climate Change and the Financial Services Sector: An Appreciation of the UNEPFI Study," 28 *Geneva Papers on Risk and Insurance* 382, 392–93 (2003); Matthew Paterson, "Risk Business: Insurance Companies in Global Warming Politics," *Global Environmental Politics*, Nov. 2001, pp. 18, 21–23; Michael Tucker, "Climate Change and the Insurance Industry: The Cost of Increased Risk and the Impetus for Action," 22 *Ecological Economics* 85 (1997).

165. Weart, note 121 above, ch. 8.

166. See, for example, Richard S. Lindzen and Constantine Giannitsis, "Reconciling Observations of Global Temperature Change," 29 *Geophysical Research Letters* 10.1029/2001GL014074 (June 26, 2002); Lindzen, "Can Increasing Carbon Dioxide Cause Climate Change?" 94 *Proceedings of the National Academy of Sciences* 8335 (1997); Lindzen, "Absence of Scientific Basis," 9 *National Geographic Research and Exploration* 191 (1993); Lindzen, "Some Coolness concerning Global Warming," 71 *Bulletin of the American Meteorological Society* 288 (1990).

167. S. Fred Singer, *Hot Talk Cold Science: Global Warming's Unfinished Debate* (1997).

168. See, for example, Quiang Fu et al., "Contribution of Stratospheric Cooling to Satellite-Inferred Tropospheric Temperature Trends," 429 *Nature* 56 (2004); Konstantin Y. Vinnikov and Norman C. Grody, "Global Warming Trend of Mean Tropospheric Temperature Observed by Satellites," 302 *Science* 269 (2003); Josefino C. Comiso, "Warming Trends in the Arctic from Clear Sky Satellite Observations," 16 *Journal of Climate* 3498 (2003); Carl A. Mears, Matthias C. Schabel, and Frank J. Wentz, "A Reanalysis of the MSU Channel 2 Tropospheric Temperature Record," 16 *Journal of Climate* 3650 (2003); B. D. Santer

et al., "Influence of Satellite Data Uncertainties on the Detection of Externally Forced Climate Change," 300 *Science* 1280 (2003). Cf. Jones et al., note 141 above, at 186–189. For a contrary view, see John R. Christy et al., "Error Estimates of Version 5.0 of MSU-AMSU Bulk Atmospheric Temperatures," 20 *Journal of Atmospheric and Oceanic Technology* 613 (2003).

169. See, for example, S. Fred Singer, "Climate Policy—From Rio to Kyoto—A Political Issue for 2000—and Beyond" (Hoover Institution on War, Revolution and Peace, Essay in Public Policy No. 102, 2000).

170. Singer, note 167 above, at ix.

171. Ibid., 70.

172. Ibid., 68.

173. Ibid., 5–6, 56.

174. It may not be. Raymond S. Bradley, Malcolm K. Hughes, and Henry F. Diaz, "Climate in Medieval Time," 302 *Science* 404 (2003).

175. John Whitfield, "Too Hot to Handle," 425 *Nature* 338 (2003).

176. Singer, note 167 above, at 84–87.

177. Ibid., 42.

178. The conservative mindset is well illustrated by J. R. Clark and Dwight R. Lee, "Global Warming and Its Dangers," 8 *Independent Review* 591 (2004).

179. On techniques for deriving a composite probability estimate from the differing estimates of different experts, see M. Granger Morgan and Max Henrion, *Uncertainty: A Guide to Dealing with Uncertainty in Quantitative Risk and Policy Analysis* 65–66, 164–168 (1990).

180. See, for example, Elizabeth A. Casman, M. Granger Morgan, and Hadi Dowlatabadi, "Mixed Levels of Uncertainty in Complex Policy Models," 19 *Risk Analysis* 33, 37 (1999).

181. Richard T. Woodward and Richard C. Bishop, "How to Decide When Experts Disagree: Uncertainty-Based Choice Rules in Environmental Policy," 73 *Land Economics* 492 (1997); Kenneth J. Arrow and Leonid Hurwicz, "An Optimality Criterion for Decision-Making under Ignorance," in *Uncertainty and Expectations in Economics: Essays in Honour of G. L. S. Shackle* 1 (C. F. Carter and J. L. Ford eds. 1972).

182. Details of the study will be posted at my Web site, http://home.uchicago.edu/~rposner/. The database is "ISI [Institute for Scientific Information] Journal Citation Reports."

183. For a recent example, see Colin Price, *Time, Discounting and Value*, ch. 17 (1993).

184. Kump, Kasting, and Crane, note 21 above, at 319.

185. See, for example, Edward Linare, *Climate, Data and Resources: A Reference and Guide* 310 (1992).

186. Ibid., 310–311.

187. The common-pool problem can beset a nonliving resource as well; if underground pools of oil or natural gas are unowned or unregulated, producers will have an incentive to extract the resource at too rapid a rate, since a producer who reduces his rate of extraction will merely be creating additional opportunities for his competitors. This is well understood and the response has been to require unitization (unified management of an oil or gas field) and other conservation measures.

188. See, for example, Magnuson-Stevens Fishery Conservation and Management Act, 16 U.S.C. §§ 1801 et seq.

189. M. J. Peterson, "International Fisheries Management," in *Institutions for the Earth: Sources of Effective International Environmental Protection* 249 (Peter M. Haas, Robert O. Keohane, and Marc A. Levy eds. 1993); Colin W. Clark, *Mathematical Bioeconomics: The Optimal Management of Renewable Resources* 158–164 (2d ed. 1990). See, for example, International Convention for the Conservation of Atlantic Tunas (3d rev. 2003), http://www.iccat.es/Documents/BasicTexts.pdf (visited Jan. 21, 2004). See also Oran R. Young, *International Cooperation: Building Regimes for Natural Resources and the Environment* 109–124 (1989).

190. Clark, note 189 above, at 36 and ch. 8.

191. A point emphasized in ibid., 47–50, 60–62.

192. See, for example, *Intellectual Property Rights and Biodiversity Conservation: An Interdisciplinary Analysis of the Values of Medicinal Plants* (Timothy Swanson ed. 1995); Amy B. Craft and R. David Simpson, "The Value of Biodiversity in Pharmaceutical Research with Differentiated Products," 18 *Environmental and Resource Economics* 1 (2001).

193. Ian Walden, "Preserving Biodiversity: The Role of Property Rights," in *Intellectual Property Rights and Biodiversity Conservation*, note 192 above, at 176.

194. Irven DeVore, "Extraterrestrial Intelligence? Not Likely," 950 *Annals of the New York Academy of Sciences* 276, 281 (2001).

195. Raup, note 21 above, at 68.

196. Peter M. Sheehan and Thor A. Hansen, "Detritus Feeding as a Buffer to Extinction at the End of the Cretaceous," 14 *Geology* 868 (1986); Fastovsky and Weishampel, note 21 above, at 423.

197. Raup, note 21 above, at 3–4. A lower estimate—98 to 99 percent—is given in Robert M. May, John H. Lawton, and Nigel E. Stork, "Assessing Extinction Rates," in *Extinction Rates* 1, 2 (Lawton and May eds. 1995).

198. Lomborg, note 100 above, at 249.

199. Edward O. Wilson, *The Future of Life* 14 (2002).

200. See, for example, Paul H. Williams, Kevin J. Gaston, and Chris J. Humphries, "Mapping Biodiversity Value Worldwide: Combining Higher-Taxon Richness from Different Groups," 264 *Proceedings of the Royal Society of London B* 141 (1997).

201. Lomborg, note 100 above, ch. 23; Julian L. Simon, *The Ultimate Resource 2*, ch. 31 (1996).

202. Raup, note 21 above, at 3, 108.

203. Wilson, note 199 above, at 100–102.

204. Ibid., 14.

205. See, for example, C. R. Margules and M. P. Austin, "Biological Models for Monitoring Species Decline: The Construction and Use of Data Bases," in *Extinction Rates*, note 197 above, at 183.

206. Other, similarly pessimistic estimates are listed in Ariel E. Lugo, "Estimating Reductions in the Diversity of Tropical Forest Species," in *Biodiversity* 58, 59 (E. O. Wilson and Frances M. Peter eds. 1988) (tab. 6–1). See Brian Goombridge and Martin D. Jenkins, *World Atlas of Biodiversity: Earth's Living*

Resources in the 21st Century, ch. 4 (2002), for a balanced discussion of the human impact on the rate of extinction.

207. The significance of the population projections in Figure 1.2 is discusssed below. On the correlation between population growth and biodiversity loss, see Jeffrey K. McKee et al., "Forecasting Global Biodiversity Threats Associated with Human Population Growth," 115 *Biological Conservation* 161 (2003).

208. Chris D. Thomas et al., "Extinction Risk from Climate Change," 427 *Nature* 145 (2004); J. Alan Pounds and Robert Puschendorf, "Clouded Futures," 427 *Nature* 107 (2004); Mueller, Vincent, and Jeffries, note 144 above, at 1–4.

209. Robert L. Peters, "Effects of Global Warming on Biodiversity," in *The Challenge of Global Warming*, note 147 above, at 82.

210. Omid Mohseni, Heinz G. Stefan, and John G. Eaton, "Global Warming and Potential Changes in Fish Habitat in U.S. Streams," 59 *Climatic Change* 389 (2003).

211. May, Lawton, and Stork, note 197 above, at 21.

212. Ibid., 6.

213. For a good discussion, see Kump, Kasting, and Crane, note 21 above, ch. 18.

214. See, for example, Helen M. Regan et al., "The Currency and Tempo of Extinction," 157 *American Naturalist* 1, 7 (2001), estimating that the current rate of extinction is between 17 and 377 times the background rate, with the best estimate lying between 36 and 78. These estimates are for mammalian species only. See also W. Wayt Gibbs, "On the Termination of Species," *Scientific American*, Nov. 2001, p. 40.

215. Regan et al., note 214 above, at 8.

216. Lomborg, note 100 above, at 255–256.

217. Michael Boulter, "A Dead Certainty," *Geographical Magazine*, March 2002, pp. 31, 32.

218. Raup, note 21 above, at 19–20. See also Ibid., 187–191.

219. Barry Estabrook, "Staying Alive: To What Length Should Scientists Go to Save Endangered Species?" *Wildlife Conservation*, June 2002. p. 37. See also Oliver A. Ryder et al., "DNA Banks for Endangered Animal Species," 288 *Science* 275 (2000); Tom J. Cade, "Using Science and Technology to Reestablish Species Lost in Nature," in *Biodiversity*, note 206 above, at 279. Other such organizations include the Consultative Group on International Agricultural Research, the Millennium Seed Bank Project, and the National Plant Germplasm Center.

220. Such questions relating to biodiversity as whether we have a duty to leave nature alone—a position forcefully criticized in Jonathan Baert Wiener, "Law and the New Ecology: Evolution, Categories, and Consequences," 22 *Ecology Law Quarterly* 325 (1995).

221. Paul K. Anderson, "Competition, Predation, and the Evolution and Extinction of Steller's Sea Cow, *Hydrodamalis Gigas*," 11 *Marine Mammal Science* 391 (1995).

222. David Tilman and Clarence Lehman, "Biodiversity, Composition, and Ecosystem Processes: Theory and Concepts," in *The Functional Consequences*

of Biodiversity: Empirical Progress and Theoretical Extensions 9, 11 (Ann P. Kinzig, Stephen W. Pacala, and David Tilman eds. 2002). See also Williams, Gaston, and Humphries, note 200 above, at 143; David Jablonski, "Extinction: Past and Present," 427 *Nature* 589 (2004) (suggesting that there are ten times as many genetically distinct populations as there are species).

223. Gary K. Meffe, C. Ronald Carroll, and Contributors, *Principles of Conservation Biology*, ch. 6 (1994).

224. Secretariat of the Convention on Biological Diversity, *Global Biodiversity Outlook* 112–113 (2001) (tabs. 1.15–1.16), www.biodiv.org/gbo (visited Jan. 29, 2004).

225. Sharon P. Lawler, Juan J. Armesto, and Peter Kareiva, "How Relevant to Conservation Are Studies Linking Biodiversity and Ecosystem Functioning?" in *The Functional Consequences of Biodiversity*, note 222 above, at 294, 306; William A. Brock and Anastasios Xepapadeas, "Valuing Diversity from an Economic Perspective: A Unified Economic, Ecological, and Genetic Approach," 93 *American Economic Review* 1597 (2003); Martin L. Weitzman, "The Noah's Ark Problem," 66 *Econometrica* 1279 (1998); Andrew Metrick and Martin L. Weitzman, "Conflicts and Choices in Biodiversity Preservation," *Journal of Economic Perspectives*, Summer 1998, p. 21.

226. Endangered Species Act of 1973, as amended, 16 U.S.C. §§ 1531 et seq.

227. Gardner M. Brown Jr. and Jason F. Shogren, "Economics of the Endangered Species Act," *Journal of Economic Perspectives*, Summer 1998, pp. 3, 6, 10.

228. Ibid., 16.

229. Martin I. Hoffert et al., "Advanced Technology Paths to Global Climate Stability: Energy for a Greenhouse Planet," 298 *Science* 981 (2002). See the further discussion of this issue in chapter 3.

230. See, for example, Gary S. Becker, *A Treatise on the Family* 173–174 (enlarged ed. 1991); John Cleland, "A Regional Review of Fertility Trends in Developing Countries: 1960 to 1995," in *The Future Population of the World: What Can We Assume Today?* 47 (Wolfgang Lutz ed., rev. ed. 1996).

231. Wolfgang Lutz, "Epilogue: Dilemmas in Population Stabilization," in ibid., 429, 432 (fig. 17.1).

232. Robert E. Lucas Jr., "Some Macroeconomics for the 21st Century," *Journal of Economic Perspectives*, Winter 2000, pp. 159, 163–164 and fig. 3.

233. On the pure effect of population on emissions of carbon dioxide, see Anqing Shi, "Population Growth and Global Carbon Dioxide Emissions," http://www.iussp.org/Brazil2001/s00/S09_04_Shi.pdf (Development Research Group, World Bank, June 2001).

234. See references in Cass R. Sunstein, "Beyond the Precautionary Principle," 151 *University of Pennsylvania Law Review* 1003, 1027, 1032 (2003).

235. On both the positive and the negative externalities of population growth, see Simon Kuznets, "Population Change and Aggregate Output," in *Demographic and Economic Change in Developed Countries: A Conference of the Universities-National Bureau Committee for Economic Research* 324 (1960). On the effect of population growth specifically on innovation, see Charles I. Jones, "Was an Industrial Revolution Inevitable? Economic Growth over the Very Long Run," *Advances in Macroeconomics*, vol. 1, issue 2, 2001, http://www.bepress.com/bejm/advances/vol1/iss2/art1; Michael Kremer, "Popula-

tion Growth and Technological Change: One Million B.C. to 1990," 108 *Quarterly Journal of Economics* 681 (1993).

236. Daron Acemoglu and Joshua Linn, "Market Size in Innovation: Theory and Evidence from the Pharmaceutical Industry" (M.I.T. Economics Department, Mar. 2004), http://econ-www.mit.edu/faculty/index.htm?prof_icl=acemoglu& type=paper; Rodrigo A. Cerda, *Drugs, Population and Market Size* (Ph.D. diss., University of Chicago Dept. of Economics, March 2003).

237. David D. Friedman, "What Does 'Optimum Population' Mean?" 3 *Research in Population Economics* 273 (1981).

238. This was Max Weber's central insight, and one that I have emphasized in my own work. See, for example, Richard A. Posner, *The Problematics of Moral and Legal Theory*, pt. 2 (1999).

239. Leslie, note 45 above, at 26–37.

240. Adrian Kent, "A Critical Look at Risk Assessments for Global Catastrophes" 24 *Risk Analysis* 157, 158–159 (2004).

241. Paul R. Ehrlich et al., *The Cold and the Dark: The World after Nuclear War* (1984); R. P. Turcko, et al., "Nuclear Winter: Global Consequences of Multiple Nuclear Explosions," 222 *Science* 1283 (1983).

242. Rees, note 31 above, at 30–31. For a fuller discussion, by two climatologists, see Cotton and Pielke, note 110 above, ch. 10. They conclude: "As a result of the almost total reliance on models which have numerous shortcomings, the nuclear winter hypothesis is a long way from being proven scientifically viable." Ibid., 159. Other destructive effects of nuclear and thermonuclear weapons are comprehensively discussed in *The Effects of Nuclear Weapons* (Samuel Glasstone and Philip J. Dolan eds. 1977).

243. Scott D. Sagan, *The Limits of Safety: Organizations, Accidents, and Nuclear Weapons* (1993); Charles Perrow, *Normal Accidents: Living with High-Risk Technologies* 284–293 (2d ed. 1999); Leslie, note 45 above, at 33–34.

244. National Research Council of the National Academies, *Making the Nation Safer: The Role of Science and Technology in Countering Terrorism* 40–41 (2002). See also *The Future of Nuclear Power*, note 153 above, at 65–66. For a skeptical view, see Council on Foreign Relations, "Terrorism: Questions & Answers: Making a Bomb," http://www.terrorismanswers.com/weapons/making2 .html (visited Jan. 21, 2004).

245. Peter Baker, "U.S.-Russia Team Seizes Uranium at Bulgaria Plant: Material Was Potent Enough for Bomb," *Washington Post*, Dec. 24, 2003, p. A10.

246. David Rohde, "Pakistani A-Bomb Guru Says He, Alone, Let Secrets Out," *New York Times* (late ed.), Feb. 5, 2004, p. A16; Mark Landler and David E. Sanger, "Pakistan Chief Says It Appears Scientists Sold Nuclear Data," *New York Times* (late ed.), Jan. 24, 2004, p. A1; Sanger and William J. Broad, "From Rogue Nuclear Programs, Web of Trails Leads to Pakistan," *New York Times*, Jan. 4, 2004, § 1, p. 1.

247. Joseph Cirincione, *Deadly Arsenals: Tracking Weapons of Mass Destruction* 115–116 (2002). See also Amy F. Woolf, "Nuclear Weapons in Russia: Safety, Security, and Control Issues" CRS-4 to –6 (Congressional Resarch Service Brief IB98038, Apr. 11, 2003).

248. Frank Barnaby, *How to Build a Nuclear Bomb and Other Weapons of Mass Destruction* 117 (2003).

249. Ibid., 36.

250. Ibid., 18.

251. Frank N. von Hippel, "Revisiting Nuclear Power Plant Safety," 299 *Science* 201 (2003); Barnaby, note 248 above, at 157–162.

252. Ibid., 37–39; National Research Council, note 244 above, at 41–51; Joby Warrick, "Study Raises Projection for 'Dirty Bomb' Toll," *Washington Post*, Jan. 13, 2004, p. A2.

253. Susan R. Owens, "Waging War on the Economy: The Possible Threat of a Bioterrorist Attack against Agriculture," 3 *EMBO Reports* 111 (2002); National Research Council, note 244 above, at 77–79.

254. Michael E. Peterson, "Antiterrorism and Foot-and-Mouth Disease: Is the United States Prepared?" in *The Gathering Biological Warfare Storm*, note 253 above, at 9; Advisory Panel to Assess Domestic Response Capabilities for Terrorism Involving Weapons of Mass Destruction, *First Annual Report to the President and the Congress. Assessing the Threat* 12–16 (RAND Corp. Dec. 15, 1999).

255. The literature on this is already extensive. For a comprehensive recent analysis, see Committee on Research Standards and Practices to Prevent the Destructive Application of Biotechnology and National Research Council of the National Academies, *Biotechnology Research in an Age of Terrorism* (2004). For an earlier discussion, also excellent though already slightly dated, see *The New Terror: Facing the Threat of Biological and Chemical Weapons* (Sidney D. Drell, Abraham D. Sofaer, and George D. Wilson eds. 1999), esp. Steven M. Block's paper "Living Nightmares: Biological Threats Enabled by Molecular Biology," in ibid., 39. See also British Medical Association, *Biotechnology, Weapons and Humanity* (1999). A fine short treatment is Michael J. Ainscough, "Next Generation Bioweapons: Genetic Engineering and BW," in *The Gathering Biological Warfare Storm* 253 (Jim A. Davis and Barry R. Schneider eds., 2d ed. 2002), and a good popular treatment is Judith Miller, Stephen Engelberg, and William Broad, *Germs: Biological Weapons and America's Secret War* (2001), esp. ch. 12.

256. Muhammad Q. Islam and Wassim N. Shahin, "Applying Economic Methodology to the War on Terrorism," 31 *Forum for Social Economics* 7 (2001), and studies cited there.

257. See, for example, Walter Enders and Todd Sandler, "Terrorism: Theory and Applications," in *Handbook of Defense Economics*, vol. 1, pp. 213, 239 (Keith Hartley and Todd Sandler eds.1995); Eli Berman and David D. Laitin, "Rational Martyrs vs. Hard Targets: Evidence on the Tactical Use of Suicide Attacks" (University of California at San Diego and Stanford University, n.d.).

258. Jonathan B. Tucker, "Bioterrorism: Threats and Responses," in *Biological Weapons: Limiting the Threat* 283, 291 (Joshua Lederberg ed. 1999). See also Bruce Hoffman, *Inside Terrorism*, ch. 4 (1998); Walter Enders and Todd Sandler, "Is Transnational Terrorism Becoming More Threatening?" 44 *Journal of Conflict Resolution* 307 (2000).

259. Robert A. Pape, "The Strategic Logic of Suicide Terrorism," 97 *American Political Science Review* 343, 355–356 (2003).

260. See, for example, National Science and Technology Council, *Nanotechnology Research Directions*, note 68 above, at 156. For a lucid description of bioengineering, see McHughen, note 82 above, chs. 2–3. A succinct sum-

mary of the dangers of "engineered viruses" can be found in Rees, note 31 above, at 54–57.

261. Barnaby, note 248 above, at 48–51, 123–124; David A. Koplow, *Smallpox: The Fight to Eradicate a Global Scourge* 89 (2003).

262. Committee on Research Standards and Practices, note 253 above, at 18.

263. John Heilprin, "Bioterror Concerns Raised at Universities," Associated Press Online, Nov. 21, 2003, http://www.cbn.com/CBNNews/Wire/031121f.asp.

264. Committee on Research Standards and Practices, note 253 above, at 19–21; Richard Preston, "The Bioweaponeers," *New Yorker*, March 9, 1998, p. 52.

265. NTI (Nuclear Threat Initiative), "North Korea Profile—Biological" (April 2003), http://www.nti.org/e_research/profiles/NK/57_276.html.

266. Cirincione, note 247 above, at 9.

267. Barnaby, note 248 above, at 119–120; Jessica Stern, "Dreaded Risks and the Control of Biological Weapons," *International Security*, Winter 2002–2003, pp. 89, 96–97.

268. U.S. Dept. of State, "Patterns of Global Terrorism, 2002" (Dept. of State Publication 11038, April 2003, App. B), www.state.gov/s/ct/rls/pgtrpt/2002/pdf.

269. U.N. Security Council Committee Established Pursuant to Resolution 1267 (1999) concerning Al-Qaida and the Taliban and Associated Individuals and Entities, "The New Consolidated List of Individuals and Entities Belonging to or Associated with the Taliban and Al-Qaida Organisation as Established and Maintained by the 1267 Committee," www.un.org/Docs/sc/committees/1267/1267ListEng.htm (visited Feb. 12, 2004).

270. David E. Kaplan, "Aum Shinrikyo (1995)," in *Toxic Terror: Assessing Terrorist Use of Chemical and Biological Weapons* 207 (Jonathan B. Tucker ed. 2000).

271. Ibid., 212.

272. Bruce Hoffman, "The Confluence of International and Domestic Trends in Terrorism," *Terrorism and Political Violence*, Summer 1997, pp. 1, 4.

273. Committee on Research Standards and Practices, note 253 above, at 25–27; Rees, note 31 above, at 57–58.

274. Ronald J. Jackson et al., "Expression of Mouse Interleukin-4 by a Recombinant Ectromelia Virus Suppresses Cytolytic Lymphocyte Responses and Overcomes Genetic Resistance to Mousepox," 75 *Journal of Virology* 1205, 1206 (2001); Jon Cohen, "Designer Bugs," *Atlantic Monthly*, July/Aug. 2002, pp. 113, 115. Why didn't the scientists want to juice up mousepox to the point at which it would kill mice rather than just make them infertile? Probably because a disease that kills the host may not spread, depending on the interval between becoming infected and dying and how widely scattered the target population is. Mice are not social animals. A mouse that died within minutes or hours of being infected might not have time to infect any other mice.

275. Cf. John Pickrell, "Imperial College Fined over Hybrid Virus Risk," 293 *Science* 779 (2001). This is an old worry about gene splicing. See, for example, Perrow, note 243 above, at 293–303. It is one of the worries about genetically modified crops.

276. Note 274 above.

277. See also the detailed description in Richard Preston, *The Demon in the Freezer: A True Story* 222–223 (2002), of how the St. Louis scientists, in a repli-

cation discussed below of the Australian experiment, spliced the IL-4 gene into the mousepox virus.

278. Barnaby, note 248 above, at 44–45.

279. Hugh Pennington, "Smallpox and Bioterrorism," 81 *Bulletin of the World Health Organization* 762, 763–765 (2003).

280. Ibid., 765.

281. Ibid., 764.

282. Pape, note 259 above, at 356–357.

283. Joseph Barbera et al., "Large-Scale Quarantine Following Biological Terrorism in the United States: Scientific Examination, Logistics and Legal Limits, and Possible Consequences," 286 *JAMA (Journal of the American Medical Association)* 2711, 2712 (2001).

284. Ibid., 2714. Studies of smallpox as a bioweapon, such as Edward H. Kaplan, David L. Craft, and Lawrence M. Wein, "Analyzing Bioterror Response Logistics: The Case of Smallpox," 185 *Mathematical Biosciences* 33 (2003), that assume an effective vaccine are of limited value in assessing the gravity of a deliberate smallpox pandemic. The virus might well be genetically modified to defeat existing vaccines, in which event, as noted in the text, quarantining might be infeasible.

285. Pennington, note 279 above, at 764. See also Jonathan B. Tucker, *Scourge: The Once and Future Threat of Smallpox* 36, 232 (2001).

286. Michael T. Osterholm and John Schwartz, *Living Terrors: What America Needs to Know to Survive the Coming Bioterrorist Catastrophe*, ch. 5 (2000); Madeline Drexler, "The Germ Front: Experts Differ over Whether Chemical and Biological Warfare Pose a Mass Threat—But They Agree That We Need a Stronger Public-Health Response," *American Prospect*, Nov. 5, 2001, pp. 26, 28.

287. Tucker, note 285 above, at 202–206; Stern, note 267 above, at 94–95.

288. National Research Council, note 244 above, at 22–23. Methods and materials for gene splicing of the vaccinia virus are described in great detail in Supplement 43 to *Current Protocols in Molecular Biology*, vol. 3 (1998). See also "Boom, or Bust?" 426 *Nature* 598, 601 (2003).

289. William J. Broad, "Bioterror Researchers Build a More Lethal Mousepox," *New York Times* (late ed.), Nov. 1, 2003, p. A8. The work of the St. Louis scientists had already been described in detail in Preston, note 277 above, at 217–228.

290. Broad, note 289 above.

291. Ibid.

292. Michael Balter, "On the Trail of Ebola and Marburg Viruses," 290 *Science* 923, 925 (2000).

293. Goldsby et al., note 3 above, at 423–425.

294. Preston, note 264 above, at 56.

295. National Science Board, *Science and Engineering Indicators—2002*, vol. 1, pp. 3–25 (National Science Foundation, NSB–02–01, 2002) (tab. 3.18). See also Michael S. Teitelbaum, "Do We Need More Scientists?" *Public Interest*, Fall 2003, pp. 40, 51.

296. Committee on Research Standards and Practices, note 253 above, at 18.

297. "Future Direction of the Department of Energy's Office of Science," Hearing before Subcomm. on Energy of H.R. Comm. on Science, 107th Cong.,

2d sess. 23 (ser., July 25, 2002) (statement of Jerome I. Friedman). On the declining interest of native-born Americans in science study and careers, see National Science Board, note 295 above, at 0–6; National Science Board, *The Science and Engineering Workforce: Realizing America's Potential* (National Science Foundation, NSB 03–69, Aug. 14, 2003), http://www.nsf.gov/nsb/documents/2003/nsb0369/nsb0369.pdf.

298. Advisory Panel, note 255 above, at 24–25. The panel's report emphasizes other practical difficulties that a terrorist group would encounter in trying to launch a devastating biological attack. Ibid., 20–26. See also Amy E. Smithson, *Ataxia: The Chemical and Biological Terrorism Threat and the US Response* (Stimson Center Rep. No. 5, 2002), http://www.stimson.org/cwc/ataxia.htm; Karl Lowe, "Analyzing Technical Constraints on Bio-Terrorism: Are They Still Important?" in *Terrorism with Chemical and Biological Weapons: Calibrating Risks and Responses* 53, 55 (Brad Roberts ed. 1997). But these difficulties have lessened since 1999 owing to rapid progress in biotechnology.

299. Arnold M. Ludwig, *The Price of Greatness: Resolving the Creativity and Madness Controversy* 161–162 (1995); David Mechanic, Scott Bilder, and Donna M. McAlpine, "Employing Persons with Serious Mental Illness," *Health Affairs*, Sept./Oct. 2002, pp. 242, 251.

300. Ibid.

301. For a brief summary of the coming horrors, see Central Intelligence Agency, Directorate of Intelligence, "The Darker Bioweapons Future," http://www.fas.org/irp/cia/product/bw1103.pdf (Nov. 3, 2003); also Stern, note 267 above, at 111.

302. See index references to "chemical weapons" in Barnaby, note 248 above, at 177; also Michael L. Moodie, "The Chemical Weapons Threat," in *The New Terror*, note 253 above, at 5.

303. For a good introduction to cyberterrorism, see Gregory J. Rattray, "The Cyberterrorism Threat," in *The Terrorism Threat and U.S. Government Response: Operational and Organizational Factors* 79 (James M. Smith and William C. Thomas eds. 2001).

304. Anne W. Branscomb, "Rogue Computer Programs and Computer Rogues: Tailoring the Punishment to Fit the Crime," in *Computers, Ethics and Social Values* 89, 99 (Deborah G. Johnson and Helen Nissenbaum eds. 1995).

305. The estimate is by a consulting firm called Computer Economics. Its estimates are thought by many observers to be exaggerated. See, for example, Michelle Delio, "Find the Cost of (Virus) Freedom," http://www.wired.com/news/infostructure/0,1377,49861,00.html (visited Aug. 5, 2003).

306. CERT Coordination Center webpage, http://www.cert.org/stats/cert_stats.html#incidents (visited Jan. 27, 2004). CERT/CC, funded primarily by the U.S. Department of Defense and other federal agencies, is a reporting center for Internet security problems.

307. For a useful discussion, see Abraham D. Sofaer and Seymour E. Goodman, "Cyber Crime and Security: The Transnational Dimension," in *The Transnational Dimension of Cyber Crime and Terrorism* 1 (Abraham D. Sofaer and Seymour E. Goodman eds. 2001); also Barnaby, note 248 above, at 166–168. On the vulnerability of government computer networks, see Robert F. Dacey, "Information Security—Serious and Widespread Weaknesses Persist at

Federal Agencies" (General Accounting Office Rep. No. GAO/AIMD–00–295 B–286154, Sept. 6, 2000).

308. National Research Council of the National Academies et al., *Cybersecurity of Freight Information Systems: A Scoping Study* 3 (Transportation Research Board Special Report 274).

309. National Research Council, note 244 above, ch. 5. Some scenarios for terrorist attacks on the Internet are described in National Research Council of the National Academies, Computer Science and Telecommunications Board Division of Engineering and Physical Sciences, Committee on the Internet under Crisis Conditions: Learning from Sept. 11, *The Internet under Crisis Conditions: Learning from September 11* 54–60 (2003).

310. National Research Council of the National Academies, Computer Science and Telecommunications Board, "Summary of Discussions at a Planning Meeting on Cyber-Security and the Insider Threat to Classified Information" (Nov. 1–2, 2000).

311. For a vivid disaster scenario combining computer viruses with physical attacks on key Internet facilities such as root servers, see Jonathan Adams et al., "Bringing Down the Internet," *Newsweek International*, Nov. 3, 2003, p. 52.

312. Bruce Schneier, *Secrets and Lies: Digital Security in a Networked World* 31–36 (2000). See also Christian Parenti, *The Soft Cage: Surveillance in America: From Slavery to the War on Terror* (2003); Shawn C. Helmes, "Translating Privacy Values with Technology," 7 *Boston University Journal of Science and Technology Law* 288, 292 (2001); Christopher S. Milligan, "Facial Recognition Technology, Video Surveillance, and Privacy," 9 *Southern California Interdisciplinary Law Journal* 295, 304 (1999); Sheri A. Alpert, "Symposium Paper: Privacy and Intelligent Highways: Finding the Right of Way," 11 *Santa Clara Computer and High Technology Law Journal* 97, 98 (1995).

313. Simson Garfinkel, *Database Nation: The Death of Privacy in the 21st Century* 82–83 (2000).

314. For an excellent discussion, see Peter P. Swire and Robert E. Litan, *None of Your Business: World Data Flows, Electronic Commerce, and the European Privacy Directive* (1998).

315. Richard A. Posner, *The Economics of Justice* 147–148 (1981).

316. The costs of loss of privacy are well summarized in Andrew Song, "Technology, Terrorism, and the Fishbowl Effect: An Economic Analysis of Surveillance and Searches" (Harvard Law School, Berkman Center for Internet and Society, Research Publication No. 2003–04, May 2003), http://cyber.law.harvard.edu/home/uploads/207/2003–04.pdf.

317. Alan F. Westin, *Privacy and Freedom* 33–34 (1967).

318. National Research Council of the National Academies, *Cryptography's Role in Securing the Information Society* 101–104 (Kenneth W. Dam and Herbert S. Lin eds. 1996).

319. David Brin, *The Transparent Society: Will Technology Force Us to Choose between Privacy and Freedom?* (1998).

320. David Friedman, "The Case for Privacy," http://www.daviddfriedman.com/Academic/privacy_chapter/privacy.htm (visited Jan. 27, 2004).

321. Calogero, note 45 above, at 197.

322. The direct and especially the indirect economic consequences of 9/11 have been considerable. For an excellent analysis, see "Economic Consequences of Terrorism," 71 *OECD Economic Outlook* 117 (2002).

323. Lewis, note 34 above, at 115.

324. Chapman and Morrison, note 28 above, at 37.

325. Howard Kunreuther and Mark Pauly, "Insurance Decision Making and Market Behavior" (Feb. 7, 2000), http://www.nber.org/~confer/2000/inss00/howard.pdf; Paul Slovic et al., "Preference for Insuring against Small Losses: Insurance Implications," 44 *Journal of Risk and Insurance* 237 (1977).

Chapter 2

1. National Science Board, *Science and Engineering Indicators—2002*, vol. 1, pp. 3–6 (National Science Foundation, NSB–02–01, 2002).

2. The number of scientific personnel in 14 foreign countries is believed to have grown over the same period from 1,048,818 to 1,658,805, which translates into an annual growth rate of almost 3 percent. UNESCO Institute for Statistics, "Personnel Engaged in R & D by Category of Personnel," *Unesco Statistical Yearbook* (1999), http://www.uis.unesco.org/TEMPLATE/html/sc_consult.html; UNESCO Institute for Statistics, "Personnel Engaged in R & D by Category of Personnel" (2002), http://www.uis.unesco.org/TEMPLATE/html/Exceltables/science/View_Table_R&D_Personnel_by_Category.xls. The 14 countries are Belgium, Bulgaria, Canada, Cuba, France, Germany, Hungary, Ireland, Italy, Japan, South Korea, the Netherlands, Spain, and the United Kingdom. Obviously, important countries have been left out, such as China and Russia, which between them, according to the UNESCO statistics, had more than 1 million scientific workers in 1999. On the worldwide growth in R&D expenditures, see Robert M. May, "The Scientific Investments of Nations," 281 *Science* 49 (1998).

3. The source of these figures is *Analytical Perspectives: Budget of the United States Government, Fiscal Year 2004* 171–189 (Feb. 2003) (tabs. 8–2, 8–3), http://www.whitehouse.gov/omb/budget/fy2004/pdf/spec.pdf.

4. Office of Management and Budget, "2003 Report to Congress on Combating Terrorism" 37 (Sept. 2003).

5. See, for example, Daniel S. Greenberg, *Science, Money, and Politics: Political Triumph and Ethical Erosion* 206 (2001); Daniel Sarewitz, *Frontiers of Illusion: Science, Technology, and the Politics of Progress* 55 (1996); Christine Y. O'Sullivan et al., "The Nation's Report Card: Science 2000," National Center for Education Statistics, Jan. 2003, http://nces.ed.gov/nationsreportcard/ (visited Mar. 30, 2004).

6. An example is discussed in Daniel Read and M. Granger Morgan, "The Efficacy of Different Methods for Informing the Public about the Range Dependency of Magnetic Fields from High Voltage Power Lines," 18 *Risk Analysis* 603 (1998).

7. Teresa A. Smith et al., *Profiles of Student Achievement in Science at the TIMSS International Benchmarks: U.S. Performance and Standards in an International Context* 10, 12 (2000) (figs. 1 and 2). "TIMSS" stands for the Trends in International Mathematics and Science Study.

8. National Science Board, note 1 above, at 1–18 to 1–20.

9. Jon D. Miller, "The Measurement of Civic Scientific Literacy," 7 *Public Understanding of Science* 203, 217 (1998) (tab. 5); Jon D. Miller, Rafael Pardo, and Fujio Niwa, *Public Perceptions of Science and Technology: A Comparative Study of the European Union, the United States, Japan, and Canada* 60 (1997) (tab. 23).

10. Ibid., 75 (tab. 25).

11. Jon D. Miller, "The Scientifical: Americans Are Evenly Divided on the Existence of Extraterrestrial Visitors, and Half Don't Believe in the Theory of Evolution," *American Demographics*, June 1987, pp. 26, 28.

12. National Science Board, note 1 above, at 7–10 to 7–11, 7–36 to 7–37.

13. Jon D. Miller, "Civic Scientific Literacy: A Necessity in the 21st Century," *FAS [Federation of American Scientists] Report*, Jan.–Feb. 2002, p. 3 (2002).

14. Morris H. Shamos, *The Myth of Scientific Literacy* 90 (1995).

15. Ibid., 89.

16. Miller, note 13 above, at 4.

17. Miller, note 9 above, at 216–217 and tab. 5.

18. Harvey A. Averch, *A Strategic Analysis of Science and Technology Policy*. ch. 5 (1985).

19. National Science Board, note 1 above, at 1–35 to 1–37.

20. Ibid., 1–37 to 1–38.

21. Richard A. Posner, *Public Intellectuals: A Study of Decline*. ch. 6 (2001); Richard A. Posner, *The Problematics of Moral and Legal Theory* 68–85 (1999).

22. P. C. W. Davies and J. R. Brown, "The Strange World of the Quantum," in *The Ghost in the Atom: A Discussion of the Mysteries of Quantum Physics* 1. 20–26 (Davies and Brown eds. 1986).

23. Ibid., 6–7; Emil Polturak and Nir Gov, "Inside a Quantum Solid," 44 *Contemporary Physics* 145 (2003).

24. Paul A. Tipler and Ralph A. Llewellyn, *Modern Physics* 215 (4th ed. 2003) (emphasis in original).

25. Davies and Brown, note 22 above, at 14–15; G. G. Adamian, N. V. Antoneko, and W. Scheid, *Nuclear Physics* 387–390 (1999).

26. Greenberg, note 5 above, at 464.

27. Cf. Miriam Amit and Michael N. Fried, "High-Stakes Assessment as a Tool for Promoting Mathematical Literacy and the Democratization of Mathematics Education," 21 *Journal of Mathematical Behavior* 499, 512 (2002).

28. David A. Sousa, *How the Special Needs Brain Learns* 139, 140 (2001). See also Joan Shapiro and Rebecca Rich, *Facing Learning Disabilities in the Adult Years* 74 (1999).

29. National Science Board, note 1 above, at 7–12 to 7–15.

30. Sarewitz, note 5 above, at 55.

31. As emphasized in George Basalla, *The Evolution of Technology* (1988); Henry Petroski, *The Evolution of Useful Things* (1993).

32. Mary Bellis, "Famous Inventions: A to Z," www.inventors.about.com/library/bl/bl12.htm (visited Oct. 6, 2003).

33. Humphrey Taylor, "Majorities Continue to Believe in Global Warming and Support Kyoto Treaty" (Harris Poll #56, Oct. 23, 2002).

34. Barry R. Bloom, "Bioterrorism and the University: The Threats to Security—and to Openness," *Harvard Magazine*, Nov.–Dec. 2003, pp. 48, 51.

35. Ibid., 52.

36. Ibid.

37. Paula E. Stephan, "The Economics of Science," 34 *Journal of Economic Literature* 1199, 1220 (1996).

38. Paul J. Piccard, "Scientists and Public Policy: Los Alamos, August-November, 1945," 18 *Western Political Quarterly* 251, 258 (1965).

39. A particularly vivid example, which would be well worth reading were it not *so* gloomy, is Olaf Stapledon, *Last and First Men: A Story of the Near and Far Future* (1931). In it, among other near-term horrors, America goes crazy and kills the entire population of Europe with poison gas; among the long-term horrors, the sun begins a rapid disintegration only 20,000 years into the future.

40. Joshua Lederberg, "Foreword: J. B. S. Haldane's *Daedalus* 1923—70 Years Before and After," in *Haldane's* Daedalus *Revisited* vii (Krishna R. Dronamraju ed. 1995).

41. The novel and Clinton's proposal are unwarrantedly derided in Stephen S. Hall, "Science-Fiction Policy," *M.I.T.'s Technology Review*, Nov.–Dec. 1998, p. 92. Preston is a genuine expert on bioterrorism; see works by him cited in chapter 1 of this book. Hall commits the standard fallacy of assuming that because bioterrorism has not yet claimed many victims, there is nothing to worry about.

42. Kenneth Chang, "Armageddon Blasts Science," July 2, 1998, http://more .abcnews.go.com/sections/science/DailyNews/armageddon98071.html.

43. "Frequently Asked Questions," http://www.matrix-at.org/faq.htm (visited Feb. 12, 2004). Resistance to the program by a number of states appears to be killing it. John Schwartz, "Privacy Fears Erode Support for a Network to Fight Crime," *New York Times* (late ed.), Mar. 15, 2004, p. C1.

44. Peter B. Lloyd, "Glitches in *The Matrix* . . . And How to Fix Them," in *Taking the Red Pill: Science, Philosophy, and Religion in* The Matrix 103 (Glenn Yeffeth ed. 2003).

45. Andrew Pollack, "With Tiny Brain Implants, Just Thinking May Make It so," *New York Times* (national ed.), Apr. 13, 2004, p. D5.

46. Jo Twist, "Brain Waves Control Video Game," *BBC News*, Mar. 24, 2004, http://newsvote.bbc.co.uk/mpapps/pagetools/print/news.bbc.co.uk/1/hi/tech nology/3485918.stm.

47. Edward Castronova, "Virtual Worlds: A First-Hand Account of Market and Society on the Cybernian Frontier" 10 (CESifo Working Paper No. 618, Dec. 2001). For a lucid description and helpful analysis of virtual worlds, with many references, see Gregory Lastowka and Dan Hunter, "The Laws of the Virtual Worlds," 92 *California Law Review* 3 (2004).

48. See, for example, Paul Fontana, "Finding God in *The Matrix*," in *Taking the Red Pill*, note 44 above, at 159. Thus I was being imprecise when I said that a kiss saved Neo from dying; he *did* die, and was resurrected by the kiss. The distinction is important to the movie's religious imagery.

49. Ray Kurzweil, "The Human Machine Merger: Are We Headed for *The Matrix?*" in Ibid., 185, 196. Recall my discussion of his benign view of AI in chapter 1.

50. Fontana, note 48 above, at 181.

51. Robert J. Sawyer, "Artificial Intelligence, Science Fiction, and *The Matrix*," in *Taking the Red Pill*, note 44 above, at 45.

52. See, for example, Gary Westfahl, *Cosmic Engineers: A Study of Hard Science Fiction* (1996); Connie Willis, "Science in Science Fiction: A Writer's Perspective," in *Chemistry and Science Fiction* 21 (Jack H. Stocker ed. 1998); Frederik Pohl, "Science Fiction: Stepchild of Science," 97 *Technology Review* 57 (1997). On the teaching of science by means of science fiction, see Leroy W. Dubeck, Suzanne E. Moshier, and Judith E. Boss, *Fantastic Voyages: Learning Science through Science Fiction Films* (2d ed. 2003).

53. Stephen Hawking, "Foreword," in Lawrence M. Krauss, *The Physics of Star Trek* xi, xiii (1995).

54. For example, John Gray, "Ethically Engineered," *Times Literary Supplement*, Jan. 16, 2004, p. 9.

55. National Science Board, note 1 above, at 7–35. See also Athena Andreadis, *To Seek Out New Life: The Biology of* Star Trek 264–265 (1998).

56. David M. Rorvik, "Ecology's Angry Lobbyist: Dr. Paul Ehrlich Argues That the Chief Cause of Pollution Is Overpopulation," *Life*, April 21, 1970, p. 42.

57. Paul R. Ehrlich, "Are There Too Many of Us?" *McCall's*, July 1970, p. 46.

58. Ibid., 46, 104.

59. Peter Collier, "Ecological Destruction Is a Condition of American Life: An Interview with Ecologist Paul Ehrlich," *Mademoiselle*, April 1970, pp. 189, 293.

60. Paul R. Ehrlich, "Population Overgrowth . . . The Fertile Curse," *Field and Stream*, June 1970, p. 38.

61. Ronald Bailey, "Earth Day Then and Now," *Reason*, May 2000, pp. 18, 20, 22, 24.

62. Julian L. Simon, *The Ultimate Resource 2* 35–36 (1996)

63. ABC News, "Nightline Transcript," Jan. 22, 1991, p. 12 (interview of Carl Sagan and others by Ted Koppel).

64. Gina Kolata, "For Radiation, How Much Is Too Much?" *New York Times* (late edition), Nov. 27, 2001, p. F1.

65. See, for example, Simon Reeve and Colin McGhee, *The Millennium Bomb: Countdown to a £400 Billion Catastrophe* (1996).

66. Margaret Atwood, *Oryx and Crake: A Novel* 180 (2003).

67. Posner, *Public Intellectuals*, note 21 above, 148–150.

68. Gregg Easterbrook, "We're All Gonna Die! But It Won't Be from Germ Warfare, Runaway Nanobots, or Shifting Magnetic Poles: A Skeptical Guide to Doomsday," *Wired*, July 2003, p. 151.

69. Ibid., 152. In fairness to Easterbrook, the dumb title may not have been of his devising. Magazine editors often title articles without consulting the author.

70. Ibid., 154.

71. Alastair Hay, "Japan's Secret Weapon," 427 *Nature* 396 (2004).

72. Easterbrook, note 68 above, at 154.

73. Ibid.

74. Freeman J. Dyson, "The Future Needs Us," *New York Review of Books*, Feb. 13, 2003, pp. 11.

75. See also Gregg Easterbrook, "Warming Up: The Real Evidence for the Greenhouse Effect," *New Republic*, Nov. 8, 1999, p. 42; Easterbrook, "Climate

Change: How W. Can Save Himself on Global Warming," *New Republic*, July 23, 2001, p. 22. In the second article, Easterbrook proposes that global-warming policy place more emphasis on reducing methane, which as we know is indeed a more dangerous greenhouse gas, pound for pound, than carbon dioxide. Whether it requires more emphasis than carbon dioxide, when the latter is a much bigger factor in global warming, may be doubted; but it certainly deserves considerable emphasis because of its potential to trigger a catastrophic runaway greenhouse effect.

76. Easterbrook, note 68 above, at 157.

77. Ibid.

78. Near-Earth Object Science Definition Team, *Study to Determine the Feasibility of Extending the Search for Near-Earth Objects to Smaller Limiting Diameters* 18–19 (NASA Aug. 22, 2003).

79. Easterbrook, note 68 above, at 157.

80. Ibid.

81. Posner, *Public Intellectuals*, note 21 above, at 425.

82. Gregg Easterbrook, "The Big One: The Real Danger is Nuclear," *New Republic*, Nov. 5, 2001, p. 24. See also Easterbrook, "Term Limits: The Meaninglessness of 'WMD,'" *New Republic*, Oct. 7, 2002, p. 22.

83. Critically discussed in Howard P. Segal, *Technological Utopianism in American Culture* (1985), and Segal, *Future Imperfect: The Mixed Blessings of Technology in America* (1994).

84. Howard Margolis, *Dealing with Risk: Why the Public and the Experts Disagree on Environmental Issues* (1996), esp. ch. 6.

85. M. F. Perutz, "The Threat of Biological Weapons," *New York Review of Books*, Apr. 13, 2000, pp. 44, 48 (quoting Harry Sokolski).

86. Stephen Moore and Julian L. Simon, *It's Getting Better All the Time: Greatest Trends of the Last 100 Years* 178 (2000). Talk about dumb titles!

87. Perutz, note 85 above, at 49.

88. Dyson, note 74 above, at 12.

89. Charles Perrow, *Normal Accidents: Living with High-Risk Technologies* 299–300 (2d ed. 1999).

90. Dyson, note 74 above, at 12. Cf. Richard Pierre Claude, *Science in the Service of Human Rights* (2002).

91. See note 3 above.

92. Dyson, note 74 above, at 13.

93. Ibid.

94. Bjørn Lomborg, *The Skeptical Environment: Measuring the Real State of the World* 286 (2001).

95. See also Anthony C. Fisher and Urvashi Narain, "Global Warming, Endogenous Risk, and Irreversibility," 25 *Environmental and Resource Economics* 395, 396 (2003).

96. This is the first row of a table of random numbers created by means of the Randbetween (0,1) function of the Microsoft Excel spreadsheet program.

97. Arne Öhman, "Fear and Anxiety as Emotional Phenomena: Clinical Phenomenology, Evolutionary Perspectives, and Information-Processing Mechanisms," in *Handbook of Emotions* 511, 518–520 (Michael Lewis and Jeannette M. Haviland eds. 1993). People's propensity to mistake random sequences for

patterns is discussed in Paul Slovic, Howard Kunreuther, and Gilbert White, "Decision Processes, Rationality and Adjustment to Natural Hazards," in *The Perception of Risk* 1, 11 (Paul Slovic ed. 2000).

98. See, for example, Peter M. Sandman, *Responding to Community Outrage: Strategies for Effective Risk Communication* (1993).

99. See, for example, Michael B. Gerrard and Anna W. Barber, "Asteroids and Comets: U.S. and International Law and the Lowest-Probability, Highest-Consequence Risk," 6 *New York University Environmental Law Journal* 4, 17 (1997–1998).

100. See, for example, Amos Tversky and Daniel Kahneman, "Extensional versus Intuitive Reasoning: The Conjunction Fallacy in Probability Judgment," in *Heuristics and Biases: The Psychology of Intuitive Judgment* 19 (Thomas Gilovich et al. eds. 2002); Paul H. Rubin, *Darwinian Politics: The Evolutionary Origin of Freedom* 169–171 (2002).

101. See, for example, Richard R. Nelson and Sidney G. Winter, *An Evolutionary Theory of Economic Change* (1982); Nelson and Winter, "Evolutionary Theorizing in Economics," *Journal of Economic Perspectives*, Spring 2002, pp. 23, 33–39.

102. The 1950 figure is based on the 1950 *World Almanac* and the 2002 *CIA World Factbook*, which lists the independence day of each country, enabling the number of countries that were already independent in 1950 to be determined.

103. William D. Nordhaus and Joseph G. Boyer, "Requiem for Kyoto: An Economic Analysis of the Kyoto Protocol," *Energy Journal*, Special Issue, 1999, pp. 93, 118.

104. Christoph Böhringer and Andreas Löschel, "Economic Impacts of Carbon Abatement Strategies," in *Controlling Global Warming: Perspectives from Economics, Game Theory and Public Choice* 105 (Christoph Böhringer, Michael Finus, and Carsten Vogt eds. 2002).

105. James C. Murdoch and Todd Sandler, "The Voluntary Provision of a Pure Public Good: The Case of Reduced CFC Emissions and the Montreal Protocol," 63 *Journal of Public Economics* 331 (1997).

106. National Assessment Synthesis Team, *Climate Change Impact on the United States: The Potential Consequences of Climate Variability and Change* (2001); Alexander E. MacDonald, "The Wild Card in the Climate Change Debate," 17 *Issues in Science and Technology* 51 (2001).

107. Nordhaus and Boyer, note 103 above, at 126.

108. Martin Rees, *Our Final Hour: A Scientist's Warning: How Terror, Error, and Environmental Disaster Threaten Humankind's Future in This Century—On Earth and Beyond* 95 (2003).

109. Nordhaus and Boyer, note 103 above, at 98. Rates, not rate, because Nordhaus and Boyer assume that the discount rate will decline to 2.3 percent by the year 2100 and 1.4 percent by the year 2300. Ibid.

110. For a good discussion of discounting to present value, specifically of environmental costs and benefits, see Daniel A. Farber, "From Here to Eternity: Environmental Law and Future Generations," 2003 *University of Illinois Law Review* 289.

111. Cf. Thomas C. Schelling, "Intergenerational Discounting," 23 *Energy Policy* 395, 397 (1995). The prospects for an altruistic U.S. foreign policy are

debunked in Jack L. Goldsmith and Eric A. Posner, *A Theory of International Law* (University of Chicago Law School, unpublished, 2003), esp. ch. 10.

112. *Report of the [U.K.] Task Force on Potentially Hazardous Near Earth Objects*, ch. 9 (Sept. 2000).

113. Greenberg, note 5 above, app. tab. 2 following p. 477. For detailed statistics on U.S. and foreign R&D; see National Science Board, note 1 above, ch. 4.

114. Ibid., 5–42; Greenberg, note 5 above, app. tab. 3 following p. 477. However, there are recent indications that U.S. scientific preeminence may be declining, in part because of increased scientific research in Asia, especially China. William J. Broad, "U.S. Is Losing Its Dominance in the Sciences," *New York Times* (national ed.), May 3, 2004, p. A1.115. *Report of the [U.K.] Task Force on Potentially Hazardous Near Earth Objects*, note 112 above, at 24. The limited activities of other countries with respect to the asteroid menace are summarized in Ibid., 25–27. See also, to the same effect, Clark R. Chapman, Daniel D. Durda, and Robert E. Gold, "The Comet/Asteroid Impact Hazard: A Systems Approach" 2 (SwRI White Paper, Feb. 24, 2001), http://www.internationalspace .com/pdf/NEOwp-Chapman-Durda-Gold.pdf.

116. John J. Mearsheimer, "The False Promise of International Institutions," *International Security*, Winter 1994/1995, pp. 5, 19–21.

117. Possible methods of international cooperation to defend against asteroid strikes are discussed constructively in Evan R. Seamone, Note, "When Wishing on a Star Just Won't Do: The Legal Basis for International Cooperation in the Mitigation of Asteroid Impacts and Similar Transboundary Disasters," 87 *Iowa Law Review* 1091 (2002).

118. National Research Council of the National Academies, *Biotechnology Research in an Age of Terrorism: Confronting the Dual Use Dilemma* (2003). According to Nicholas Wade, "Panel of Scientists Supports Review of Biomedical That Research Terrorists Could Use," *New York Times* (late edition), Oct. 9, 2003, p. A1, the panel's recommendations have been taken under advisement by President Bush's science advisor (technically, the Director of the Office of Science and Technology in the Executive Office of the President)—who is none other than John H. Marburger, III, who was the director of the Brookhaven National Laboratory when RHIC was built and in that capacity appointed the panel of physicists that conducted the RHIC risk assessment.

119. National Research Council, note 118 above, at 13–14.

120. Regina M. A. A. Galhardi, "Brazilian Policy for Biotechnology: A Critical Review," 21 *Science and Public Policy* 395 (1994).

121. Jonathan B. Tucker, "Preventing the Misuse of Pathogens: The Need for Global Biosecurity Standards," *Arms Control Today*, June 2003, pp. 3, 6.

122. Ibid., 3.

123. "Introduction," in *Biotechnology in Latin America: Politics, Impacts, and Risks* xvii, xxiv (N. Patrick Peritore and Ana Karina Galve-Peritore eds. 1995).

124. National Research Council, note 118 above, at 17.

125. M. J. Peterson, "International Fisheries Mangement," in *Institutions for the Earth: Sources of Effective International Environmental Protection* 249 (Peter M. Haas, Robert O. Keohane, and Marc A. Levy eds. 1993); *The Economics of International Environmental Agreements* (Amitrajeet A. Batabyal ed. 2000).

126. Joseph Cirincione, *Deadly Arsenals: Tracking Weapons of Mass Destruction* 114–122 (2002); Amy F. Woolf, "Nuclear Weapons in Russia: Safety, Security, and Control Issues" (Congressional Resarch Service Report IB98038, Apr. 11, 2003); Richard G. Lugar, "Act Enables U.S. to Negate Threats: Updates to the Law Allow Nation to Go Anywhere in the World to Seize Weapons," *Indianapolis Star*, Nov. 30, 2003, p. 1E. The Bush Administration initially reduced funding for Russian nuclear material security, but later restored the funding to its previous level. Cirincione, above, at 116.

127. Richard A. Posner, *Law, Pragmatism, and Democracy*, ch. 5 (2003). For illustrative contributions to public choice theory, see Robert D. Cooter, *The Strategic Constitution* (2000); Daniel A. Farber and Philip P. Frickey, *Law and Public Choice: A Critical Introduction* (1991), George J. Stigler, *The Citizen and the State: Essays on Regulation* (1975); James M. Buchanan and Gordon Tullock, *The Calculus of Consent: Logical Foundations of Constitutional Democracy* (1962); Jonathan R. Macey, "Public Choice and the Law," in *The New Palgrave Dictionary of Economics and the Law*, vol. 3, p. 171 (Peter Newman ed. 1998); Stephen P. Magee, William A. Brock, and Leslie Young, *Black Hole Tariffs and Endogenous Political Theory: Political Economy in General Equilibrium* (1989); Richard A. Posner, "Theories of Economic Regulation," 5 *Bell Journal of Economics and Management Science* 335 (1974).

128. Richard A. Meserve, "Global Warming and Nuclear Power," 303 *Science* 433 (2004).

129. Stephan, note 37 above, at 1217.

130. John Marburger, "Science Policy in the 21st Century" 2 (Office of Science and Technology Policy, Executive Office of the President, Nov. 2, 2003), http://spacsun.rice.edu/~neal/pdfs/marburger.pdf.

131. Tim Josling and H. Wayne Moyer, "The Common Agricultural Policy of the European Community: A Public Choice Interpretation," in *The Political Economy of International Organizations: A Public Choice Approach* 286 (Roland Vaubel and Thomas D. Willett eds. 1991); Norman Scott, "Protectionism in Western Europe," in *Protectionism and World Welfare* 371, 385–392 (Dominick Salvatore ed. 1993).

132. Robert Roy Britt, "Why We Fear Ourselves More Than Asteroids," Mar. 26, 2002, http:www.space.com/scienceastronomy/solarsystem/asteroid_fears_020326-1.html. See generally Michael B. Gerrard, "Risks of Hazardous Waste Sites versus Asteroid and Comet Impacts: Accounting for the Discrepancies in U.S. Resource Allocation," 20 *Risk Analysis* 895 (2000).

133. Near-Earth Object Science Definition Team, *Study to Determine the Feasibility of Extending the Search for Near-Earth Objects to Smaller Limiting Diameters* (NASA Aug. 22, 2003), which I cited extensively in chapter 1.

134. But notice that the article on asteroid collisions by Gerrard and Barber, note 99 above, was published in an environmental law journal.

Chapter 3

1. For a simplified cost-benefit analysis of defenses against asteroid collisions, see Anthony E. Boardman et al., *Cost-Benefit Analysis: Concepts and Practice* 160–161 (2d ed. 2001).

2. *Protecting Public Health and the Environment: Implementing the Precautionary Principle* (Carolyn Raffensperger and Joel A. Tickner eds. 1999); *Interpreting the Precautionary Principle* (Tim O'Riordan and James Cameron eds. 1994); Jonathan B. Wiener, "Whose Precaution After All? A Comment on the Comparison and Evolution of Risk Regulatory Systems," 13 *Duke Journal of Comparative and International Law* 207 (2003).

3. As powerfully argued in Cass R. Sunstein, *Risk and Reason: Safety, Law, and the Environment* 33–52 (2002).

4. As in Joel A. Tickner, "A Map toward Precautionary Decision Making," in *Protecting Public Health and the Environment*, note 2 above, at 162, 163. See also Christian Gollier, Bruno Jullien, and Nicolas Treich, "Scientific Progress and Irreversibility: An Economic Interpretation of the 'Precautionary Principle,'" 75 *Journal of Public Economics* 229 (2000).

5. "The Relativistic Heavy Ion Collider (RHIC): A Premier Facility for Nuclear Physics Research," http://www.bnl.gov/bnlweb/PDF/Factsheet/FS-RHIC .pdf (visited Mar. 30, 2004). Surprisingly for a public project, so far the actual costs have been below the estimated costs: 2001: $113.6 million; 2002: $114.6 million; 2003: $118.0 million; 2004: $121.1 million. (The figures for 2001 and 2002 are from the *U.S. Dept. of Energy FY 2002 Budget Request* 30, http://fire.pppl.gov/DOE_FY2002_Budget.pdf. The 2003 and 2004 figures are from *Twenty Year Planning Study for the RHIC Facility* 26 (Appendix 4 Budget Table for FY 2004), http://www.bnl.gov/henp/docs/20year_BNL71881.pdf.)

6. Arnon Dar, A. De Rújula, and Ulrich Heinz, "Will Relativistic Heavy-Ion Colliders Destroy Our Planet?" 470 *Physics Letters B* 142, 146 (1999).

7. R. L. Jaffe et al., "Review of Speculative 'Disaster Scenarios' at RHIC," 72 *Reviews of Modern Physics* 1125, 1138 (2000). These estimates, it should be noted, were made before RHIC went into operation. The significance of this qualification is discussed in the last section of the chapter (before the summary), where I return to the issue of RHIC's safety.

8. Derek Parfit, *Reasons and Persons* 75 (1984).

9. E. J. N. Wilson, *An Introduction to Particle Accelerators*, ch. 13 (2001). Of the 10,000 or so particle accelerators in the world, however, the vast majority are low-energy accelerators used for medical research and therapy, manufacturing materials used in computers, and other purposes unrelated to research in particle physics. Ibid., 185.

10. Steven Weinberg, *Facing up: Science and Its Cultural Adversaries*, ch. 2 (2001). The story of the SSC debacle is told in Daniel S. Greenberg, *Science, Money, and Politics: Political Triumph and Ethical Erosion* 404–410 (2001).

11. U.S. Congress, Congressional Budget Office, *Risks and Benefits of Building the Superconducting Super Collider* 17 (U.S. Government Printing Office Oct. 1988).

12. For illustrations of both points, see Committee for Economic Development, *America's Basic Research: Prosperity through Discovery: A Policy Statement by the Research and Policy Committee of the Committee for Economic Development* 8–10 (1998).

13. On which see Ronald N. Kostoff, "Assessing Research Impact: US Government Retrospective and Quantitative Approaches," 21 *Science and Public Policy* 13 (1994); Nicholas S. Vonortas, "New Directions for US Science and

Technology Policy: The View from the R&D Assessment Front," 22 *Science and Public Policy* 19 (1995).

14. See, for example, Zvi Griliches, *R&D and Productivity: The Econometric Evidence* (1998); Charles I. Jones and John C. Williams, "Measuring the Social Return to R&D," 113 *Quarterly Journal of Economics* 1119 (1998).

15. See, for example, Griliches, note 14 above, at 251–255, on the effects of scientific research on agricultural productivity, and Edwin Mansfield, "Academic Research Underlying Industrial Innovations: Sources, Characteristics, and Financing," 77 *Review of Economics and Statistics* 55 (1995), on the effects of academic research on drugs, instruments, and data processing.

16. Zvi Griliches, *R&D, Education, and Productivity: A Retrospective* 68, 70 (2000); Committee for Economic Development, note 12 above, at 11.

17. See the particularly helpful discussion in Richard R. Nelson, "The Simple Economics of Basic Scientific Research," 67 *Journal of Political Economy* 297 (1959).

18. William M. Landes and Richard A. Posner, *The Economic Structure of Intellectual Property Law* 305–308 (2003).

19. Computed from NSF/SRS, *National Patterns of R&D Resources: 2000 Data Update* tab. 2B: National Expenditures for Basic Research from Funding Sectors to Performing Sectors: 1993–2000, http://www.nsf.gov/sbe/srs/nsf01309/start.htm (visited Jan. 21, 2004).

20. Ron Kostoff, "Evaluating Federal R&D in the United States," in *Evaluating R&D Impacts: Methods and Practice* 163, 174–175 (Barry Bozeman and Julia Melkers eds. 1993).

21. See, for example, *Valuing Environmental Preferences: Theory and Practice of the Contingent Valuation Method in the US, EU, and Developing Countries* (Ian J. Bateman and Kenneth G. Willis eds. 1999); *Determining the Value of Non-Marketed Goods: Economic, Psychological, and Policy Relevant Aspects of Contingent Valuation Methods* (R. J. Kopp, W. W. Pommerehne, and N. Schwarz eds. 1997); W. Michael Hanemann, "Valuing the Environment through Contingent Valuation," *Journal of Economic Perspectives*, Autumn 1994, p. 19. For a strong defense of the method, see Richard T. Carson, Nicholas E. Flores, and Norman F. Meade, "Contingent Valuation: Controversies and Evidence," 19 *Environmental and Resources Economics* 173 (2001).

22. As emphasized in Amartya Sen, "The Discipline of Cost-Benefit Analysis," in *Cost-Benefit Analysis: Legal, Economic, and Philosophical Perspectives* 95, 113 (Matthew D. Adler and Eric A. Posner eds. 2001). On this and other weaknesses of contingent evaluation as a tool of policy, see *Contingent Valuation: A Critical Assessment* (Jerry A. Hausman ed. 1993); Peter A. Diamond and Jerry A. Hausman, "Contingent Valuation: Is Some Number Better than No Number?" *Journal of Economic Perspectives*, Fall 1994, p. 45.

23. For a list of a hundred physics books for the general public, including the three I've mentioned, see Hans Christian von Baeyer and Edith V. Bowers, "Resource Letter PBGP–1: Physics Books for the General Public," 72 *American Journal of Physics* 135 (2004). But the authors err in calling Hawking's *A Brief History of Time* "comprehensible to anyone with a high school science background." Ibid., 137. It is an extremely difficult book. That it sold nine million copies, Bruce V. Lewenstein, "Science Books since World War II" 2 (forthcom-

ing in *History of the Book in America*, to be published by Cambridge University Press), is a tribute to the power of fads.

24. National Research Council of the National Academies, Astronomy and Astrophysics Survey Committee, *Astronomy and Astrophysics in the New Millennnium* 140–142 (2001).

25. Brian Greene, *The Elegant Universe: Superstrings, Hidden Dimensions, and the Quest for the Ultimate Theory* x (1999). "Widespread yearning" should be taken with a grain of salt. It is unlikely that Greene's lecture audiences are representative of the population, even the highly educated population, as a whole.

26. The sources for these data are: Sharon G. Sullivan, "Prices of U.S. and Foreign Published Materials," in *The Bowker Annual: Library and Trade Book Almanac* 491, 500 (48th ed., Dave Bogart ed. 2003) (tab. 6); and Nielsen BookScan, an international sales data monitoring and analysis service for the English-language book industry worldwide.

27. *AEC Authorizing Legislation Fiscal Year 1970*, Hearings before the Joint Committee on Atomic Energy. 91st Cong., 1st sess., pt. 1, p. 113 (U.S. Govt. Printing Office 1969). In fact, Wilson anticipated practical spinoffs from the accelerator. Ibid., 115.

28. Philip Kitcher, "What Kinds of Science Should Be Done," *in Living with the Genie: Essays on Technology and the Quest for Human Mastery* 201, 205–211 (Alan Lightman, Daniel Sarewitz, and Christina Desser eds. 2003).

29. On all three points, see discussion and references in Bruno S. Frey and Alois Stutzer, "What Can Economists Learn from Happiness Research?" 40 *Journal of Economic Literature* 402, 409–418 (2002).

30. Ibid., 413–416; Richard A. Easterlin, "The Economics of Happiness," *Daedalus*, Spring 2004, pp. 26, 31; Easterlin, "Does Economic Growth Improve the Human Lot? Some Empirical Evidence," in *Nations and Households in Economic Growth: Essays in Honor of Moses Abramovitz* 89 (Paul A. David and Melvin W. Reder eds. 1974); Bruno S. Frey and Alois Stutzer, *Happiness and Economics: How the Economy and Institutions Affect Well-Being* 76–77 (2002); Richard Layard, "Income and Happiness: Rethinking Economic Policy" (Lionel Robbins Lecture at the London School of Economics, Feb. 2003), http://cep .lse.ac.uk/events/lectures/layard/RL040303.pdf.

31. Samuel Fankhauser, *Valuing Climate Change: The Economics of the Greenhouse* 119–120 (1995).

32. Ibid., ch. 8.

33. Richard Newell and William Pizer, "Discounting the Benefits of Climate Change Mitigation: How Much Do Uncertain Rates Increase Valuations?" 1, 13–14 (Dec. 2001), http://www.pewclimate.org/docUploads/econ%5Fdiscounting %2Epdf. I return to this point later in the chapter.

34. Richard N. Cooper, "International Approaches to Global Climate Change," *World Bank Research Observer*, Aug. 2000, pp. 145, 153–154.

35. Parfit, note 8 above, at 357.

36. As advocated in John Broome, *Counting the Cost of Global Warming* 108, 133 (1992).

37. See, for example, besides Broome, note 36 above, Kenneth J. Arrow, "Discounting, Morality, and Gaming," in *Discounting and Intergenerational*

Equity 13 (Paul R. Portney and John P. Weyant eds. 1999); Richard L. Revesz, "Environmental Regulation, Cost-Benefit Analysis, and the Discounting of Human Lives," 99 *Columbia Law Review* 941 (1999); Andrew Caplin and John Leahy, "The Social Discount Rate" (National Bureau of Economic Research Working Paper 7983 Oct. 2000), http://www.nber.org/papers/w7983; Lawrence B. Solum, "To Our Children's Children's Children: The Problem of Intergenerational Ethics," 35 *Loyola of Los Angeles Law Review* 163 (2001).

38. Newell and Pizer, note 33 above, at 15–16. For a similar argument, see Martin L. Weitzman, "Why the Far-Distant Future Should Be Discounted at Its Lowest Possible Rate," 36 *Journal of Environmental Economics and Management* 201 (1998).

39. Ibid., 201–202.

40. Philip M. Fearnside, "Time Preference in Global Warming Calculations: A Proposal for a Unified Index," 41 *Ecological Economics* 21 (2002).

41. See, for example, Thomas D. Lauricella and Constance Mitchell, "Coca-Cola Joins Disney at the Very Long End with a Sale of $150 Million of 100–Year Bonds," *Wall Street Journal*, July 23, 1993, p. C15. The article reports that Walt Disney Company had issued $300 million of 100–year bonds just a few days earlier, but that these were the first 100–year bond issues in a half century. It is noteworthy that both Coca-Cola and Disney have a very long history of successful operations, which, consistent with the dinosaur-human comparison in chapter 1, suggests that they indeed are pretty likely to be around for another century.

42. These are canvassed in *Cost-Benefit Analysis: Legal, Economic, and Philosophical Perspectives*, note 22 above. See also Richard A. Posner, *Frontiers of Legal Theory* 121–141 (2001). I use the term "ethical" rather than "moral" because "ethical" has broader connotations. The ethical question is: "What is to be done?" The moral question is: "What is the morally correct thing to do?"

43. The variety of possible regulatory methods is discussed in Carolyn Fischer and Richard Newell, "Environmental and Technology Policies for Climate Change and Renewable Energy" (Resources for the Future Discussion Paper, Sept. 2003), http://www.rff.org/~newell/Renewtech%206.pdf. For a comprehensive discussion of taxation as an instrument for regulating the environment, see A. Lans Bovenberg and Lawrence H. Goulder, "Environmental Taxation and Regulation," in *Handbook of Public Economics*, vol. 3, p. 1471 (Alan J. Auerbach and Martin Feldstein eds., 2d ed. 2002).

44. Gary S. Becker and Casey B. Mulligan, "Deadweight Costs and the Size of Government," 46 *Journal of Law and Economics* 293 (2003).

45. For lucid descriptions of some of these methods, see Klaus S. Lackner, Patrick Grimes, and Hans-J. Ziock, "Capturing Carbon Dioxide from Air," http://www.lackner.eee.columbia.edu/Papers/Air%20Extraction/CaptureFromAir.pdf (visited Jan. 15, 2004); Judith C. Chow et al., "Separation and Capture of CO_2 from Large Stationary Sources and Sequestration in Geological Formations," 53 *Journal of the Air and Waste Management Association* 1172 (2003); Elizabeth J. Wilson, Timothy L. Johnson, and David W. Keith, "Regulating the Ultimate Sink: Managing the Risks of Geologic CO_2 Storage," 37 *Environmental Science and Technology* 3476 (2003). See also Timothy L. Johnson and David W. Keith, "Fossil Electricity and CO_2 Sequestration: How Natural Gas Prices, Initial Con-

ditions and Retrofits Determine the Cost of Controlling CO_2 Emissions," 32 *Energy Policy* 367 (2004). The Wilson, Johnson, and Keith article, above, at 3477, points to possible dangers associated with the storage of carbon dioxide; should it escape in great quantity suddenly, the results could be devastating. Carbon dioxide is denser than air and so would tend to hug the ground, and breathing air that is more than 10 percent carbon dioxide can be fatal. A more substantial worry is a carbon "burp"—that carbon dioxide injected underground or piped to ocean bottoms or fixed in carbonates would eventually return to the atmosphere, augmenting the warming effect of the carbon dioxide emissions that were not being sequestered.

46. On the elasticity of demand for fossil fuels, see Bjorn Larsen and Anwar Shah, "World Fossil Fuel Subsidies and Global Carbon Emissions" 7 (World Bank Policy Research Working Paper WPS 1002, Oct. 1992); Clare Smith, Stephen Hall, and Nick Mabey, "Econometric Modelling of International Carbon Tax Regimes," 17 *Energy Economics* 133 (1995); Noureddine Krichene, "World Crude Oil and Natural Gas: A Demand and Supply Model," 24 *Energy Economics* 557 (2002); Salman Saif Ghouri, "Oil Demand in North America: 1980–2020," 25 *OPEC Review* 339 (2001); John C. B. Cooper, "Price Elasticity of Demand for Crude Oil: Estimates for 23 Countries," 27 *OPEC Review* 1 (2003).

47. Lawrence H. Goulder, "Environmental Taxation and the Double Dividend: A Reader's Guide," 2 *International Tax and Public Finance* 157 (1995).

48. The tax-subsidy trade-off is discussed in the pollution context in Ian W. H. Parry, "On the Implications of Technological Innovation for Environmental Policy" (Resources for the Future, Aug. 2001), http://www.rff.org/Documents/RFF-DP-01–44.pdf. See also Parry, William A. Pizer, and Carolyn Fischer, "How Large Are the Welfare Gains from Technological Innovation Induced by Environmental Policies?" 23 *Journal of Regulatory Economics* 237 (2003); Parry, "Pollution Regulation and the Efficiency Gains from Technological Innovation," 14 *Journal of Regulatory Economics* 229 (1998).

49. Economists' estimates of the price effects of compliance with the Kyoto Protocol are summarized in Bruce Yandle, "The Precautionary Principle as a Force for Global Political Centralization: A Case-Study of the Kyoto Protocol," in *Rethinking Risk and the Precautionary Principle* 170–171 (Julian Morris ed. 2000).

50. Ibid., 167, 170.

51. The option approach to global warming is discussed in William D. Nordhaus, *Managing the Global Commons: The Economics of Climate Change*, ch. 8 (1994).

52. Benoît Morel et al., "Pesticide Resistance, the Precautionary Principle, and the Regulation of *Bt* Corn: Real Option and Rational Option Approaches to Decisionmaking," in *Battling Resistance to Antibiotics and Pesticides: An Economic Approach* 184 (Ramanan Laxminarayan ed. 2003).

53. As argued in Ian William Holmes Parry, *Policy Analysis of Global Warming Uncertainties*, ch. 3 (Ph.D. diss., University of Chicago Dept. of Economics, Dec. 1993). See also Stephen H. Schneider, B. L. Turner II, and Holly Morehouse Garriga, "Imaginable Surprise in Global Change Science," 1 *Journal of Risk Research* 165 (1998). Parry skirted the issue in his formal analysis by assuming that the trigger point was at least 15 years in the future. He was

writing in 1993, 11 years ago, and in the intervening years the evidence of global warming, the concentration of greenhouse gases in the atmosphere, and recognition of the possibility of abrupt global warming have all increased.

54. Richard A. Posner, *Economic Analysis of Law* § 6.12 (6th ed. 2003), and references in ibid., p. 197 n. 5; particularly helpful is W. Kip Viscusi, *Rational Risk Policy: The 1996 Arne Ryde Memorial Lectures*, ch. 4 (1998). A paper by Viscusi and Joseph E. Aldy, "The Value of a Statistical Life: A Critical Review of Market Estimates throughout the World," 27 *Journal of Risk and Uncertainty* 5 (2003), is a comprehensive, up-to-date review of the literature.

55. Viscusi and Aldy, note 54 above, at 6, 63. One recent study, however, presents evidence that the value of life may be as low as $1.54 million. Orley Ashenfelter and Michael Greenstone, "Using Mandated Speed Limits to Measure the Value of a Statistical Life," 112 *Journal of Political Economy* S226 (2004). But we'll see that my analysis is not highly sensitive to estimates of the value of life within a very broad range.

56. Milton C. Weinstein, Donald S. Shepard, and Joseph S. Pliskin, "The Economic Value of Changing Mortality Probabilities: A Decision-Theoretic Approach," 94 *Quarterly Journal of Economics* 373, 384 (1980).

57. Viscusi and Aldy, note 54 above, at 29–30.

58. Ibid., 19–21 (tab. 2), 27–28 (tab. 4).

59. Clark R. Chapman and David Morrison, "Impacts on the Earth by Asteroids and Comets: Assessing the Hazard," 367 *Nature* 33, 38 (1994). See also Charles Perrow, *Normal Accidents: Living with High-Risk Technologies* 324–328 (2d ed. 1999); Paul Slovic, Baruch Fischhoff, and Sarah Lichtenstein, "Facts and Fears: Understanding Perceived Risks," in *The Perception of Risk* 137 (Paul Slovic ed. 2000). For an extended discussion of the psychology of risk perceptions, with many references, see Sunstein, *Risk and Reason*, note 3 above, at 33–52.

60. Slovic, Fischhoff, and Lichtenstein, note 59 above, at 151 (tab. 8.6).

61. Cass R. Sunstein, "Probability Neglect: Emotions, Worst Cases, and Law," 112 *Yale Law Journal* 61 (2002).

62. W. Kip Viscusi and Richard J. Zeckhauser, "Sacrificing Civil Liberties to Reduce Terrorism Risks," 26 *Journal of Risk and Uncertainty* 99, 116 (2003) (tab. 8).

63. Howard Kunreuther, Nathan Novemsky, and Daniel Kahneman, "Making Low Probabilities Useful," 23 *Journal of Risk and Uncertainty* 103 (2001); Gerd Gigerenzer and Ulrich Hoffrage, "How to Improve Bayesian Reasoning without Instruction: Frequency Formats," 102 *Psychological Review* 684 (1995).

64. Viscusi and Aldy, note 54 above, at 40.

65. W. Kip Viscusi and William N. Evans, "Utility Functions That Depend on Health Status: Estimates and Economic Implications," 80 *American Economic Review* 353, 369 (1990).

66. See, for example, Cass R. Sunstein, "Terrorism and Probability Neglect," 26 *Journal of Risk and Uncertainty* 121 (2003).

67. Pub. Law 107–297, 116 Stat. 2322. The Act is due to expire in 2005; it is uncertain at this writing whether it will be renewed.

68. Stacey Kalberman, "Terrorism Risk Insurance," in Anthony H. Anikeef et al., *Homeland Security Law Handbook* 153 (2003), esp. p. 158. On the challenge

that the risk of terrorist attacks or other catastrophes poses to the insurance industry, see generally Patricia Grossi and Howard Kunreuther, *Catastrophic Modeling: A New Approach to Managing Risk*, ch. 10 (unpublished, Nov. 13, 2003); Jeffrey R. Brown et al., "An Empirical Analysis of the Economic Impact of Federal Terrorism Reinsurance" (National Bureau of Economic Research Working Paper 10388, Mar. 2004); Howard Kunreuther, Erwann Michel-Kerjan, and Beverly Porter, "Assessing, Managing and Financing Extreme Events: Dealing with Terrorism" (National Bureau of Economic Research Working Paper 10179, Dec. 2003); Jeffrey R. Brown, Randall S. Kroszner, and Brian H. Jenn, "Federal Terrorism Risk Insurance" (National Bureau of Economic Research Working Paper 9271, Oct. 2002); David M. Cutler and Richard J. Zeckhauser, "Reinsurance for Catastrophes and Cataclysms" (National Bureau of Economic Research Working Paper 5913, Feb. 1997).

69. For useful discussions, varying in pessimism, see Baruch Fischhoff, "Assessing and Communicating the Risks of Terrorism," in *Science and Technology in a Vulnerable World: Supplement to AAAS Science and Technology Policy Yearbook 2003* 51 (Albert H. Teich, Stephen D. Nelson, and Stephen J. Lita eds. 2002); Jessica Stern, "Dreaded Risks and the Control of Biological Weapons," *International Security*, Winter 2002–2003, pp. 89, 99–102; Gordon Wood, "Quantifying Insurance Terrorism Risk, " 2002, http://www.nber.org/~confer/2002/insw02/woo.pdf (visited May 23, 2004).

70. Jay Davis, "Epilogue: A Twenty-First Century Terrorism Agenda for the United States," in *The Terrorism Threat and U.S. Government Response: Operational and Organizational Factors* 269, 275 (James M. Smith and William C. Thomas eds. 2001).

71. Milton Leitenberg, "Biological Weapons and 'Bioterrorism' in the First Years of the 21st Century" (July 10, 2002), http://www.puaf.umd.edu/CISSM/People/milton_files/bw%2021st%20c.pdf. He will hate this book, therefore.

72. See, for example, Laurie Garrett, "The Nightmare of Bioterrorism," *Foreign Affairs*, Jan./Feb. 2001, p. 76.

73. Robert P. Kadlec, "Bookends: Two Views of the Biological Threat," http://www.homelandsecurity.org/Journal/Commentary/Kadlec_Commentary.htm (visited Jan. 15, 2004).

74. See the helpful discussion in Michael Abramowicz, "Information Markets, Administrative Decisionmaking, and Predictive Cost-Benefit Analysis" 53–57 (AEI-Brookings Joint Center for Regulatory Studies Working Paper No. 5, 2003), http://www.aei-brookings.org/admin/authorpdfs/page.phys?icl=284.

75. Office of Management and Budget, "2003 Report to Congress on Combating Terrorism" 37 (Executive Office of the President, Sept. 2003), http://www.whitehouse.gov/omb/inforeg/2003_combat_terr.pdf.

76. Anthony H. Anikeeff et al., *Homeland Security Law Handbook* (2003), esp. chs. 4, 8, 11.

77. See, for example, William K. Rashbaum and Judith Miller, "New York Police Take Broad Steps in Facing Terror," *New York Times*, Feb. 15, 2004, § 1, p. 1.

78. NASA Office of Space Science, "NASA Announcements Opportunity, Appendix A.2.8: Near Earth Object Observations," http://research.hq.nasa.gov/code_s/nra/current/nra-03-oss-01/appendA2.html (visited Jan. 15, 2004); testimony of Dr. Lindley Johnson at a Science, Technology, and Space Hearing on

Near Earth Objects (NEO) before S. Comm. on Commerce, Science & Transportation, Apr. 7, 2004, http://commerce.senate.gov/hearings/testimony.cfm?id=1147&wit_id=3241. On the history of proposals for asteroid defenses, see Charles T. Rubin, "Asteroid Collisions and Precautionary Thinking," in *Rethinking Risk and the Precautionary Principle* 105, 112–119 (2000).

79. *Report of the [U.K.] Task Force on Potentially Hazardous Near Earth Objects* 24 (Sept. 2000).

80. See, for example, "The Hard Rain," *Economist*, Sept. 11, 1993, p. 81.

81. National Research Council of the National Academies, Astronomy and Astrophysics Survey Committee, *Astronomy and Astrophysics in the New Millennium* 107 (2001). See also http://www.lsst.org.

82. *Analytical Perspectives, Budget of the United States Government, Fiscal 2004: 8. Research and Development* 185–186 (Feb. 2003) (tab. 8–4), http://www.whitehouse.gov/omb/budget/fy2004/pdf/spec.pdf.

83. Jenifer B. Evans, Frank C. Shelly, and Grant H. Stokes, "Detection and Discovery of Near-Earth Asteroids by the LINEAR Program," 14 *Lincoln Laboratory Journal* 199 (2003). It was LINEAR, by the way, that spotted the small asteroid (30-meter diameter) that missed the earth by 26,500 miles on March 18, 2004. Robert Roy Britt, "Earth Safe from Ultra-Close Asteroid Flyby Today," Mar. 18, 2004, http://www.space.com/scienceastronomy/asteroid_flyby_040318.html.

84. Barnaby J. Feder, "Some Businesses Take Initiative to Voluntarily Reduce Emissions," *New York Times* (national ed.), Dec. 1, 2003, p. C9.

85. Ferenc L. Toth, "Climate Policy in Light of Climate Science: The ICLIPS Project," 56 *Climatic Change* 7 (2003). See also Thomas Bruckner et al., "Methodological Aspects of the Tolerable Windows Approach," 56 *Climate Change* 73 (2003).

86. 16 U.S.C. § 1533(b)(2); New Mexico Cattle Growers Association v. U.S. Fish & Wildlife Service, 248 F.3d 1277 (10th Cir. 2001); Amy Sinden, "The Economics of Endangered Species: Why Less Is More in the Economic Analysis of Critical Habitat Designations," 28 *Harvard Environmental Review* 129 (2004). The snail-darter case is Tennessee Valley Authority v. Hill, 437 U.S. 153 (1978).

87. Gardner M. Brown Jr. and Jason F. Shogren, "Economics of the Endangered Species Act," *Journal of Economic Perspectives*, Summer 1998, pp. 3, 13–15.

88. Sinden, note 86 above, at 180–183, 202–207.

89. *Risk versus Risk: Tradeoffs in Protecting Health and the Environment* (John D. Graham and Jonathan Baert Wiener eds. 1995); Stern, note 69 above.

90. Ibid., 113–114.

91. As in Stern's article, which is otherwise a first-rate review of the danger of bioterrorism and the possible responses to it.

92. This theme is emphasized in the work of Gerd Gigerenzer and his associates. See note 63 above and Gerd Gigerenzer, Peter M. Todd, and the ABC Research Group, *Simple Heuristics That Make Us Smart* (1999).

93. Gary S. Becker, "A Comment on the Conference on Cost-Benefit Analysis," in *Cost-Benefit Analysis*, note 22 above, at 313, 315–316.

94. See, for example, Sunstein, *Risk and Reason*, note 3 above, at 30–31 (tab. 2.1); Stephen Breyer, *Breaking the Vicious Circle: Toward Effective Risk Regulation* 24–27 (1993) (tab. 5).

95. Sunstein, *Risk and Reason*, note 3 above, at 30–31 (tab. 2.1).

96. Frank Ackerman and Lisa Heinzerling, *Priceless: On Knowing the Price of Everything and the Value of Nothing* (2004).

97. Jaffe et al., note 7 above.

98. The three are Wit Busza, Robert L. Jaffe, and Jake Sandweiss. The fourth assessor, Frank Wilczek, is a theoretical high-energy physicist, not an experimenter. But the data that he constructs theories to explain come from experiments conducted in particle accelerators, such as RHIC. (The information in this note was obtained from a Google search under the names of the four scientists.)

99. This is apparent from the statements by Wilczek quoted in David Voss, "Making the Stuff of the Big Bang," 285 *Science* 1194, 1195 (1999).

100. Edward Farhi and R. L. Jaffe, "Strange Matter," 30 *Physical Review D* 2379, 2390 (1984).

101. Thomas May, Mark P. Aulisio, and Ross D. Silverman, "The Smallpox Vaccination of Health Care Workers: Professional Obligations and Defense against Bioterrorism" 26 (Hastings Center Report, Sept.–Oct. 2003).

102. Francesco Calogero, "Might a Laboratory Experiment Destroy Planet Earth?" 25 *Interdisciplinary Science Reviews* 191, 193 (2000).

103. Adrian Kent, "A Critical Look at Risk Assessments for Global Catastrophes," 24 *Risk Analysis* 157, 161 (2004). The reference is to Dar, De Rújula, and Heinz, note 6 above.

104. From the application of the formula $(1 - p)^n$; see introduction and chapter 2.

105. Kent, note 103 above, at 163.

106. Ibid., 164.

107. Jaffe et al., note 7 above, at 1132, 1135–1136.

108. Voss, note 99 above, at 1195.

109. An atom has a neutral charge because it has the same number of protons, which have a positive charge, and electrons, which have a negative charge. All the protons are in the nucleus, along with neutrons, which having a neutral charge don't affect the overall charge of the nucleus and hence of the atom.

110. See, for example, Martin Rees, *Our Final Hour: A Scientist's Warning: How Terror, Error, and Environmental Disaster Threaten Humankind's Future in This Century—On Earth and Beyond* 123–124 (2003).

111. Jaffe et al., note 7 above, at 1136–1138.

112. Calogero, note 102 above, at 196. This distinction, or "loophole" as they put it, is acknowledged by Dar, De Rújula, and Heinz, note 6 above.

113. J.-P. Blaizot et al., "Study of Potentially Dangerous Events During Heavy-Ion Collisions at the LHC: Report of the LHC Safety Study Group" (CERN 2003–001, Feb. 28, 2003), http://doc.cern.ch/yellowrep/2003/2003–001/p1.pdf..

114. Ibid., 2.

115. Jes Madsen, "Intermediate Mass Strangelets Are Positively Charged," 85 *Physical Review Letters* 4687 (2000).

116. Blaizot et al., note 113 above, at 3.

117. Ibid., 6.

118. Jaffe et al., note 7 above, at 1128–1129.

119. Blaizot et al., note 113 above, at 5.

120. Ibid.

121. Ibid.

122. Rees, note 110 above, at 128.

123. Wilson, note 9 above, ch. 14.

Chapter 4

1. Richard A. Posner, *Antitrust Law* (2d ed. 2001).

2. See, for example, Richard A. Posner, *Frontiers of Legal Theory* 37 (2001), discussing the "Hand Formula" for determining negligence.

3. Richard A. Posner, *Economic Analysis of Law* (6th ed. 2003).

4. Richard P. Feynman, Robert B. Leighton, and Matthew Sands, *The Feynman Lectures on Physics*, vol. 1, p. 1–1 (1965) (emphasis in original).

5. In its *Directory of Law Teachers 1992–1993* and *Directory of Law Teachers* 2002–2003.

6. Posner, note 2 above, at 4–14.

7. See its Web site at http://www.aaas.org/spp/sfrl/committees/ncls.

8. Computed from the biographical data in the *2004 Almanac of the Federal Judiciary* (Megan Chase ed. 2004).

9. On the broader issue of specialized versus generalist courts, see, for example, Richard A. Posner, *The Federal Courts: Challenge and Reform*, ch. 8 (1996); Rochelle C. Dreyfuss, "Forums of the Future: The Role of Specialized Courts in Resolving Business Disputes," 61 *Brooklyn Law Review* 1 (1995).

10. Thomas G. Field, "Pursuing Transparency through Science Courts," in *Proceedings from the VALDOR Symposium on Values in Decisions on Risk* 228 (K. Anderson ed. 1999); Morris H. Shamos, *The Myth of Scientific Literary* 206–210 (1995).

11. Arthur Kantrowitz, "Proposal for an Institution for Scientific Judgment," 156 *Science* 763 (1967), and, for criticism, Albert R. Matheny and Bruce A. Williams, "Scientific Disputes and Adversary Procedures in Policy-Making," 3 *Law and Policy Quarterly* 341 (1981).

12. For criticism of the original proposal, and a suggested alternative, see Nancy Ellen Abrams and R. Stephen Berry, "Mediation: A Better Alternative to Science Courts," *Bulletin of the Atomic Scientists*, April 1977, p. 50.

13. William M. Landes and Richard A. Posner, *The Economic Structure of Intellectual Property Law*, ch. 12 (2003); Landes and Posner, "An Empirical Analysis of the Patent Court," 71 *University of Chicago Law Review* 111 (2004).

14. John R. Allison and Mark A. Lemley, "How Federal Circuit Judges Vote in Patent Validity Cases," 27 *Florida State University Law Review* 745, 751–752 (2000).

15. Janet Stidman Eveleth, "Maryland Launches First Business and Technology Court in Nation," *[Maryland State] Bar Bulletin*, Mar. 2003, p. 1.

16. Francesco Calogero, "Might a Laboratory Experiment Destroy Planet Earth?" 25 *Interdisciplinary Science Reviews* 191, 193 (2000). I discussed his proposal in chapter 3.

17. For references supporting these points, and the concept of science courts more broadly, see Sven Timmerbeil, "The Role of Expert Witnesses in German and U.S. Civil Litigation," 9 *Annual Survey of International and Com-*

parative Law 163 (2003); M. Neil Browne, Carrie L. Williamson, and Linda L. Barkacs, "The Perspectival Nature of Expert Testimony in the United States, England, Korea, and France," 18 *Connecticut Journal of International Law* 55 (2002); LeRoy L. Kondo, "Untangling the Tangled Web: Federal Court Reform through Specialization for Internet Law and Other High Technology Cases," 2002 *UCLA Journal of Law and Technology* 1 (2002); George P. Smith, "Judicial Decisionmaking in the Age of Biotechnology," 13 *Notre Dame Journal of Law, Ethics, and Public Policy* 93 (1999); Carl B. Meyer, "Science and Law: The Quest for the Neutral Expert Witness: A View from the Trenches," 12 *Journal of Natural Resources and Environmental Law* 35 (1996–1997).

18. Peter Gorner and Ronald Kotulak, "U. of C. to Lead the Fight against Deadliest Diseases: $35 Million Backs Bioterror Battle," *Chicago Tribune*, Sept. 5, 2003, metro section, p. 1.

19. See, for example, Richard B. Stewart and Jonathan B. Wiener, *Reconstructing Climate Policy: Beyond Kyoto* (2003).

20. Thomas Bernauer, "The Effect of International Environmental Institutions: How We Might Learn More," 49 *International Organization* 351, 353 (1995).

21. Daniel Bodansky, "The Legitimacy of International Governance: A Coming Challenge for International Environmental Law?" 93 *American Journal of International Law* 596, 598 (1999).

22. As argued in ibid.

23. Freedom House, "Freedom in the World," http://www.freedomhouse .org/ratings/index.htm (visited Jan. 6, 2004); Center for International Development and Conflict Management of the University of Maryland, "Polity IV Project," http://www.cidcm.umd.edu/inscr/polity/#data (visited Jan. 6, 2004).

24. The argument that follows was made to me by John Mearsheimer in conversation.

25. For an exemplary study, see David A. Kay, *The Functioning and Effectiveness of Selected United Nations Systems Programs* (1980). Little is known, in general, however, concerning the conditions for effective international institutions. Bernauer, note 20 above.

26. Donald J. Boudreaux and A. C. Pritchard, "Rewriting the Constitution: An Economic Analysis of the Constitutional Amendment Process," 62 *Fordham Law Review* 111 (1993).

27. John K. Setear, "The President's Rational Choice of a Treaty's Preratification Pathway: Article II, Congressional-Executive Agreement, or Executive Agreement?" 31 *Journal of Legal Studies* S5 (2002).

28. As emphasized in Barry Kellman, "Responses to the September 11 Attacks: An International Criminal Law Approach to Bioterrorism," 25 *Harvard Journal of Law and Public Policy* 721 (2002).

29. David Fischer, *History of the International Atomic Energy Agency: The First Forty Years* 454 (1997). Fischer's overall assessment of the agency is positive. Ibid., ch. 13. For a darker assessment, see Carla Anne Robbins, "Nuclear Fission: An Atomic Bargain Hampers the Hunt for Illicit Weapons," *Wall Street Journal*, Apr. 8, 2004, p. A1.

30. U.S. Dept. of Energy, Environment, Safety, and Health Division, "Accelerator Safety," http://www.sc.doe.gov/sc-80/sc-83/accelerator.shtml (visited

Jan. 14, 2004). See also U.S. Dept. of Energy, "Safety of Accelerator Facilities" (DOE O 420.2, Nov. 5, 1998); U.S. Dept. of Energy, "Guidance for an Accelerator Facility Safety Program" (DOE 5480.25 GUIDANCE, Sept. 1, 1993).

31. David Forrest, "Regulating Nanotechnology Development" (Foresight Institute, Mar. 23, 1989), http://www.foresight.org/NanoRev/Forrest1989.html.

32. See, for example, "As One Door Closes . . . ," 427 *Nature* 190 (2004).

33. See the next subsection of this chapter for details; also National Research Council of the National Academies, *Biotechnology Research in an Age of Terrorism: Confronting the Dual Use Dilemma* 42–44 (2003). For a comprehensive description and analysis of legal measures for combating bioterrorism, see Victoria Sutton, *Law and Bioterrorism* (2003). Contrary to some news reports, however, it does not appear that the visa restrictions are significantly limiting enrollments of foreign students in U.S. university science programs. Jeffrey Mervis, "Is the U.S. Brain Gain Faltering?" 304 *Science* 1278 (2004).

34. For a useful summary of the nation's antibioterrorism efforts, see Victoria Sutton, "Law and Science Drive Technology in the War against Bioterrorism" (forthcoming in *Technology in Society*).

35. See also Jonathan B. Tucker, "Preventing the Misuse of Pathogens: The Need for Global Biosecurity Standards," *Arms Control Today*, June 2003, pp. 3, 5.

36. Some of these measures predate 9/11. Sutton, note 34 above, at 9–10.

37. William M. Landes and Richard A. Posner, *The Economic Structure of Tort Law*, ch. 9 (1987); Stephen Shavell, "Liability for Harm versus Regulation of Safety," 13 *Journal of Legal Studies* 357 (1984); Donald Wittman, "Prior Regulation versus Post Liability: The Choice between Input and Output Monitoring," 6 *Journal of Legal Studies* 193 (1977).

38. For an excellent discussion, see Lawrence O. Gostin, "When Terrorism Threatens Health: How Far Are Limitations on Personal and Economic Liberties Justified?" 55 *Florida Law Review* 1105 (2003).

39. National Research Council, note 33 above, at 61.

40. Ibid., 34.

41. Public Law 107–56, Oct. 26, 2001, § 817

42. Rebecca L. Sigmund, "Immigration and Border Security," in Anthony H. Anikeef et al., *Homeland Security Law Handbook* 213, 221 (2003).

43. National Research Council, note 33 above, at 27.

44. Ibid., ch. 3.

45. An exception is John C. Yoo, "BCW Treaties and the Constitution," in *The New Terror: Facing the Threat of Biological and Chemical Weapons* 269 (Sidney D. Drell, Abraham D. Sofaer, and George D. Wilson eds. 1999).

46. I expand on this theme in Richard A. Posner, *Law, Pragmatism, and Democracy*, ch. 8 (2003).

47. W. Kip Viscusi and Richard J. Zeckhauser, "Sacrificing Civil Liberties to Reduce Terrorism Risks," 26 *Journal of Risk and Uncertainty* 99 (2003).

48. As suggested in Richard A. Posner, "Security versus Civil Liberties," *Atlantic Monthly*, Dec. 2001, p. 46, and Donald A. Dripps, "Terror and Tolerance: Criminal Justice for the New Age of Anxiety," 1 *Ohio State Journal of Criminal Law* 9, 34 (2003).

49. Near v. Minnesota, 283 U.S. 697, 716 (1931).

50. United States v. Progressive, Inc., 467 F. Supp. 990 (W.D. Wis.), appeal dismissed without opinion, 610 F.2d 819 (7th Cir. 1979); see Christina Ramirez, "The Balance of Interests between National Security Controls and First Amendment Interests in Academic Freedom," 13 *Journal of College and University Law* 179, 196–197 (1986).

51. Rice v. Paladin Enterprises, Inc., 128 F.3d 233 (4th Cir. 1997). See also United States v. Barnett, 667 F.2d 835 (9th Cir. 1982).

52. W. Seth Carus, "Unlawful Acquisition and Use of Biological Agents," in *Biological Weapons: Limiting the Threat* 211, 227 (Joshua Lederberg ed. 1999).

53. 22 C.F.R. §§ 120.1 et seq.

54. Ramirez, note 50 above, at 185. See also Lloyd V. Berkner, "Secrecy and Scientific Progress," 123 *Science* 783, 786 (1956); Dawn Levy, "Satellite Research Grounded: Stanford, Other Universities Oppose Regulatory Change," *Stanford Report*, May 24, 2000, http:/news-service.stanford.edu/news/2000/may24/itar-524.html.

55. Raymond A. Zilinskas and Jonathan B. Tucker, "Limiting the Contribution of the Open Scientific Literature to the Biological Weapons Threat," Dec. 2002, http://www.homelandsecurity.org/journal/Articles/Tucker.html.

56. Ramirez, note 50 above, at 197.

57. National Science Board, *Science and Engineering Indicators—2002*, vol. 1, p. 3–30 (National Science Foundation, NSB–02–01, 2002).

58. Terry v. Ohio, 392 U.S. 1 (1968).

59. 50 U.S.C. §§ 1801 et seq.; see John C. Yoo, "Judicial Review and the War on Terrorism" 40–46 (Law School, University of California at Berkeley, 2003).

60. Edmond v. Goldsmith, 183 F.3d 659, 663 (7th Cir. 1999), affirmed under the name City of Indianapolis v. Edmond, 531 U.S. 32 (2000).

61. Ibid., 44. See also Florida v. J.L., 529 U.S. 266, 273–274 (2000), where the Court remarked: "We do not say, for example, that a report of a person carrying a bomb need bear the indicia of reliability we demand for a report of a person carrying a firearm before the police can constitutionally conduct a frisk."

62. See, besides Posner, note 46 above, ch. 8, Alan M. Dershowitz, *Why Terrorism Works* (2003); Oren Gross, "Chaos and Rules: Should Responses to Violent Crisis Always Be Constitutional?" 112 *Yale Law Journal* 1011 (2003), esp. pp. 1018–1021; Sanford Levinson, "'Precommitment' and 'Postcommitment': The Ban on Torture in the Wake of September 11," 81 *Texas Law Review* 2013 (2003); Dripps, note 48 above; Eric A. Posner and Adrian Vermeule, "Accommodating Emergencies," 56 *Stanford Law Review* 605 (2003); Yoo, note 59 above. For illustrative criticism, see Philip B. Heymann, *Terrorism, Freedom, and Security: Winning without War* (2003); Stephen J. Schulhofer, *The Enemy Within: Intelligence Gathering, Law Enforcement, and Civil Liberties in the Wake of September 11* (2002); *The War on Our Freedoms: Civil Liberties in an Age of Terrorism* (Richard C. Leone and Greg Anrig, Jr., eds. 2003).

63. See generally Daryl J. Levinson, "Collective Sanctions," 56 *Stanford Law Review* 345 (2003).

64. Eric Posner and John Yoo, "Reign of Terror: Is the Enemy in Us?" *Chicago Tribune*, Jan. 18, 2004, p. C1.

65. Jeffrey Rosen, *The Naked Crowd: Reclaiming Security and Freedom in an Anxious Age*, ch. 2 (2004).

66. "Boom, or Bust?" 426 *Nature* 598 (2003) (emphasis added).

67. Ibid., 599.

68. Michael Ignatieff, *The Lesser Evil: Political Ethics in an Age of Terror* 141 (2004).

69. This is an implication of Mark Bowden's interesting article "The Dark Art of Interrogation," *Atlantic Monthly*, Oct. 2003, p. 51.

70. Dershowitz, note 62 above, at 137.

71. Ibid., 148.

72. The argument is made by Henry Shue in his "Response [to Sanford Levinson, "The Debate on Torture: War against Virtual States," *Dissent*, Summer 2003, p. 79], *Dissent*, Summer 2003, pp. 90, 91.

73. Ibid., 91.

74. Posner, note 46 above, at 273.

75. Dershowitz, note 62 above, ch. 4.

76. United States v. Leon, 468 U.S. 897, 923 (1984).

77. Michael Ignatieff, "Lesser Evils: What It Will Cost Us to Succeed in the War on Terror," *New York Times Magazine*, May 2, 2004, pp. 46, 48.

78. Peter G. Chronis, "Airlines Have New 'Security' Screen; Secret System Raises Discrimination Question," *Denver Post* (second ed.), Jan. 1, 1998, p. B1.

79. See, for example, American Liberties Union, "MATRIX: Myths and Reality," Feb. 10, 2004, http://www.aclu.org/Privacy/Privacy.cfm?ID=14894&c=130, criticizing the MATRIX project that I mentioned in chapter 2.

80. For a notable exception, see Christian Parenti, *The Soft Cage: Surveillance in America: From the Civil War to the War on Terror* (2003).

81. For a good discussion of cybercrime and existing and proposed punishments for it, see Anne W. Branscomb, "Rogue Computer Programs and Computer Rogues: Tailoring the Punishment to Fit the Crime," in *Computers, Ethics and Social Values* 89 (Deborah G. Johnson and Helen Nissenbaum eds. 1995).

82. Not exactly, though close enough for my purposes. Suppose we start with 10,000 prisoners. The deterrent effect of the increased punishment reduces the number to 9,900, but each serves a 1 percent longer term, and $9,900 \times 1.01 = 9,999$, which means that there is one fewer prisoner.

Conclusion

1. Alfred W. Crosby, *America's Forgotten Pandemic: The Influenza of 1918*, ch. 15 (1989).

2. Lee R. Kump, James F. Kasting, and Robert G. Crane, *The Earth System* 320 (2d ed. 2004).

Index

cyberterrorists, 243–245; synergies with other forms of terrorism, 85–86

Maddox, John, 112
Manhattan Project, 192, 203
Marburger, John, 31, 274 n. 47, 299
  n. 118, 300 n. 130
Maryland Business and Technology
  Case Management Programs, 211
Matrix, The, 106–109
May, Robert, 63, 261, 284 n. 197, 285
  n. 211
Mearsheimer, John, 299 n. 116, 311
  n. 24
Meteorites, 24
Methane, as greenhouse gas, 47, 165;
  as potential source of natural gas, 59
Michaels, Patrick, 53–54
Mill, John Stuart, 146–147
Monkeypox, 24
Montreal Protocol, 125
Moore, Stephen, 116
Moore, Thomas Gale, 46, 279 n. 118
Morrison, David, 29, 168, 273 nn. 28,
  31, 293 n. 324, 306 n. 59
Mousepox, Australian experiment,
  77–78, 82, 129, 227; St. Louis experi-
  ment, 80–81

Nanometer, 35; defined, 12. *See also*
  Nanotechnology
Nanotechnology, 35–37; danger of run-
  away nanomachines, 36–38, 114,
  117, 253; potential use in computers,
  41; tolerable-windows analysis, 186;
  weaponization of, 37. *See also* Car-
  bon sequestration
NASA (National Aeronautics and Space
  Administration), 136–137, 180–181,
  183–184, 188, 250–251. *See also*
  Asteroid collisions
National Conference of Lawyers and
  Scientists, 206–207
Natural resources, markets in, 58–61;
  potential exhaustion of, 58–59
Near-Earth Object Science Definition
  Team, 179, 181
Near v. Minnesota, 312 n. 49
Newell, Richard, 153–154, 303 n. 33,
  304 nn. 38–39, 43
Nineteen Eighty-Four. See Orwell
Nordhaus, William, 44, 46, 49–50, 126,
  279 nn. 106, 117, 280 nn. 131–132,
  136, 298 nn. 103, 107, 109

Nuclear (and thermonuclear) war and
  weaponry, 71–75, 111, 115, 132
Nuclear energy, 51–52
Nuclear proliferation, 74, 117, 132, 220,
  247
Nuclear winter, 72–75
Nunn-Lugar Act, 132

Office of Science and Technology Pol-
  icy, 183, 299 n. 118
Oklahoma City bombing, 74
Orwell, George, 88, 102–103, 106
Oryx and Crake. See Atwood
Outbreak, 105–106
Ozone layer in stratosphere. *See*
  Chlorofluorocarbons

Parry, Ian, 305 nn. 48, 53
Particle accelerators, privatization of,
  147–148, 252; social benefits of,
  142–148, 150, 192. *See also* Depart-
  ment of Energy; Strangelet disaster
  scenario; names of particular acceler-
  ator facilities
Patents, 9, 144, 160; patent court, 210
Pattern recognition, 119–120
Perutz, M. F., 116–117, 297 nn. 85, 87
Pesticides, 23
Phase transition, 31
Philander, George, 281 n. 139
Physics, high-energy. *See* Particle accelerators
Pizer, William, 153–154, 303 n. 33, 304
  nn. 38–39
Popper, Karl, 202
Population, determinants of growth of,
  68; external effects of, 39, 63, 68–71,
  186, 259–260
Precautionary principle, 140, 148–150
Preston, Richard, 104, 289 nn. 264, 277,
  290 n. 294
Privacy, 87–89; as political good,
  88–89
Probability, 18–19, 113, 195–196; difficulty of comprehending small probabilities, 120–121, 167–168, 248–249;
  difficulty of thinking in terms of,
  versus frequency, 9–10, 90, 121–122,
  169, 246, 248; Monte Carlo simulations, 29; nonquantifiable, 171–172;
  probability neglect, 168, 188;

Probability (*continued*), significance of interval over which assesssed, 13, 119, 155, 191–192; subjective, 172, 194–195. *See also* Statistics

Project BioShield, 177

Psychology, 9–11, 90; pattern recognition, 119–120. *See also* Probability; Rationality

Public choice theory, 118, 133–138, 264. *See also under* Global warming

Public Health Security and Bioterrorism Preparedness and Response Act of 2002, 226

Punishment. *See* Legal regulation

Quarantines versus isolation, 79

Quarks, strange. *See* Strangelet disaster scenario

Rationality, 14; evolutionarily adaptive limitations of, 16–17

Recombinant DNA technology. *See* Gene splicing

Rees, Martin, 30, 35–38, 43, 72, 112, 195, 253, 273 nn. 31, 34–35, 274 nn. 38, 45, 48, 276 n. 72, 278 nn. 102, 103, 280 n. 125, 287 n. 242, 298 n. 108, 309 n. 110, 310 n. 122

Regulation, cap and trade, 60–61, 127. *See also* Legal regulation

Relativistic Heavy Ion Collider (RHIC), 30–32; adequacy of technical safety analysis, 192–196; cost-benefit analysis, 140–143, 173, 187–196; RHIC–II, 32, 185–186, 196–197; risk assessment, 141, 189–195, 252, 256–257; social benefits of, 141–148, 150

Replication, 37–38. *See also* Crystal conversion; Nanotechnology

Research, limiting publication, 227, 230–231; private and social returns to basic research, 135–136, 143–144; restrictions on freedom of, 221–224, 226–228; valuation of basic, 144–148. *See also* Innovation; Particle accelerators; Science

RHIC. *See* Relativistic Heavy Ion Collider

Rice v. Paladin Enterprises, Inc., 313 n. 51

Risk, versus uncertainty, 171–175. *See also* Probability; Risk aversion

Risk assessment, 189–196

Risk aversion, 55, 71, 163; as basis of precautionary principle, 140, 150

Risk-risk assessment, 186

Ritonavir conversion incident, 34–35, 43

Robots and robotics. *See* Artificial intelligence; *Matrix*

Rosen, Jeffrey, 236, 313 n. 65

Sagan, Carl, 111

Schumpeter, Joseph, 61

Science, and legal profession, 200–209; and legal professoriat, 204–206; and religiosity, 95, 109; character, incentives, psychology, and intelligence of scientists, 98–100, 116–117, 189–190, 201–203, 252; education in, 93–95; expert scientific witnesses, 212–213; federal R&D budget, 93, 134, 143–144; foreign science students in United States, 82, 99, 221–224, 226, 231–232; foreign scientists in United States, 82; how to measure value of, 143–148; in legal education, 95, 97, 203–207; judicial versus scientific culture, 201–202; legal regulation of, 9, 216–244; limitations of scientists as policy makers, 100; natural sciences contrasted with economics, 200–201; natural sciences contrasted with social sciences, 200–203; philosophy of, 202; popular books on, 145–146; problem of scientific illiteracy, 93–98; progress of relative to other human endeavors, 70; screening of scientists for terrorist risk, 224, 226; uncritical veneration of by lay public, 97–98; versus technology, 98; worldwide growth of scientific and engineering employment, 92. *See also* Law and science; Science court; Science fiction; Science Policy

Science court, 209–213; appellate versus trial, 210–211; foreign, 213

Science fiction, 100–110; and religion, 108–109

Science policy, 8, 100, 213–215, 252.
 See also Law and science; Science
Security Studies Program (M.I.T.), 214
Shamos, Morris, 94, 294 n. 14
Simon, Julian, 110–111, 116, 284
 n. 201, 296 n. 62, 297 n. 86
Sims, The, 107
Singer, S. Fred, 54–55, 57–58, 282
 n. 167, 283 nn. 169–173, 176–177
Smalley, Richard E., 276 n. 74
Smallpox, 5, 24, 79–80; gene spliced,
 78–83, 114. *See also* Bioterrorism
Snowball earth, 4–5, 47–48
Species, definition of, 66; number of,
 62–68. *See also* Endangered Species
 Act
Stanford Linear Accelerator Center, 147
Stapledon, Olaf, 295 n. 39
Statistics, difficulty of thinking rationally
 in terms of, 9–10, 119–120, 187.
 See also Probability
Steller's sea cow, 65–66
Strangelet disaster scenario, 30–35, 90,
 114, 141, 182, 187, 189–196, 251;
 public choice analysis, 133–134;
 tolerable-windows analysis,
 185–186. *See also* Relativistic Heavy
 Ion Collider (RHIC)
Student and Exchange Visitor Information System, 226
Sulfur dioxide, cap and trade regulation
 of, 60–61, 127
Sunstein, Cass, 168, 270 n. 25, 286
 n. 234, 301 n. 3, 306 nn. 59, 61, 66,
 309 n. 95
Superconducting Super Collider, 134,
 143
Surveillance, as catastrophic risk,
 86–89; constitutionality of, 232–234;
 electronic, 86–89, 262; MATRIX project, 86, 107, 314 n. 79

Taxation. *See* Global warming, emissions taxes
Technology, contribution of to economic welfare, 15–16; dual-use
 issue, 15, 81, 124, 260; economics of,
 123–124; externalities, 124; social
 consequences of, 6–8. *See also* Innovation; Science
Terminator, 109

Terrorism, 262–263; 9/11 attacks, 174,
 176; collective punishment, 235;
 information markets in, 175–176;
 insurance against, 172, 176; nuclear,
 73–75; risk of, 171–172; types of
 terrorist, 76–77; use of torture to
 prevent, 235–242; willingness to
 pay to prevent, 168, 170. *See also*
 Bioterrorism; Civil liberties; Cyberterrorism
Terrorism Risk Insurance Act of 2002,
 172, 176
Terry v. Ohio, 313 n. 58.
Test of time, 62
Thomas Jefferson Science Foundation
 Program (U.S. Department of State),
 214
Threat assessment, 182–183
Tolerable-windows approach. *See*
 under Cost-benefit analysis
Torture, 235–242; as catastrophic risk,
 238; warrants, 239–240
Tucker, Jonathan, 129, 299
 nn. 121–122, 312 n. 35

Unabomber, 77
United Nations, 216, 218
United States v. Leon, 314 n. 76
United States v. Progressive, Inc., 313
 n. 50
Unmanned Aerial Vehicles, 42–43
USA PATRIOT Act, 226, 234
Utilitarianism, 70; average versus total,
 153

Vaccines, 81. *See also* Bioterrorism, by
 gene splicing; Viruses
Value of life, asymptotic relation between size of risk and value,
 165–170, 180, 188–189, 191, 249;
 economic method of estimation of,
 165–171; variance in estimates across
 different types of risk, 188
Virtual worlds, 107–108
Viruses, 38; computer; mutation of,
 22–23; vaccinia virus, 80. *See also*
 Cyberterrorism; Mousepox;
 Smallpox
Viscusi, W. Kip, 269 n. 19, 306 nn. 55,
 57, 62, 64–65, 312 n. 47
Volcanic eruptions, 29

Printed in the United States
135353LV00005B/37/A

6736277R0

Made in the USA
Lexington, KY
17 September 2010